Energy Risk Management: A Primer for the Utility Industry

Andrew S. Hyman
Michael J. Denton, Ph.D.
Leonard S. Hyman
Bradford G. Leach
Gary A. Walter

Foreword by
Robert M. Anderson
Executive Director
Committee of Chief Risk Officers

Public Utilities Reports, Inc.

This publication is designed to provide accurate and authoritative information in regard to the subject matter covered. It is sold with the understanding that the publisher is not engaged in rendering legal, accounting, or other professional service. If legal advice or other expert assistance is required, the services of a competent professional person should be sought. *(From a Declaration of Principles jointly adopted by a Committee of the American Bar Association and a Committee of Publishers.)*

First Printing, June 2006

Library of Congress Cataloging-in-Publication Data

Energy risk management: a primer for the utility industry / Andrew S. Hyman . . . [et al.]; foreword by Robert M. Anderson.
   p. cm.
  ISBN-13: 978-0-910325-18-9 (perfect bound) 1. Public utilities. 2. Energy industries. 3. Risk management. I. Hyman, Andrew S., 1969-
   HD2763.E54 2006
   333.79068'1—dc22

                    2006015199

To my lovely wife Adiel, and our daughter Julia Marina, whose sleep habits defy any mathematical law.

Andrew S. Hyman

Andrew S. Hyman is marketing director at Fiske Walter Capital Management, a commodity trading advisor. Prior to employment at Fiske Walter, he was director of weather risk services at Weathernews Americas, an affiliate of the world's largest publicly traded, full service weather company. Before that, he worked at the Global Energy, Utilities, and Mining Group at PricewaterhouseCoopers, where he produced the firm's *Energy Trading Glossary*.

Mr. Hyman is the co-chairman of the Chicago steering committee of the Professional Risk Managers International Association (PRMIA). He has been a member of the steering committee since its inception. He co-authored *America's Electric Utilities: Past, Present and Future* and *The Water Business: Understanding the Water and Wastewater Industry*, both published by Public Utilities Reports. He also contributed to *Weather Derivatives: An Introduction* published by the ICFAI University Press in India. In addition, Mr. Hyman has also written articles on energy and weather risk management and presented to numerous audiences on these topics.

He has a B.S. in applied physics from Tufts University, a master of public policy from Vanderbilt University, and a master of arts in geography from the University of Illinois at Urbana-Champaign.

Mr. Hyman lives in Chicago with his wife Adiel and his daughter Julia.

Michael J. Denton, Ph.D.

Michael J. Denton, Ph.D. is a Senior Manager at Risk Capital, LLC. Within the advisory services team, he provides quantitative risk management, asset valuation, and commodities trading expertise to energy clients. He has consulted for more than 40 utility organizations and is recognized in *Who's Who in Finance and Industry, America and The World*.

Most recently, Mr. Denton was a Senior Vice President of the Analytics team at SunGard Energy Systems, where he designed risk measurement and valuation methods for energy trading operations. Prior to his work at SunGard, Mr. Denton served as a management consultant for Theodore Barry & Associates, Metzler & Associates, and Utilities International, Inc. He also has held positions at Sargent & Lundy and Amoco Oil, specializing in energy and generation engineering.

Mr. Denton has published numerous academic and trade articles on strategic risk management and the energy markets and is a registered professional engineer in Indiana. His doctoral thesis research focused on deregulated spot markets for electric power. In addition, Mr. Denton serves on the board of the International Foundation for Research in Experimental Economics.

Mr. Denton earned his Ph.D. in Economics from the University of Arizona, his M.B.A. in Finance from the University of Chicago, and his B.A. in Power Systems Engineering from Purdue University.

Leonard S. Hyman, CFA

Leonard S. Hyman is President of Private Sector Advisors, Inc. and senior consultant associate at R.J. Rudden Associates, a Black and Veatch Company. He was previously a senior industry advisor to Salomon Smith Barney.

From 1978 to 1994, as head of the Utility Research Group and first vice president at Merrill Lynch, Mr. Hyman supervised and maintained equity research on foreign and domestic energy and telecommunication utilities. He was a member of privatization teams for offerings of British, Spanish, Mexican, Argentine, and Brazilian utilities and consultant for other restructuring studies. Prior to joining Merrill Lynch, he was a partner at a New York Stock Exchange member firm, H.C. Wainwright, and an officer at Chase Manhattan Bank.

Mr. Hyman has written and spoken on utility finance and deregulation, presenting papers on four continents. He has testified before Congress, served on four advisory panels for the U.S. Congress Office of Technology Assessment, and has served on an advisory panel for the National Science Foundation. He was a member of task forces on: electric utility efficiency for Pennsylvania; fusion and other energy sources for NASA; and system reliability for NERC's blue ribbon task force. He has served on the advisory board of the Electric Power Research Institute (EPRI), and is presently on the advisory boards of the International Foundation for Research in Experimental Economics, and EnerTech Capital.

He is co-author of *America's Electric Utilities: Past, Present and Future, The New Telecommunications Industry: Meeting the Competition, The Water Business: Understanding the Water Supply and Wastewater Industry* and *Unlocking the Benefits of Restructuring: A Blueprint for Transmission*. He also is the editor of *The Privatization of Public Utilities*, and has contributed to other books and professional journals.

For more than a decade, Mr. Hyman was cited by *Institutional Investor* as one of the leading research analysts in his field. He is a Chartered Financial Analyst (CFA). He holds a B.A. from New York University, where he was elected to Phi Beta Kappa, and an M.A. in economics from Cornell University.

Bradford G. Leach

Bradford G. Leach is Senior Director of Electricity and Natural Gas Research at the New York Mercantile Exchange. Currently, he is responsible for research related to the NYMEX electricity and natural gas futures contracts. He also supervises research related to the development of electricity and natural gas NYMEX OTC clearing contracts. Additional responsibilities include research related to weather derivatives, emissions, and energy e-commerce.

Mr. Leach joined the NYMEX Research Department in 1986 as the research analyst responsible for the development of the NYMEX natural gas futures contract. Prior to joining the NYMEX research staff, Mr. Leach was associated with the American Paper Institute where he was involved in the development of natural gas and electricity policy for the pulp and paper industry. He is a graduate of Columbia University.

Gary A. Walter

Gary A. Walter is the CEO and Principal of Fiske Walter Capital Management Ltd., a commodity trading advisor.

Before starting Fiske Walter Capital Management, Mr. Walter was Principal at Marold Capital Management LLC. Prior to working at Marold, Mr. Walter worked at the John S. & James L. Knight Foundation in Miami, Florida, where he was Performance and Risk Manager. Knight is one of the largest private foundations in the United States with over $2.2 billion in investments. Mr. Walter developed and automated highly sophisticated systems for performance reporting and risk management. He served as liaison between the Knight Foundation and all investment managers globally and nationwide.

Mr. Walter received his M.B.A. from Florida International University, a Master of Divinity from Columbia International University in South Carolina, and a B.S. degree from the University of Illinois.

He currently resides with his wife Katie in Glen Ellyn, Illinois, a suburb of Chicago.

TABLE OF CONTENTS

LIST OF TABLES AND FIGURES

Tables

CHAPTER 5

CHAPTER 6

CHAPTER 7

CHAPTER 8

FOREWORD

It still surprises me that all boards of directors have not *demanded* basic, enterprise-wide risk information. In my three years as executive director of the Committee of Chief Risk Officers (CCRO), the risk management organization of the energy industry, I have seen how boards of directors and corporate officers capture value from the insights furnished by risk adjusted information. These risk-aware managers use risk information in deciding how to allocate capital between different investment opportunities, in designing the internal controls that assure management knows what is going on, and in assessing performance in a way that takes into account whether the returns are good enough relative to the risk involved. The smart risk-aware managements share that information with investors, regulators and other stakeholders, and create greater confidence in the firm, its decisions, and in its securities.

But — despite the benefits — many boards fail to make that demand.

Yet, I can assure you, with great confidence, firms whose boards and managements remain uninformed about the risks within their enterprises will not, with any regularity, find themselves listed among the industry's best performers. If you are still among the risk-uninformed, I wish I could take you inside the best performers in the industry — you would then demand risk adjusted financial information for your board, and make sure executives apply that information when making decisions.

Some managements claim the chief executive officer "takes care of" risk, somehow, when making decisions. Some believe that well designed operating procedures constitute risk management. Some see no reason for risk management because the firm does not engage in "risky" energy trading. Those attitudes not only demonstrate poor governance and risk oversight, but they also reveal a firm at a competitive disadvantage due to an inability to take advantage of risk information that remains hidden from use.

So why don't more people within the energy industry (both producers and users) deploy and benefit from readily available best practices to acquire and then use risk information, in order to better understand and manage risk? I think many directors and executives lack basic knowledge about risk information and how they can use it. After all, what good is information if you don't know how to use it? Perhaps the emphasis on expertise and higher mathematics, and the association of risk management with the trading function, has kept risk information from its most important users — those at the board and chief executive level. Knowledge, at that level, requires both information and understanding how to use that information. All too often, boards receive the risk information, but do not know what to do with it. I have seen, first hand, how boards and executives — without means to understand and utilize risk information — either ignore it, or even worse, close down the risk management department to save money.

With that in mind, I am particularly pleased Andrew Hyman asked me to write the introduction to *Energy Risk Management: A Primer for the Utility Industry.* Aimed at directors and management, it not only looks at the big picture, but also examines the building blocks needed to construct a risk management program. This book should help to close the risk knowledge gap.

Nowadays, managements can no longer excuse their inaction by claiming that recognized standards for risk practices do not exist. They do. Any company can benefit from robust risk-adjusted information about its current and planned business activities, and develop appropriate practices to manage that risk. Setting up a risk analysis and management function is more cost effective than ever before. In fact, risk knowledge has never been more readily available in the energy area, because of the CCRO, whose benefits include white papers that lay out best practices for energy risk management for all to see, and ongoing membership efforts to "raise the bar" regarding risk management practices found in the best companies across our industry.

I hope you will enjoy — as I do — the knowledge that risk awareness brings to the management of a company's operations and growth plans. I encourage you to press your management to learn more, and even get them to join the CCRO in order to develop risk management experience throughout the organization. (Members of the CCRO range from giant to small firms, regulated and unregulated. They all share a common interest in understanding the impact of risk on current and planned businesses.) After reading this book, I am sure you will gain an appetite for more knowledge of risk.

ROBERT M. ANDERSON

Executive Director
Committee of Chief Risk Officers

PREFACE

Risk management: the term conjures up visions of corporate law enforcement types reining in free wheeling traders and investigating fraud, and of directors deciding to get the firm out of "risky" activities. Risk management, in reality, is about making decisions in the face of uncertainty, that is, risk. Unfortunately, many people tend to steer away from the topic because of two misconceptions: that a firm that does not engage in derivative or other trading activities does not incur risk, and that risk management is too difficult to understand.

This book explains the basics of risk management, with emphasis on the risks of the energy business. It examines not just the obvious trading decisions but also other business decisions and policies that involve risk, as well as how nondecisions create risk. It uses simple examples to illustrate the principles of risk management. It has been designed for corporate directors and staff, policy makers, regulators, legislators, investors, and sellers and consumers of energy, who want an understanding of what risks exist, and how they might be managed, without the complications of technical jargon and higher mathematics.

The book is divided into eight sections that provide a systematic approach to risk management for utilities, energy companies, and their customers.

The first section, Chapter 1, analyzes the *Need for Risk Management*, and why utilities and energy companies need to apply risk management within their businesses.

The second section, *The Basics* (Chapters 2-6), discusses terminology and techniques that relate to risk management, along with a systematic framework that allows companies to manage risks effectively. It examines common risks that organizations face, and misconceptions, such as that derivatives are dangerous. It shows how risk management needs to start with the attention of the board and top management, or it will not be taken seriously. It explains the basics of how to shift risk using derivatives, and analyzes basis, which helps determine the effectiveness of hedging strategies.

The third section, *Core Risks*, examines how to manage the key risk that utilities and energy companies face: the risk from volatile energy prices and weather variability.

The fourth section, *Other Market Risks* (Chapters 9-13), examines risks, which while not the core risks of the business nevertheless can have a significant impact on an organization's financial health. These include foreign exchange risk, interest rate risk, equity risk, credit risk and the risks that arise from choice of trading venue.

The fifth section, *Risks Within the Business*, examines the broad world of operational risk and the topic that Sarbanes-Oxley has brought to the attention of boards and managers — fraud.

Given that utilities and energy companies operate in a highly regulated environment, it isn't surprising that regulation and government can be major sources of risk. The sixth section, *Regulation and Government* (Chapters 16 and 17), explains the basics of regulation and the risks that result from it.

The last section, *Experimental Economics* (Chapter 18), illustrates how insights from this relatively new field can greatly improve the setting of risk limits and governance of trading operations.

Finally the book concludes with three appendices that will serve as a ready reference for those who need to understand and apply risk management. Appendix A lists the important contracts that energy companies and utilities need to consider. Appendix B explains common measures related to risk, such as value at risk, and how to interpret them. Finally, the book concludes with Appendix C, a glossary of nearly 900 vital energy trading and risk management terms, which cuts through the jargon and allows the reader to understand the often confusing terminology that can prevent a sound understanding of risk management.

We hope that this book will clarify, and maybe even demystify the field of energy risk management for the reader.

Andrew S. Hyman

Identifying Risks and Evaluating Prospects

In approaching energy risk management, you must first identify the risk, then evaluate it. Then decide whether to incur the risk at all, or whether to manage the risk. Managing a risk means trying to find ways to limit or eliminate the impact of a particular circumstance on the participant in the market. Risk management costs money, so one has to balance that cost against the potential for loss. Remember, too, that risk involves more than the chance of encountering the odd disaster. Not earning a return commensurate with the risk incurred produces a loss of capital as surely as a natural disaster. Risk managers have to know the risks before they devise plans to manage them.

A household products company planning to introduce a new soap bar to the market would want to know, in advance of the introduction, whether the public would buy the product. So, it would conduct a market research survey of potential customers to determine their preferences in terms of size, color, scent, and price. It would ascertain the availability of the key ingredient that would differentiate the new soap from others on the market. It would estimate the time interval before competitors came to the market with a similar product. With all that information, it would estimate the size of the market, expected sales volume, costs, and profitability. It would consider other risks, as well, such as the possibility that consumers might change their buying habits, perhaps favoring liquid soap instead of bars of soap. The company will weigh the risks of launching the new product against the expected rewards before proceeding. Once it makes the decision to go forward, it will take steps to assure success, or limit the risk of failure. For instance, it might tie up the supply of the key ingredient at a fixed price, secure shelf space in supermarkets, and launch an advertising campaign that convinces consumers that no soap cleans better. Occasionally the process fails, spectacularly, as in the cases of the Edsel and New Coke, but Ford never bet the company on the success of the Edsel, and Coca Cola quickly reinstated the old product when consumers rejected the new one. Successful companies know how to limit bets and stop losses.

Energy companies, however, have committed billions of dollars to projects and products without taking the risk minimizing precautions that our hypothetical soap company would take. They did bet the company and they did not cut the losses. Regulators formulated new markets without determining what customers wanted, and those markets failed to attract consumers. Neither the energy companies nor the regulators recognized or evaluated the risks to be incurred, and both the companies and their customers suffered the consequences, with costs measured in the tens of billions of dollars.

As an example, during the late 1960s and early 1970s, the regulated electric utility industry engaged in an enormous building program based on the expectation that demand for electricity would continue to grow at the same rate as it had in the past, despite the fact that the price of electricity had begun to rise, whereas in the past it had fallen continuously. The industry knew what customers wanted, had no reason to ask them, or even consider that the normal laws of supply and demand might apply in the electricity market. Demand did slow down, leaving the industry with an enormous burden of underused facilities. Hardly anyone had considered the risk that the projections would not pan out.

During the 1990s, builders of new generating plants took enormous risks without considering the consequences that might ensue if their assumptions for the market were wrong. They thought that the utilities would retire old power stations, thereby enlarging the market for the modern generating plants. That did not happen. They acted as if the vast expansion of generating capacity would not affect the availability and price of natural gas, but it did. They did not consider the possibility that the collapse of one huge, but dishonestly run, energy company would cause the bond rating agencies and bankers to question the activities of honestly run, but imprudently financed, energy merchants, and thereby constrict the flow of capital to those companies. As a consequence of not understanding the market that they had entered, and not taking proper precautions, the energy companies suffered more than the embarrassment of an unsuccessful product launch. Many went bankrupt.

For convenience, we might divide the risk discovery and evaluation process into four categories: market research, industrial research, scenario analysis and synthesis. We could use some of the same research, analysis and information gathering techniques for much of the process.

Traditional market research requires contact with potential customers to find out what they like, what they will pay, and how much they will buy at different prices, but statistical analysis of past customer activities might provide sufficient information for many decisions about customer behavior.

Industrial research requires an examination of what happens when the firm attempts to deliver the product (how suppliers will act, how competitors will react) because the firm does not act in a vacuum.

By engaging in market and industrial research, the firm should gain a better idea of the demand for its product, the cost of supplying it, and how the competitive picture could change over time. Analyzing that information should help the firm reduce the overall risk of doing business, and indicate which specific risks require management.

Analyzing prospects in the gas or electric market involves a more complicated process than figuring out the market for a soap. Gas and electric firms operate within networks and competitors share the use of those networks. They may have the ability to impede the delivery of a competitor's product. Participants in the market will seek ways to take advantage of rigid auction or operating rules in a way to "jack up" prices to customers who have been forced to buy at those markets. Ultimate customers may not pay the cost of production of the energy, at particular times, so they do not react to astronomical prices by cutting back on demand, which gives sellers the opportunity to overcharge at peak periods. The analysis must not only take into account the peculiarities of the industry's structure, but also what might happen if the rules were changed to allow more normal market conditions.

With all those complications (and more), the market participant (or regulator) might have to build a mathematical model that simulates the market. In the model, mathematical formulas approximate how participants would react to changing circumstances. (For instance, a rise in the price of natural gas and a drop in the price of coal would cause power producers to shift production from gas-fired to coal-fired power stations.) The simulation permits the modelers to test how the market participants would fare under different circumstances. The usefulness of the model, however, depends on the correctness of the formulas, whether the model includes enough of the factors that affect the outcome ("variables" in statistical parlance) in the real world, and whether a model based on past events will work as technology and market structures change. Some models, in a sense, skip the issue of reality. The model builder assumes that the market participants act in the economically rational manner so dear to textbooks, and runs the model to determine what those computer-like market participants would do. Models, of course, are only as good as the information put into them. They probably do not reflect the changes that will take place in a dynamic, evolving marketplace, but they should help the users understand the interactions within the market.

Unfortunately, real people might not act in accordance with the mathematical formulas from the old textbooks, especially when they act within a shifting, imperfect market in which bending or breaking or taking advantage of rules can pay off. Economists, however, have devised experiments to test how people would act in various types of markets, operating under different sets of rules. The economists design computerized versions of the market or network, with people acting as market participants, making decisions and affecting the market just as real market participants would. What looks like a computer game provides insight into how market participants can gain or lose from various situations, including the configuration of the network. Experimental economics offers a new way of testing the market.

Model building and experimental economics provide insight into what might happen under specified conditions, but it is not practical to build models or design experiments for every possibility, and modelers might not know how to build one for the type of event that has not happened before. That is where scenario building and analysis comes in. Market participants need to consider what would happen if certain big (and possibly unlikely) events would occur, and what they might have to do if such events take place. What if domestic natural gas supply declined at a faster rate than predicted? What if flat plate lighting reduced electricity demand by 10%? What if war engulfed the entire Middle East? What if fuel cells go into mass production? Not all scenarios are equally probable, of course, but facing up to possibilities is part of the process of risk assessment.

Finally, those in charge must synthesize all the information, consider the likelihood of success or failure, and determine how to minimize (at the lowest possible cost) those risks that would endanger the success of the enterprise. That management of risk could take many forms, from making transactions that protect against swings in fuel prices to making sure that the firm has the financial strength to allow it to survive unexpected business difficulties. In some cases, risk management means saying, "If we face a particular risk, we don't want to be in the business at all." Obviously, market participants cannot avoid risk altogether, but, properly prepared, they can avoid unnecessary or intolerable risks and manage the level of the risk that they choose to incur.

Utilities and Energy Companies Need Risk Management

The utility business ain't what it used to be, certainly not since it morphed into the energy business. At one time, the utility business was considered safe — after all, didn't the government guarantee returns? However, industry restructuring exposed companies to uncertainty, especially in fuel and power prices. Now utilities and their spinoffs, the energy merchants, must confront risk — and how they manage that risk will determine their success. Let's take a look at the recent events in the energy business that illustrate the need for good risk management.

Risk Seemed Exciting — For a While

At the onset of restructuring, once staid utilities embraced the excitement of risk and trading. Regulated utilities with captive customers seemed boring. Managers wanted to be in on the excitement — and that meant energy trading. Companies that engaged in the exciting businesses saw their stock prices climb. Companies wanted to be like Enron, or so it seemed.

When returns are high, stockholders are happy, and corporate leaders, such as Ken Lay of Enron, are exalted.[1] Higher risk, however, usually accompanies higher returns — and the concept of risk was new to many utilities.[2] In 2000 and 2001, the wholesale market boomed. Generators and traders earned large profits. In order to get a bigger piece of this business, unregulated subsidiaries of major utilities borrowed heavily to expand their generation, marketing, and trading capabilities.[3]

However, when the US economy slowed down in 2001, the producers and marketers faced a glut of generation. Prices fell. These unfavorable market conditions occurred as many generators and traders faced the need to pay debts incurred to build or buy their power plants. In addition, in the fall of 2001, Enron went bankrupt. Enron's departure from the markets decreased liquidity. Many market-makers were on the other side of deals with Enron, and consequently were caught short, meaning they didn't get what they paid for or get paid for what they delivered. Companies became more wary of the parties with whom they traded. Liquidity decreased in the markets, and the number of creditworthy players dwindled.

The falloff in business — and the maturing debt payments — forced many companies to renegotiate debt payments on unfavorable terms or sell assets at fire sale prices.[4] Many companies saw their credit ratings drop. In certain cases, when their credit ratings fell below investment grade, that set off triggers in their debt covenants that required the companies to accelerate debt payments. This combination of events drove some marketing affiliates of solvent utilities into default or bankruptcy. Although the affiliates may have operated independently of parent companies, the parents did not escape unharmed. They faced major asset impairment charges. Xcel reported a $2.9 billion asset impairment charge for the failure of its NRG subsidiary in 2002.[5] And so much of this chaos was due to a firm that was going to change the world — Enron.

Enron

At one time, Enron seemed to represent the future of the energy and utility world, with its excitement, pizzazz, and a glitzy headquarters under construction in Houston.[6] It was, supposedly, filled with trading geniuses always figuring out more ways to make money — gobs of it — for a parent that everyone was trying to keep up with or copy. This was a bad model for the utility industry to follow. Enron collapsed, dramatically, in 2001, plunging from high-flyer to bankrupt. Enron's CEO Ken Lay was indicted for engaging in illegal activities at Enron, following guilty pleas by former officers of the firm, who admitted to wrongdoing. In going down, the firm took along the auditing firm of Arthur Andersen, a major provider of accounting and consulting services to the utility sector.

For many, Enron represented the paradigm of how to succeed in the restructured energy market. Enron portrayed itself as being very smart — and utilities as being — well — dumb.[7] It set up its own energy trading platform, known as EnronOnline, supposedly the energy market of the future, a platform on which buyers and sellers would meet and transact business. However, that market also allowed Enron to see who was buying and selling commodities and permitted Enron to exploit that information in a way that would not be allowed on a regulated exchange.[8]

Enron performed a disservice to risk management. After its fall, boards of directors and Wall Streeters became wary of using derivatives and risk management tools — they thought using the instruments made their companies like Enron. That was a mistake.

Just because companies avoid derivatives, does not mean that they avoid risk. The risk remains, like an untreated disease. It won't go away just because certain drugs, that can be misused, are not used to treat the disease.

Enron's fall contributed to the passage of the Sarbanes-Oxley law, which increased the regulatory burden on U.S. registered companies. But Enron was not the only entity to bring discredit to the energy markets.

Wash Trading and Index Scandal

The other scandal spurred by the drive to trade, was the wash trading outbreak of 2002. Wash trading (or round trip trading) is:

> Entering into, or purporting to enter into, transactions to give the appearance that purchases and sales have been made, without incurring market risk or changing the trader's market position. The Commodity Exchange Act prohibits wash trading.[9]

Power traders engaged in wash trading to boost their reported volume and revenues — although the trades did not boost their profitability. Some traders were compensated based on their trading volume, so they wanted to boost the numbers. In other cases, companies tried to boost their revenues to raise their standings in tables of major energy traders, which they viewed as a way to gain a higher profile in the industry. Needless to say, when word leaked about these trades, confidence in the trading industry fell further. Although some made the

3

case that the trades were not illegal, the Commodity Futures Trading Commission did not take that view and extracted significant fines from energy traders for wash trading.

At the same time, it was reported that many trading companies had improperly reported the nature of trades they made to index publishers, These indices of energy prices were used to settle various forward and futures contracts. Traders improperly reported trade details to these publications in ways designed to manipulate the market.[10]

Avoid Increased Regulatory Scrutiny

A utility often has an often adversarial relationship with its regulators, who can determine its economic future. The one thing the industry does not need is misguided regulation. One way to prevent that from happening is to pay careful attention to risk management and apply its lessons to prevent a recurrence of the above problems — or something even worse — in the future.

Notes

[1]For a detailed look at the history of Enron and its leadership, see Bethany McLean and Peter Elkind's book, *The Smartest Guys in the Room: The Amazing Rise and Scandalous Fall of Enron* (New York: Portfolio, 2003). This book illustrates what happens when a company does not follow the basic principles of risk management.

[2]In thinking about the relation between risk and return, it will be helpful to look at the bond and equity markets to emphasize this relationship. For example, a corporate bond trades at a premium to a treasury bond with the same maturity and face value, because the corporation is seen as a greater credit risk for nonpayment than the US government. A bondholder requires the higher return to compensate for the greater risk on nonpayment. The same applies to the equity markets, where equity demands a risk premium over debt. Equity is riskier, because in the event of bankruptcy, the claims of shareholders are subsidiary to those of debt holders.

[3]Standard & Poor's, *Industry Surveys: Electric Utilities,* 7 August 2003, p. 2.

[4]*Ibid.*

[5]Justin C. McCann, Standard & Poor's *Industry Surveys: Electric Utilities,* 7 August 2003, p. 3.

[6]Bethany McLean and Peter Elkind, *The Smartest Guys in the Room: The Amazing Rise and Scandalous Fall of Enron* (New York: Portfolio, 2003), p. 239.

[7]McLean and Elkind, *op. cit.*, p. 241.

[8]McLean and Elkind, *op. cit.*, pp. 221-224.

[9]Commodity Futures Trading Commission, *The CFTC Glossary: A Guide to the Language of the Futures Industry.* Available on the World Wide Web at: *http://www.cftc.gov/files/opa/cftcglossary.pdf.*

[10]For example, see the Commodities Futures Trading Commission's enforcement order against Coral Energy (an affiliate of Shell), which the company settled for $30 million for alleged market manipulation. Available on the World Wide Web at: *http://www.cftc.gov/files/enf/04orders/enfcoral-order.pdf.*

Dealing with Risk:
Terminology and Techniques

To manage risk, it is necessary to define risk and its various aspects. Through the understanding provided by a common language, the reader can learn the seven basic techniques for managing risk, and better understand the role of a risk manager, and the challenge of risk management.

Terminology

Managing risk requires an understanding of risk and the terms used to measure it. These definitions come from Mehr and Cammack's *Principles of Insurance*, a classic in the field. But wait, some may say, energy firms aren't insurance companies — there's no connection. Wrong. The insurance industry has grown and prospered by understanding risk and how to profit from it. It would be unwise to ignore the experience of an industry that has existed for hundreds of years and has some of the largest financial institutions in this country amongst its members. Here are the basic terms needed to understand risk. To illustrate the terms, let's consider them in the context of an everyday risk — being involved in an automobile collision.

Risk is "uncertainty about loss."[1] Every time a driver proceeds in his automobile, he faces the possibility of colliding with another automobile, pedestrian, or tree and the consequent damage to his vehicle and person. However, the driver does not know if he will be involved in a collision on that trip — this uncertainty is the risk he faces.

Chance of Loss is the probable number of losses arising from a given number of exposures expressed as a fraction:[2]

$$\text{Chance of loss} = \frac{\text{Probable number of losses}}{\text{Number of exposures}}$$

Say, for example, you play a game by rolling a fair six-sided die. You win if an even number appears on top after a roll, and lose if an odd number appears. There are three winning possibilities and three losing possibilities — a total of six possibilities.

$$\text{Chance of loss} = 3/6 = 1/2 = 50\%.$$

In the case of automobile accidents in the United States of America in 2002, the **chance of loss**, with loss the probability of a vehicle occupant dying was:

$$\text{Chance of loss} = \frac{37232 \text{ vehicle occupant fatalities}}{2880 \text{ billion vehicle miles traveled}} = \frac{1.29 \text{ fatalities}}{100 \text{ million vehicle miles traveled}^3}$$

Peril is a "cause of loss."[4] This could be another vehicle or a fixed object along the side of the road that, through impact, causes damage to the vehicle — or a driver's own actions that lead to a collision and resultant property damage and loss of life.

Hazard is a condition that increases the chance of loss.[5] Some drivers are more hazardous than others. For example, males age 16-20 are almost nine times as likely to be involved in a fatal accident as are females in between ages 55-64.[6] Insurance companies use this rating to charge higher insurance rates to males 16-20 than females 55-64, as the chance of loss from a young male driver far exceeds that of the female age 55-64.

Loss is "the unintentional decline in, or disappearance of value, arising from a contingency."[7] For the automobile occupant, this loss could consist of property damage to the vehicle, injury, or loss of life.

With these definitions, it is possible to understand the six techniques for managing risk.

Framework

The techniques are from Mehr and Cammack and represent a systematic way to examine risks and approach them to create an effective risk management stratagem. Solutions to some problems may use one or a combination of techniques. Again, the principles will be illustrated within the context of the risks arising from operating an automobile.

Technique One: Avoid Risks

The simplest way to avoid risk is to not expose yourself to hazards. This may work at times in particular areas of business — for example a company may choose to stay out of a particular business such as nuclear power. However, a business cannot avoid risk completely. Investors commit capital to a firm with the expectation of earning a return on investment — they put their capital at risk. For putting that capital at risk, they expect a return exceeding that from a risk free investment — such as a Treasury bond. If a business wishes to maintain access to capital and to function as a going entity, it will have to engage in risky business — although it can choose how much risk it wishes to take on.

Think of the choice to use an automobile. The only way to be certain of staying out of a car crash is not to travel by car. Of course, those who wish to travel will have to choose some other method of transportation — which will bring attendant risks with it. In many parts of the USA, lack of an automobile significantly restricts mobility and access to work. In this case, avoiding risk can significantly restrict the opportunity to earn a living, or the ability to easily access necessities — such as groceries.

No risk, no reward.

Technique Two: Bear the Risk

Some organizations may choose to bear all risks on their own rather than take out insurance or use other financial tools for protection. These organizations may see self-insurance (bearing all the risk) as a way to save money by not paying for insurance. However, if they cannot afford their losses, they're in trouble.[8]

An organization should choose to bear risk as a result of a conscious, informed decision, not simply as a default choice. Choosing to bear risk may make sense, when the decision is accompanied by a careful analysis of the costs and benefits of a chosen path. However, it would be negligent to bear risk simply out of ignorance (when an organization neglects to make a careful inventory of its risks) or from the misconception that inaction on risk is superior to action. For example, an energy company may choose not to use energy derivatives to protect against price increases in a fuel, as it feels derivatives are "dangerous." (This fallacy will be dealt with in the next chapter.) Just because the company has not shifted the risk to another party with derivatives (*see Technique Five*) does not mean the risk goes away — prices can still move in a way that could be adverse to the company's fortunes. By choosing not to act (or by not acting through ignorance about risk) the organization has consciously or unconsciously chosen to bear risk. Fuel prices will react to market forces — not the energy company's needs.

Again, the example of an automobile driver provides a good way to illustrate risk bearing. When a driver operates an automobile, he exposes himself to the risk of being involved in an accident, and facing financial claims against his person and assets (in addition to actual physical harm) if deemed liable for some or all of the losses stemming from the crash. Without automobile insurance, the driver would have to bear all financial risk stemming from the crash, which could cause him to forfeit his financial and real assets in the event that a civil judgment is returned against him. In some locales, drivers are allowed to self-insure — in others, automobile liability insurance is required. However, even when a driver has automobile collision insurance, he often bears risk through the deductible on his policy. For example, a car owner has a comprehensive policy with a $500 deductible. A tree branch falls on his car while it is parked on the street and breaks a windshield. The repairs will cost $1500. He is responsible for paying damages to his car up to $500, to repair it, after which the the insurance company will pay the remaining $1000. This is a good example of two risk management techniques coexisting — **bearing risk** and **shifting risk** (*Technique Five*).

Financial institutions might not lend to small to medium-sized organizations that choose to bear all risks, because losses could cripple the business and prevent repayment of loans. Even when risk bearers do obtain credit, it may be at a higher cost than for an organization with less risk, because the exposure to potential **losses** increases the chance of an adverse credit event — such as a loan default. Organizations may also face significant credit risks if they are forced to pay out for a major loss or misfortune.

Technique Three: Reduce the Hazard

Avoid the conditions that increase the chance of a loss. Many of the major debacles of recent years (Enron, wash trading, collapse of power markets) resulted from failure to effectively manage trading operations and those employees that engaged in risky business — and who violated company policies. Allowing persistent violation of company policies, not having policies in place, or not having people who understand how to manage the risks the organization faces, create a hazardous environment that can increase the chances of losses for the company. Going forward, the best way to reduce the hazard is to implement policies and procedures, led by the right people, that enforce the risk management goals of the senior leadership of the organization. This translates into paying careful attention to corporate governance and implementation of governance policies.

Certain conditions and behaviors can increase the chance of loss. For example, if a car has tires that are severely underinflated, this condition increases the chances of a blowout of a tire that could cause a car to go out of control and crash. Certain behaviors, such as driving while intoxicated and running through stop signs (analogous to violation of company policies) increase the chance of getting involved in an accident. Actions such as making sure that a car's tires are properly inflated and driving responsibly reduce the hazards of automobile operation.

Technique Four: Reduce the Loss

Take steps to reduce the **losses** arising from a **peril.**

Given the large number of risk exposures that an organization faces, it is likely that a peril will affect the company, causing a loss. This loss may occur because of a failure to remedy certain hazards, or for reasons that could not have been foreseen. What is important is to be prepared for the loss: have policies and procedures in place, and prepared people, to deal with losses — and to minimize losses when they take place.

For example, a fire extinguisher on the premises will not stop a fire from igniting, but its use can reduce fire damage. Companies with trading operations need to react quickly to adverse market conditions and set up strategies in advance that contain provisions to reduce losses when faced with adverse market moves.

For a driver in a car, who may be in an accident, wearing a seat belt is a technique to reduce loss, because wearing the belt reduces the chance of death or injury in an accident, as well as the severity of injury received.

Technique Five: Shift the Risk

One way to get rid of risk is to pass it along to someone else. Often this is done for a price, or because the other side of the deal sees potential for profit. However, just because the other side may make money, doesn't mean that shifting risk is a bad business deal. Think of the driver who purchases automobile insurance. For a modest outlay he can protect his assets from a lawsuit and minimize the financial adversity that could stem from his car being stolen or damaged.

One way that businesses can shift risk, besides using insurance, is through the use of financial risk management tools, such as derivatives, that allow the firms to shift the risk of price increases or decreases to other parties. Derivatives are financial products that derive their value from the price of another commodity or the value of an index number. Later chapters will outline the basic types of derivatives and how to use them to manage financial risk from unpredictable energy prices.

Other ways to shift risk are through subcontracting and leasing. For example, if a utility has not had much success in operating a nuclear plant, but still wants the power that comes from the plant, it could subcontract the operation to a company that specializes in running nuclear plants and has a strong track record in making problematic plants profitable. As part of the operating agreement, the buyer of the services can receive financial guarantees from the subcontractor, which could mitigate the costs of an unreliable plant — a source of financial certainty that the utility couldn't manage when it ran the plant on its own.

When an item is leased, the owner, not the user, assumes responsibility for the financial risk. For example, someone rents a car on vacation. If the car is stolen in the course of a trip, the renter is not financially responsible for the theft. In addition, the rental car company will provide another car to allow the traveler to proceed on his way. By renting the car, the traveler transfers the risks of car theft that could disrupt a trip onto the rental car agency.

The way an organization structures itself can also play a role in shifting risk. For example, when a company is incorporated, shareholders risk only the capital they have invested. In an unincorporated business, if the assets of the business are insufficient to meet creditors' claims, then the assets of the owners can be called upon. By incorporating, some of the risk of a business failure moves from the owners to creditors, due to the principle of limited liability.

Technique Six: Reduce the Risk

Remember, risk is about uncertainty. Quantifying the probability of events reduces uncertainty. Drivers know that cars get stolen, but they don't know whose car will be stolen — they have a high level of uncertainty. However, if automobile owners are pooled by an insurance company, then a large data set can be assembled. Via the law of large numbers, the insurance company can quantify the chance of an automobile being stolen, given such factors as the model type, where it is housed, and whether it has a theft prevention system. Knowing the probability of a car being stolen reduces risk. Increasing the pool of insured reduces risk, making losses predictable enough to calculate premiums. Insurance companies desire the largest number of policy holders to better quantify risk and to spread it over a large group to minimize the possibility of multiple claims related to a single event. Some insurers did not have diverse portfolios in 1992, with heavy exposure in Southeast Florida, and were devastated by Hurricane Andrew.

Applying the Principles of Risk Management

Now the question arises: how to put it all together. That will become clearer as we work through the different risk areas that face an energy firm. Keep these thoughts in mind throughout:

The job of risk analysis is keyed to finding the answer to two basic questions: (1) what can cause loss? and (2) how much loss can it cause? The risk manager must be prepared to answer these questions whether he is engaged in decision making for a large corporation or merely engaged in planning his own family security.[9]

With that overall mandate, it is possible to see the benefit of using a structured framework to give an outline of the job for the risk manager. The role of the risk manager boils down to these tasks:

(1) to discover the risk problems to be solved
(2) to consider the ways to deal with the problem
(3) to decide what appears to be the most efficient
    way to deal with the problem
(4) to implement the decision
(5) to evaluate the results.[10]

Armed with an understanding of the terminology and techniques of risk management, it is now possible to start looking at the risks facing energy companies and what to do about them.

Notes

[1]Robert I. Mehr and Emerson Cammack, *Principles of Insurance*; Fourth Edition (Homewood, Illinois: Richard D. Irwin, Inc. 1966), p. 24.

[2]Mehr and Cammack, *op. cit.*, p. 17.

[3]National Highway Traffic Safety Administration, *Traffic Safety Facts 2002: A Compilation of Motor Vehicle Crash Data from the Fatality Analysis Reporting System and the General Estimates System* (Washington, DC: U.S. Department of Transportation, January 2004).

[4]Mehr and Cammack, *op. cit.*, p. 22.

[5]*Ibid.*

[6]National Highway Traffic Safety Administration, *op. cit.*, p. 98.

[7]Mehr and Cammack, *op. cit.*, p. 23.

[8]Cammack and Mehr provide an apt illustration of how a company may assume more risk than it expected:

"Often when risk is assumed, there is an attempt to build up a sinking fund to offset possible losses. Just how successful this method will be in handling risk depends upon the circumstances. For example, businessmen sometimes accumulate sinking funds to meet uncertainty, in the erroneous belief that they are conducting a scientifically based operation. Let us assume that the manager of a store that has never suffered a fire loss begins to cast a covetous eye at the firm's annual fire insurance bill. The manager is very prevention-conscious, to the extent of having monthly fire drills; and he is never out of arm's reach of a fire extinguisher. He decides that he will self-insure his fire risk. Instead of renewing his insurance, he puts the premium into a newly created account, 'Fire Self-Insurance Fund.' (As will soon become apparent, this is an erroneous use of the term 'self insurance.') One evening, when the manager has locked up his extinguisher for the night, a hungry rat, who is new in the building and has missed the fire drills, gnaws into the casing of an electric line and causes a short circuit, which before morning, has started a fire that cannot be extinguished. Where is the self insurance fund then? Perhaps there is a loss of $100,000 to be offset by a fund of $2,000"; pp. 27-28.

[9]*Ibid.*

[10]Cammack and Mehr, *op. cit.*, p. 51.

Common Risks and Misconceptions

Uncertainty is inescapable. Risk permeates life and business. Energy suppliers are not immune — and they weren't before industry restructuring. Few businesses, however, face such a variety of risks: everything from hurricanes to regulators to squirrels chewing through wires. Fraud, of course, has been a risk since biblical days.[1] Risk cannot be escaped through ignorance — management needs to understand and manage the uncertainty it confronts.

Price Uncertainty

Restructuring of energy markets has magnified the effects of volatile fuel prices, because it is harder to pass costs on to customers, unlike under regulation. For example, what happens when an electric distributor has an obligation to serve its customers at a capped rate, but it has to buy power in an unregulated market? In such a case it can, theoretically, face an unlimited risk on the fuel side and limited return from the customers. During the California power crisis, this spread between the power purchase price and the retail revenue caused Pacific Gas & Electric, one of the nation's largest energy suppliers, to go bankrupt.[2]

However, prudent risk management minimizes the damage of price volatility. A firm can switch fuels or suppliers, diversify its fuel sources (a form of reducing risk), or hedge purchases and sales, which transfers the risk to other parties.

Weather Uncertainty

Weather dominates the energy business. Temperatures determine energy usage and revenues. A warm winter reduces revenues for a gas company and cool summers cut sales at electric companies. Storms interrupt service and annoy customers. Weather can contribute to larger scale disruptions. During the California power crisis, water levels behind dams dropped, which meant less hydropower than normal. Utilities that relied on hydropower had to buy in the spot market — when there was power — at high prices, which they could not pass on to their customers.

Interest Rates

Although, at the time of this writing, interest rates are comparatively low, they may rise. In the 1970s, interest rates rose dramatically, which increased costs of debt financing. Utilities cannot control interest rates, but tools exist to mitigate the risk.

Foreign Exchange

Many energy suppliers have overseas operations accompanied by foreign currency risk. A fall of the overseas currency relative to the dollar could dramatically reduce earnings in comparison to projections. A devaluation could cause overseas assets to fall in value, requiring write-downs that could affect credit agreements.

Credit

After a company's credit rating falls, it pays higher costs for borrowing and may be restricted from trading with certain counterparties, which could affect its ability to purchase power in a market and fulfill commitments to customers and counterparties.

Stock Price

Companies like their stock prices to rise. Yet, the stock price can vary outside the firm's control. However, financial tools can mitigate possible financial consequences of that risk — especially of a falling stock price.

Asset Values

In 2001, Ford Motor Company had to write down the value of its palladium inventory by one billion dollars.[3] Ford had purchased the palladium — at a peak in the palladium market — for use in its catalytic converters. Palladium prices plummeted after the purchase. According to accounting rules, the commodity's value must be marked-to-market, so Ford's inventory suffered an "impairment" of its value, which led to

the charge of roughly one billion dollars to Ford's fourth quarter earnings, all because the company did not protect the value of a volatile
commodity.

What to Do About the Risks

The way the energy supplier approaches risks can help avoid the harm
or ease the pain.

Chapter Two outlined the six basic techniques for managing risk:

> 1) Avoid the risk.
> 2) Bear the risk.
> 3) Reduce the hazard.
> 4) Reduce the loss.
> 5) Shift the risk (hedge).
> 6) Reduce the risk (diversify).

The technique that causes the greatest concern for managers and
boards of directors is *Technique 5: Shift the Risk*, or **hedging**,
because it brings the element of financial **derivatives** into play. The
"D-Word" seems to strike terror in the hearts of corporate boards and
regulators. After all, didn't Procter & Gamble, Gibson Greetings, and
Orange County collectively lose almost two billion dollars on
derivatives in the 1990s?[4] Their fear is misplaced. Derivatives are
simply financial instruments that derive their value from an underlying
financial instrument, commodity price, or index value. Consider, for
instance, the *hedge*, defined as:

> **hedge (economic)** — The initiation of a position in a futures or
> options market that is intended as a temporary substitute for the
> sale or purchase of the actual commodity. An example is the sale
> of futures contracts in anticipation of future sale of cash com-
> modities as a protection against potential price declines or the
> purchase of futures contracts in anticipation of future purchases
> of cash commodities as a protection against the possibility of
> increasing costs.[5]

When used to manage risk, derivatives (hedging in this case) allow
one organization to shift its risk to another party. The recipient of the

risk may be another hedger, or possibly a speculator, who seeks to profit from changes in the prices of the contracts.

Hedging is not speculation, *and the two should not be confused!* The main question that corporate boards will have to wrestle with is what policy they wish to implement, hedging or speculation, and understand the difference between the two. They need to understand how derivatives fit in with corporate policy. For example, Orange County was not engaged in the derivatives market to manage its risk exposures, but used derivatives as a way to increase investment returns, although the county officials did not appear to understand the difference of the risks involved.[6] It will be up to a corporate board to assure that its wishes are respected by the trading operations of the firm, as discussed in Chapter 4.

Conclusion

Management needs to acknowledge the risks inherent to the energy supply business and use a combination of techniques to manage those risks. Just because a company doesn't use derivatives doesn't mean it will avoid problems. The risk will still remain, but the company will have lost a tool to deal with it. Risk doesn't go away, but managers who fail to deal with it effectively do.

Notes

[1] In Chapter 29 of Genesis, Laban deceived Jacob when instead of delivering Rachel as payment for services rendered, he delivered his less attractive daughter, Leah.

[2] The California Power Crisis occurred in 2000-2001. Because of the way the power markets were restructured, the major utilities were forced to buy power in the spot market — at a market price — and sell it, in many cases, below cost, to consumers. In addition, market manipulation, and lack of in-state generation, led to power shortages and rolling blackouts in many parts of the state. The financial strain hurt Edison International and, as mentioned above, drove Pacific Gas & Electric into bankruptcy.

[3] Ford Motor Company, Form 10-K for the fiscal year ended 2001, p. FS-17.

[4] Frank Partnoy, *F.I.A.S.C.O.: Blood in the Water on Wall Street* (New York, W.W. Norton, 1997), pp. 93-94; pp. 157-158.

[5] Committee of Chief Risk Officers, *Glossary*. Definition for **hedge (economic)**.

[6] Frank Partnoy, *op. cit.*, pp. 157-176.

Risk Management Starts at the Top

The chief executive of a failed corporation says, "I didn't know what was going on. The chief financial officer made all those decisions. I couldn't have been expected to understand them." The collapsed energy merchant had a chief risk officer who had put in place an expensive risk management system that did not protect the firm. The hedge fund with tight risk management rules failed because it had violated its own risk rules. What went wrong?

Perhaps the corporate structure became too large and complex for anyone to know what was going on, a risk that deserves, but rarely receives, management attention. Perhaps the directors and managers viewed risk management as an administrative burden rather than as a tool for decision making, a window-dressing procedure to deflect criticism. Perhaps management decided to ignore guidelines because it had in front of it a deal too good to pass up.

Risk management serves a real purpose only if executive officers and directors embrace it as an integral part of business strategy. Otherwise, it is nothing more than a bureaucratic exercise that lulls the management and directors into a false sense of security.[1] Those at the top, who oversee the organization, need to determine its rationale for being involved in energy markets, its objectives, and the policies and procedures to assure the firm meets its objectives and stays in line with the overall goals regarding strategy and risk.[2] If the board of directors and senior management do not explicitly develop and proclaim these goals and explain them to those in charge of executing them, then the policy will evolve by default from the actions of those who are involved in either trading or making the decisions that affect the firm's exposure to risk.

The board and senior management need to make a priority of enforcing their policies and procedures — and not permitting deviations.[3] If the rules are not enforced, then the systematic flouting of the rules will produce a new policy by default — one that most likely will be contrary to the board's wishes.[4] If the rules need revision, that is a job for the board to decide —not the traders on the desk.[5]

Business Strategy Shapes Risk Management Style

As a start, management must determine the purpose of its activities that require the risk management. Not having a clear notion of business strategy creates risk.

Firms Need to Decide Why They're Trading in the Energy Markets

To simplify the situation, think of the energy trading function as having three purposes:

1. *Trading for profit* — Less politely referred to as "speculation," trading energy for profit is no different than trading common stocks, soybeans, or tulip bulbs. A market exists. It is volatile. The trader hopes to earn a profit by selling a product on the market at a higher price than the purchase price. The trading business is a high-risk volatile enterprise, which requires strict trading rules and supervision to prevent the kind of rogue trading that can bring down the firm.[6] It requires a capitalization befitting the risk profile, and a keen awareness of the risks on the part of management and directors.

2. *Hedging* — Energy buyers or sellers may have a prosaic use for risk management. They do not intend to make a killing in the energy markets. They just want some assurance of the price at which they will buy or sell energy, or to shift some of the risk that they might contract to buy or sell at too high or low a price. Hedging costs money, but it also lowers risk, which lessens the cost of capital. Businesses or consumers who do not view their primary activity as speculation on energy prices should hedge. Those who hedge should regard the activity as a way to lower risk rather than to make money. Risk managers of hedgers have to keep the policy focused on cutting risk, and not allow any eager prognosticator to turn the policy toward speculation, "just this one time."

3. *Using trading to build other businesses* — Often called "trading around the assets," this strategy views energy trading as a

means to build up an associated business. For instance, the firm owns power plants, and views operation of those plants as its real business. But the power plants have to sell the electricity that they produce. A trading operation might help to market the output from the power plants, and might find ways to reduce the price risks involved in selling that electricity on the markets. This type of trading has a specific goal, to enhance the value of the generating assets. It should operate within risk guidelines that prevent it from engaging in other activities, or it will develop other purposes, and probably, raise the level of risk.

In effect, the organization must align risk management with the priorities of the organization, and then stick to the priorities set. Aligning risk management with priorities does not mean something like looser risk management for speculative ventures in order to let them speculate. It means setting procedures that control the activities undertaken. Changing the priorities leaves the firm operating with risk management procedures designed for the previous priority. In addition, the risk managers must apply their standards throughout the organization, lest risk activities shift from risk intolerant to risk tolerant divisions within the enterprise.

Role of Risk Managers

The risk manager does not establish the firm's risk policy. The board of directors does (or should do) that. The risk manager (or the chief risk officer) implements board policy. That means that the board of directors must, consciously, decide the level of risk it wishes the corporation to incur. This willingness to accept or avoid risk sends a message to employees, shareholders, and creditors. The risk manager may have helped the board to formulate the risk policy, but should not have formulated the policy for the perfunctory approval of the board. The risk manager then has to implement the board's policies throughout the organization. Given that the risk manager may have no line authority, and may have to work through senior executives who have their own agendas for the operations under their supervision, it is essential that everyone understand that risk management policies derive from the authority of the board of directors. Otherwise, the risk manager becomes, in the eyes of the line management, just one more meddlesome bean counter sent in by central staff to harass and annoy those who know what the business really is all about. Brett Friedman and Tim

Essaye of the consultancy Risk Capital enunciate the type of authority the CRO (Chief Risk Officer) needs:

> Failure to give the CRO sufficient independence and authority typically results in the business functions ignoring the CRO's recommendations and marginalizing risk management within the organization. Business unit and trading managers must respect the CRO and his authority for the position to be successful.[7]

Once policies are in place, the risk manager must monitor activities within the organization, not an easy task in a large firm. Monitoring, furthermore, has to go beyond collecting pieces of paper that claim compliance with the rules. Employees who cheat do not fill out forms explaining what they are doing. Monitoring may require cross-checks and alert supervisors who can spot unusual activities. (Organizations shooting for low risk levels may have to avoid certain activities for no other reason than they cannot monitor the risks taken with great enough certainty.)

The risk manager, then, has to compare activities underway with the policy guidelines, make necessary changes in risk management procedures to assure compliance with the guidelines, and report back to the board on a regular basis.

The risk manager might, instead, report to one of the top executives, such as the chief financial officer. That chain of command might work well in an organization that, as a matter of policy, engages in minimally risky activities. The indirect line of command, however, may remove the board from active discussion of risk management, and may not make clear to the board that some seemingly low risk activities really involve high risk to the corporation. Risk management, probably, requires explicit discussion by boards. In addition, the compensation of the risk management staff needs to be independent of, and not tied to, the performance of the energy trading business or market operations.[8] Otherwise, the trading organization can hold the risk managers hostage by controlling compensation, advancement, or allocation of resources.

Oversight of Trading

In designing a corporate structure for a trading operation, it is essential to separate the operation and oversight of the front, middle, and back offices.

The front office executes the firm's strategies with respect to trading and managing risk through the purchase and sale of energy and related derivatives. The role of the front office consists of executing deals, initial recording of the specific terms and conditions of a transaction, and related transaction support roles (*e.g.,* scheduling and nominations). Because of the potential trouble the front office can get the firm into, the infrastructure to control it — usually the middle office — needs to be totally separate.

The middle office polices and controls the front office, and needs to be independent of it. Its function is to assure that the front office complies with policies and risk limits as well as validating the models that are used to place a value on elements of the trading portfolio. (At Enron, traders often valued their own deals, which did not create transparent reporting.) The middle office functions fit well within the corporate risk management function.

The back office plays a vital role in controls by taking care of the accounting and financial reporting (reconciliation of trades, accounts receivable and payable) related to the settlement of trades. It is important that the back office be separate from the front office. All too often problems build up because, when a trader who has losses can take care of his own accounting, he can make sure trades go into a drawer rather than into a trading system that reveals his losses. The back office plays a vital role in preventing this from happening.

Conclusion

The real business of risk management starts at the top. Although risk management often is portrayed as some highly mathematical and arcane practice, ultimately the risk management policies and procedures are designed to help the energy company meet its financial and operational goals. Although the senior level managers and boards do not need to be mathematicians, it is important they they understand the basics of risk management and set the direction that it needs to follow — and make sure that the policies and procedures are followed. Otherwise their decisions about the company's direction will be invalidated, with potentially disastrous consequences.

Notes

[1]The risk management staff at Enron was routinely ignored and was quite ineffectual in pressing its case according to Bethany McLean's and Peter Elkind's book, *The Smartest Guys in the Room: The Amazing Rise and Scandalous Fall of Enron* (New York: Portfolio, 2003).

[2]This process is discussed in great detail in the Committee of Chief Risk Officers Organizational Independence and Governance Working Group's white paper on governance. Committee of Chief Risk Officers: *Governance and Controls*, Volume 2 of 6, 19 November 2002, p. 3.

[3]The collapse in 2005 of China Aviation Oil occurred because traders persistently flouted risk controls.

[4]In the case of China Aviation Oil that new policy led to bankruptcy and the jailing of the CEO.

[5]Traders are known to be very aggressive and will push limits in search of trading profits, without always considering risk. When they are trading with their own money that is one thing, but if they are risking the company's resources, that means they need to hew to the rules.

[6]Peter Thal Larsen, "Today Leeson Would Work for a Hedge Fund," *Financial Times*, 21 February 2005, p. 16.

[7]Brett Friedman and Tim Essaye, "Corporate Risk: What Does Management Really Know?" *Public Utilities Fortnightly*, Volume 143, No. 2, February 2005, p. 56.

[8]Committee of Chief Risk Officers: *Introduction and Executive Summaries of CCRO Recommendations*, Volume 1 of 6, 19 November 2002, pp. 9-10.

Shifting Risk with Derivatives:
The Building Blocks

Derivatives practitioners like to portray themselves as members of a quantitative mystic brotherhood (or sisterhood) that few can enter. In reality, they use tools based on simple building blocks that perform a simple purpose: they allow those affected by price volatility to shift the risk to other parties. Derivatives are nothing more than financial products that derive their value from an underlying commodity price, security price, or index number. This chapter provides basic explanations of how to use derivatives to manage financial risk from unpredictable price moves.

Tools of Risk Management

Derivatives grow out of forward contracts, futures, options, and swaps.

Forward and futures contracts enable buyers and sellers to fix a price in advance on an item they will either receive or deliver in the future. Knowing the price allows buyers, known as *longs*, and sellers, known as *shorts*, to transfer the risk that prices will rise or fall in the future.

Forward Contracts

In a *forward contract*:

> . . . a commercial buyer and seller agree upon delivery of a specified quality and quantity of goods at a specified future date. . . . A price may be agreed upon in advance, or there may be agreement that the price will be determined at the time of delivery.[1]

Forward contracts are privately negotiated and not necessarily standardized. Buyers and sellers customize contracts to their needs. Customization creates liquidity risk, however, because the specialized nature of the contracts makes it hard to sell or transfer them to others, a major disadvantage if the conditions change and the contract no longer serves the needs of the buyer (long) or seller (short).

Futures Contracts

A *futures contract* resembles a forward contract, but has certain legal features. It is:

> . . . a legally binding agreement, made on the selling floor [or electronic equivalent] of a futures exchange, to buy or sell a commodity or financial instrument sometime in the future. Futures contracts are standardized according to the quality, quantity, and delivery time and location for each commodity. The only variable is price, which is discovered on an exchange trading floor [or electronic trading system].[2]

In the United States, futures contracts can only trade on licensed contract markets, commonly known as *futures exchanges*, which the Commodities Futures Trading Commission has licensed to trade futures and options.[3] Although standardized, futures contracts frequently have flexibility regarding the quality of the product delivered. To increase liquidity, for certain contracts, commodities of higher or lower quality than the specified grade may be delivered at a respective premium or discount to the contract grade.[4]

One key advantage of futures contracts over forward contracts is that the buyer does not have to take delivery of the commodity, and the seller does not have to make delivery of the commodity. In fact, only a small percentage of traded contracts ever result in delivery.[5] This low delivery rate occurs because of a procedure known as *covering*, or *offset*, which is a:

> situation that occurs when, instead of taking delivery, the buyer of a futures contract reverses the position by selling the [same] contract [month] before the delivery date; a contract writer can reverse this short position by purchasing the [same] contract [month].[6]

In contrast, forward contracts cannot be easily liquidated through an offsetting trade, because their specialized nature restricts their usefulness for the overall marketplace. Furthermore, buyers and sellers of futures contracts can easily cover their positions, because they don't place their transactions with each other, but with the clearinghouse of the exchange. A *clearinghouse* is:

> An agency or separate corporation of a futures exchange that is responsible for settling trading accounts, clearing trades, collecting and maintaining margin monies, regulating delivery, and reporting trading data. Clearinghouses act as third parties to all futures and options contracts, acting as a buyer to every clearing member seller and a seller to every clearing member buyer.[7]

This clearing/credit management function is another key advantage of futures contracts over privately negotiated derivatives, because the clearinghouse guarantees the contracts. Thanks to the clearinghouse, individual buyers and sellers do not have to know the creditworthiness of their opposite numbers in a sale. Another advantage of standardized contracts, although they are less effective than forward contracts in fitting specific needs, is that they trade in a liquid market. The party that no longer wishes involvement in the transaction can get out of the contract. A long can sell the contract to someone else, and a short can buy it back from someone else.

Forward and futures contracts enable buyers and sellers to fix a price in advance on an item they will either receive or deliver at a future date. By knowing the price, the buyers and sellers can transfer the risk that prices will rise or fall in the future, assuring a certain price for a transaction.

Futures

Futures can be used to fix a price, which shifts the risk of price volatility on a good that will be purchased or sold in the near future. Futures provide an effective *hedge*, because the price of the futures correlates highly with the value of the cash commodity. This phenomenon, known as "convergence," is "the tendency for prices of physicals and futures to approach one another, usually during the delivery month."[8]

Long Hedge

A long hedge assures that the buyer can buy a commodity at a given price at a specified future date. The long hedge provides protection against increasing prices. If a hedger purchases a futures contract, and the price of the underlying commodity increases, the purchaser can use the profits realized by the futures contract (selling it at a profit) to counteract the price increase in the cash market, thereby protecting himself against the price increases. By purchasing a futures contract, the buyer has locked in a price and minimizes the effect of upward price movements.[9]

On the other hand, if the price of the commodity falls, the futures contract will decrease in value, and the hedger will take a loss on the futures contract. However, that loss will be offset by the fact that the cash commodity has fallen in price, so what is lost on the futures contract is gained by the ability to buy the commodity at a lower price. The goal of these transactions is not to save money but to reduce the uncertainty about a future price. Shifting the risk increases the certainty of a future price, allowing the buyer to project cash flows with more assurance.

When looking at the examples, please remember that reducing risk has a financial value, and making a smaller profit when taking a lower risk is not a bad business outcome as opposed to making a bigger profit when taking a higher risk.

Example of Using a Long Futures Contract to Hedge a Purchase (Table 5-1)

Consider an oil refinery that needs to purchase crude oil to refine into gasoline and other refined petroleum products. It is February. Refinery management needs to purchase crude oil for the May production run. Currently the oil it refines, West Texas Intermediate Crude (WTI), trades in the forward market for $45.00 per barrel (bbl) as does the futures contract. To protect against a price increase, the refiner purchases, in February, a June long futures contract for $45.00/bbl.[10]

Rising Prices

In May, the price in both the futures and spot markets rises to $50.00/bbl. The refiner sells the futures contract for $50.00/bbl, making a profit of $5.00/bbl. The refiner then buys the crude in the spot market for $50.00/bbl. However, the refiner applies the $5.00/bbl profit on the futures trade to the cash purchase, so the effective cost of each barrel is now $45.00. Because the refiner hedged its purchase, it avoided the shock of the price increase, which the seller of the futures contract had to bear.

Table 5-1

Using Long Futures to Hedge Crude Oil Purchases

Rising Oil Prices

Date	Spot Market	Futures Market
February	WTI Spot is $45.00/bbl	Buy June WTI Futures at $45.00/bbl
May	WTI Spot is $50.00/bbl	Sell June WTI Futures at $50.00/bbl
Change	$5.00/bbl loss	$5.00/bbl gain
Spot Price when Oil is Purchased		$50.00/bbl
Gain on Futures Position		-$5.00/bbl
Net Purchase Price		$45.00/bbl

Falling Oil Prices

Date	Spot Market	Futures Market
February	WTI Spot is $45.00/bbl	Buy June WTI Futures at $45.00/bbl
May	WTI Spot is $40.00/bbl	Sell June WTI Futures at $40.00/bbl
Change	$5.00/bbl gain	$5.00/bbl loss
Spot Price when Oil is Purchased		$40.00/bbl
Loss on Futures Position		+$5.00/bbl
Net Purchase Price		$45.00/bbl

Falling Prices

On the other hand, what if the price had fallen? In May, the price in the futures and spot markets falls to $40.00/bbl. The refiner sells the futures contract for $40.00/bbl, losing $5.00/bbl. However, because the price in the spot market has fallen, the refiner buys the crude in the spot market for $40.00/bbl, a savings of $5.00/bbl over the price seen in February. The refiner adds the $5.00/bbl loss on the futures to the cash purchase, so the effective cost of each barrel is now $45.00.

Although the refiner may have paid less had it not hedged, it would not have protected itself against rising prices. The purpose of the hedge, however, was to minimize risk, not minimize prices. The hedge accomplished that, because the refiner fixed a price in advance.

Short Hedge

A short hedge permits a seller to fix a future sale price on a commodity, to protect against price declines. If a hedger sells a futures contract, and the price of the underlying commodity decreases, the seller can use the profits realized by the futures contract (buying it back at a lower price) to counteract the price decrease in the cash market, thereby protecting himself against the price decreases. By selling a futures contract, the buyer locks in a price and minimizes the effect of downward price movements.

Example of Using a Short Futures Contract to Hedge a Sale (Table 5-2)

Consider an oil producer that sells crude oil to refiners. It is February. The producer expects to sell oil in May when refiners begin to blend gasoline for the summer driving season. Currently the oil it sells, West Texas Intermediate Crude (WTI), trades in the spot market for $45.00 barrel, as does the futures contract. To protect against a price decrease, the producer, in February, sells a June futures contract for $45.00/bbl.

Falling Prices

In May, the prices in the futures and spot markets fall to $40.00/bbl. The producer buys back the futures contract for $40.00/bbl, making $5.00/bbl. However, because the price in the spot market has fallen, the producer sells the crude in the spot market for $40.00/bbl. The producer adds the $5.00/bbl gain on the futures contract to the cash sale, so the effective sale price of each barrel is now $45.00.

Because the producer hedged its sale, it avoided the shock of the price drop — which the buyer of the futures contract had to bear.

Rising Prices

In May, the prices in the futures and spot markets rise to $50.00/bbl. The producer buys back the futures contract for $50.00/bbl, losing $5.00/bbl. The producer then sells the crude in the spot market for $50.00/bbl. After the producer applies the $5.00/bbl loss on the futures trade to the cash sale, the effective sale price of each barrel is now $45.00.

Although the producer may have sold the crude at a higher effective price had it not hedged, it would not have protected itself against a price drop. The purpose of the hedge, remember, was to minimize risk, not increase revenues.

Table 5-2

Using Short Futures to Hedge Crude Oil Sales

	Falling Oil Prices	
Date	**Spot Market**	**Futures Market**
February	WTI Spot is $45.00/bbl	Sell June WTI Futures at $45.00/bbl
May	WTI Spot is $40.00/bbl	Buy June WTI Futures at $40.00/bbl
Change	$5.00/bbl loss	$5.00/bbl gain
Spot Price when Oil is Sold		$40.00/bbl
Gain on Futures Position		+$5.00/bbl
Net Sale Price		$45.00/bbl
	Rising Oil Prices	
Date	**Spot Market**	**Futures Market**
February	WTI Spot is $45.00/bbl	Sell June WTI Futures at $45.00/bbl
May	WTI Spot is $50.00/bbl	Buy June WTI Futures at $50.00/bbl
Change	$5.00/bbl gain	$5.00/bbl loss
Spot Price when Oil is Sold		$50.00/bbl
Loss on Futures Position		-$5.00/bbl
Net Sale Price		$45.00/bbl

Margins and Mark-to-Market Procedures

Futures and short options positions are highly leveraged transactions. Remember, the buyer or seller of a futures contract and the writer of an option contract have created a financial obligation that will be filled at a time in the future. To maintain integrity in their marketplaces, exchanges require the buyers and the sellers of futures contracts and options writers to post a performance bond, known as *margin*, as a good faith deposit to assure that they will meet their financial obligations under the contract. When a customer initiates a futures transaction, he is required to post *initial margin*. As the contract trades, the daily gains or losses from the trading are added to or subtracted from the balance in the account. If the equity in the account falls below a threshold, known as *maintenance margin*, the customer is required to return the margin to the initial margin level (which is higher than maintenance margin).[11] This is known as a *margin call*. If the account holder fails to meet the margin call, the broker is entitled to liquidate the account holder's position, because the broker is responsible for clearing the trade. Table 5-3 depicts five days in the oil futures markets, which will help clarify these concepts.

Five Days in the Oil Futures Markets (Table 5-3).

On *Monday*, 4 April 2005, two traders simultaneously initiate positions in the NYMEX WTI futures. Trader A goes long one contract at the settlement price of $57.01/bbl, and Trader B goes short one contract at the settlement price of $57.01/bbl. Each posts initial margin of $4,725.

On *Tuesday*, 5 April 2005, the contract falls to $56.04/bbl, down $0.97/bbl. Trader A loses $970, and his account falls to $3,755. Trader B, however, gains $970, and his account now holds $5,695.

On *Wednesday*, 6 April 2005, the contract falls another $0.19/bbl to $55.85/bbl. Trader A loses $190 and his account falls to $3,565. Trader B gains $190 and his account now totals $5,885.

On *Thursday*, 7 April 2005, the contract falls $1.74/bbl to $54.11/bbl. Trader A loses $1,740 and the balance in his account falls to $1,825, below the maintenance margin of $3,500/contract. Now Trader A's broker calls Trader A up and has him deposit $2,900 to bring him back to the initial margin of $4,725. Trader B gains $1,740 and his account now totals $7,625.

On *Friday*, the market falls $0.79 to settle at $53.32/bbl. Trader A loses $790 to have his account fall to $3,935. Trader B has a gain of $790, which makes his account now total $8,415.

Table 5-3

Mark-to-Market and Margin

NYMEX WTI Futures
Initial Margin of $4,725.00 per contract
Maintenance Margin of $3,500 per contract
Contract is 1,000 U.S. barrels (42,000 gallons)

Five Days in the Crude Oil Futures Markets
4 April 2005 to 8 April 2005

Day	Settlement Price ($/bbl)	Trader A (Long) Account Balance	Trader B (Short) Account Balance
Monday	$57.01	Buy 1 WTI Futures Contract	Sell 1 WTI Futures Contract
		$4,725 initial margin	$4,725 initial margin
Tuesday	$56.04	-$970 market loss	+$970 market gain
		($0.97/bbl loss × 1000 bbls)	($0.97/bbl gain × 1000 bbls)
		= $3,755 account total	= $5,695 account total
Wednesday	$55.85	− $190 market loss	+ $190 market gain
		($0.19/bbl loss × 1000 bbls)	($0.19/bbl gain × 1000 bbls)
		$3,565 account total	$5,885 account total
Thursday	$54.11	− $1,740 market loss	+ 1,740 market gain
		($1.74/bbl loss × 1000 bbls)	($1.74/bbl gain × 1000 bbls)
		= $1,825 account balance	= $7,625 account balance
		+ $2,900 margin call to bring account up to initial level	
		= $4,725 account total after margin call	
Friday	$53.32	− $790 market loss	+ 790 market gain
		($0.79/bbl loss × 1000 bbls)	($0.79/bbl gain × 1000 bbls)
		= $3,935 account balance	= $8,415 account balance

Certain conclusions can be drawn from a review of these daily transactions:

1. The losses for the long (Trader A) equate to the gains of the short (Trader B) with the opposite position. Trading is a zero sum game — one party's losses equate to the other party's gains.

2. The energy markets can be quite volatile — it's very easy to lose money! A rapid drawdown in a company's margin account could have significant implications for cash flows. The tremendous demands that trading (as opposed to hedging) can make on a firm's capital need to be fully considered before a board or senior executives endorse such a program. (Remember, the trader's are trading with the firm's money, not their own.)

3. In futures markets, a trader can use a small amount of leverage to control a large position. When the traders started out, for $4,725, they controlled a contract worth $57,010 — a leverage of over 12:1. (One dollar of margin controlled about $12 of contract.) This leverage can produce tremendous gains and losses. Trader B, for an initial outlay of $4,725, has a profit of $3,690 — a 78% increase in his portfolio in a week of trading. On the other hand, Trader A has lost $3,690 of his capital and had to tie up another $2,900 to keep his position open.

These mark-to-market examples should not serve as a reason to avoid the markets to manage risk. They just point out what market participants need to understand before they jump into trading. The risks involved in a speculative trading program should give boards pause before they approve a speculative trading program, or even an "optimization" program.

Options

Options are contracts that convey the right, but not the obligation, to buy or sell a particular good (the *underlying asset*) at some time in the future, at a certain price, for a limited time period that ends on the option's expiration date. A *call option* gives the holder the right to buy the underlying asset at a certain price, for a limited time period. A *put option* gives the holder the right to sell the underlying asset at a given price for a limited time period. The *strike price* or *exercise price is* "the price at which the futures contract underlying a call or put option can be purchased (if a call) or sold (if a put)."[12] To *exercise an option* means "to elect to buy or sell, taking advantage of the right (but not the obligation) conferred to the owner of an option contract."[13] An option that is profitable to exercise is known as *in-the-money*. A call option goes in-the-money when its "strike price is below the current price of the underlying futures contract."[14] A put option goes in-the-money when "its strike price is above the current price of the underlying futures contract."[15] The *breakeven point* is "the underlying futures price at which a given options strategy is neither profitable nor unprofitable. For call options, it is the strike price plus the premium. For put options, it is the strike price minus the premium."[16]

For options buyers, also known as *holders of the options*, options are less risky than forward or futures contracts, because risk is limited to the payment of the premium required to purchase the option.[17] The most that buyers can lose is the cost of the option (the *premium*). However, that low risk profile does not apply to the seller of the option, also known as the *option writer* or *option grantor.*[18] The option writer has "the obligation (if assigned) to BUY (short put option), or SELL (short call option) a futures contract at a specific price on or before an expiration date."[19] Options exchanges randomly assign option writers to fulfill the options that option holders exercise. The option writer assumes the risk of assignation in exchange for receipt of the buyer's premium. In the same way, an insurer receives a premium to bear a policyholder's risk for the duration of an insurance policy. Consequently, the option writer exposes himself to unlimited risk as long as he holds the written contract. He can cancel his obligation by *offsetting* through a purchase of the opposite obligation (a long call or long put) of the same expiration date and strike price on the options market.

The value of an option is based on the:

1. *Price of the underlying asset relative to the option's exercise price* — Options are worth more when the underlying price is near the strike price, because those options have a better chance of going in-the-money.

2. *Time to expiration* — An option with a longer life is more valuable, because it increases the amount of time for the underlying asset to hit the strike price.

3. *Volatility of the price of the underlying asset* — With a more volatile asset, there is a greater chance that the underlying asset will hit the strike price during the option's life.

4. *Interest rates* — Rates affect the cost of financing options.

Higher interest rates tend to lead to higher premiums, which may reduce the profitability of the option.[20]

The various options models that exist, such as the well known Black-Scholes, use the above variables to come to a theoretical price that can guide trading and risk management decisions.[21]

Because option buyers make a one-time payment on an option, their liabilities do not fluctuate daily, as do futures contracts. The most they can lose is the premium — and they pay that when they purchase the option. Hence, there are no mark-to-market procedures for options buyers. Options writers, however, are subject to risk from price fluctuations. Consequently, exchanges require option writers to post margin because their positions are subject to losses in the same way as futures contracts. The accounts of options writers are marked-to-market on a daily basis and margin calls are made when margin levels fall below the maintenance level.[22]

Example of Using Long Calls to Hedge a Purchase (Table 5-4)

Consider an oil refinery that needs to purchase crude oil to refine into gasoline and other refined petroleum products. It is February. The refinery needs to purchase crude oil for its May production run. It has considered using futures, but wants to be able to take advantage of drops in the price of oil. It decides to hedge using long calls. Currently the oil it uses in the refinery, West Texas Intermediate Crude (WTI), trades in the spot market for $45.00 per barrel. To protect against a price increase, the refiner purchases, in February, a June call with a strike price of $45.00/bbl for a $2.50/bbl premium.[23]

Rising Prices

In May, the price in the spot market rises to $50.00/bbl. The option goes in the money. The refiner sells the call option for $5.00/bbl, making a profit of $2.50/bbl. The refiner then buys the crude in the spot market for $50.00/bbl. The refiner, however, applies the $2.50/bbl profit on the option to the cash purchase, so the effective cost of each barrel is $47.50. Because the refiner hedged its purchase, it lessened the size of the price increase.

Table 5-4

Using Long Calls to Hedge Crude Oil Purchases

Rising Oil Prices

Date	Spot Market	Options Market
February	WTI Spot is $45.00/bbl	Buy June WTI $45.00/bbl Call for $2.50/bbl premium
May	WTI Spot is $50.00/bbl	Sell June WTI $45.00/bbl Call for $5.00 premium
Change	$5.00/bbl loss	$2.50/bbl gain
Spot Price when Oil is Purchased		$50.00/bbl
Gain on Options Position		-$2.50/bbl
Net Purchase Price		$47.50/bbl

Falling Oil Prices

Date	Spot Market	Options Market
February	WTI Spot is $45.00/bbl	Buy June WTI $45.00/bbl Call for $2.50/bbl premium
May	WTI Spot is $40.00/bbl	Options Expire Worthless
Change	$5.00/bbl gain	$2.50/bbl loss
Spot Price when Oil is Purchased		$40.00/bbl
Loss on Options Position		+$2.50/bbl
Net Purchase Price		$42.50/bbl

Falling Prices

On the other hand, what if the price had fallen? In May, the price in the spot market falls to $40.00/bbl. The call option expires worthless. However, because the price in the spot market has fallen, the refiner buys the crude in the spot market for $40.00/bbl, a savings of $5.00/bbl over the price indicated by the markets in February. The refiner adds the $2.50/bbl loss on the options to the cash purchase, so the effective cost of each barrel is $42.50. By using the option, the refiner benefits more from the fall in prices than by using a futures contract, because the amount spent on the option, the premium of $2.50, does not cancel out the value of the price drop, as would happen with a short futures contract.

Although the refiner may have paid less had it not hedged, it would not have protected itself against an upward price move.

Example of Using Long Puts to Hedge a Sale (Table 5-5)

Consider an oil producer that sells crude oil to refiners. It is February. The producer will sell oil in May to refiners that will blend gasoline for the summer driving season. Currently the oil it sells, West Texas Intermediate Crude (WTI), trades in the spot market for $45.00 per barrel. To protect against a price decrease, the producer, in February, buys a June put with a strike price of $45.00/bbl for a premium of $2.50/bbl.

Falling Prices

In May, the price in the spot market falls to $40.00/bbl and the option is now worth $5.00/bbl. The producer sells the contract for $5.00/bbl, making $2.50/bbl. However, because the price in the spot market has fallen, the producer sells the crude in the spot market for $40.00/bbl. The producer adds the $2.50/bbl gain on the futures to the cash sale, so the effective sale price of each barrel is now $42.50.

Because the producer hedged its sale, it lessened the impact of the price drop that it suffered — passing on some of the financial pain to the seller of the options contract.

Rising Prices

In May, the spot market price rises to $50.00/bbl. The put option expires worthless The producer then sells the crude in the spot market for $50.00/bbl. After the producer applies the $2.50/bbl loss on the options to the cash sale, the effective sale price of each barrel is $47.50.

Although the producer would have sold the crude at a higher effective price had it not hedged, it would not have had protection against a price drop.

Table 5-5

Using Long Puts to Hedge Crude Oil Sales

Falling Oil Prices

Date	Spot Market	Options Market
February	WTI Spot is $45.00/bbl	Buy June WTI $45.00/bbl Puts for $2.50/bbl premium
May	WTI Spot is $40.00/bbl	Sell June WTI $45.00/bbl Puts for $5.00 premium
Change	$5.00/bbl loss	$2.50/bbl gain
Spot Price when Oil is Sold		$40.00/bbl
Gain on Options Position		+$2.50/bbl
Net Sale Price		$42.50/bbl

Rising Oil Prices

Date	Spot Market	Options Market
February	WTI Spot is $45.00/bbl	Buy June WTI $45.00/bbl Puts for $2.50/bbl premium
May	WTI Spot is $50.00/bbl	Options Expire Worthless
Change	$5.00/bbl gain	$2.50/bbl loss
Spot Price when Oil is Sold		$50.00/bbl
Loss on Options Position		-$2.50/bbl
Net Sale Price		$47.50/bbl

Collar

The collar is a variant for using options, which reduces the cost of using options to manage risk. Collars are created by the purchase (or sale) of a call offset by the sale (or purchase) of a put. The calls and puts are both out of the money and have the same expiration month.[24]

If the income from selling the put (call) matches the cost of buying the call (put), the creator of the collar has constructed a costless way to fix a future price range for buying or selling a commodity, known in the trade as a *costless collar.*

41

Example of Using a Collar (Table 5-6a and 5-6b)

For these examples, assume the current price of oil is $45.00/bbl and the $47.50 call trades at $1.25/bbl and the $42.50 put trades at $1.25/bbl.

Using a Collar to Cap Price Range *(Table 5-6a)*

Crude oil currently trades at $45.00/bbl. The refiner is concerned about price increases and wants to set a cap on price by using options, but at a lower cost than buying calls outright. The refiner sells a $42.50/bbl put for $1.25/bbl and buys the $47.50/bbl call for $1.25/bbl. Now the minimum price the refiner will pay for oil will be $42.50/bbl and the maximum will be $47.50/bbl. Here is an analysis of how a collar can cap a price.

Table 5-6a

Collars

Collar is instituted when oil trades at $45.00/bbl
$47.50/bbl call option trades at $1.25/bbl when collar is instituted
$42.50/bbl put option trades at $1.25/bbl when collar is instituted

Using a Collar to Cap Prices
(Sell $42.50/bbl put and Buy $47.50/bbl call)

		Case 1 Oil Falls to $40.00/bbl	Case 2 Oil Stays at $45.00/bbl	Case 3 Oil Climbs to $50.00/bbl
1	Initial Cost of Call	-$1.25	-$1.25	-$1.25
2	Revenue from Sale of Put	$1.25	$1.25	$1.25
3	Initial Cost of Collar	$0.00	$0.00	$0.00
4	Cost of Short Put at Expiration	-$2.50	$0.00	$0.00
5	Value of Call at Expiration	$0.00	$0.00	$2.50
6	Combined Profit or Loss	-$2.50	$0.00	$2.50
7	Final Effective Cost of Oil	$42.50	$45.00	$47.50

After, New York Mercantile Exchange: A Guide to Energy Hedging, pp. 58-59.

Oil falls to $40.00/bbl

Line 1: The refiner buys the $47.50/bbl call for $1.25/bbl.

Line 2: The refiner sells the $42.50/bbl put for 1.25/bbl.

Line 3: The sale and purchase cancel each other out to create a zero outlay.

Line 4: At expiration, the short put costs the seller $2.50/bbl. (The put expires $2.50 below its strike price, and the seller is required to pay that difference to the option holder.)

Line 5: The call is worth zero at expiration. (It expires beneath its strike price.)

Line 6: This is the sum of lines 1-5. This is a loss of $2.50/bbl.

Line 7: The loss of $2.50/bbl is added to the purchase price of $40.00/bbl for a final effective cost of oil of $42.50/bbl.

Oil stays at $45.00/bbl

Line 1: The refiner buys the $47.50/bbl call for $1.25/bbl.

Line 2: The refiner sells the $42.50/bbl put for 1.25/bbl.

Line 3: The sale and purchase cancel each other out to create a zero outlay.

Line 4: At expiration, the short put expires worthless, because the market price is greater than the strike price. (It makes no sense to sell oil at $42.50/bbl when the market trades at $45.00/bbl.)

Line 5: The call is worth zero at expiration because it expires beneath its strike price. (It does not make sense to exercise the call — why would someone want an option to buy oil for $47.50/bbl when the market price is $45.00/bbl?)

Line 6: This is the sum of lines 1-5. There is no net profit or loss.

Line 7: Because there is no net profit or loss, the final effective cost of oil is the same as the market price: $45.00/bbl.

Oil climbs to $50.00/bbl

Line 1: The refiner buys the $47.50/bbl call for $1.25/bbl.

Line 2: The refiner sells the $42.50/bbl put for 1.25/bbl.

Line 3: The sale and purchase cancel each other out to create a zero outlay.

Line 4: At expiration, the short put expires worthless, because the market price is greater than the strike price. (It makes no sense to sell oil at $42.50/bbl when the market trades at $50.00/bbl.)

Line 5: The call is worth $2.50/bbl at expiration, because the right to buy oil for $47.50/bbl is now worth $2.50/bbl.

Line 6: This is the sum of lines 1-5. This is a gain of $2.50/bbl.

Line 7: The gain of $2.50/bbl is subtracted from the purchase price of $50.00/bbl for a final effective price of oil of $47.50/bbl.

Using a Collar to Create a Floor Range (Table 5-6b)

Crude oil currently trades at $45.00/bbl. The producer is concerned about price decreases and wants to set a floor using options, but at a lower cost than buying puts outright. The producer buys a $42.50/bbl put for $1.25/bbl and sells the $47.50/bbl call for $1.25/bbl. Now the minimum price the producer will receive for oil will be $42.50/bbl and the maximum will be $47.50/bbl. Here is an analysis of how a collar can provide a price floor.

Table 5-6b

Using a Collar to Create a Price Floor
(Buy $42.50/bbl put and Sell $47.50/bbl call)

		Case 1 Oil Falls to $40.00/bbl	Case 2 Oil Stays at $45.00/bbl	Case 3 Oil Climbs to $50.00/bbl
1	Initial Cost of Put	-$1.25	-$1.25	-$1.25
2	Revenue from Sale of Call	$1.25	$1.25	$1.25
3	Initial Cost of Collar	$0.00	$0.00	$0.00
4	Cost of Short Call at Expiration	$0.00	$0.00	-$2.50
5	Value of Put at Expiration	$2.50	$0.00	$0.00
6	Combined Profit or Loss	$2.50	$0.00	-$2.50
7	Final Effective Price of Oil	$42.50	$45.00	$47.50

After, New York Mercantile Exchange: A Guide to Energy Hedging, pp. 58-59.

Oil falls to $40.00/bbl

Line 1: The producer buys the $42.50/bbl put for $1.25/bbl.

Line 2: The producer sells the $47.50/bbl call for $1.25/bbl.

Line 3: The sale and purchase cancel each other out to create a zero outlay.

Line 4: At expiration, the short call expires worthless, because the owner of the call will not exercise a call to buy oil at $47.50/bbl when market prices are $40.00/bbl.

Line 5: The put is worth $2.50/bbl at expiration, because the right to sell oil for $42.50/bbl is now worth $2.50/bbl.

Line 6: This is the sum of lines 1-5. This is a gain of $2.50/bbl.

Line 7: The gain of $2.50/bbl is added to the sale price of $40.00/bbl for a final effective price of oil of $42.50/bbl.

Oil stays at $45.00/bbl

Line 1: The producer buys the $42.50/bbl put for $1.25/bbl.

Line 2: The producer sells the $47.50/bbl call for $1.25/bbl.

Line 3: The sale and purchase cancel each other out to create a zero outlay.

- *Line 4*: At expiration, the short call does not cost the seller anything, because the owner does not exercise the option. (It makes no sense to exercise a call to buy oil at $47.50/bbl when oil trades at $45.00/bbl.)

Line 5: The put is worth zero at expiration, because it expires above its strike price.

Line 6: This is the sum of lines 1-5. There is no net profit or loss.

Line 7: Because there is no net profit or loss, the final effective price of oil is the same as the market price: $45.00/bbl.

Oil climbs to 50.00/bbl

Line 1: The producer buys the $42.50/bbl put for $1.25/bbl.

Line 2: The producer sells the $47.50/bbl call for $1.25/bbl.

Line 3: The sale and purchase cancel each other out to create a zero outlay.

Line 4: At expiration, the short call costs the seller $2.50/bbl. (The call expires $2.50 above its strike price, and the seller is required to pay that difference to the option holder.)

Line 5: The put is worth zero at expiration. (It expires above its strike price.)

Line 6: This is the sum of lines 1-5. This is a loss of $2.50/bbl.

Line 7: The loss of $2.50/bbl is subtracted from the sale price of $50.00/bbl for a final effective price of oil of $47.50/bbl.

Swaps

Swaps are derivatives in which two parties agree to exchange (swap) a price risk exposure for a given time period. Because swaps may be privately negotiated, they can be highly customized to meet all sorts of risks. In commodities, swaps are used to protect against price fluctuations. Most swaps involve a periodic exchange of cash flows between two parties, with one paying a fixed cash flow and the other a variable amount relative to a given benchmark. By combining swaps with a position in the cash market, companies can lock in a price for commodities they wish to buy or sell.

Example of Using Swaps to Fix a Price (Table 5-7)

Here is a simple example of a swap. An oil refiner wishes to protect against an increase in crude price and a producer wishes to protect itself against a fall in price. They could make a deal to exchange payments depending on the price of oil. Say that each determined that $45.00 bbl represented the point of profitability. If the price of oil falls below $45.00/bbl, then the refiner pays the producer the difference between $45.00/bbl and the market price. If the price equals $45.00/bbl, no payments are exchanged. If the price is greater than $45.00/bbl, the producer pays the refiner the difference between the current oil price and $45.00/bbl. This way both the refiner and producer are assured a price of 45.00/bbl.

Table 5-7

Using Swaps to Manage Price Risk

Price	What Happens?	How much money changes hands?
Oil Price < $45.00/bbl	Refiner Pays Producer	$45.00/bbl - Oil Price/bbl
Oil Price = $45.00/bbl	No money changes hands	None
Oil Price > $45.00/bbl	Producer Pays Refiner	Oil Price/bbl - $45.00/bbl

Conclusion

Derivatives allow buyers and sellers to neutralize risk by profiting from "the selfsame events that inflict losses in the commercial arena."[25] Proper use of derivatives lessens risk — derivatives should not be used to increase an organization's risk exposure.

Derivatives are less complex than generally supposed. They are built from simple building blocks. Organizations should apply derivatives to manage risk — not create more risk through misapplication.

Notes

[1]Commodities Futures Trading Commission. *The CFTC Glossary: A Guide to the Language of the Futures Industry.* Last revised March 2005. Available on the World Wide Web at: *http://www.cftc.gov/files/opa/cftcglossary.pdf.* Definition for **Forward Contract.**

[2]Chicago Board of Trade. *Glossary.* Available on the World Wide Web at: *http://www.cbot.com/cbot/pub/page/0,3181,1059,00.html.* Definition for **Futures Contract.**

[3]Commodities Futures Trading Commission, *op. cit.* Definition for **Contract Market.**

[4]Futures Industry Institute, *Futures and Options Course* (Washington, D.C.: Futures Industry Institute, 1995), p. 31.

[5]Market participants usually make deals in the cash markets, but use the futures to take care of financial risk, not to actually take or make delivery. This is because the futures markets specify delivery at a certain point — which may not be convenient for buyer or seller. For example a gasoline dealer in Seattle would not find it convenient to take delivery of a futures contract on NYMEX gasoline because the delivery point is New York Harbor, and the dealer would then have to arrange transportation, as opposed to receiving delivery from a pipeline in the Northwest. However, the price in Seattle will be related to the NYMEX price, allowing it to be used as a hedge. Chapter 6 on *basis* discusses the relation between futures markets prices and the local cash markets.

[6]Gary Smith, *Financial Assets, Markets, and Institutions* (Lexington, MA: D.C. Heath and Company, 1993), p. A34.

[7]Chicago Board of Trade, *op. cit.* Definition for **Clearinghouse.**

[8]Commodities Futures Trading Commission, *op. cit.* Definition for **Convergence.**

[9]These examples are modifications of those used in the Futures Industry Institute's *Futures and Options Course,* cited in footnote 4, pp 32-33.

[10]Hedgers use the futures contract that is closest to the month, but not before, their actual cash transaction. This increases the effectiveness of the hedge.

[11]Initial margin is higher than maintenance margin for speculators. For hedgers, their initial margin is usually the same as the maintenance margin. Exchanges make this distinction, because hedgers face only basis risk, which is typically lower than the risks of futures markets price moves.

[12]Chicago Board of Trade, *op. cit.* Definition for **Strike Price.**

[13]Commodities Futures Trading Commission, *op. cit.* Definition for **Exercise.**

[14]Chicago Board of Trade, *op. cit.* Definition for **In-the-Money Option.**

[15] *Ibid.*

[16] New York Mercantile Exchange, *Glossary of Terms* (New York: New York Mercantile Exchange, 2000). Definition for **Breakeven Point.** Available on the World Wide Web at: *http://www.nymex.com/media/glossary.pdf.*

[17] John Nyhoff, *Options for Beginners* (Chicago: Chicago Mercantile Exchange, no date), p. 4.

[18] John Nyhoff, *op. cit.*, p. 9.

[19] John Nyhoff, *op. cit.,* p. 8.

[20] Mark J. Powers, *Getting Started in Commodity Futures Trading* (Cedar Falls, IA: Investor Publications, 1983), p. 235.

[21] In dealing with options, users will also come across some terms known as "The Greeks." These are measures of the sensitivity of an option's price to certain variables. These definitions of the "The Greeks" are from the Committee of Chief Risk Officers *Glossary.*

> **delta** — A measure of the sensitivity of the option value to a small change in the price of the **underlying** asset/**contract**. The delta is the ratio of the change in the value of the option and the (small) change in the price of the underlying. Delta is called the first derivative of the option value with respect to the price of the underlying.
>
> **gamma** — A measure of the sensitivity of the option delta value to a small change in the price of the **underlying** asset/**contract**. Gamma is called the second derivative of the option value with respect to the price of the underlying.
>
> **rho** — A measure of the sensitivity of the option value to a small change in the risk-free interest rate.
>
> **theta** — A measure of the sensitivity of the option value to a small change in the time to expiration.
>
> **vega** — A measure of the sensitivity of the option value to a small change in the *implied volatility* of the **underlying** asset/**contract**.

Source: Committee of Chief Risk Officers. *Best Practices*, Volume 6 of 6. *Glossary*, 19 November 2002. Available on the World Wide Web at: *http://www.ccro.org/pdf/glossary.pdf.*

[22] Mark-to-market is: Part of the "daily *cash flow* system used by US **futures exchanges** to maintain a minimum level of **margin equity** for a given futures or **option contract position** by calculating the gain or loss in each contract position resulting from changes in the price of the futures or option contracts at the end of each **trading** session." These amounts are added or subtracted to each account balance. Source: Commodities Futures Trading Commission. *The CFTC Glossary: A Guide to the Language of the Futures Industry.* Last revised March 2005. Available on the World Wide

Web at: *http://www.cftc.gov/files/opa/cftcglossary.pdf.*

[23] Actually, when traded on the NYMEX, these are options on crude oil futures, but to simplify the explanation, the options are considered based on the crude oil spot prices. In reality, the principle is the same, with the futures functioning as the underlying, as opposed to the crude oil spot price.

[24] New York Mercantile Exchange, *A Guide to Energy Hedging,* (New York: New York Mercantile Exchange, 1999), p. 58. Available on the World Wide Web at: *http://www.nymex.com/media/energyhedge.pdf.*

[25] Philip McBride Johnson, *Derivatives: A Manager's Guide to the World's Most Powerful Financial Instruments* (New York: McGraw-Hill, 1999), p. 26.

Basis

In the transactions discussed in Chapter 5, the spot and the futures markets perfectly canceled each other out, which does not happen frequently in real markets, because futures and cash markets do not always move in lockstep. Futures markets and cash markets can be highly volatile, but the relationship *between the markets* tends to be more stable, which makes hedging possible. This relationship between markets is called *basis*. A change in basis between the implementation and offset of a hedge can affect the performance of a hedge. Basis risk is usually less than price risk.[1]

What is Basis?

Basis is the difference between *Cash Price* and *Futures Price*, usually the difference between the cash price and the "nearby"[2] futures contract month.[3] Basis is measured relative to the futures month. If crude oil trades in the cash market for $45.00/bbl and the nearby month trades at $50.00 bbl, the basis is "$5.00 under." If the cash markets traded at $55.00 and the futures market at $50.00, then the basis is "$5.00/over."

Where does Basis Come From?

Basis arises primarily from the three factors that differentiate the cash markets from a futures markets, namely delivery of a particular amount of a commodity of a specific grade at a specific point and time:

> *Quality/Grade*: The futures contract specifies delivery of a commodity of a particular quality. Goods with a higher quality will command a premium and those of a lesser quality will be worth less. Sometimes a commodity, such as jet fuel, does not have a futures contract available to hedge, and a close commodity, such

51

as distillate fuel oil is used, although the correlation may not be as strong as desired, which create significant basis differences.

Delivery Point: The contract specifies delivery at a certain place. As can be imagined with deliveries of physical commodities, transportation costs can make a great deal of difference in the price a commodity commands. In addition, local markets may have their own dynamics, due to weather, such as a local cold snap, or supply breakdown that drives up local prices, regardless of futures markets trends.

Time: A futures contract may not exist that will match the time when the cash market transaction is made. For example a hedger may have to hedge with a futures contract that expires a few months after the cash transaction.

Describing Change in Basis *(Figure 6-1)*

When the difference between cash and futures prices widens (becomes more positive or less negative) basis "strengthens" and short hedgers benefit. Because short hedgers desire basis to increase, they are considered "long the basis."

When the difference between cash and futures prices narrows (becomes less positive or more negative) basis "weakens" and long hedgers benefit. Because long hedgers desire basis to decrease, they are considered "short the basis."

Implications for Risk Management Strategies

Let us reconsider the example used in Chapter 5, where a perfect hedge managed to cancel out the movements in the cash market, now taking into account what happens to the long and short hedges when the variability of basis comes into play.

Figure 6-1

Strengthening and Weakening Basis

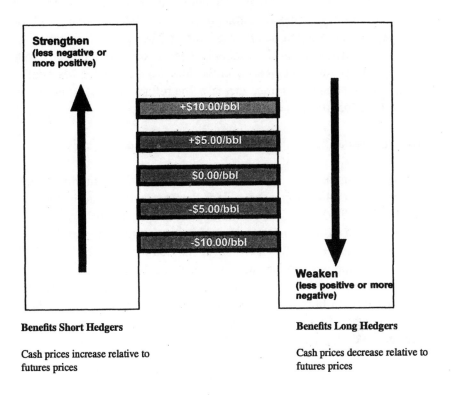

Benefits Short Hedgers

Cash prices increase relative to
futures prices

Benefits Long Hedgers

Cash prices decrease relative to
futures prices

After, Chicago Board of Trade. *Agricultural Futures and Options: A Home Study Course*, p. 11.

Basis and Longs (Short the Basis)

Example of Using a Long Futures Contract to Hedge a Purchase (Tables 6-1a and 6-1b)

Consider an oil refinery that will purchase crude oil to refine into gasoline and other refined petroleum products. It is February and the refinery needs to purchase crude oil for its May production run. Currently the oil it uses in the refinery, West Texas Intermediate Crude (WTI), trades for $45.00/barrel in the forward market for May delivery. To protect against a price increase, the refiner purchases, in February, a June long futures contract for $46.00/bbl.[4]

Rising Crude Oil Prices with Strengthening Basis (Table 6-1a)

In May, the price in the spot market rises to $50.00/bbl and the futures price rises to $48.00/bbl. The refiner then buys the crude in the spot market for $50.00/bbl. The refiner applies the $2.00/bbl profit on the futures to the cash purchase, so the effective cost of each barrel is now $48.00/bbl. Note that the increase in the futures price did not fully cancel out the spot price increase, because basis strengthened by $3.00/bbl. Strengthening basis hurts long hedgers because the futures contract fails to blunt the full impact of the adverse cash move. Still, the refiner benefited from hedging, because the hedge reduced the impact of the cash price move by $2.00/bbl.

Rising Crude Oil Prices with Weakening Basis (Table 6-1a)

In May, the price in the futures and spot market rises to $50.00/bbl. The refiner sells the futures contract for $54.00/bbl, making a profit of $8.00/bbl. The refiner then buys the crude in the spot market for $50.00/bbl. The refiner applies the $8.00/bbl profit on the futures to the cash purchase, so the effective cost of each barrel is now $42.00. Because the basis weakened by $3.00/bbl, the hedge reduced the impact of the adverse price move even more than the perfect hedge.

Table 6-1a

Using Long Futures to Hedge Crude Oil Purchases

Rising Oil Prices

Strengthening Basis

Date	Spot Market	Futures Market	Basis
February	WTI Spot is $45.00/bbl	Buy June WTI Futures at $46.00/bbl	– $1.00/bbl
May	WTI Spot is $50.00/bbl	Sell June WTI Futures at $48.00/bbl	+ $2.00/bbl
Change	$5.00/bbl loss	$2.00/bbl gain	+ $3.00/bbl

Spot Price when Oil is Purchased	$50.00/bbl
Gain on Futures Position	– $2.00/bbl
Net Purchase Price	$48.00/bbl

Weakening Basis

Date	Spot Market	Futures Market	Basis
February	WTI Spot is $45.00/bbl	Buy June WTI Futures at $46.00/bbl	– $1.00/bbl
May	WTI Spot is $50.00/bbl	Sell June WTI Futures at $54.00/bbl	– $4.00/bbl
Change	$5.00/bbl loss	$8.00/bbl gain	– $3.00/bbl

Spot Price when Oil is Purchased	$50.00/bbl
Gain on Futures Position	– $8.00/bbl
Net Purchase Price	$42.00/bbl

Falling Crude Oil Prices with Strengthening Basis (Table 6-1b)

In May, the price in the spot market falls to $40.00/bbl and the futures market falls to $38.00/bbl. The refiner sells the futures contract for $38.00/bbl, losing $8.00/bbl. However, because the price in the spot market has fallen, the refiner buys the crude in the spot market for $40.00/bbl, a savings of $5.00/bbl, over what it would have paid by buying in the forward market in February. The refiner adds the $8.00/bbl loss on the futures to the cash purchase, so the effective cost of each barrel is now $48.00, which is more than the forward price quoted in February. Strengthening basis hurts long hedgers because increasing basis reduces the savings from the drop in cash prices. However, the cash prices could have just as likely increased, and the lack of hedge could have hurt the refiner.

Falling Crude Oil Prices with Weakening Basis (Table 6-1b)

In May, the price in the spot market falls to $40.00/bbl and the futures market falls to $44.00/bbl. The refiner sells the futures contract for $44.00/bbl, losing $2.00/bbl. However, because the price in the spot market has fallen, the refiner buys the crude in the spot market for $40.00/bbl, a savings of $5.00/bbl over what it would have paid for a forward contract in February. The refiner adds the $2.00/bbl loss on the futures to the cash purchase, so the effective cost of each barrel is now $42.00. Although the hedger lost money on the hedge, because the basis weakened, the drop in cash price overwhelmed the loss from the futures, leading to a lower price than for the perfect hedge in Chapter 5.

Basis and Shorts (Long the Basis)

Short Hedge

A short hedge allows a seller to fix a future sale price on a commodity to protect against price declines. If a hedger sells a futures contract, and the price of the underlying commodity decreases, the seller can use the profits realized by the futures contract (buying the contract back at a lower price) to counteract the price decrease in the cash market. By selling a futures contract, the buyer has locked in a price and can minimize the effect of downward price movements.

Table 6-1b

Using Long Futures to Hedge Crude Oil Purchases

Falling Oil Prices

Strengthening Basis

Date	Spot Market	Futures Market	Basis
February	WTI Spot is $45.00/bbl	Buy June WTI Futures at $46.00/bbl	− $1.00/bbl
May	WTI Spot is $40.00/bbl	Sell June WTI Futures at $38.00/bbl	+ $2.00/bbl
Change	$5.00/bbl gain	$8.00/bbl loss	+ $3.00/bbl

Spot Price when Oil is Purchased	$40.00/bbl
Loss on Futures Position	+ $8.00/bbl
Net Purchase Price	$48.00/bbl

Weakening Basis

Date	Spot Market	Futures Market	Basis
February	WTI Spot is $45.00/bbl	Buy June WTI Futures at $46.00/bbl	− $1.00/bbl
May	WTI Spot is $40.00/bbl	Sell June WTI Futures at $44.00/bbl	− $4.00/bbl
Change	$5.00/bbl gain	$2.00/bbl loss	− $3.00/bbl

Spot Price when Oil is Purchased	$40.00/bbl
Loss on Futures Position	+ $2.00/bbl
Net Purchase Price	$42.00/bbl

Example of Using a Short Futures Contract to Hedge a Sale (Tables 6-2a and 6-2b)

Consider an oil producer that sells crude oil to refiners. It is February and the refiner expects to sell oil in May to refiners that blend gasoline for the summer driving season. Currently the oil it sells, West Texas Intermediate Crude (WTI), trades in the May forward cash market for $45.00 barrel. To protect against a price decrease, the producer, in February, sells a June futures contract for $46.00/bbl.

Falling Crude Oil Prices with Strengthening Basis (Table 6-2a)

In May, the price in the futures and spot market falls to $40.00/bbl and the futures contract falls to $38.00/bbl. The producer buys back the futures contract for $38.00/bbl, making $8.00/bbl. However, because the price in the spot market has fallen, the producer sells the crude in the spot market for $40.00/bbl. The producer adds the $8.00/bbl gain on the futures contract to the cash sale, so the effective sale price of each barrel is now $48.00. Because the basis strengthened, the gain from the futures exceeded the loss in the cash market, and the hedge performed better than the perfect hedge.

Falling Crude Oil Prices with Weakening Basis (Table 6-2a)

In May, the price in the spot market falls to $40.00/bbl. The producer buys back the futures contract for $44.00/bbl, losing $2.00/bbl. However, because the price in the spot market has fallen, the producer sells the crude in the spot market for $40.00/bbl. The producer adds the $2.00/bbl gain on the futures to the cash sale, so the effective sale price of each barrel is now $42.00. Because the basis weakened, the loss from the cash market exceeded the gain in the futures market, and the hedge performed worse than the perfect hedge, but better than no hedge at all.

Table 6-2a

Using Short Futures to Hedge Crude Oil Sales

Falling Oil Prices

Strengthening Basis

Date	Spot Market	Futures Market	Basis
February	WTI Spot is $45.00/bbl	Sell June WTI Futures at $46.00/bbl	− $1.00/bbl
May	WTI Spot is $40.00/bbl	Buy June WTI Futures at $38.00/bbl	+ $2.00/bbl
Change	$5.00/bbl loss	$8.00/bbl gain	+ $3.00/bbl

Spot Price when Oil is Sold	$40.00/bbl
Gain on Futures Position	+ $8.00/bbl
Net Sale Price	$48.00/bbl

Weakening Basis

Date	Spot Market	Futures Market	Basis
February	WTI Spot is $45.00/bbl	Sell June WTI Futures at $46.00/bbl	− $1.00/bbl
May	WTI Spot is $40.00/bbl	Buy June WTI Futures at $44.00/bbl	− $4.00/bbl
Change	$5.00/bbl loss	$2.00/bbl gain	− $3.00/bbl

Spot Price when Oil is Sold	$40.00/bbl
Gain on Futures Position	+ $2.00/bbl
Net Sale Price	$42.00/bbl

Rising Crude Oil Prices with Strengthening Basis (Table 6-2b)

In May, the price in the spot market rises to $50.00/bbl. The producer buys back the futures contract for $48.00/bbl, losing $2.00/bbl. The producer then sells the crude in the spot market for $50.00/bbl. After the producer applies the $2.00/bbl loss on the futures to the cash sale, the effective sale price of each barrel is now $48.00. Because the basis strengthened, the gain from the cash market exceeded the loss in the futures market, and the hedge performed better than the perfect hedge.

Rising Crude Oil Prices with Weakening Basis (Table 6-2b)

In May, the price in the spot market rises to $50.00/bbl. The producer buys back the futures contract for $54.00/bbl, losing $8.00/bbl. The producer then sells the crude in the spot market for $50.00/bbl. After the producer applies the $8.00/bbl loss on the futures to the cash sale, the effective sale price of each barrel is now $42.00. Because the basis weakened, the loss from the futures market exceeded the gain in the cash market, and the hedge performed worse than the perfect hedge. Although the producer may have sold the crude at a higher price in the cash market in May, had it not hedged, it would not have been protected against a price drop.

Table 6-2b

Using Short Futures to Hedge Crude Oil Sales

Rising Oil Prices

Strengthening Basis

Date	Spot Market	Futures Market	Basis
February	WTI Spot is $45.00/bbl	Sell June WTI Futures at $46.00/bbl	− $1.00/bbl
May	WTI Spot is $50.00/bbl	Buy June WTI Futures at $48.00/bbl	+ $2.00/bbl
Change	$5.00/bbl gain	$2.00/bbl loss	+ $3.00/bbl

Spot Price when Oil is Sold	$50.00/bbl
Loss on Futures Position	− $2.00/bbl
Net Sale Price	$48.00/bbl

Weakening Basis

Date	Spot Market	Futures Market	Basis
February	WTI Spot is $45.00/bbl	Sell June WTI Futures at $46.00/bbl	− $1.00/bbl
May	WTI Spot is $50.00/bbl	Buy June WTI Futures at $54.00/bbl	− $4.00/bbl
Change	$5.00/bbl gain	$8.00/bbl loss	− $3.00/bbl

Spot Price when Oil is Sold	$50.00/bbl
Loss on Futures Position	− $8.00/bbl
Net Sale Price	$42.00/bbl

Basis Swap (Table 6-3)

Although basis tends to be more predictable, and less volatile than the individual cash and futures prices, its variability creates uncertainty for those using derivatives to transfer risk. One common way to manage this risk is through a basis swap. In a basis swap, two parties select a basis level to create a swap based on a particular basis level. They exchange payments based on the level, effectively neutralizing the effects of basis. The party that benefits from strengthening basis will pay the party that is hurt by strengthening basis and the party that benefits from weakening basis will pay the party that is hurt by weakening basis.

Example (Table 6-3)

Consider the basis in Table 6-1a, which at the start of the hedging process is 1.00 under May (– $1.00/bbl). In the first hedge, basis strengthens to 2.00 over May (+ $2.00/bbl). In this case, the short hedger (who benefits from strengthening basis) pays the long hedger (who is hurt by strengthening basis) the amount that basis changes: $3.00/bbl. In the second hedge, basis weakens to 4.00 under May (– $4.00/bbl). In this case, the long hedger (who benefits from weakening basis) pays the short hedger (who is hurt by weakening basis) the amount that basis changes: $3.00/bbl. The swap reduces the basis risk for both parties.

Table 6-3

Using Swaps to Manage Basis Risk

Price	What Happens?	How much money changes hands?	How much money changes hands?
Basis Strengthens above – $1.00	Short Hedger pays Long Hedger	New Basis – (– $1.00)	$2.00 – (– $1.00) = $3.00
Basis stays at – $1.00	No money changes hands	None	None
Basis Weakens below – $1.00	Long Hedger Pays Short Hedger	– $1.00 – New Basis	– $1.00 – (– $4.00) = $3.00

Conclusion

Although basis risk is usually less than price risk, it must be considered in order to create effective hedges. In addition, knowledge about basis can help effectively time hedges. If a seller has kept careful basis records, and institutes a hedge when basis is weak and expected to strengthen, its hedges may be more effective than not using that information. Likewise, a long hedger that analyzes basis records and institutes a long hedge when basis is likely to weaken, will also create more effective hedges in the long run. Basis is an important concept for understanding hedging and managing a hedging program.

Notes

[1] Chicago Board of Trade, *Agricultural Futures and Options: A Home Study Course.* (Chicago: Board of Trade of the City of Chicago, 1998), p. 13.

[2] The nearby month is the nearest delivery month for a futures contract.

[3] Basis can be specified relative to any futures contract month; it is helpful to note the month, however, to avoid confusion with the nearby month.

[4] Hedgers use the futures contract that is closest to the month, but not before, their actual cash transaction. This increases the effectiveness of the hedge.

Energy Price Risk

Volatile fuel prices are one of the main risks that energy suppliers face. Energy resources are among the most volatile commodities. Unpredictable prices make it difficult to plan for the future or to meet earnings targets. Energy suppliers need to understand their options regarding price risk and ways to manage it, utilizing the risk framework outlined in Chapter Two. Energy market participants can choose from one or several of the six risk management techniques.

Technique One: Avoid Energy Price Risk

Avoiding energy price risk is the most difficult strategy for a company that wishes to remain in the energy business. A company, however, can choose to avoid use of one commodity or fuel in order to avoid the risks associated with that commodity. But, choosing to totally avoid a fuel may have significant opportunity costs. For example, a generating company may wish to avoid the price shocks of the natural gas market. That decision to forego natural gas, though, would also mean a decision to forego ownership of peaker plants. Since a company's baseload supply would only take it so far, it might have to buy extra power at a premium price when demand is high in the cash market. Thus, by avoiding use of natural gas and the supposed risks of the market, the company winds up facing other fuel price risks.

An energy supplier avoids energy price risks with enormous difficulty.

Technique Two: Bear Energy Price Risk

When deciding to bear energy price risk, an organization must make that decision in a conscious manner, that is to **choose** to bear energy price risk after an analysis of the risk and available means to mitigate it. It may decide:

    1. It can afford to bear a particular risk.

2. It is more cost-effective to bear the risk than to mitigate it over the long run.

3. Tools do not exist to mitigate a particular risk.

When making the decision, the organization must carefully study the risks posed by volatile energy prices — not only where prices have moved in the past, but also where they may move in the future. Statistical techniques can provide numbers for "what if" scenarios to stress test a company's ability to weather price spikes or price drops.

The organization should not inadvertently take on a risk — by either arbitrarily dismissing risk mitigation or by not fully studying risks and being aware of the means to mitigate them. Ignoring the problem does not provide a cost effective solution to it. Risk will not go away because an organization fails to perceive it or to pay attention to risks that it knows exists.

Technique Three: Reduce the Hazard

Reducing the hazards from volatile energy prices requires decreasing the exposure to conditions that increase the chance of a loss, that is, reducing the hazards of price spikes by regulating the amount of exposure that a company has to volatile markets whose rapid price moves could produce dire financial consequences for the firm.

To reduce hazards, a company should carefully select those who direct the purchase and sale of energy commodities, assuring that their personalities are right for the job. It is essential, as well, to put in place policies and procedures that ensure that the firm's trading policy is implemented as the board and management desires. For example, if a company wants its trading desk to operate in a conservative manner, it should not staff the desk with traders who have a background in speculative trading. That would be a recipe for disaster, because traders can be very good at fooling managers — even auditors — who do not understand how trading desks work.

Probably the best way to reduce the hazards of volatile prices, is to have a board of directors and management that have a solid understanding of the price risks that a company faces, and the tools available to deal with those risks. Those individuals need not be traders themselves, but they should understand the risks that arise from a free market, the techniques available to manage risk, and the strengths and weaknesses of those techniques. They should understand how derivatives work and how they can be misused by individuals through ignorance or avarice.

Technique Four: Reduce the Loss

Reducing loss means taking steps to reduce the **losses** arising from a **peril**. In this case, the peril consists of price movements that could adversely affect the financial health of an energy supplier and possibly its customers. Some may occur very quickly. When these movements happen, there may be little time to react — or formulate plans. A company needs to have a plan that will tell its managers what to do when contingencies arise.

Technique Five: Shift the Risk

Shifting the risk of adverse price moves should figure prominently in the strategies for managing fuel price risk. The many tools devoted to shifting risks create a sizable market with significant depth that enables companies to shift risk in an efficient manner. This section explains how to apply the principles of forwards, futures, options, and swaps that were outlined in Chapter 5. When shifting risk, and using these tools, remember that derivatives should be used to neutralize risk by profiting from "the self-same events that inflict losses in the commercial arena."[1] Proper use lessens risk — *derivatives should not be used to increase an organization's risk exposure, unless the organization is out to speculate — not manage risk.*

Forwards

The simplest example of shifting risk is using a forward contract, whereby a buyer (seller) agrees to buy (sell) a specific amount and quality of a commodity, fuel or power, at a particular time in the future, with specific provisions for delivery.

Forward contracts are non-standardized and privately negotiated between buyers and sellers. Lack of standardization causes problems, because customized contracts are hard to sell or transfer to others, if either of the parties wish to get out of the deal.

Actually, forward contracts are part of everyday life. Anytime a traveler purchases an airline ticket prior to his trip, he makes a forward contract with an airline. In exchange for payment, the airline agrees to provide the traveler with a commodity — a seat — at a particular time in the future and of a particular quality and price. Upon making the deal, the traveler takes a financial risk that the airline will still be in business and able to fly him to his destination on the given date. In addition, in exchange for a fixed price that would protect him against a higher fare, the traveler gives up the chance to buy the ticket at a lower price in the future.

The same principle applies in the power market. Say a distribution company feels it might be short 100 MW of power for sixteen hours in the coming day. In order to assure that it has enough power, it goes into the day ahead market and buys power for delivery *into its distribution system* at $75/MWh. The total value of the transaction is:

Total price = $75/MWh × 100 MW × 16 hours = $120,000

Now as the next day dawns, there are a number of ways the forward contract could turn out, with particular consequences for the distributor.

1. The price in the market turns out to be higher than $75/MWh. In this case, buying the forward contract has protected the buyer against a higher price.

2. The market trades at $75/MWh, so the contract purchaser has accurately priced the contract.

3. The market falls below $75/MWh, but the company still needs the power. In this case, the company has achieved price certainty, but missed out on a chance to achieve a lower price in the market. Say the price falls to $50/MWh. In this case, the forward purchase costs the company $40,000 more than if it had stayed in the spot market. This shows one possible weakness of dealing in a less than liquid market. For example, prices might have started to fall right after the company agreed to purchase the contract. The company, as a result, might have wanted to get out of the contract quickly, and lock in a lower price. However, the seller of the contract had little incentive to break the contract — why

should the seller take a lower price? This inability to get out of a deal is a distinct disadvantage of forward contracts compared with futures. The forward markets contrast with liquid markets — such as exchange traded futures and options — where the depth of the markets often allows buyers and sellers to exit their positions in a way that can minimize losses from adverse market moves. This does not mean that a forward sale is bad, just that when one deals in an illiquid market, the chances for **reducing losses** when faced with an adverse price move are minimized.

4. The company does not need the power on the following day, yet because it has bought a forward contract, it can't exit the position. It is stuck with a contract it does not need. Ideally, the buyer would like to unload the contract in the power markets. However, since the company bought a customized contract — for delivery into *its* distribution network — it would need to find a buyer with its same needs. If it is the only power buyer in the area, this may be difficult. If it cannot resell the power in its area, it may have to try to sell it and reroute it through the transmission network — for a fee, of course.

These examples illuminate a prime weakness of customized contracts. Although it may be simpler to use a forward contract rather than to use a standardized contract with the necessary calculations to account for basis risk (as discussed in Chapter 6), this ease comes at a price of decreased liquidity.

This again raises an issue for boards and managers when they make policies on what types of derivatives to use. They must consider liquidity when deciding on which instruments the firm will use. In the electric markets the volume of exchange-traded, highly liquid contracts is negligible compared to the overall size of the market.

Exchange Traded Futures and Options

This section examines the use of exchange traded derivatives — futures and options — as a way to shift energy price risk. The examples will come from the natural gas futures and options markets, which are heavily traded and liquid.

Futures

Futures can be used to fix a price, thereby shifting the risk of price volatility on a good that will be purchased or sold in the near future. Futures provide an effective hedge, because the price of the futures contract correlates highly with the value of the cash commodity. This phenomenon is known as *convergence*, which is, "the tendency for prices of physicals and futures to approach one another, usually during the delivery month."[2] The futures markets allow market participants to shift risk in a liquid, transparent market.

Essentially futures can be used in the same situations as forward contracts, but because the contracts can be offset, the futures allow the holders of positions to exit adverse price moves in a way that forwards do not permit.

Long Hedge

One problem that market participants face is how to shift the risk of price increases. Long futures positions allow a buyer to transfer risk of price increases.

Example of Using a Long Futures Contract to Hedge a Purchase (Table 7-1)

Consider a generator that needs natural gas to power its peaker plants. It is February. It will need gas for July during the peak summer season. Currently natural gas trades in the forward market for $7.00/MMBtu as does the Henry Hub futures contract. To protect against a price increase, the generator purchases, in February, an August Henry Hub long futures contract for $7.00/MMBtu.[3]

Rising Prices

In July, the price in the futures and spot market rises to $8.00/MMBtu. The generator sells the futures contract for $8.00/MMBtu, making a profit of $1.00/MMBtu. The generator then buys the gas in the spot market for $8.00/MMBtu. However, the generator applies the $1.00/MMBtu profit on the futures to the cash purchase, so the effective cost of each MMBtu is now $7.00. Because the generator hedged its purchase, it avoided the shock of the price increase, which the seller of the futures contract had to absorb.

Table 7-1

Using Long Futures to Hedge Natural Gas Purchases

Rising Natural Gas Prices

Date	Spot Market	Futures Market
February	Henry Hub Spot is $7.00/MMBtu	Buy August Henry Hub Futures at $7.00/MMBtu
July	Henry Hub Spot is $8.00/MMBtu	Sell August Henry Hub Futures at $8.00/MMBtu
Change	$1.00/MMBtu loss	$1.00/MMBtu gain
Spot Price when Gas is Purchased		$8.00/MMBtu
Gain on Futures Position		-$1.00/MMBtu
Net Purchase Price		$7.00/MMBtu

Falling Natural Gas Prices

Date	Spot Market	Futures Market
February	Henry Hub Spot is $7.00/MMBtu	Buy August Henry Hub Futures at $7.00/MMBtu
July	Henry Hub Spot is $6.00/MMBtu	Sell August Henry Hub Futures at $6.00/MMBtu
Change	$1.00/MMBtu gain	$1.00/MMBtu loss
Spot Price when Gas is Purchased		$6.00/MMBtu
Loss on Futures Position		+$1.00/MMBtu
Net Purchase Price		$7.00/MMBtu

Falling Prices

On the other hand, what if the price had fallen?

In July, the price in the futures and spot market falls to $6.00/MMBtu. The generator sells the futures contract for $6.00/MMBtu, losing $1.00/MMBtu. However, because the price in the spot market has fallen, the generator buys the gas in the spot market for $6.00/MMBtu, a savings of $1.00/MMBtu. The generator adds the $1.00/MMBtu loss on the futures to the cash purchase, so the effective cost of each MMBtu is now $7.00. Although the generator may have paid less had it not hedged, it would not have protected itself against an upward price move. However, the purpose of the hedge was to minimize risk, not minimize prices. The hedge accomplished that, because the generator fixed a price in advance.

Although the first hedge may seem to look like a winner, and the second looks like a loser, that is the wrong way to look at the examples. (The generator might have committed to sell its output in July at a fixed price, so it was essential to fix the price of the generator's main cost, fuel.) The role of these transactions is not to provide a profit center for the generator, but to insulate it against price swings. If it actually knew the direction of prices, then it wouldn't need to hedge. Who knows that? The upward price swing could have been painful for the company and canceled out any benefits from trying to bear all risk in the cash markets. It is important to remember that hedging is possible, because for the most part, the futures markets and cash markets are highly correlated.

Short Hedge

For every long hedger, there is a short hedger to take the other side of the position. A short hedger uses futures contracts to assure that it can sell a commodity at a given price at a time in the future or protect the value of an inventory.

Example of Using a Short Futures Contract to Hedge a Sale (Table 7-2)

Consider a gas producer that sells gas to electric generators. It is February. The producer will sell a large volume of gas in July when generators operate their peaker plants. Currently, gas trades in the forward market for $7.00 MMBtu, as does the Henry Hub futures contract. To protect against a price decrease, the producer, in February, sells an August futures contract for $7.00/MMBtu.

Falling Prices

In July, the price in the futures and spot market falls to $6.00/MMBtu. The producer buys back the futures contract for $6.00/MMBtu, making $1.00/MMBtu. However, because the price in the spot market has fallen, the producer sells the gas in the spot market for $6.00/MMBtu. The producer adds the $1.00/MMBtu gain on the futures to the cash sale, so the effective sale price of each MMBtu is $7.00.

Because the producer hedged its sale, it avoided the impact of the price drop.

Table 7-2

Using Short Futures to Hedge Natural Gas Sales

Falling Natural Gas Prices

Date	Spot Market	Futures Market
February	Henry Hub Spot is $7.00/MMBtu	Sell August Henry Hub Futures at $7.00/MMBtu
July	Henry Hub Spot is $6.00/MMBtu	Buy August Henry Hub Futures at $6.00/MMBtu
Change	$1.00/MMBtu loss	$1.00/MMBtu gain

Spot Price when Natural Gas is Sold	$6.00/MMBtu
Gain on Futures Position	+$1.00/MMBtu
Net Sale Price	$7.00/MMBtu

Rising Natural Gas Prices

Date	Spot Market	Futures Market
February	Henry Hub Spot is $7.00/MMBtu	Sell August Henry Hub Futures at $7.00/MMBtu
July	Henry Hub Spot is $8.00/MMBtu	Buy August Henry Hub Futures at $8.00/MMBtu
Change	$1.00/MMBtu gain	$1.00/MMBtu loss

Spot Price when Natural Gas is Sold	$8.00/MMBtu
Loss on Futures Position	-$1.00/MMBtu
Net Sale Price	$7.00/MMBtu

Rising Prices

In July, the price in the futures and spot market rises to $8.00/MMBtu. The producer buys back the futures contract for $8.00/MMBtu, losing $1.00/MMBtu. The producer then sells the gas in the spot market for $8.00/MMBtu. After the producer applies the $1.00/MMBtu loss on the futures to the cash sale, the effective sale price of each MMBtu is now $7.00.

Although the producer may have sold the gas at a higher effective price had it not hedged, it would not have protected itself against a price drop. The purpose of the hedge was to minimize risk, not increase prices. The hedge accomplished that, because the producer fixed a price in advance. The producer earned less, but it also took less of a chance, and lower risk often is accompanied by lower return.

Options

Example of Using Long Calls to Hedge a Purchase (Table 7-3)

Consider the generator that needs to purchase gas to power its peaker plants in July. It has considered using futures, but wants to take advantage of drops in the price of gas, which an option allows. It decides to hedge using long calls. In February, gas trades in the forward market for $7.00 MMBtu as does the futures contract. To protect against a price increase, the generator purchases, in February, an August call with a strike price of $7.00/MMBtu for a $0.50/MMBtu premium.[4]

Rising Prices

In July, the price in the spot market rises to $8.00/MMBtu and the option goes in the money. The generator sells the call option for $1.00, making a profit of $0.50/MMBtu. The generator then buys the gas in the spot market for $8.00/MMBtu. The generator applies the $0.50/MMBtu profit on the option to the cash purchase, making the effective cost of each MMBtu $7.50. Because the generator hedged its purchase, it lessened the size of the price increase.

Falling Prices

On the other hand, what if the price had fallen? In July, the price in the futures and spot market falls to $6.00/MMBtu. The call option expires worthless. Because the price in the spot market has fallen, the generator can buy the gas in the spot market for $6.00/MMBtu, a savings of $1.00/MMBtu. The generator adds the $0.50/MMBtu loss on the options to the cash purchase, so the effective cost of each MMBtu is now $6.50. By using the option, the generator was able to benefit more from the fall in prices than by using the futures.

Although the generator may have paid less had it not hedged, it would not have protected itself against an upward price move.

Table 7-3

Using Long Calls to Hedge Natural Gas Purchases

Rising Natural Gas Prices

Date	Spot Market	Options Market
February	Henry Hub Spot is $7.00/MMBtu	Buy August Henry Hub $7.00/MMBtu Calls for $0.50/MMBtu premium
July	Henry Hub Spot is $8.00/MMBtu	Sell August Henry Hub $7.00/MMBtu Calls for $1.00 premium
Change	$1.00/MMBtu loss	$0.50/MMBtu gain

Spot Price when Natural Gas is Purchased	$8.00/MMBtu
Gain on Options Position	-$0.50/MMBtu
Net Purchase Price	$7.50/MMBtu

Falling Natural Gas Prices

Date	Spot Market	Options Market
February	Henry Hub Spot is $7.00/MMBtu	Buy August Henry Hub $7.00/MMBtu Calls for $0.50/MMBtu premium
July	Henry Hub Spot is $6.00/MMBtu	Options Expire Worthless
Change	$1.00/MMBtu gain	$.50/MMBtu loss

Spot Price when Natural Gas is Purchased	$6.00/MMBtu
Loss on Options Position	+$0.50/MMBtu
Net Purchase Price	$6.50/MMBtu

Example of Using Long Puts to Hedge a Sale (Table 7-4)

Consider a gas producer that sells to generators. It is February. Gas sales will boom in July when generators must meet summer peak demands. Currently gas trades in the forward market for $7.00/MMBtu, as does the futures contract. To protect against a price decrease, the producer, in February, buys an August put with a strike price of $7.00/MMBtu for a premium of $0.50/MMBtu.

Falling Prices

In July, the price in the spot market falls to $6.00/MMBtu and the option is now worth $1.00/MMBtu. The producer sells the contract for $1.00/MMBtu, making $0.50/MMBtu. Because the price in the spot market has fallen, the producer sells the gas in the spot market for $6.00/MMBtu. The producer adds the $0.50/MMBtu gain on the futures to the cash sale, so the effective sale price of each MMBtu is now $6.50.

Because the producer hedged its sale, it lessened the impact of the price drop.

Rising Prices

In July, the price in the futures and spot market rises to $8.00/MMBtu. The put option expires worthless. The producer then sells the gas in the spot market for $8.00/MMBtu. After the producer applies the $0.50/MMBtu loss on the futures to the cash sale, the effective sale price of each MMBtu is now $7.50.

Although the producer may have sold the gas at a higher effective price had it not hedged, it would not have protected itself against a price drop. The purpose of the hedge, though, was to minimize risk, not increase prices. By using the option, the gas producer could benefit more from the rise in prices than by using the futures.

Table 7-4

Using Long Puts to Hedge Natural Gas Sales

Falling Natural Gas Prices

Date	Spot Market	Options Market
February	Henry Hub Spot is $7.00/MMBtu	Buy August Henry Hub $7.00/MMBtu Puts for $0.50/MMBtu premium
July	Henry Hub Spot is $6.00/MMBtu	Sell August Henry Hub $7.00/MMBtu Puts for $1.00/MMBtu premium
Change	$1.00/MMBtu loss	$0.50/MMBtu gain

Spot Price when Natural Gas is Sold	$6.00/MMBtu
Gain on Options Position	+$0.50/MMBtu
Net Sale Price	$6.50/MMBtu

Rising Natural Gas Prices

Date	Spot Market	Options Market
February	Henry Hub Spot is $7.00/MMBtu	Buy August Henry Hub $7.00/MMBtu Puts for $0.50/MMBtu premium
July	Henry Hub Spot is $8.00/MMBtu	Options Expire Worthless
Change	$1.00/MMBtu gain	$0.50/MMBtu loss

Spot Price when Natural Gas is Sold	$8.00/MMBtu
Loss on Options Position	-$0.50/MMBtu
Net Sale Price	$7.50/MMBtu

Collar

The collar is still another variant for using options. It reduces the cost of using options to manage risk. Collars are created by the purchase (or sale) of a call offset by the sale (or purchase) of a put. The calls and puts are both out of the money and have the same expiration month.[5]

If the income from selling the put (call) matches the cost of buying the call (put), the creator of the collar has created a costless way to fix a future price range for buying or selling a commodity, the so-called *costless collar.*

Examples of Using a Collar (Tables 7-5a and 7-5b)

For these examples, assume the February price of gas is $7.00/MMBtu and the August $7.50 call is trading at $0.25/MMBtu and the August $6.50 put is trading at $0.25/MMBtu.

Table 7-5a

Collars

Collar is instituted when gas trades at $7.00/MMBtu
$7.50/MMBtu call option trades at $0.25/MMBtu when collar is instituted
$6.50/MMBtu put option trades at $0.25/MMBtu when collar is instituted

Using a Collar to Cap Prices
(Sell $6.50/MMBtu put and Buy $7.50/MMBtu call)

		Case 1 Natural Gas Falls to $6.00/MMBtu	Case 2 Natural Gas Stays at $7.00/MMBtu	Case 3 Natural Gas Climbs to $8.00/MMBtu
1	Initial Cost of Call	-$0.25	-$0.25	-$0.25
2	Revenue from Sale of Put	$0.25	$0.25	$0.25
3	Initial Cost of Collar	$0.00	$0.00	$0.00
4	Cost of Short Put at Expiration	-$0.50	$0.00	$0.00
5	Value of Call at Expiration	$0.00	$0.00	$0.50
6	Combined Profit or Loss	-$0.50	$0.00	$0.50
7	Effective Cost of Natural Gas	$6.50	$7.00	$7.50

After, New York Mercantile Exchange: A Guide to Energy Hedging, pp. 58-59.

Using a Collar to Cap Price Range

Gas trades in February at $7.00/MMBtu, and a generator, concerned about price increases, wants to set a cap using options, but at a lower cost than buying calls outright. The generator sells a $6.50/MMBtu put for $0.25/MMBtu and buys the $7.50/MMBtu call for $0.25/MMBtu. Now the minimum price the generator will pay for gas is $6.50/MMBtu and the maximum is $7.50/MMBtu. In the example shown, the gain and loss of the put and call cancel each other out. Here is an analysis of how a collar can cap a price.

Gas falls to $6.00/MMBtu

Line 1: The generator buys the $7.50/MMBtu call for $0.25/MMBtu.

Line 2: The generator sells the $6.50/MMBtu put for $0.25/MMBtu.

Line 3: The sale and purchase cancel each other out to create a zero outlay.

Line 4: At expiration, the short put costs the seller $0.50/MMBtu. (The put expires $0.50 below its strike price, and the seller is required to pay that difference to the option holder.)

Line 5: The call is worth zero at expiration (it expires beneath its strike price).

Line 6: This is the sum of lines 1-5. This is a loss of $0.50/MMBtu.

Line 7: The loss of $0.50/MMBtu is added to the purchase price of $6.00/MMBtu for a final effective cost of gas of $6.50/MMBtu.

Gas stays at $7.00/MMBtu

Line 1: The generator buys the $7.50/MMBtu call for $0.25/MMBtu.

Line 2: The generator sells the $6.50/MMBtu put for $0.25/MMBtu.

Line 3: The sale and purchase cancel each other out to create a zero outlay.

Line 4: At expiration, the short put expires worthless, because the market price is greater than the strike price. (It makes no sense to sell gas at $6.50/MMBtu when the market trades at $7.00/MMBtu.)

Line 5: The call is worth zero at expiration because it expires beneath its strike price. (It does not make sense to exercise the call — why would someone want an option to buy gas for $7.50/MMBtu when the market price is $7.00/MMBtu?)

Line 6: This is the sum of lines 1-5. There is no net profit or loss.

Line 7: Because there is no net profit or loss, the final effective cost of gas is the same as the market price: $7.00/MMBtu.

Gas climbs to $8.00/MMBtu

Line 1: The generator buys the $7.50/MMBtu call for $0.25/MMBtu.

Line 2: The generator sells the $6.50/MMBtu put for $0.25/MMBtu.

Line 3: The sale and purchase cancel each other out to create a zero outlay.

Line 4: At expiration, the short put expires worthless, because the market price is greater than the strike price. (It makes no sense to sell gas at $6.50/MMBtu when the market trades at $7.50/MMBtu.)

Line 5: The call is worth $0.50/MMBtu at expiration, because the right to buy gas for $7.50/MMBtu is now worth $0.50/ MMBtu.

Line 6: This is the sum of lines 1-5. This is a gain of $0.50/MMBtu.

Line 7: The gain of $0.50/MMBtu is subtracted from the purchase price of $8.00/MMBtu for a final effective cost of gas of $7.50/MMBtu.

Using a Collar to Create a Floor Range *(Table 7-5b)*

Natural gas currently trades at $7.00/MMBtu. A producer is concerned about price decreases and wants to set a floor using options, but at a lower cost than buying puts outright. The generator buys a $6.50/MMBtu put for $0.25/MMBtu and sells the $7.50/MMBtu call for $0.25/MMBtu. Now the minimum price the producer will receive for gas will be $6.50/MMBtu and the maximum will be $7.50/MMBtu. In the example shown, the gain and loss of the call and put cancel each other out. Here is an analysis of how a collar can provide a price floor.

Table 7-5b

Using a Collar to Create a Price Floor
(Buy $6.50/MMBtu put and Sell $7.50/MMBtu call)

		Case 1 Natural Gas Falls to $6.00/MMBtu	Case 2 Natural Gas Stays at $7.00/MMBtu	Case 3 Natural Gas Climbs to $8.00/MMBtu
1	Initial Cost of Put	-$0.25	-$0.25	-$0.25
2	Revenue from Sale of Call	$0.25	$0.25	$0.25
3	Initial Cost of Collar	$0.00	$0.00	$0.00
4	Cost of Short Call at Expiration	$0.00	$0.00	-$0.50
5	Value of Put at Expiration	$0.50	$0.00	$0.00
6	Combined Profit or Loss	$0.50	$0.00	-$0.50
7	Effective Price of Natural Gas	$6.50	$7.00	$7.50

After, New York Mercantile Exchange: A Guide to Energy Hedging, pp. 58-59.

Gas falls to $6.00/MMBtu

Line 1: The producer buys the $6.50/MMBtu put for $0.25/MMBtu.

Line 2: The producer sells the $7.50/MMBtu call for $0.25/MMBtu.

Line 3: The sale and purchase cancel each other out to create a zero outlay.

Line 4: At expiration, the short call expires worthless, because the owner of the call will not exercise a call to buy gas at $7.50/MMBtu when market prices are $6.00/MMBtu.

Line 5: The put is worth $0.50/MMBtu at expiration, because the right to sell gas for $6.50/MMBtu is now worth $0.50/MMBtu.

Line 6: This is the sum of lines 1-5. This is a gain of $0.50/MMBtu.

Line 7: The gain of $0.50/MMBtu is added to the sale price of $6.00/MMBtu for a final effective price of gas of $6.50/MMBtu.

Gas stays at $7.00/MMBtu

Line 1: The producer buys the $6.50/MMBtu put for $0.25/MMBtu.

Line 2: The producer sells the $7.50/MMBtu call for $0.25/MMBtu.

Line 3: The sale and purchase cancel each other out to create a zero outlay.

Line 4: At expiration, the short call does not cost the seller anything, because the owner does not exercise the option. (It makes no sense to exercise a call to buy gas at $7.50/MMBtu when gas trades at $7.00/MMBtu.)

Line 5: The put is worth zero at expiration, because the spot price at expiration exceeds the put option's strike price.

Line 6: This is the sum of lines 1-5. There is no net profit or loss.

Line 7: Because there is no net profit or loss, the final effective price of gas is the same as the market price: $7.00/MMBtu.

Gas climbs to $8.00/MMBtu

Line 1: The producer buys the $6.50/MMBtu put for $0.25/MMBtu.

Line 2: The producer sells the $7.50/MMBtu call for $0.25/MMBtu.

Line 3: The sale and purchase cancel each other out to create a zero outlay.

Line 4: At expiration, the short call costs the seller $0.50/MMBtu. (The call expires $0.50 above its strike price, and the seller is required to pay that difference to the option holder.)

Line 5: The put is worth zero at expiration, because the spot price at expiration exceeds the put option's strike price.

Line 6: This is the sum of lines 1-5. This is a loss of $0.50/MMBtu.

Line 7: The loss of $0.50/MMBtu is subtracted from the sale price of $8.00/MMBtu for a final effective cost of gas of $7.50/MMBtu.

Swaps

Swaps are, usually, privately negotiated (not exchange traded) derivatives, in which two parties agree to exchange (swap) a price risk exposure for a given time period. Because swaps are privately negotiated, they can be customized to meet all sorts of risks. In commodities, swaps are used to protect against price fluctuations. Most swaps involve a periodic exchange of cash flows between two parties, with one paying a fixed cash flow and the other a variable amount relative to a given benchmark. By combining swaps with a position in the cash market, companies can lock in a price for commodities they wish to buy or sell. Again, because most swaps are customized and privately negotiated, it may be difficult to exit them, as with forward contracts, if holding the swap is no longer advantageous for a particular party.

Table 7-6

Using Swaps to Manage Price Risk

Price	What Happens?	How much money changes hands?
Natural Gas Price < $7.00/MMBtu	Generator Pays Producer	$7.00/MMBtu - Natural Gas Price/MMBtu
Natural Gas Price = 7.00/MMBtu	No money changes hands	None
Natural Gas Price > $7.00/MMBtu	Producer Pays Generator	Natural Gas Price/ MMBtu - $7.00/MMBtu

Using a Swap to Fix a Price (Table 7-6)

Here is a simple example of a swap. Say a generator wishes to protect itself against an increase in natural gas prices and a natural gas producer wishes to protect itself against a fall in price. The two parties could make a deal to exchange payments depending on the price of natural gas. Say each determined that $7.00/MMBtu represented the point of profitability. If the price of gas falls below $7.00/MMBtu, then the generator pays the producer the difference between $7.00/MMBtu and the current price. If the price equals $7.00/MMBtu, no payments are exchanged. If the price is greater than $7.00/MMBtu, the producer pays the generator the difference between the current natural gas price and $7.00/MMBtu. This way both the generator and producer are assured a price of $7.00/MMBtu.

Technique Six: Reduce the Risk

One way to reduce price risk is to diversify sources of supply and demand, creating a portfolio of price risks, of the sort one finds in modern portfolio theory. Two tenets of this theory are that:

1. When faced with two investments that have the same return, investors would prefer the one that has lower risk (standard deviation of returns).

2. When faced with two investments that have the same risk, investors would prefer the investment with the higher return.

If an energy supplier depends on one fuel, it exposes itself to all the risks that come with using that fuel — such as supply interruptions and price variability. Think of an independent power producer that has its generator hooked up to one gas line. It is a captive market for its gas supplier — if the supplier does not deliver or the prices are too high, the generator may be precluded from producing power or generating power at a profit. If the generator had other fuel or energy sources available, it could reduce its risk by setting up a diversified fuel portfolio.[6]

In devising the diversified portfolio, the generator would consider how the fuel prices are correlated. Although past prices may not predict future prices, looking at the price relationships between different fuels, may provide insights into how to diversify fuels and minimize risk. Some relationships may derive from the nature of the fuels involved — for example oil and natural gas prices often move together because they are derived from similar sources or wells. Others have a weaker relationship — by their very nature. For example, uranium and natural gas come from different sources and are purchased through entirely different channels. Or if a generating company has a hydropower component, those costs are mostly fixed, and the cost of production will

83

not, in most cases, have any correlation to the prices paid for natural gas, and so would add diversification to a portfolio. Or, in another way, the forces that govern the supply of water for a hydropower operation — snowpack in a watershed for example — are determined by hydrology, not the forces in the natural gas market. So, it is very likely that the costs of running a hydropower plant would not correlate strongly with prices for natural gas. Thus combining a hydropower operation with a natural gas-fired power plant, would reduce the risk for an operator dependent on natural gas for fuel.

Conclusion

Ultimately, the fact of being in the energy business requires an energy supplier to face risk — and to decide to do something about that risk — whether through action or inaction. Every action uses one or more of the six techniques for managing risk, including the often dangerous decision to ignore risk or bear risk simply because management fears, but does not understand, the risk management tools that are there for its asking. Lack of knowledge is not an excuse for those who have a fiduciary duty to safeguard a company and its assets — as techniques have evolved to manage risk — and none too soon: with concerns growing about declining oil supplies, and with many energy sources located in unstable parts of the world, uncertainty about energy prices will not go away — if anything it may increase in the future.

Notes

[1] Johnson, Philip McBride, *Derivatives: A Manager's Guide to the World's Most Powerful Financial Instruments* (New York: McGraw-Hill, 1999), p. 26.

[2] Commodities Futures Trading Commission, *op. cit.* Definition for **Convergence.**

[3] Hedgers use the futures contract that is closest to the month, but not before, the actual cash transaction. This increases the effectiveness of the hedge.

[4] Actually, when traded on the NYMEX, these are options on natural gas futures, but to simplify the explanation, the options are considered based on the natural gas spot prices. In reality, the principle is the same, with the futures functioning as the underlying, as opposed to the natural gas spot price.

[5] New York Mercantile Exchange, *A Guide to Energy Hedging* (New York: New York Mercantile Exchange 1999), p. 58.

[6] This fuel portfolio could be compared to an investment portfolio and the principles of

Markowitz's portfolio theory applied. Consider an electric utility with a retail price for customers that is fixed for a given period by a regulator, while at the same time it purchases its fuel in the open market. It would be possible to model the portfolio and examine the effects of varying fuel choices on the overall fuel risk for a generator. Consider the following hypothetical two-fuel input model.

Let W_1 = the weight of fuel 1 in the generating fuel mix

Let W_2 = the weight of fuel 2 in the generating fuel mix

$W_1 + W_2 = 1$

Let R_1 = Return from producing power with fuel 1 (This equals the retail revenue minus the fuel cost)

Let R_2 = Return from producing power with fuel 2 (This equals the retail revenue minus the fuel cost)

Let R_p = Return of Portfolio

Let S_1 = Standard deviation of R_1

Let S_2 = Standard deviation of R_2

Let S_p = Standard Deviation of Portfolio

cov = covariance between two variables. Covariance is a measure of the relationship between two variables. Variables with a positive covariance have a direct relationship. Variables with a negative covariance have an inverse relationship. Variables with zero covariance do not have a mathematical relationship.

According to Modern Portfolio Theory:

$$R_p = W_1 R_1 + W_2 R_2$$
$$Sp = [W_1^2 S_1^2 + W_2^2 S_2^2 + 2W_1 W_2 \, cov(R_1 R_2)]^{-1/2}$$

Thus the risk of the portfolio depends on the variability of the individual variables, as well as the **relationship** between the variables. This relationship allows two portfolios to have the same return, but depending on the relationship between the elements of the portfolio, they may have different risks associated with them. When two portfolios have the same return, the preferred portfolio is the one with the lower risk.

Although this example uses two portfolio elements, the analysis can be expanded to using an infinite number of elements. However, increasing the number of variables increases the number of computations required, significantly. Matrix algebra is useful when dealing with more than three variables for ease of computation.

Source: This material has been modified from, "An Introduction to Matrix Algebra," by Jim Finegan, CFA in *Financial Engineering News*, September/October 2004, pp. 15-20.

Weather Risk

Few businesses have performance so closely tied to the weather as does the energy sector. Significant weather risks include, temperature, precipitation, and extreme events. The 1998 power crisis in the Midwest was brought on by higher than expected temperatures, which led to higher than normal demand at a time when there was inadequate supply capacity to meet the demand at the offered prices. The California Power crisis developed when there was insufficient hydropower available to meet the needs of California customers, thus requiring the purchase of more expensive power, often from outside the state, which permitted many of the financial manipulations that destroyed the California utility restructuring and led to the bankruptcy of Pacific Gas & Electric.

Wind can have significant effects on power markets — and not just from toppling over transmission towers. Lack of wind can deny transmission lines the cooling they need, which means less transmission of power through lines.[1] In 2004, hurricanes damaged oil and gas rigs and decreased their production.[2] The weather can cause other problems due to environmental regulations. Consider an ozone non-attainment area. Under certain weather conditions (sunny and warm, usually in summer) pollutants may exceed thresholds, causing regulators to shut down or curtail operations of polluting industries, such as oil refineries or power plants.

Although the weather may not be controllable, companies can choose their responses to changing weather by developing a risk management plan designed to deal with the vagaries of weather. Managing weather risk can affect profitability. In the past, utilities could pass on weather related costs to captive customers. What happens now that customers have a choice, or regulators no longer allow passthroughs? The management of weather risk could prove crucial to a company's viability.

Temperature and Profitability

Weather drives utility revenues. Utilities essentially hold portfolios of revenue streams analogous to long positions. They should think that way when dealing with the risks. In summer an electric utility holds a long position in cooling degree days. The higher the number of cooling degree days, the higher the revenues. In winter, a gas company holds a long position in heating degree days. With more heating degree days, the company sells a higher volume of gas. Utility revenues consist of two components — price of energy sold and quantity sold. Weather affects both components.

Avoid the Risk

In reality, it is not possible to avoid overall "weather risk" unless the company wants to exit the atmosphere. However, by choosing its markets and fuel sources, a company can avoid certain weather risks. It is important to remember that choosing to avoid risks may prevent a company from seizing opportunities to create returns. For example, the 2004 hurricane season in North America was costly for companies with oil and gas platforms and pipelines in the Gulf of Mexico. A company that decides to avoid offshore hurricane risks may shut itself out of future opportunities for domestic offshore hydrocarbon production. The decision to avoid risk needs has to be compared with the opportunity cost of losing out on profitable exploration and production opportunities.

Given that weather is difficult to predict, weather risk, *in toto*, cannot be avoided. This does not mean that specific weather risks cannot be avoided, though. A company needs to decide which weather risks it wishes to incur or avoid. Different regions have different weather characteristics. When choosing to avoid a weather risk, it is important to also look at the cost of the avoidance. A power company that wants to avoid the risks of trees falling on its wires in high winds will face a higher cost from burying its wires in an effort to avoid windstorm risk. Whatever the case, an energy or utility company cannot avoid weather risk. This should be accepted and built into the company's strategic and short-term planning. The risks should be explicitly acknowledged, and plans to deal with them developed and implemented.

Bear the Risk

Given the inherent difficulty of avoiding risk, it is likely that energy companies will bear weather risk regularly.

The decision to bear weather risk is a decision that needs to be made consciously by a board/management in its risk management planning.

Although weather can be unpredictable, climate records can be used to develop statistical probabilities of events or temperatures. As anyone who follows weather reports knows, weather forecasts can be inaccurate. However, seasonal climate is more predictable — it usually cools off in winter and warms up in summer. These probabilities can be combined with the costs of the events or temperature ranges to estimate the financial risks of pursuing various risk management options. Of course, choosing to bear risk is one of those options. Before choosing to bear risk, a board or senior decision-makers need to understand the potential costs of that decision.

Reduce the Hazard

Reducing weather hazards consists of avoiding the conditions that increase the chance of a loss. To reduce hazards, it helps to do a systematic analysis of not only the hazards the firm faces, but also the potential financial benefits from reducing the hazards and the costs of sticking with the status quo. For example, as mentioned earlier, a utility faces a greater hazard of a distribution disruption if its wires are strung from poles rather than placed underground. In the past, this decision in favor of overhead lines may have been justified because it cost less than placing wires underground. Customers, who bore the inconvenience and expenses of any disruption, were not usually given an explicit choice between overhead or underground lines. Some customers may value reliability (a lower risk) and want to pay a higher price for better service. Comprehensive analysis of weather risk might point out new opportunities for the firm — such as providing more reliable, weather resistant distribution, as a differentiating factor or as a premium service.

With energy companies, one of the most common losses arises from adverse temperature events. The energy company can work on planning its operation and infrastructure in ways that will reduce the chances of losses from adverse weather events.

Common Weather Hazards

Temperature Spike in Summer

One of the dangers of a temperature spike in summer for an electric company is that it might not have enough power to meet demand, or it may have to buy power at an elevated price in the market to meet higher demand from needs such as air conditioning. In the less regulated market of today, the firm may not be able to pass on that cost increase to customers — yet it still has an obligation to serve them. Oftentimes the power demands of businesses and residential customers may peak at the same time, creating strain on the distribution system. What can be done?

Putting in place methods to reduce the peaks, before they happen could significantly reduce the hazards of temperatures spikes. For example:

1. Introduce real time pricing of power based on system demand, and have feedback systems so customers can adjust their power usage when demand spikes, and thereby reduce strains on the system.

2. Consider the risk of adding a load, as well as the potential return when considering new customers. If a utility expects to be short power and an overly warm summer is expected, then it may look at two customers differently. Say two customers apply with equal annual power loads. One is a multiplex movie theater with high summer air conditioning needs coincidental with the summer peak, and the other is a nursery that will use more power in winter for lighting and heating. The two customers may offer the same return, but one produces a higher risk for the system (the multiplex).

This discussion assumes of course that the utility or the energy supplier can refuse a customer. If it cannot, it must find ways to price its product to reflect the customer-specific risks.

Storm Damage

For customers, the most visible effect of weather on utility operations is when they lose their power in a storm. This usually occurs when high winds knock trees onto power lines. Obviously one way to reduce the hazard is through prudent tree pruning programs. The most dramatic way to reduce the hazard would be to put power lines underground. In the past utility companies emphasized the cost of this path, without giving customers a choice of choosing the reliability of their distribution system. Going forward, as mentioned earlier, perhaps a utility could make a business of providing more reliable power. Whatever the case, when planning new transmission and distribution, the risk of a system should be factored in when analyzing costs — this may change the economics of a system and alter thinking about how to design it.

Mild Temperatures

How can one reduce the hazard of mild temperatures? Gas companies do poorly when winters are warm, and power companies suffer when summers are mild. The key may lie, again, in examining what types of customers to add, and perhaps customers to shed. When adding customers it is important to not only look at the rates they may pay, but the risks from adding them to the system — and to consider how the customer's power demands could affect the company's financial risks from mild temperatures. Perhaps it may be more beneficial, at times, to add customers whose loads are not highly weather dependent.

Reduce the Loss

Take steps to reduce the **losses** arising from a **peril**.

The Peril of Weather Induced High Demand

For electric markets, the peril of weather induced high demand can be very expensive, if the firm does not have the power to meet its customers' needs. The firm, in advance, needs to have policies and procedures in place to deal with such contingencies. In many cases, it will cut off customers with interruptible contracts. Or a utility may turn off air conditioners of residential customers that have agreed to cutoffs, in exchange for a reduction in rates. Of course, these shutoffs, if repeated often, may undermine the impression that customers have of a utility, and drive them away. Perhaps a system of real time pricing or automated metering to reduce demand in a selective manner may prove a more palatable way to reduce losses. Distributed generation, by being closer to the customer, may also effectively reduce losses, by powering up quickly to make up for lost power sources or by coming on line quickly to meet peaks.

The Peril of Mild Weather

During a period of mild weather, a utility may have excess generating capacity or excess gas on hand. During periods of low demand in its home region, it may wish to have plans on hand to market the power or sell some gas to areas that are short power or gas. Or, a company may wish to investigate ways to sell options on its plants to sell power to those that may need it.

Transfer the Risk

The standard derivatives are good for controlling price risk. However, they do not protect energy suppliers and users from non-monetary forces, such as weather, that drive volume of demand. For example, a generating company could have locked in a high summer price for its power, but a very cool summer would not generate the volume of business it needs to meet its profit targets. Weather derivatives are tools to manage that volumetric risk based on heating and cooling degree-days.

Heating degree-days are measures of the coolness of the weather. A heating degree-day (HDD) is the number of degrees Fahrenheit by which the average temperature on a day falls below 65°F (18°C). For degree day purposes, the average temperature is determined by adding the day's maximum temperature to the day's minimum temperature and dividing by two. The developers of this measure considered 65°F (18°C) as the point at which people start turning on their heaters, and therefore a proxy for the coolness of the weather in estimating energy demand. There is a positive relationship between the number of heating degree-days and demand for electric power and natural gas for heating purposes.

A cooling degree-day (CDD) measures how hot the weather is. A cooling degree-day is the number of degrees Fahrenheit by which the average temperature on a day exceeds 65°F (18°C). The developers of this measure considered 65°F (18°C) as the point at which people start turning on their air conditioners, and therefore a proxy for heat in estimating energy demand. There is an extremely strong relationship between the number of cooling degree-days and demand for electric power for air conditioning purposes, one of the heaviest power loads in summer.

For example, generating companies make money in the summer when there is high demand for their power. However, a cool summer could hurt their profits, if their profitability is tied to volume in their rate design, because few people will use their air conditioners and the capacity is underutilized.

Heating and cooling degree-day derivatives allow an energy user to "buy" a temperature level to minimize the effects of temperature volatility. The Chicago Mercantile Exchange features exchange-traded weather derivatives based on heating and cooling degree-days measured at O'Hare Airport and other locations. The contracts work by assigning a value of $20.00 to each heating or cooling degree-day for the US futures contracts (Table 8-1).[3]

Table 8-1

Weather Futures Contracts with Ticker Symbols
Traded on Chicago Mercantile Exchange (CME)

United States Contracts

City	Monthly HDD	Monthly CDD	Seasonal HDD	Seasonal CDD
Atlanta	H1	K1	HS1	KS1
Chicago	H2	K2	HS2	KS2
Cincinnati	H3	K3	HS3	KS3
New York	H4	K4	HS4	KS4
Dallas	H5	K5	HS5	KS5
Philadelphia	H6	K6	HS6	KS6
Portland	H7	K7	HS7	KS7
Tucson	H8	K8	HS8	KS8
Des Moines	H9	K9	HS9	KS9
Las Vegas	H0	K0	HS0	KS0
Boston	HW	KW	A0	B0
Houston	HR	KR	A2	B2
Kansas City	HX	KX	A4	B4
Minneapolis	HQ	KQ	A5	B5
Sacramento	HS	KS	A9	B9
Salt Lake City	HU	KU	A7	B7
Detroit	HK	KK	A8	B8
Baltimore	HV	KV	A3	B3

European Contracts

City	Monthly HDD	Monthly CDD	Seasonal HDD	Seasonal CDD
London	D0	G0	P0	V0
Paris	D1	G1	P1	V1
Amsterdam	D2	G2	P2	V2
Berlin	D3	G3	P3	V3
Essen	D4	G4	P4	V4
Stockholm	D5	G5	P5	V5
Rome	D9	G9	P9	V9
Madrid	DQ	GQ	PQ	VQ
Barcelona	D8	G8	P8	V8

Asian Contracts

City	Monthly Average Temperature	Seasonal Average Temperature
Tokyo	G6	V6
Osaka	G7	V7

Long Hedge

One problem market participants face is how to shift the risk of cost increases caused by weather conditions. Long futures positions allow a buyer to transfer risk of the increased costs due to the weather.

Example of Using a Long Futures Contract to Hedge a Purchase (Table 8-2)

Consider a shopping center in Chicago, which heats with gas. Each HDD in winter costs it $20.00 in heating bills. It is June. The winter forecast is for 5,000 HDDs. To protect against a cold winter, the shopping center, purchases a long seasonal HDD futures contract (September to May).

Rising HDDs

In April, as the contract nears the end of its life, the price in the futures market rises to 6,000 HDDs (the winter's total). The shopping center sells the futures contract for $120,000 making a profit of $20,000. The shopping center then pays its heating bill of $120,000. However, the shopping center applies the $20,000 profit on the futures to the gas bill, so the bill is reduced to $100,000. Because the shopping center hedged the weather, it avoided the financial shock of cold weather, which the seller of the futures contract had to absorb.

Falling HDDs

On the other hand, what if the HDDs had fallen?

In April, the price in the futures market falls to 4,000 HDDs (the season's total). The shopping center sells the futures contract for $80,000, losing $20,000. However, because the warmer temperatures reduce gas consumption, the shopping center's heating bill falls to $80,000. The shopping center adds the $20,000 loss on the futures to the gas bill, so the effective cost of heating is now $100,000.

Although the shopping center may have paid less had it not hedged, it would not have protected itself against a cold winter. However, the purpose of the hedge was to minimize risk, not minimize gas bills. The hedge accomplished that, because the shopping center fixed its winter HDDs in advance.

Table 8-2

Using Long Futures to Hedge a Cool Winter

Rising HDDs

Date	Utility Bill	Futures Market
June	Expected costs: 5,000 HDDs ($100,000)	Buy Seasonal HDD Futures for 5,000 HDDs ($100,000)
April of Following Year	Actual HDDs: 6,000 ($120,000)	Sell Back Seasonal HDD Futures for 6,000 HDDs ($120,000)
Change	$20,000 shortfall	$20,000 gain

Heating Bill	$120,000.00
Gain on Futures Position	-$20,000.00
Net Cost	$100,000.00

Falling HDDs

Date	Utility Bill	Futures Market
June	Expected costs: 5,000 HDDs ($100,000)	Buy Seasonal HDD Futures for 5,000 HDDs ($100,000)
April of Following Year	Actual HDDs: 4,000 ($80,000)	Sell Back Seasonal HDD Futures for 4,000 HDDs ($80,000)
Change	$20,000 windfall	$20,000 loss

Heating Bill	$80,000.00
Loss on Futures Position	+ $20,000.00
Net Cost	$100,000.00

Short Hedge

A short hedger uses weather futures contracts to protect against a fall in CDDs or HDDs (a mild season).

Example of Using a Short Futures Contract to Hedge a Sale (Table 8-3)

Consider a gas utility that sells gas to the shopping center in Chicago. It is June and the winter forecast is for 5,000 HDDs, and the seasonal futures contract trades at 5,000 HDDs. To protect against a mild winter, the utility, in June, sells a seasonal HDD futures contract for 5,000 HDDs ($100,000).

Falling HDDs

In April, the price in the futures market falls to 4,000 HDDs (the season's total). The gas utility buys back the futures contract for $80,000, making $20,000. However, because the winter was mild, the gas utility only sold $80,000 worth of gas. The utility adds the $20,000 gain on the futures to the season's sales, so it has $100,000 of sales for the winter. Because the utility hedged its sale, it avoided the impact of a mild winter.

Rising HDDs

In April, the price in the futures market rises to 6,000 HDDs (the season's total). The utility buys back the futures contract for $120,000 losing $20,000. However, because of the cold weather, the utility sells $120,000 of gas. After the utility applies the $20,000 loss on the futures to the season's sales, the effective seasonal revenue is $100,000.

Although the utility may have made more money, had it not hedged, it would not have protected itself against a mild winter. The purpose of the hedge was to minimize risk, not increase sales. The hedge accomplished that, because the utility fixed a weather level in advance. The utility earned less, but it also took less of a chance, and lower risk often is accompanied by lower return.

Table 8-3

Using Short Futures to Hedge a Warm Winter

+1 HDD = -$20.00 move in futures contract
1 HDD = $20.00 of revenues for utility

Falling HDDs

Date	Utility Revenues	Futures Market
June	Expected revenues: 5,000 HDDs ($100,000)	Sell Seasonal HDD Futures for 5,000 HDDs ($100,000)
April of Following Year	Actual HDDs: 4,000 ($80,000)	Buy Back Seasonal HDD Futures for 4,000 HDDs ($80,000)
Change	$20,000 shortfall	$20,000 gain

Actual Revenues	$80,000.00
Gain on Futures Position	+ $20,000.00
Net Sales Revenue	$100,000.00

Rising HDDs

Date	Utility Revenues	Futures Market
April	Expected revenues: 5,000 HDDs ($100,000)	Sell Seasonal HDD Futures for 5,000 HDDs ($100,000)
April of Following Year	Actual HDDs: 6,000 $120,000)	Buy Back Seasonal HDD Futures for 6,000 HDDs ($120,000)
Change	$20,000 windfall	$20,000 loss

Actual Revenues	$120,000.00
Loss on Futures Position	-$20,000.00
Net Sales Revenue	$100,000.00

Options

Example of Using Long Calls to Hedge a Purchase (Table 8-4)

Consider the shopping center that needs to purchase gas for heating in the winter. It has considered using futures, but wants to take advantage of drops in HDDs if there is a mild winter, which an option allows. It decides to hedge using long calls. The forecast is for a 5,000 HDD Heating Season. To protect against a cold winter, the shopping center purchases, in June, a seasonal call with a strike price of 5,000 HDDs for a 500 HDD ($10,000) premium.[4]

Rising HDDs

By April, the heating season totals 6,000 HDDs and the option goes in the money. The shopping center sells the call option for 1,000 HDDs, making a profit of $10,000. The shopping center applies the $10,000 profit to its heating bill of $120,000, reducing the bill to $110,000. Because the shopping center hedged its weather it lessened the impact of the cold weather.

Falling HDDs

On the other hand, what if the HDDs had fallen? By April, the heating season totals 4,000 HDDs, and the option expires worthless. However, because the winter was mild, the shopping center only had an $80,000 heating bill. The shopping center then adds the $10,000 loss on the options to the cash purchase, so the effective heating bill is now $90,000. By using options, the shopping center was able to benefit more from the fall in prices than by using the futures.

Although the shopping center may have paid less had it not hedged, it would not have protected itself against cooler than expected temperatures.

Table 8-4

Using Long Calls to Hedge a Cool Winter

1 HDD = 1 tick = $20.00

Rising HDDs

Date	Utility Bill	Options Market
June	Expected costs: 5,000 HDDs ($100,000)	Buy Seasonal 5,000 HDD strike Calls for 500 ticks (HDDs) ($10,000)
April of Following Year	Actual HDDs: 6,000 ($120,000)	Sell Seasonal HDD Calls for 1,000 ticks (HDDs) ($20,000)
Change	$20,000 shortfall	$10,000 gain

Heating Bill	$120,000.00
Gain on Options Position	-$10,000.00
Net Cost	$110,000.00

Falling HDDs

Date	Utility Bill	Options Market
June	Expected costs: 5,000 HDDs ($100,000)	Buy Seasonal 5,000 HDD strike Calls for 500 ticks (HDDs) ($10,000)
April of Following Year	Actual HDDs: 4,000 ($80,000)	Options Expire Worthless
Change	$20,000 windfall	$10,000 loss

Heating Bill	$80,000.00
Loss on Options Position	+ $10,000.00
Net Cost	$90,000.00

Example of Using a Long Put to Hedge a Sale (Table 8-5)

Consider a gas utility that sells gas to shopping centers for heating in winter. It is June. The forecast is for a winter with 5,000 HDDs. To protect against a mild weather, the utility, in June, buys a seasonal put with strike price of 5,000 HDDs for a premium of 500 HDDs ($10,000).

Falling HDDs

By April, the heating season totals 6,000 HDDs and the option goes in the money. The utility sells the option for $20,000 making $10,000. Because the winter was mild, the utility only sold $80,000 worth of gas. The utility adds the $10,000 gain on the option to its revenues, with its effective revenue totaling $90,000.

Because the utility hedged its weather, it lessened the impact of the mild winter.

Rising HDDs

By April, the seasonal HDDs total 6,000. The cold weather has created $120,000 in sales. The put option expires worthless. After the utility applies the $10,000 loss on the option to its revenues, the effective revenues now total $110,000. Although the utility may have had higher revenues had it not hedged, it would not have protected itself against a mild winter. The purpose of the hedge, though, was to minimize risk, not increase sales. By using the option, the gas utility could benefit more from the rise in HDDs than by using the futures.

Collar

The collar is still another variant for using options. It reduces the cost of using options to manage risk. Collars are created by the purchase (or sale) of a call offset by the sale (or purchase) of a put. The calls and puts are both out of the money and have the same expiration month.[5]

If the income from selling the put (call) matches the cost of buying the call (put), the creator of the collar has created a costless way to fix a future price range for buying or selling a commodity, the so-called *costless collar.*

Table 8-5

Using Long Puts to Hedge a Warm Winter

1 Tick = 1 HDD = $20.00

Falling HDDs

Date	Utility Revenues	Options Market
June	Expected revenues: 5,000 HDDs ($100,000)	Buy Seasonal 5,000 HDD Puts for 500 ticks ($10,000)
April of Following Year	Actual HDDs: 4,000 ($80,000)	Sell Seasonal HDD Puts for 1,000 ticks ($20,000)
Change	$20,000 shortfall	$10,000 gain

Actual Revenues	$80,000.00
Gain on Options Position	+ $10,000.00
Net Sales Revenue	$90,000.00

Rising HDDs

Date	Utility Revenues	Options Market
April	Expected revenues: 5,000 HDDs ($100,000)	Buy Seasonal 5,000 HDD Puts for 500 ticks ($10,000)
April of Following Year	Actual HDDs: 6,000 ($120,000)	Options Expire Worthless
Change	$20,000 windfall	$10,000 loss

Actual Revenues	$120,000.00
Loss on Options Position	-$10,000.00
Net Sales Revenue	$110,000.00

Examples of Using a Collar (Table 8-6a and 8-6b)

For these examples, assume that in June the forecast is for a 5,000 HDD heating season, with the 5,500 HDD call trading at $2,500 and the 4,500 HDD put trading at $2,500.

Using a Collar to Cap Price Range (Table 8-6a)

In June the winter forecast is for 5,000 HDDs, and a shopping center, concerned about increased outlays, wants to set a cap using options, but at a lower cost than buying calls outright. The shopping center sells a 4,500 HDD put for $2,500 and buys the 5,500 HDD call for $2,500. Now the minimum price the shopping center will pay for gas is 4,500 HDDs ($90,000) and the maximum is 5,500 HDDs ($110,000). In the example shown, the gain and loss of the put and call cancel each other out. Here is an analysis of how a collar can cap costs.

Table 8-6a

Collars

Collar is instituted — forecast is for winter with 5,000 HDDs
5,500 HDD call option trades at 125 ticks ($2,500)
4,500 HDD put option trades at 125 ticks ($2,500)

Using a Collar to Cap Costs
(Sell 4,500 HDD put and Buy 5,500 HDD call)

		Case 1 Seasonal HDDs Fall to 4,000	Case 2 Seasonal HDDs Total 5,000	Case 3 Seasonal HDDs Rise to 6,000
1	Initial Cost of Call	-$2,500	-$2,500	-$2,500
2	Revenue from Sale of Put	$2,500	$2,500	$2,500
3	Initial Cost of Collar	$0	$0	$0
4	Cost of Short Put at Expiration	$10,000	$0	$0
5	Value of Call at Expiration	$0	$0	$10,000
6	Combined Profit or Loss	-$10,000	$0	$10,000
7	Gas Bill	$80,000	$100,000	$120,000
8	Adjusted Gas Bill	$90,000	$100,000	$110,000

After, New York Mercantile Exchange: A Guide to Energy Hedging, pp. 58-59.

Seasonal HDDs fall to 4,000

Line 1: The shopping center buys the 5,500 HDD call for $2,500.

Line 2: The shopping center sells the 4,500 HDD put for $2,500.

Line 3: The sale and purchase cancel each other out to create a zero outlay.

Line 4: At expiration, the short put costs the seller $10,000. (The put expires 500 HDDs below its strike price, and the seller is required to pay that difference to the option holder.)

Line 5: The call is worth zero at expiration (it expires beneath its strike price).

Line 6: This is the sum of lines 1-5. This is a loss of $10,000.

Line 7: The loss of $10,000 is added to the gas bill of $80,000 for a final effective cost of gas of $90,000.

Seasonal HDDs finish at 5,000

Line 1: The shopping center buys the 5,500 HDD call for $2,500.

Line 2: The shopping center sells the 4,500 HDD put for $2,500.

Line 3: The sale and purchase cancel each other out to create a zero outlay.

Line 4: At expiration, the short put expires worthless, because the market price is greater than the strike price. (It makes no sense for the holder of the put to sell the contract at 4,500 HDDs when the market trades at 5,000 HDDs.)

Line 5: The call is worth zero at expiration because it expires beneath its strike price. (It does not make sense to exercise the call — why would the holder of the call want to buy a contract for 5,500 HDDs when the market price is 5,000 HDDs?)

Line 6: This is the sum of lines 1-5. There is no net profit or loss.

Line 7: Because there is no net profit or loss, the final effective cost of gas is the same as the market price: $100,000.

Seasonal HDDs Climb to 6,000

Line 1: The shopping center buys the 5,500 HDD call for $2,500.

Line 2: The shopping center sells the 4,500 HDD put for.$2,500.

Line 3: The sale and purchase cancel each other out to create a zero outlay.

Line 4: At expiration, the short put expires worthless, because the market price is greater than the strike price. (It makes no sense for the holder of the put to sell the contract at 4,500 HDDs when the market trades at 5,500 HDDs.)

Line 5: The call is worth $10,000 at expiration, because the right to buy the contract for 5,500 HDDs is now worth $10,000.

Line 6: This is the sum of lines 1-5. This is a gain of $10,000.

Line 7: The gain of $10,000 is subtracted from the purchase price of $120,000 for a final effective cost of gas of $110,000.

Using a Collar to Create a Floor Range (Table 8-6b)

The winter forecast is for a heating season of 5,000 HDDs. A gas utility is concerned about a mild winter and wants to put in a floor using options, but at a lower cost than buying puts outright. The gas utility buys a 4,500 HDD put for $2,500 and sells the 5,500 HDD call for $2,500. Now the minimum price the utility will receive for the gas it sells will be $90,000 and the maximum will be $110,000. In the example shown, the gain and loss of the call and put cancel each other out. Here is an analysis of how a collar can provide a price floor.

Table 8-6b

Collars

Collar is instituted — forecast is for winter with 5,000 HDDs
5,500 HDD call option trades at 125 ticks ($2,500)
4,500 HDD put option trades at 125 ticks ($2,500)

Using a Collar to Create a Price Floor
(Buy 4,500 HDD put and Sell 5,500 HDD call)

		Case 1 Seasonal HDDs Fall to 4,000	Case 2 Seasonal HDDs Total 5,000	Case 3 Seasonal HDDs Rise to 6,000
1	Initial Cost of Put	-$2,500	-$2,500	-$2,500
2	Revenue from Sale of Call	$2,500	$2,500	$2,500
3	Initial Cost of Collar	$0	$0	$0
4	Cost of Short Call at Expiration	$0	$0	-$10,000
5	Value of Put at Expiration	$10,000	$0	$0
6	Combined Profit or Loss	$10,000	$0	$10,000
7	Revenue	$80,000	$100,000	$120,000
8	Net Sales Revenue	$90,000	$100,000	$110,000

After, New York Mercantile Exchange: A Guide to Energy Hedging, pp. 58-59.

If Seasonal HDDs Fall to 4,000

Line 1: The utility buys the 4,500 HDD put for $2,500.

Line 2: The utility sells the 5,500 HDD call for $2,500.

Line 3: The sale and purchase cancel each other out to create a zero outlay.

Line 4: At expiration, the short call expires worthless, because the owner of the call will not exercise a call to buy a contract for 5,500 HDDs when the market price is 4,000 HDDs.

Line 5: The put is worth $10,000 at expiration, because the right to sell the contract for 4,500 HDDs is now worth $10,000.

Line 6: This is the sum of lines 1-5. This is a gain of $10,000.

Line 7: The gain of $10,000 is added to the sales of $80,000 for net revenues of $90,000.

If Seasonal HDDs Stay at 5,000

Line 1: The utility buys the 4,500 HDD put for $2,500.

Line 2: The utility sells the 5,500 HDD call for $2,500.

Line 3: The sale and purchase cancel each other out to create a zero outlay.

Line 4: At expiration, the short call does not cost the seller anything, because the owner does not exercise the option. (It makes no sense to exercise a call to buy the contract at 5,500 HDDs when it trades at 5,000 HDDs.)

Line 5: The put is worth zero at expiration, because it expires above its strike price.

Line 6: This is the sum of lines 1-5. There is no net profit or loss.

Line 7: Because there is no net profit or loss, the net sales revenue is the same as the market price: $100,000.

If Seasonal HDDs Climb to 6,000

Line 1: The utility buys the 4,500 HDDs put for $2,500.

Line 2: The utility sells the 5,500 HDDs call for $2,500.

Line 3: The sale and purchase cancel each other out to create a zero outlay.

Line 4: At expiration, the short call costs the seller $10,000. (The call expires 500 HDDs above its strike price, and the seller is required to pay that difference to the option holder.)

Line 5: The put is worth zero at expiration (it expires above its strike price).

Line 6: This is the sum of lines 1-5. This is a loss of $10,000.

Line 7: The loss of $10,000 is subtracted from the $120,000 in sales, creating net revenues of $110,000.

Swaps

Swaps are, usually, privately negotiated (not exchange traded) derivatives, in which two parties agree to exchange (swap) a price risk exposure for a given time period. Because swaps are privately negotiated, they can be customized to meet all sorts of risks. In commodities, swaps are used to protect against price fluctuations. Most swaps involve a periodic exchange of cash flows between two parties, with one paying a fixed cash flow and the other a variable amount relative to a given benchmark. By combining swaps with a position in the cash market, companies can lock in a price for commodities they wish to buy or sell. Again, because most swaps are customized and privately negotiated, it may be difficult to exit them, as with forward contracts, if holding the swap is no longer advantageous for a particular party.

Using a Swap to Fix a Price (Table 8-7)

Here is a simple example of a swap. Say a merchant generator wishes to protect against a mild summer and a cinema operator that has high air conditioning bills wants to protect itself against a very hot summer that could hurt its profits. The generator's profits will be imperiled if the seasonal CDDs fall below 900 and the cinema operator's bills will be onerous if the cooling season exceeds 900 CDDs. The generator and cinema operator agree to a swap.

The two parties could make a deal to exchange payments depending on the seasonal CDDs. If the seasonal CDD total falls below 900, then the cinema owner pays the generator $100 for each CDD below 900. If the seasonal CDDs total 900, no payments are exchanged. If the seasonal CDDs are greater than 900, the generator pays the cinema $100 for each CDD below 900. This way both the generator and utility are assured a cooling season of 900 CDDs.

Table 8-7

Using Swaps to Manage Price Risk

CDD's	What Happens?	How much money changes hands?
Seasonal CDDs < 900	Cinema Owner Pays Generator	(900 CDDs − Actual CDDs) × $100/CDD
Seasonal CDDs = 900	No money changes hands	None
Seasonal CDDs > 900	Generator Pays Cinema Owner	(Actual CDDs − 900 CDDs) × $100/CDD

Data Series and Data Cleaning

Of course, not all weather risks will be located in the same location as the weather station that is used for the settlement of the weather contracts traded at the Chicago Mercantile Exchange. In that case, it will be helpful to compare the data series for the site where the weather risk needs to be managed, with the data series of the weather station used to settle the contract, essentially a form of basis risk.

In addition, although weather data series may be long, they may have certain data problems. Often the official weather station for an area may have moved — often multiple times, which can create concerns about data quality. There may be gaps in data that need to be interpolated or estimated. This often requires the skills of a meteorologist or climatologist specializing in analysis of these data series.

Insurance[6]

Many of those who need to manage risk, may wonder why not use insurance to manage weather risk? In certain cases, when dealing with damages from low-probability, high cost events, insurance, such as property insurance may be available for energy companies. For example, if a hurricane knocks out a generating station, insurance would most likely pay the owner to repair or rebuild the plant.[7] However, if a heat wave causes tremendous spikes in the power markets for another company, that other company would have a tough time making a claim for damages.

First, let's look at the types of insurance that may cover weather risks and then the nature of what risks are considered insurable, and which risks aren't insurable.[8]

Here are some criteria for insurable risks. Risks that do not meet these criteria may be better suited for other forms of risk management.[9]

1. The risk of loss must be definite with respect to time and place and hard to falsify. Death is a good example of definite loss.

2. The risk is unexpected. A generating plant being hit by a tornado qualifies, while the gradual depreciation of a generator from ordinary wear and tear does not.

3. The peril must create a significant financial loss. It would make sense to insure a power plant against tornado damage, but not against minor storm losses.

4. The loss needs to be calculable. In advance, it would be relatively straightforward to calculate a loss from a weather event that destroys a transmission tower, but it would be hard to quantify, in advance, the cost of a heat wave for a distribution company that purchases power on the open market (or whose system collapses under heavy load).

5. The insurance must be affordable. If the premiums are prohibitively high, the risk may not be insurable.

6. There must be a large pool of companies with similar insured risks, which will allow the insurance company to aggregate risks, and through the law of large numbers to predict losses. This could create a problem for many common weather phenomena, because they are inherently regional. A given region may only have one or two utilities that are dealing with weather risk. It may be hard for an insurance company to obtain the large data sets needed to predict losses for that particular energy operation.

7. The loss must not happen to a large number of insureds simultaneously. Otherwise the insurance company would face an extremely large payout at one time, which could imperil its finances. In the past, when insurance companies insured risks in one area, a large fire in one city could cause a company to go bankrupt, if its business was local. If a mild winter hit one large geographic region, and an insurance company had sold a lot of mild weather policies in that area, the company could face significant losses. This could make it hard to insure against large climatic events such as mild winters or summers.

Weather Insurance

The insurance industry has provided insurance for weather events for a long time. Insurance has been available for weather related damage, such as rainfall and hail. Rain insurance has been available to compensate for damage caused by rain and loss of income from rain (such as a baseball game being canceled due to rain).[10] Multiple peril crop-hail insurance policies cover perils for crops covered weather perils such as hail, drought, too much heat or moisture, flooding, wind, tornadoes, sleet, hurricanes, frost, freezes, and snow.[11]

Utilities need to carefully consider their weather insurance options when transferring weather related risk. Insurance companies have extensive experience and pools of expertise in dealing with and analyzing weather risk. Energy companies should actively engage their insurers when seeking to manage risk. In addition to the expertise, insurance companies are significant financial intermediaries with large derivatives portfolios. They may be able to help craft a solution that uses multiple risk management strategies to create a plan that best fits the needs of the insured.

Reduce the Risk (diversify)

One way to reduce weather risk is to have operations in locations with non-correlated weather risks. Once again, it is possible to apply the Markowitz model to create a weather portfolio. Of course, the correlations will be built around historical data, although they can also be based on forecasts, but the uncertainty within weather forecasts will need to be considered if this option is chosen. It may be possible to create a portfolio with weather diversification based on measures such as HDDs and CDDs. Think of an independent power producer or merchant generator. When assembling a generating portfolio, if all the plants are within the same regional climate, then the loads most likely will be coincident. Although the generator may have many plants, that may not reduce risk much if they are all idle or active at the same time. Say two locations could be assembled that have little correlation in terms of weather events. Here is an example based on the Markowitz discussion used in Chapter 7.

Example of Risk Reduction for a Merchant Generator (Table 8-8)

Consider a merchant generator that has a power plant that it operates in New York. It has an opportunity to expand its business into three cities, Chicago, Dallas, and Tucson. In each it can collect the same revenue stream as in New York City. The generator wants to reduce its risk by buying another power plant in a non-correlated weather market. The revenue streams will be evenly balanced between two plants, with each providing $100,000 per cooling season. Let us assume that the standard deviation of the returns is the same as the standard deviation of cooling degree days for the cooling season.

Table 8-8
Seasonal CDDs

Year	New York	Chicago	Dallas	Tucson
1995	1308.5	1161	2350	2754
1996	1064.5	652	2476	2878.5
1997	1093.5	622	2220	2927
1998	1277.5	956.5	3116.5	2609.5
1999	1370	895	2639.5	2592.5
2000	1025.5	722.5	2773	2983
2001	1308	814.5	2324.5	2944
2002	1355	1007	2292	2878.5
2003	1111.5	659.5	2364	2958.5
2004	1149.5	574.5	2228.5	2768
Mean	1206.35	806.45	2478.4	2829.35
Variance	16944.3917	37407.3583	81904.9333	20185.8917
Standard Deviation	130.170625	193.40982	286.19038	142.077062

Covariance

	New York	Chicago	Dallas	Tucson
New York	16944.3917	19671.714	1841.844	-10853.442

Portfolio Standard Deviation

	New York	Chicago	Dallas	Tucson
New York	130.2	153.0	160.1	62.10

Let W_1 = Weight of revenues from New York power plant = 0.5

Let W_2 = Weight of revenues from 2nd plant = 0.5

Let R_1 = Return from the New York Power plant = \$100,000

Let R_2 = Return from second power plant = \$100,000

Let R_p = Return of Portfolio

Let S_1 = Standard deviation of R_1

Let S_2 = Standard deviation of R_2

Let S_p = Standard Deviation of Portfolio

$$R_p = W_1 R_1 + W_2 R_2$$

$$S_p = [W_1^2 S_1^2 + W_2^2 S_2^2 + 2 W_1 W_2 \, \text{cov}(R_1 R_2)]^{1/2}$$

The goal of the company's weather analysis is to add the city that creates the least weather risk, so that the company can intelligently minimize the risk for its portfolio. The data is given for the past ten cooling seasons. The last ten years are often used for a data set, because of recent warming trends in urban areas due to the urban heat island effect.[12] Table 8-8 shows the variances of cooling degree days for each city and the covariances for each city's weather with that of New York City. Then, the portfolio risk for each combination is determined.

There are some interesting conclusions from the analysis. The first is that diversification does not always reduce risk. Expanding into Chicago or Dallas would actually increase the company's weather risk. In those cases, the company would have been better off had it not diversified. The expansion into Tucson, however, would create a less risky portfolio, and allow the firm to reduce its risk by over 50%.

Regulatory Aspects

In the fall of 2003, the Massachusetts Department of Telecommunications and Energy (DTE) denied the Keyspan Corporation's subsidiary, Boston Gas, a Weather Stabilization Clause (WSC) that would increase rates and shift the company's weather risk away from the shareholders to the ratepayers. This denial was pushed by Massachusetts Attorney General Reilly, who argued that if Boston Gas had weather stabilization clauses in its rate agreement, the company would not need to enter into weather hedging arrangements. This meant that, Boston Gas would transfer the risk of weather volatility to its customers. The Boston Gas ruling has the potential to spread to other commissions and change the way they look at weather risk.[13]

Also, this raises another question: what happens if a utility makes a rate deal, and bases its rates on a presumed temperature pattern? What happens if for example, a gas utility has a series of warm winters, which cause its revenues to fall? Does the utility go to the commission and reopen the case, or should it have used weather derivatives to protect against such a contingency?

Thoughts on the Future

Why can't weather derivatives be used to help develop alternative energy schemes? One of the main problems with wind and solar energy is the unpredictability of the wind or the sun. The current method of dealing with this risk is to have geographic diversification of wind farms or solar power entities. Why not create derivatives based on solar flux or wind energy to allow these risks to be transferred to counterparties and provide a steady stream of financial wind or sunshine that can reduce the risk from variable weather?

Conclusion

The degree to which weather risk affects the financial health of an energy company depends on the steps that the company takes to manage those risks. The tools and techniques are there for those that wish to use them.

When the investment community compares two similar firms — one of which blames the weather for poor earnings and another that has taken steps to manage the financial risks of that same weather, which will look better? That is a question that managers and board members need to ask when they approach weather risk, especially when they can't easily pass it on to ratepayers anymore. The weather isn't going away, but without proper management, companies might get washed away.

Notes

[1] Tapani Seppa and Dale Douglass, "Safe Weather Assumptions for Line Ratings." *Electrical World,* January/February 2001, pp 21-22.

[2] Jaime Kammerzell. "GoM Platforms Damaged, Lost." *Offshore*, Volume 64, Number 11, November 2004, p. 14.

[3] In Europe the contract is 20.00 pounds times the degree-day amount. In Asia the contract is ¥250,000 times the Pacific Rim Index, based on average temperatures.

[4] Actually, when traded on the CME, these are options on degree-day futures, but to simplify the explanation, the options are considered based on the actual degree-days. In reality, the principle is the same, with the futures functioning as the underlying, as opposed to the actual degree-day index.

[5] New York Mercantile Exchange, *A Guide to Energy Hedging* (New York: New York Mercantile Exchange, 1999), p. 58.

[6] Insurance is: "A contract or device for transferring risk from a person, business, or organization to an insurance company that agrees, in exchange for a premium, to pay for losses through an accumulation of premiums." Source: *Property Casualty Basics*, 7th edition, BISYS Educational Services. Atlanta, 2000, p. 3.

[7] Certain types of insurance are highly relevant for risk management for energy companies. Property insurance protects a firm against the financial loss from damage to, or loss of, property. Business income insurance pays a company for losses when a peril forces it to stop operating. Business interruption insurance covers income that is lost from an accident that damages a covered item. Business liability insurance protects from liability that arises from the businesses' operations.

[8]When thinking about the limitations of using insurance, it is important to understand how insurance is priced. The insurance company needs to be able to cover the expected loss as well as compensation for bearing risk. The total of these risks determines the premium it charges. The compensation for bearing risk includes the administrative costs of providing the insurance as well as a profit for the insurance company.

By definition:

Expected Value of Loss = Probability of Loss × Value of Loss

The premium = Expected Value of Loss + Return to Insurance Company for Bearing risk

Assume probability of loss = 1% (.01)

Let Value of Loss = $100,000

Expected Value of Loss = (.01) × $100,000 = $1,000.00

Return to Insurance Company for Bearing Risk = $1,000.00 (A benefit/premium ratio of 50% can often be typical in insurance according to Smith, see below.

Premium = Expected Value of Loss + Return to Insurance Company for
Bearing Risk
= $1,000.00 + $1,000.00
= $2,000.00

After Gary Smith. *Financial Assets, Markets, and Institutions* (Lexington, Massachusetts: D.C. Heath and Company, 1993), pp. 532-534.

[9]These criteria are taken from *Property Casualty Basics*, 7th edition (BISYS Educational Services, Atlanta, 2000), p. 5.

[10]Robert I. Mehr and Emerson Cammack, *Principles of Insurance*, Fourth Edition (Homewood, Illinois: Richard D. Irwin, Inc., 1966), p. 294.

[11]Mehr and Cammack, *op. cit.*, pp. 295-296.

[12]Robert Dischel, "Black-Scholes Won't Do." Available on the world Wide Web at: *http://www.financewise.com/public/edit/energy/weatherrisk/wthr-options.htm.*

Geoffrey Considine, Ph.D. "Introduction to Weather Derivatives." Available on the world Wide Web at: *http://www.cme.com/files/weatherde.pdf.*

[13]Weather Risk Management Association, "WRMA Applauds Ruling on Keyspan Weather Stabilization Clause." Press Release, 16 December 2003. Available on the World Wide Web at: *http://librarydocs.wrma.org/librarydocs/bc51_wrma/public/file607.doc.*

Foreign Exchange

At one time, utilities in the United States were domestic affairs, whose only foreign exchanges involved hosting visiting delegations of foreign utility executives, with the exception of cooperation with Canada on utility operations and imports of gas. However, industry restructuring in the 1980s and 1990s prompted US utilities to venture overseas, to the frequent detriment of shareholders. In addition, privatized European utilities, with cash on hand, acquired US companies and exposed themselves to foreign exchange risk, when they acquired an income stream in a currency that has dropped significantly in value since their acquisitions. For example, German utility giant RWE bought American Water Works just in time to have its earnings diluted as the dollar fell 8% against the euro.

Consider the situation of a European utility that bought a US operation at the beginning of the European Monetary Union. Within three years, the dollar fell 40% against the euro. Would the income of the acquired utility have increased enough in the same three years to offset the drop in the value of the dollar? Not likely. After all, utilities are regulated businesses that exhibit slow growth. What does a 40% currency devaluation do to a balance sheet when it is translated into euros? Not good things.

Not only European utilities have had currency trouble. AES, a US stock market darling in the 1990s, had extensive operations in Latin America, a region known for volatile currencies. AES's income from its Brazilian subsidiaries fell significantly due to currency devaluation, which conveniently occurred when AES was in the midst of a credit crunch — and the company was forced to sell assets.

For energy companies outside the US that try to avoid exchange rate risk by staying in their own market, that will be tough, because the major energy contracts — notably oil and gas — are denominated in dollars. This creates significant currency risks for oil traders and buyers in countries whose currency is not the dollar.[1] Consider the interaction of exchange rates and oil prices between January 2002 and January 2005. In January of 2002, oil traded at $25/barrel and it took 1.11

euros to buy a dollar. In January of 2005, oil traded at $50/barrel and it took 0.77 euros to buy a dollar.

Consider how exchange rate changes affected the price of oil.

January 2002: $25/barrel × 1.11 euros/dollar = 27.75 euros/barrel

January 2005: $50/barrel × 0.77/euros/dollar) = 38.50 euros/barrel

US producers would have a 100% increase in the price of the crude they sold. For a euro denominated producer, the fall in the dollar against the exchange rate meant that its crude price only increased 39%. Refiners in Europe might have benefited from the euro's rise against the dollar, because they could buy their raw material for fewer euros.

In these days of transnational utility investments, and international trade in energy products, foreign exchange risk has to be studied and managed in order to minimize the adverse risks that come from currency exposures.

Overview of Foreign Exchange (Forex) Trading

The exchange rate (e) is the ratio between the foreign currency and the domestic currency:

$$e = \text{Domestic Currency/Foreign Currency}$$

If it takes 1.30 dollars to buy 1 euro, the exchange rate is 1.30 dollars/euro. (Conversely, a dollar is worth 1/1.30 euros = 0.77 euros.) This means that a visitor to the US from Europe would only need 0.77 euros to buy one dollar, while a tourist going to Europe from the US would need 1.30 dollars to buy one euro.

Determinants of Foreign Exchange Rates

The exchange rate is the price to purchase a particular currency. Exchange rates are driven by the demand for a particular currency with respect to another. If more people want to buy dollars with euros than want to buy euros with dollars, then the dollar will appreciate against the euro. If more people want to buy euros with dollars than buy dollars with euros, then the euro will appreciate against the dollar. Companies should attempt to minimize the adverse effects of currency movements.

Just comparing prices provides a simple framework to assess exchange rates. That is, the domestic price of an item in one country should equal the domestic price of the same item in another country.[2] For example, if a dress sells in Spain for 50 euros, and the exchange rate is $1.30/euro, then the dress should sell in the United States for $65.00. If the prices get significantly out of line, this may be a sign that an exchange rate is due for a correction. For example, if the dresses sold for 50 euros in Spain and $50.00 in the USA, yet the exchange rate was $1.30/euro, when the exchange rate implied by the dresses was 1:1, this might be a sign that the euro was overvalued relative to the dollar and due for a fall. (Some governments, however, attempt to maintain the value of their currencies at artificial values, and do so for extended periods of time, until market forces overwhelm the efforts.) Essentially this "law of one price" leads to the formulation of the exchange rate.[3]

With:

$$e = p_d / p_f$$

where e = exchange rate

p_d = domestic price index

p_f = foreign price index

Δ = change

and

$$\%\Delta e = \%\Delta p_d - \%\Delta p_f$$

Thus, if US prices increase at a rate of 3% and overseas prices increase at a rate of 5%, then the exchange rate will fall by 2%, that is, overseas currencies will fall 2% in relation to the dollar.

Avoid the Risk

It is difficult to fully avoid currency risk, because currency movements and government efforts to manage exchange rates can affect the domestic economy. In addition, energy companies outside the US, and those that deal in energy products priced in dollars, notably oil and gas, cannot avoid the effects of exchange rate differentials on the prices at which they either buy or sell petroleum products.

To avoid direct foreign exchange risk, however, a company can restrict its operations entirely to one country and not engage in overseas empire building. Actually, given the experiences of a number of US utilities, maybe that isn't such a bad idea after all.

Loans in Different Currencies

More cross-border transactions create more currency risk. If a US company has a European subsidiary, it makes more sense for the subsidiary to seek financing in its home currency, rather than for the parent to obtain financing in the USA. In this way, the local subsidiary will avoid the risk that it borrows money in a currency whose value goes up while it collects revenues needed to pay that debt in a currency whose value declines.

Bear the Risk

Choosing to do business overseas, or to operate in an economy where the currencies freely trade, exposes the firm to currency risk of varying degrees. The currency risks have two elements:

1) Currency risks that the company chooses to embrace.

This currency risk appears when a company chooses to incur exchange rate risk by engaging in a cross-border transaction such as:

    a) Buying an overseas operation

    b) Buying equipment from overseas

    c) Seeking financing overseas — whether through a stock exchange listing or bond placement.

For example, if a windpower company contracts to buy a number of large wind turbines from a European company for 100 million euros at a point when it costs $1.25 to buy one euro, the company appears to have a liability of $125 million dollars. However, if the dollar drops and it now costs $1.35 to buy one euro, when the company has to pay for the turbines, it pays $135 million — $10 million more than it expected to pay when it initiated the transaction.

2) Currency risks that are forced on the company due to governmental or market decisions in a macro-economy.

The second type of currency risk is an indirect risk, a sort of secondary effect arising from governmental or market responses to a move in the currency markets. For example, if a government decides to defend its currency, and intervenes in the market by raising interest rates to alter currency flows, this change in interest rates could affect the domestic economy, as well as the value of the currency.

If price levels appreciate because of currency devaluations, this too could affect a utility's operations. A rise in general price levels could lead to a central bank taking anti-inflationary moves that would slow down the economy, which could adversely affect the volume of energy sales. Or, the rise in prices could affect the utility's profitability, because it could not raise its regulated prices as quickly as prices rise.

When entering cross-border transactions, a conscious decision needs to be made about what to do about currency risk. A decision not to do anything means that the company has chosen to bear currency risk. In today's global economy, companies face systemic risk from decisions made to change currency valuations that could affect the company's finances — for example when a central bank takes operations to defend its currency, which wind up affecting overall price levels.

Reduce the Hazard

The degree or risk that a company faces from currency valuations depends on how it structures its operations. It needs to set up and finance operations in a way that reduces the exposures to potentially adverse currency events. For example, an American company buys an overseas operation in the UK. That UK operation needs financing. If the UK operation seeks funding from the US parent, it faces the risk of adverse price moves that may make the loan more expensive than financing in the UK. When repatriating funds to the US, exchange rates may again cause the income stream to be diminished. Minimizing the exposure to financing that requires cross-border transfers reduces the hazard of currency risk. To reduce the hazard, the overseas operation seeks financing in its local market, rather than moving currencies across borders. This decision needs to be made after taking into account the financing opportunities in each region where the company has operations.

In addition, when choosing currencies to deal in — and countries to invest in — the stability of the currency (which often correlates with the economy) needs to be considered when investing. A company can reduce the hazard of an adverse currency move by investing in operations in countries with more stable currencies, or in ones that have the same currency as the investor nation (as in within the Eurozone for European companies) or in countries that denominate in the dollar for US companies.

Also to reduce the hazards of dealing in foreign exchange, the right people need to staff the currency desk. Since foreign exchange is not the utility's main business, but a service necessary to do business overseas, the utility should consider having a bank handle its foreign exchange transactions, or if necessary, its own trading desk to deal in these transactions, with the explicit understanding that the foreign exchange transactions are to facilitate the business and not act as a profit center. It may be best to hand these transactions off to a bank that has extensive foreign exchange dealings, with the oversight of a risk manager whose mandate is to minimize the risk the portfolio faces.

Reduce the Loss

Currency markets can move rapidly, making it hard to react quickly and minimize losses, unless plans are in place beforehand. Consider a US company that plans to buy a European company for 1 billion euros, at a time when the euro is trading at $1.25/euro — or $1.250 billion. The US company has arranged financing, but it only arranged a line of credit for $1.250 billion. Now, one month after the deal was announced, the dollar falls to $1.35/euro — the purchase now costs $1.350 billion — and the deal falls through because of the lack of credit. Had this company factored in exchange rate risk — and had a plan in place, it might have been able to make its deal happen.

Shift the Risk

The principles of shifting risk apply also to currencies. Extremely liquid futures and options markets, as well as swaps markets exist to transfer risk. An illustration based on the futures markets will be used to describe the transactions.

Using Long Futures to Hedge a Foreign Currency Transaction (Table 9-1)

Consider a US company that wishes to purchase a Spanish utility for € 500 million.[4] It faces a risk that the dollar could fall relative to the euro between the time that it announces the deal in January and the completion of the purchase in May. It can hedge that risk by going long 500 million of euro futures on the Chicago Mercantile Exchange. Each euro futures contract is for 125,000 euros, so the utility goes long 4000 contracts at a price of $1.25/euro — $625 million. If the dollar weakens, and the dollar falls to $1.30/euro, had the company not hedged it would have had to pay $25 million more (125,000 euros × $.05/euro × 4000 contracts) than it expected at the beginning of the process. On the other hand if the dollar had strengthened to $1.20/euro then the loss on the hedge would have negated the gain in the spot market, but the risk would have been shifted.

Table 9-1

Using Long Futures to Hedge Currency Risk

Dollar Weakens		
Date	**Spot Market**	**Futures Market**
January	Euro Forward Market Trades at $1.25	Buy Euro Futures at $1.25
May	Euro Trades at $1.30	Sell Euro Futures at $1.30
Change	$.05/Euro loss	$ .05/Euro gain
Spot Price on 1 May		$1.30/Euro
Gain on Futures Position		-$.05/Euro
Resulting Exchange Rate		$1.25/Euro

Dollar Strengthens		
Date	**Spot Market**	**Futures Market**
January	Euro Forward Market Trades at $1.25	Buy Euro Futures at $1.25
May	Euro Trades at $1.20	Sell Euro Futures at $1.20
Change	$ .05/Euro gain	$.05/Euro loss
Spot Price on 1 May		$1.20/Euro
Loss on Futures Position		+$.05/Euro
Resulting Exchange Rate		$1.25/Euro

Using Short Futures to Hedge a Foreign Currency Transaction (Table 9-2)

Now consider the US company in the year after it has bought the Spanish utility. In January it expects to repatriate € 12,500,000 in May after the close of the first quarter. The company faces a risk of a strengthening dollar, which could hurt that cash flow. Consequently, the US utility decides to hedge by shorting 100 euro futures contract on the Chicago Mercantile Exchange at $1.25/euro. In the first case, the dollar strengthens to $1.20/euro. Had the company not hedged, the company would have repatriated the money at an exchange rate of $1.20/euro, which would have meant income of $15,000,000 as opposed to the hedged income of $15,625,000 (a shortfall of 4%). In the event that the dollar weakens, however, the loss on the hedge balances out the gain in the spot market. The hedge, however, was designed to shift the risk of adverse currency moves, which it accomplished.

Options

As in other markets, there are extensive foreign currency options that can be used to shift risk, with calls and puts used in a parallel to the long and short examples given above.

Swaps

Swaps are a highly liquid market in forex. In currency swaps, two parties exchange assets or liabilities denominated in different currencies.[5] Say a utility that has Spanish operations believes that it can better finance its operations in the US, because it has good credit there. It will arrange a dollar/euro swap with a Spanish company that wants dollars, but wishes to obtain its financing in the Eurozone. Assume that the exchange rate is $1.20/euro. The US company will issue $6 million in bonds and the Spanish company will issue € 5 million in bonds. The US company gets the € 5 million it needs and the Spanish company obtains $6 million. In swapping liabilities, the US company will pay the Spanish company's interest and principal in euros, while the Spanish company pays in dollars, the interest and principal the US company owes its bondholders. The companies have effectively swapped their debts by exchanging liabilities.

Table 9-2

Using Short Futures to Hedge Currency Risk

Dollar Strengthens

Date	Spot Market	Futures Market
January	Euro Forward Market Trades at $1.25	Sell Euro Futures at $1.25
April	Euro Trades at $1.20	Buy Euro Futures at $1.20
Change	$.05/Euro loss	$ .05/Euro gain

Spot Price on 1 May	$1.20/Euro
Gain on Futures Position	+$.05/Euro
Resulting Exchange Rate	$1.25/Euro

Dollar Weakens

Date	Spot Market	Futures Market
January	Euro Forward Market Trades at $1.25	Sell Euro Futures at $1.25
April	Euro Trades at $1.30	Buy Euro Futures at $1.30
Change	$ .05/Euro gain	$.05/Euro loss

Spot Price on 1 May	$1.30/Euro
Loss on Futures Position	-$.05/Euro
Resulting Exchange Rate	$1.25/Euro

Reduce the Risk *(Table 9-3)*

To reduce currency risk requires diversification amongst currencies that taken together as a portfolio could reduce risks, using the Markowitz model, as used in discussion of energy price and weather risk. Again, it is difficult to actually forecast future correlations. However, past records illustrate the underlying principle of diversification and may illuminate thinking about which currencies, and consequently countries, a company may wish to invest in.

Assume an energy company has $20 million that it wishes to invest in two power plants (worth $10 million each) outside the United States that will become operational in 5 years. It has the opportunity to choose between plant projects in the Eurozone, Brazil, Canada, or Switzerland. The assets on the books will vary in value for 5 years. Which combination would create the least currency risk over that period? Table 9-3 depicts the end of year exchange rates and the portfolio values in US dollars for the four currencies from 1999-2004, and the respective means and variances of the individual portfolios. Using these data, it is possible to calculate the covariances between the portfolios, and then find the portfolio with the lowest standard deviation. Building on Markowitz's tenets outlined in Chapter 5, it appears that a portfolio consisting of one Brazilian company and one Swiss company could provide the least currency risk.[6]

Conclusion

Any company that plans to do deals overseas in search of higher returns must deal with the currency risk that goes with those deals. Major currency shifts can significantly, and adversely, affect the repatriation of income, or the value of assets or liabilities on a balance sheet. Admittedly many US utilities that made overseas investments in the 1990s have sold off those holdings, with a consequent reduction of exchange rate related earnings risk. However, the globalization of energy markets makes it difficult for even the most domestic of companies to avoid some contact with foreign exchange markets and the consequence of activities in those markets.

Table 9-3
Reducing Currency Risk

Year	Euro Exchange Rate	Euro Asset in US Dollars	Brazilian Real Exchange Rate	Brazilian Real Asset in U.S. Dollars	Canadian Dollar Exchange Rate	Canadian Dollar Asset in U.S. Dollars	Swiss Franc Exchange Rate	Swiss Franc Asset in U.S. Dollars
1999	1.007	$10,000,000	0.5528	$10,000,000	0.6925	$10,000,000	0.6277	$10,000,000
2000	0.9388	$9,322,741	0.5126	$9,272,168	0.6669	$9,629,877	0.6172	$9,832,119
2001	0.8901	$8,839,126	0.4325	$7,824,394	0.6279	$9,067,504	0.6025	$9,597,542
2002	1.0485	$10,412,115	0.2825	$5,110,169	0.6329	$9,139,240	0.7229	$11,515,940
2003	1.2597	$12,509,434	0.3454	$6,248,705	0.7738	$11,173,876	0.8078	$12,867,528
2004	1.3538	$13,443,893	0.3766	$6,813,559	0.8310	$11,999,335	0.8763	$13,958,991
Mean	1.0830	$10,754,552	0.4171	$7,544,832	0.7042	$10,168,306	0.7091	$11,295,353
Variance	0.0339	3,343,543,433,800	0.0105	$3,446,396,760,200	0.0067	$1,390,562,559,400	0.0129	$3,263,382,603,300
Standard Deviation	0.1841	$1,828,536	0.1026	$1,856,447	0.0817	$1,179,221	0.1134	$1,806,483

Covariance of Portfolios

	Euro	Real	Canadian Dollar	Swiss Franc
Euro	3.3435343e+12	-1.6537449286e+12	2.00954739e+12	3.2342784813e+12
Real		3.446396760e+12	-3.575823456e+11	-2.1410178925e+12
Canadian Dollar			1.39056215e+12	1.8211898246e+12
Swiss Franc				3.2633826003e+12

Portfolio Standard Deviation

	Euro	Real	Canadian Dollar	Swiss Franc
Euro	$1,828,536			
Real	$933,066	$1,856,447		
Canadian Dollar	$1,479,290	$1,015,110	$1,179,221	
Swiss Franc	$1,808,002	$779,061	$1,440,167	$1,806,483

Note: The spreadsheet program all only 11 digits of data to be displayed, which may lead to rounding errors.

Notes

[1] In fact, according to two authors, the fall of the dollar has forced OPEC countries to raise prices to cover exchange rate risk, because their costs are incurred in currencies beside the dollar. Source: Chris Bakewell and Chris Horsley, "Innovation Lacking in High-Tech World of Oil." *Oil & Gas Financial Journal*, Vol. II, No. 4, June 2005, p. 27.

[2] This works best in comparing similar items, and also does not consider transaction or transportation costs that may lead to differences in price.

[3] Gary Smith, *Financial Assets, Markets, and Institutions* (Lexington, Massachusetts: D.C. Heath and Company, 1993), p. 66.

[4] € is the symbol for euro.

[5] Gary Smith, *Financial Assets, Markets, and Institutions* (Lexington, Massachusetts: D.C. Heath and Company, 1993), p. 360.

[6] This of course assumes that relationships between currencies remain consistent.

Interest Rates

Debt is a major source of financing for utilities and energy companies. Changes in interest rates affect both the income statement and the balance sheet. In addition, interest rate changes can affect the valuation of assets held by company pension plans, and may affect the asset-liability matching process for defined-benefit pension plans. As borrowers, the main risk energy companies face is from rising interest rates that raise the cost of borrowing.

Interest Rate Categories

Interest rates are classified by time to pay back the principal on a loan or bond offering when issued: short-term, medium-term, and long-term. **Maturity** represents the time until the principal is repaid. Short-term instruments have maturities of less than five years.[1] Medium-term instruments have maturities between five and twelve years.[2] Long-term bonds have maturities greater than twelve years.[3] Interest rates tend to increase as the maturity of their associated instruments increases — the interest rate on a 30 year Treasury Bond is usually higher than a 10 year Treasury Note, which is usually higher than a 13 week Treasury Bill (*see* Table 10-1).[4] Longer term instruments usually have higher interest rates to compensate the lender for the greater risk associated with holding an instrument for a longer period.

Short-Term Instruments

Short-term instruments come in a variety of forms. Those with maturities of less than one year are called money market instruments. Common examples are:

• *Treasury Bills* — Short-term debt of the U.S. government. The Treasury Bill (T-Bill) interest rate is often used as the standard **risk free** interest rate that figures into many financial models such as the Capital Asset Pricing Model discussed in **Chapter 11: Equity Risk.**

Table 10-1
Yield of Bonds and Time to Maturity

	Treasury Instruments		Corporate Issuances				
Bond Period	Maturity	Interest Rate (%)	Instrument	Maturity	S&P Credit Rating	Interest Rate (%)	Premium over Treasuries
Short Term	91 Days	3.99	LIBOR*	91 days	N/A	4.34	0.35
			US CDs	91 days	N/A	4.45	0.46
Medium Term	5 years	4.38	Con Edison	5 years	A	4.90	0.52
			Duke Energy	6 years	BBB	5.30	0.92
	10 years	4.50	Con Edison	10 years	A	5.15	0.65
			Duke Energy	10 years	BBB	5.30	0.80
Long Term	25 years	5.38	Con Edison	27 years	A	5.52	0.14
			Duke Energy	27 years	BBB	6.01	0.63

* LIBOR is the London Interbank Offered Rate is the interest rate that banks borrow from each other in the London interbank market.

Source: Financial Times (3 January 2006) and www.investinginbonds.com

- *Eurodollars* — Dollars on deposit in banks outside the United States (not necessarily in Europe). Eurodollar futures on the Chicago Mercantile Exchange (CME) are used to hedge interest rates on short term borrowing.

- *Short-Term Tax Exempt* — Short-term notes issued by states, municipalities, and local government agencies that are not subject to Federal income tax.

- *Federal Agency Notes* — Short-term debt issued by government agencies or by quasi governmental agencies whose debt is not backed by the full faith and credit of the United States Government (*e.g.* Fannie Mae).

Short-term notes are discount instruments, that is their price is expressed as a fraction of the instrument's value at maturity. Interest rates for money market instruments are calculated based on a 360 day year, not a 365 day year.

Here is an example of how to calculate the interest rate on a T-Bill. Take a 13 week T-Bill that is issued at a 3% discount:[5]

$$100 \ - \ \frac{(91 \text{ days})}{(360 \text{ days})} \ \times \ 3\% \ = \ 99.9924$$

This works out to a yield of

$(100 - 99.9924) / 99.9924 = .7601\%$

Equivalent to simple interest of $= 3.0488\%$[6]

Compound interest of $= 3.0838\%$[7]

Note that the discount does not equal the interest rate.

Medium-Term Instruments

The prices of medium-term instruments are expressed as a percentage of the face value of the instrument at maturity. For example, a bond of $1000 face value that sells in the market at a price of $990 is quoted by bond market makers at 99.

Medium-Term Notes — Coupon bearing fixed rate unsecured corporate issues.

State and Municipal Bonds — Medium-term debt issued by state and local governments and authorities, such as power authorities and municipal utilities.

U.S. Treasury Notes — Borrowing by Federal government. Backed by full faith and credit of U.S. government.

Characteristics of Long-Term Instruments

Long-term instruments are more sensitive to changes in interest rates than short-term instruments.[8] Like medium-term instruments, long-term instruments, when quoted, appear with a price that is a percentage of face value. The main instruments are:

Corporate Bonds — Long-term borrowing by private, for-profit, non-governmental corporations.

U.S. Treasury Bonds — Borrowing by Federal government. Backed by full faith and credit of U.S. government. These bonds are the underlying for the Treasury Bond futures that is used to hedge long-term debt.

Basis in Bonds

When it comes to lending, the debt of the U.S. government is the benchmark that is used to determine interest rates. Investment in U.S. government securities is considered risk free, because the likelihood of the U.S. government defaulting on a loan is considered infinitesimally small. Consequently, the U.S. government also pays the lowest interest rates compared to bonds of similar maturities in the U.S. market. A corporate bond issuer would pay a higher interest rate than the comparable government bond to compensate the lender for the possibility of default on the bond payments (Table 10-1). In addition, as credit ratings worsen, the borrower tends to pay higher interest rates.

Determinants of Interest Rates

The Federal government seeks to regulate the level of economic activity to promote growth and relative price stability through fiscal and monetary policy. These policies alter the demand for money. Demand for money determines interest rates. Higher demand for money increases interest rates, and lower demand for money decreases interest rates.

Fiscal policy consists of actions by the Federal government to stimulate or slow down the economy. For example, in a recession or depression, the Federal government may spend money on public works and other government projects to stimulate the economy. It could also lower taxes in an effort to keep more money in private hands to encourage spending that will stimulate the economy, or both. When faced with an overheating economy, the Federal government could raise taxes or cut spending to reduce the inflationary effect on the economy, reducing the demand for money, which puts downward pressure on interest rates.

Monetary policy is the other side of the policy coin, which is set by the Federal Reserve Bank. The Federal Reserve Bank (the Fed) influences economic activity by altering the amount of money circulating in the economy. More money flowing means more economic activity, and inflationary pressures. Less money flowing quenches economic activity. When the Fed wants to reduce economic activity to prevent inflation it has a number of tools at its disposal:

1. *Raising the Federal Reserve rate (prime rate)*, which is the minimum rate at which the Federal Reserve will lend money to U.S. banks. The banks, in turn, will charge their customers a rate that exceeds the prime rate. The higher rates charged by banks for loans to their customers will decrease loan demand and spending in the economy.

2. *Decreasing the amount of money in circulation.* Less money in circulation tends to contract the economy.

3. *Raising reserve requirements for banks.* Reserve requirements govern the amount of depositors money that must not be loaned out from a bank. When reserve requirements are raised, banks are not able to lend as much money.

When the economy slows down, the Federal Reserve can stimulate the economy by:

4. *Decreasing the Federal Reserve rate (prime rate).* This will permit banks to lower their interest charges for customers and stimulate borrowing and investment in the economy.

131

5. *Increasing the amount of money in circulation.* More money in circulation is expansionary, and possibly inflationary.

6. *Lowering reserve requirements for banks.* Lower reserve requirements free up more bank funds for lending.

The level of interest rates in the economy affects more than the cost of borrowing money. When the Federal Reserve adjusts interest rates, this can stimulate or slow down the economy, with consequent effects on energy sales. In addition, when the Federal Reserve adjusts interest rates, this can affect the level of a company's dividend yield, with consequent effect on the stock price. Changes in interest rates, therefore, even affect those businesses that do not borrow money.

Bond Pricing

When an investor buys a bond upon its issuance, he lends money to a company. When an investor buys a bond in the open market, he purchases a security that represents money already lent to the company.

The price the investor pays is based on the estimated value of the bond to the investor — its value at redemption and the value of any interest payments. The price of a bond is a function of those values, as well as prevailing interest rates. For example, when prevailing interest rates are 8%, it would not make sense to pay full price for a bond that has a coupon that pays only 5%. A brief discussion of the mathematics of bond pricing will help clarify the principles that underlie bond pricing, and how changing interest rates affect bond prices, as well as the ability to manage those risks.

Bond prices depend on the principle of the time value of money. Consider the problem of whether you would like to receive $100 today, or $100 in one year. In an environment where that dollar can be invested, at a positive rate of return, a dollar now is worth more than a dollar a year from now.[9]

Consider, an investor who could take $100 now and invest it in a bank account at 5% interest per year. What happens to the money?

$$\$100 + (5\% \times \$100)$$

$$= \$100 + (.05 \times \$100)$$

$$= \$100 + \$5 = \$105$$

At the end of one year, the investor could have $105, so taking the $100 now is better than $100 in one year, because the principal plus the interest at the end of one year will be $105, as opposed to $100. The $105 is known as the future value of the investment. However, if the investor was offered $100 now or $105 in one year, he would be indifferent, because the investments are interchangeable. $100 now will equate to $105 in one year.

Here is an explanation of the math:

Let P = Principal = $100

Let i = Interest rate (expressed in decimal form) = .05

Let t = Number of time periods

FV = Future value

For a given year:

$$FV = P (1 + i)t$$

Therefore for one year:

$$FV = P (1 + i)^1$$
$$FV = \$100 (1 + .05)^1$$
$$= \$100 (1.05)$$
$$= \$105$$

For 5 years:

$$FV = \$100 (1+.05)^5$$
$$= \$100 (1.2763)$$
$$= \$127.63$$

This equation can be manipulated to calculate what a future series of cash flows in the future is worth today. Recall that the future value is determined by multiplying the principal (or value today) by the interest rate raised to the number of compounding periods. On the other hand, the principal could be considered the present value, and the future cash flows discounted to determine their worth now. To an investor, therefore, a bond represents a series of monetary payments he expects to receive at some time in the future. He will value the bond as the present value of the expected cash flows from interest payments (if any) and the principal received when the bond matures.

Let:

PV = Present value

t = Time period (from 1-5)

C_t = Cash flow (interest payment) at time period t

i = Interest rate

P = Principal

$$PV = \frac{C_1}{(1+i)^1} + \frac{C_2}{(1+i)^2} + \frac{C_3}{(1+i)^3} + \frac{C_4}{(1+i)^4} + \frac{C_5}{(1+i)^5} + \frac{P}{(1+i)^5}$$

$$PV = \frac{\$50}{(1+.05)^1} + \frac{\$50}{(1+.05)^2} + \frac{\$50}{(1+.05)^3} + \frac{\$50}{(1+.05)^4} + \frac{\$50}{(1+.05)^5} + \frac{\$1000}{(1+.05)^5}$$

PV = $1000

If the interest rate went up after the bond was issued, the bond would be worth less, and if interest rates fell, the bond would be worth more.[10]

Try the math. Assume that interest rates rise to 6% (0.06) or fall to 4% (0.04). Note the difference in present values.

Avoid the Risk

Given that interest is the price of money, and energy companies desire to make money, avoiding interest rate risk in a market economy is not possible. What about the company that says we don't have interest rate risk, because we don't have loans on our books? That may be true, but when the Federal Reserve raises interest rates and reduces overall economic activity, can it avoid the impact? Or when the Fed allows price levels to increase, and the costs of inputs goes up, the company faces a definite additional cost. Or when interest rates go up, and shareholders dump a stock because they can get a better yield in the bank, then interest rates have affected a company — even if it has no debt. The key item is to accept the reality and build planning into the business — so when interest rates go up or down, the company has a plan to minimize the pain or seize opportunities.

Bear the Risk

It is highly likely that a company will bear interest rate risk at some time, by choice or by default. Even when shifting risk using futures, it is highly likely that a company will have to bear some risk because of **basis risk** between Treasury instruments and corporate debt instruments.[11]

In addition to the matter of debt, as mentioned above, the rise or fall of interest rates can influence the overall business environment, which can affect the financial operations of a business in a way that may not be easy to hedge. The key item is to be aware of the risks and factor them into financing decisions by making provisions for interest rate changes.

Reduce the Hazard

The vulnerability of a company to changes in interest rates arises on two fronts. One is the sensitivity to the actual cost of money (the interest rate) and the other is to the amount of money needed at that particular interest rate.[12]

The actual interest rate that a company will pay depends on the rates in the market (such as for Treasury instruments that are used to price corporate debt), the credit rating of the company, which will determine the amount over the risk free rate that it will need to pay, and the length of time for which the loan will be sought. The company, obviously, cannot control the interest rates on Treasury instruments, as those rates are determined through interaction in a vast financial market that is beyond the company's control. However, the company has some control over the differential that it will pay compared to the risk free rate, through its credit rating. The credit rating is an assessment of a company's ability to meet its financial obligations. In addition, the level of indebtedness will determine the cost of a loan over time.

Companies need to think about how their financial decisions will affect their ratings by various agencies, and how certain financial decisions will affect the creditworthiness of the company, which consequently determines the cost of money. **Chapter 12: Credit Risk** discusses the principles of determining creditworthiness.

But, there is another factor besides the cost of money. There is also the actual amount of money needed. Why is it needed and is borrowing the recommended way to obtain those funds? If a company does a poor job of managing its receivables, and has to rely on short-term financing, then it needs to think about its financial operations and how they are run — and why they are incurring the need for short-term financing. It may help to compare, based on an analysis of publicly available documents, how a firm's ratios compare to those of its competitors. This analysis may point to room for improvement in operations that may decrease the need for borrowing of the short- or long-term variety. Of course these decisions need to be made in the context of the firm's overall financial strategy, but the question needs to be asked.

Certain ratios can be indicative of a company's financial position — and would point to a need for cash. It may pay for companies to monitor their positions and discipline their treasury operations to minimize the surprise occasions when cash may be needed. *See* the section on **liquidity ratios** in **Chapter 12: Credit Risk.**

Reduce the Loss

The key to reducing interest rate related losses lies in being prepared to deal with events that lead to losses from interest rate moves. Markets move rapidly in unpredictable ways. A sudden move in interest rates could adversely affect costs of financing.[13] To reduce losses, a firm needs a plan in place on how to deal with rapid interest rate moves and liquidity issues before they take place.

Shift the Risk

The highly liquid global interest rate futures and options markets facilitate shifting the risk of an adverse interest rate move. Futures and options exist to hedge short-term, medium-term, and long-term interest rates.

Consider a company that wishes to make a medium-term bond offering. It has set a coupon of $70 per year to be paid in two $35 semiannual installments at a time when the prevailing interest rate for discounting these notes is 7% and $70 is all the company can afford to pay. What happens if interest rates rise? The company will not be able to borrow as much money as it needed. How can it protect against that? Table 10-2 shows how to hedge using Treasury note futures. In the event that interest rates rise to 8%, the bond offering would only bring in $95,945,000 — a shortfall of $4,055,000. However, the profit from shorting 965 Treasury note futures contract, fully makes up the shortfall and provides an extra $60,725.[14] In this case, when interest rates rise, the rise in value of the short Treasury futures not only balances out the shortfall on the debt offering but also provides a slight profit.[15]

The bottom half of the table shows what could happen if interest rates fall to 6%. In that case, the debt offering would bring in $104,265,000 — a windfall of $4,265,000. On the other hand, the futures contract incurs a loss of $4,333,820, so the total debt offering now brings in $99,931,180.

Table 10-2

Using Short Futures to Hedge Interest Rates

Rising Interest Rates

Date	Spot Market	Futures market
February	Company anticipates offering of 5 year notes at 7% bringing in $100 million	T-Note Rate is 5%. Sell 965 Treasury Note futures for $96,500,000*
May	Interest Rates rise to 8% and offering brings in $95,945,000	T-Note Rate Climbs to 6%. Buy Back 965 Treasury Note Futures for $92,384,275
Change	$4,055,000 shortfall	$4,115,725 gain
Sale		$95,945,000
Gain on Futures Position		$4,115,725
Total Proceeds from Bond Sale		$100,060,725

Falling Interest Rates

Date	Spot Market	Futures market
February	Company anticipates offering of 5 year notes at 7% bringing in $100 million	T-Note Rate is 5%. Sell 965 Treasury Note futures for $96,500,000
May	Interest Rates fall to 6% and offering brings in $104,265,000	4%. Buy Back 965 Treasury note Futures for $100,833,820
Change	$4,265,000 windfall	$4,333,820 loss
Sale		$104,265,000
Loss on Futures Position		-$4,333,820
Total Proceeds from Bond Sale		$99,931,180

* Each Treasury Note Futures contract is for $100,000

Calculations for Table 10-2

Instrument	Interest Rate	Payment Period										Present Value of All Coupon Payments	Present Value of Principal	Final Bond Value (Coupon + Principal)
		1	2	3	4	5	6	7	8	9	10			
Bond	6%	$33.98	$32.99	$32.03	$31.10	$30.19	$29.31	$28.46	$27.63	$26.82	$26.04	$298.56	$744.09	$1,042.65
	7%	$33.82	$32.67	$31.57	$30.50	$29.47	$28.47	$27.51	$26.58	$25.68	$24.81	$291.08	$708.92	$1,000.00
	8%	$33.65	$32.36	$31.11	$29.92	$28.77	$27.66	$26.60	$25.57	$24.59	$23.64	$283.88	$675.56	$959.45
Treasury Note	4%	$24.51	$24.03	$23.56	$23.10	$22.64	$22.20	$21.76	$21.34	$20.92	$20.51	$224.56	$820.35	$1,044.91
	5%	$24.39	$23.80	$23.21	$22.65	$22.10	$21.56	$21.03	$20.52	$20.02	$19.53	$218.80	$781.20	$1,000.00
	6%	$24.27	$23.56	$22.88	$22.21	$21.57	$20.94	$20.33	$19.74	$19.16	$18.60	$213.26	$744.09	$957.35

Although in the second situation there is a slight shortfall, the key point, however, is that the risk of a harmful interest rate increase has been hedged. Either way, the firm can assure, that if interest rates move, the company can come close to meeting its target for proceeds from the bond offering.

The risks can also be managed with interest rate options and swaps. The principle remains the same. The important thing to study when setting up an interest rate hedge is to ask what happens to the instrument when the interest rate changes, because the actual interest rates are not traded. It is only the instruments that change in value when interest rates change. This is the relationship that is actually hedged.

Reduce the Risk

For energy companies, reducing interest rate risk through diversification is hard. When a company needs money, it has to access the money markets, and it is highly unlikely that the company will be able to reduce risk through the law of large numbers or through diversification.[16] There is an analogous concept, however, that is related to the concept of diversification. This concept, known as duration, measures the sensitivity of a portfolio's valuation to changes in interest rates. This is especially important for pension plans, where firms try to match assets (cash, bonds, and securities and other investments) with liabilities (payments to retirees). A change in interest rates could decrease the value of assets and increase the size of expected liabilities, thereby creating a shortfall that the sponsor of the pension fund would have to make up. The duration of the portfolio is a function of the maturities of the instruments chosen. For a bond, it is the average time to each payment.[17] The duration can be adjusted through the use of instruments with various maturities or through adding futures or options to the portfolio. Table 10-3 shows how the duration was calculated for the instruments used in Table 10-2 and how the hedge ratio was constructed from the durations of the 7% bond and the futures contract on the 5% Treasury note.

Table 10-3

Duration and Hedge Ratios

PV = Present Value

Duration of 7% Bond

Year	Cash Flow	PV of Cash Flow	PV of Cash Flow/Total Cash Flow	Year × PV of Cash Flow/Total Cash Flow
1	$70	$65.42	0.06542	0.0654
2	$70	$61.14	0.0611	0.1223
3	$70	$57.14	0.0571	0.1714
4	$70	$53.40	0.0534	0.2136
5	$1,070	$762.90	0.7629	3.8145
Total Cash Flow		$1000.00	Duration (Years)	4.3872

Duration of 5% T-Note

Year	Cash Flow	PV of Cash Flow	PV of Cash Flow/Total Cash Flow	Year × PV of Cash Flow/Total Cash Flow
1	$50	$47.62	0.04762	0.0476
2	$50	$45.35	0.04535	0.0907
3	$50	$43.19	0.04319	0.1296
4	$50	$41.14	0.04114	0.1645
5	$1,050	$822.70	0.82270	4.1135
Total Cash Flow		$1000	Duration (Years)	4.5460

$$\text{Hedge Ratio} = \frac{\text{Duration of 7\% Bond}}{\text{Duration of 5\% T-Note}} = \frac{4.3872}{4.5460} = 0.9651$$

Conclusion

Interest rate shocks are the last thing a company needs when it is trying to access the credit markets. When a loan offering ends up costing more than expected, this can upset carefully laid borrowing plans, which might lead to inadequate capitalization. Or an increase in interest rates could significantly devalue bond holdings in a pension portfolio that could require the firm to make up shortfalls in a defined benefit plan. As long as energy companies need money from borrowers, or have bonds in a pension portfolio, they need to have a strategy — or suite of strategies — on hand to manage the risks from unpredictable movements in interest rates that can make borrowing riskier — and more expensive.

Notes

[1] The Bond Market Association, *An Investor's Guide to Bond Basics. The Bond Market Association*, 2004, p. 4. Available on the World Wide Web at: *http://www.bond-markets.com.*

[2] *Ibid.*

[3] *Ibid.*

[4] Notes refer to unsecured debt instruments with maturities less than ten years. Richard A. Brealey and Stewart C. Myers, *Principles of Corporate Finance*: Third Edition (New York: McGraw-Hill Publishing Company, 1988), p. 579.

[5] Discount means that the instrument is sold at less than face value.

[6] Simple Interest = Quarterly interest $\times$ (365/91), or (.7601%) $\times$ (365/91) = 3.0488%.

[7] Compound interest = $(1 + i)^{365/91} - 1$, or $(1 + .007601)^{365/91} - 1 = 3.0838\%$.

[8] This is discussed in the section on **Bond Pricing**.

[9] In a deflationary environment a dollar today is worth less than a dollar in the future.

[10] A higher interest rate would mean a larger denominator than the original case, hence a smaller PV. On the other hand, a lower interest rate would mean a smaller denominator than the original case, hence a larger PV.

[11] *See* **Chapter 6: Basis** for discussion of basis.

[12] The company's borrowing costs are the product of the principal borrowed (amount of money) multiplied by the interest rate (cost of money). Requiring less principal

could lead to lower borrowing costs by the same amount as a lower interest rate depending on the circumstances.

[13]It is distinctly possible, however, that the company's pension plan finds itself in the business of holding bills or bonds for investment purposes. The sensitivity to interest rate risk for an asset management operation are more complex than those for the basic needs of financing the operations of a utility or energy company.

[14]Why not 1000 contracts? Because the value of the 5% Treasury note changes at a different rate than the 7% bond, only 965 contracts are needed to create the hedge. This ratio was determined by dividing the duration of the 7% bond by the 5% Treasury note as seen in Table 10-3, which covers the calculations of duration.

[15]Of course, the hedge may fall short a bit in another case, but if properly set up, the hedge should protect against most of the adverse price move.

[16]Of course, if the pension plan of the company is holding a portfolio of bonds for investment purposes, then the bond portfolio can be diversified through procedures along lines proposed by Markowitz and discussed in detail in **Chapter 7: Energy Price Risk**.

[17]Duration is calculated in the following manner:

PV = Present Value of Cash Flow (C_1)

V = Total Value of Bond

$$D = \frac{[PV(C_1) \times 1]}{V} + \frac{[PV(C_2) \times 2]}{V} + \frac{[PV(C_3) \times 3]}{V} \ldots$$

Source: Richard A. Brealey and Stewart C. Myers. *Principles of Corporate Finance*, Third Edition (New York: McGraw-Hill Publishing Company, 1988), p. 611.

Equity Risk

Risk decisions made within the business affect the value of the business's common stock. Value of the stock may affect the borrowing capacity of the corporation. The market's evaluation of the risk inherent in the common stock (equity) plays a part in the assessment of the return that regulators allow the utility to earn. That, in turn, affects the price that the utility charges its customers.

Too low a stock price, in an industry that raises capital from the market more than most, affects the corporation's ability to raise capital in a manner fair to existing investors. A low stock price in relation to value makes the corporation easy prey for takeover. A high price enables the firm to more easily finance expansion.

Issues of equity risk, and how the market evaluates that risk, pervade the energy business. They affect shareholders, corporations, and even customers.

Theory First

Using what is called the capital asset pricing model, portfolio managers like to talk about stock price movement in terms of two Greek letters, alpha and beta. In simplest terms, alpha measures the increase in the stock relative to the market over time, while beta measures how much the stock swings relative to swings in the market. For instance, if, over a period of five years, the market as a whole goes nowhere (rises 0% per year), but the stock goes up an average rate of 2% per year, then the stock has an alpha of 2. During that five year period, the market swings up and down many times. If the stock tends to swing twice as far as the market (it falls 20% when the market falls 10% and rises 20% when the market goes up 10%), then the stock has a beta of 2. Obviously, buyers of common stock (equity) want to find stocks with high alphas if they can. Who would not want to buy a stock that goes up more than the market over time? At the same time, they would like to minimize the risk that they take, and that is where beta comes in. When a stock rises or falls more than the market, on a regular basis, then potential investors have to worry about the possibility that they might buy the stock at the peak and have to sell it at the bottom of the valley, thereby losing a lot of money. On the other hand, they could buy at the bottom and sell at the top (every portfolio manager's dream) and earn big profits.

Note that the investor really takes two risks: market risk (how much the market moves) and specific stock risk (how much that stock moves relative to the market). The measure of specific stock risk is beta. Stocks of companies in risky businesses or of companies that engage in risky financial policies would have higher betas, generally, than those of stable, conservatively run companies. As a matter of prudence, investors should not buy high beta stocks unless they expect to earn a high return that compensates them for the risk taken.

Figure 11-1 presents an illustration of alpha and beta, comparing Stock A, Stock B and the market. In this case, neither the market nor the individual stocks show any progress over time, so alpha equals 0 for the stocks. Note that B moves half as much and A twice as much as the market. Stock A, therefore, has a beta of 2 and B has a beta of 0.5. Since nobody can be sure when the market will hit a peak or a bottom, cautious investors might opt to buy stock B, figuring that they are not likely to see a big drop in the stock price in case they purchased at the top of the market. Of course, they will not make a big profit either if they bought the stock at the bottom. They accept the lower profit potential in return for the lower chance of loss. In the energy sector, utility stocks tend to have lower betas than generating companies, energy merchants, and firms that drill for oil and gas.

Capital market theorists have devised a formula for the return that investors want to earn (also called cost of capital or required return). Equity investors want to earn the risk free rate of return (let's say, the interest rate on Treasury bills) plus a premium for risk that gets bigger as beta goes up.

Figure 11-1

How High and Low Beta Stocks Move
Relative to the Market

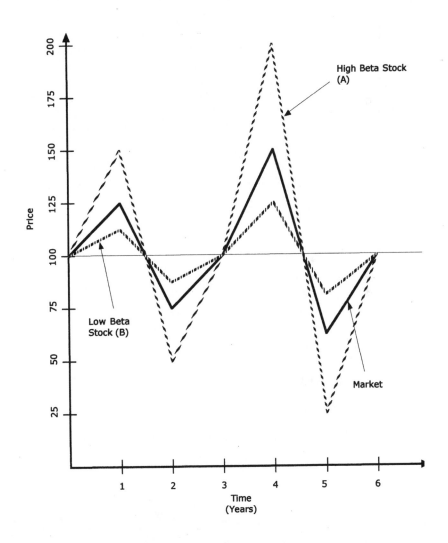

Figure 11-2 shows a graph of alpha and beta for company C. Alpha is the line's intercept of the y axis, where the x axis is at zero. Beta provides the slope of the line. In this instance, alpha equals 2 and beta equals 2.

Figure 11-2

How Price of Stock C Moves When Market Moves

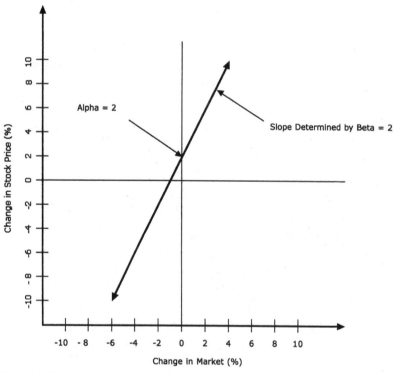

Where (all in percent):

R = required return on the security

R_f = risk free return

R_m = market rate of return

β = beta

then:

$$R = R_f + \beta\,(R_m - R_f).$$

Where does $(R_m - R_f)$ come from? Historic studies show that the stock market tends to produce a return that exceeds the risk free return by several percentage points a year. Let's say that the stock market averages a return of 9% per year while the risk free return averages 4% per year. That would indicate an equity risk premium of 5% per year. Knowing that $(R_m - R_f)$ equals 5%, and that Treasury bills currently yield 2% and the stock has a beta of 0.5, we could work out the required return (in %) as:

$$R = 2 + 0.5 \ (5) = 4.5\%.$$

If the beta were 2, then the formula would produce:

$$R = 2 + 2 \ (5) = 12\%.$$

Remember that these calculations apply to the market value of the common stock. They measure the return that the investor expects on market value.

Utility regulators like to trot out those formulas when deciding the proper return to grant the utility in a rate case. Financial engineers like to trot out the formulas when trying to justify the return that a company should accept when it makes an investment. Be wary of such calculations. First, the calculations of beta and the difference between the market return and the risk free return will vary from period to period studied. Second, returns calculated based on the past may not reflect current expectations of investors. Conditions do change. Third, beta may not be an accurate predictor of returns. Fourth, studies show that the calculation of expected returns tend to understate the returns for firms that show a low beta.[1]

Financial managers, regulators and investors must understand, as well, Modigliani and Miller's contribution to the analysis of corporate finance. M & M, as they are familiarly known in academic circles, said, basically, that a lot of fancy, financial footwork will not allow anyone to evade the number one rule of economics: there is no such thing as a free lunch. M & M held that the risk inherent in a project — not how the investor raises the money — determines the required return (also called "cost of capital").

Take the case of a power station that requires a high 20% return, because it has a lot of competitors, and does not have secure contracts to sell its output, so the buyer could expect an unsteady and insecure flow of income. The power plant might earn $200 per year, on average. It has no debt outstanding. No buyer should pay more than $1000 for that power plant, because paying a higher price would reduce the return below the necessary 20%.

Along come two potential buyers. Both can borrow money at 8%. Both think that they can raise the value of the power plant over $1,000, and both have figured out how to make the deal look good for the shareholders. Buyer A decides to raise the money by borrowing $900 and putting up $100 of stockholders' money. The more conservative Buyer B decides that so much borrowing is unsafe, so it will borrow only $500 and pay the balance with stockholders' money. Here is how they calculate the deals:

	Buyer A	Buyer B
1. Income from operations	$200	$200
2. Interest on debt	72	40
3. Net income	128	160
4. Common stock equity	100	500
5. Debt	900	500
6. Capital raised	1,000	1,000
7. Debt ratio [(5/6) × 100]	90%	50%
8. Return on equity [(3/4) × 100]	128	32
9. Return on capital [(1/6) × 100]	20	20

The common stocks of both A and B currently sell at 15 times the reported earnings of each company. The financial engineers at A believe that the deal, as contemplated, will add $1,820 to the company's market value (15 × $128 less the $100 investment) while those at B look forward to a $1,900 (15 × $160 less the $500 investment) increment to the company's market value.

Most analysts would focus on the fact that A will embark on a riskier strategy, borrowing so much money. The shareholder will earn a higher return, but also takes a bigger risk. Investors in power plants during the 1990s did just what A wants to do. They borrowed heavily to buy power stations, and many of them lost those stations to creditors. So, maybe B has the right idea.

Financial theorists, using M & M's concept, would take a different view.[2] They would concede that both A and B plan to pay the right price for the power plant, $1,000, which would produce a 20% return on the investment. Yet, here is how the financial gurus at A and B think that the market will value the facility.

	Company A	Company B
Net income × 15	$1,920	$2,400
Debt	900	500
Market valuation of plant (1+2)	2,820	2,900

Why would investors pay close to three times more than the buyers of the plant think that it is worth? Financial theorists will say that they should not, and, probably, will not. To get that valuation over $1,000, the buyer has to get the earnings above $200 or reduce the risk inherent in the investment (by convincing buyers of power to sign long-term power purchase contracts that assure the power plant of a safe flow of income). If, for instance, the buyer can figure out how to raise profits to $300 by cutting expenses, the value of the plant would rise to $1,500, while still producing a 20% return to the buyer. If the buyer finds rock solid purchasers for the power, who sign long-term contracts, that might reduce the risk level so much that buyers would settle for a 10% return, which would justify a $2,000 valuation for the much safer $200 per year stream of operating income.

Ignoring the lessons of M & M creates a risk to shareholders of acquiring companies. The acquirers think that they can engineer a higher value for the asset, so that they can get away with paying more than the real value of the asset because they think that they can convince the market to value the asset at an even higher level. Perhaps that false faith in their ability to create value, where none exists, accounts for the failure of so many mergers and acquisitions to earn cost of capital.

Putting together all the theory, taking greater financial risks at the corporation probably increases the beta of the corporation's stock, meaning that the corporation may have to raise the return it earns proportionately more than it has raised the risk level, if it hopes to increase the stock price. Taking a different view, the corporation can raise the return on common stock investment on its books by means of leverage (borrowing money at an interest rate lower than the return earned on the investment) but doing so might not add to the value of the corporation's stock in the market.

Market Risk and Individual Stock Risk

Over the decades, utility stocks have exhibited two characteristics. They have tended to move up or down less than the stock market as a whole (low beta). And they have tended to move in parallel with bonds (they are interest rate sensitive).[3] In other words, when the market goes up sharply, utility stocks move up less, and when the market takes a dive, utility stocks do not fall as much, and when interest rates rise, utility stocks tend to fall, and when interest rates fall, utility stocks tend to rise. Furthermore, the utility stocks tend to rise when the difference between return earned by the utility and interest rates widens, and fall when the differential narrows.[4] The stocks of energy merchants, generating companies and fuel producers tend to move up and down more than utilities, and are more likely to move due to changes in the prices of fuels or of electricity, resource discoveries and of the market as a whole. The investor in the average utility expects to receive a steady dividend plus some increase in stock price over time, but not an exceptional return. Investors in energy merchants, generators and fuel producers take greater risks, do not expect much in the way of dividends, but do hope for significant capital appreciation of their shares.

Investors can diversify their holdings and take other steps to limit the risk of their investments.[5] Corporations want their shares to perform well, but generally, they do not engage in transactions that allow them to make profits on an upswing in their stock prices. Nor would they own a portfolio of their own shares that might go down in value, causing them to take losses. The corporation is supposed to run a business, not play the market in its own stock.

At the same time, the board of directors of the corporation should engage in policies that enhance the value of the common stock. They do work, after all, for the shareholders, who do own the business. If the corporation makes investments that raise the risk of doing business, for instance, shareholders may not like the idea, in which case they may push down the value of the stock by selling it. That is, doing business in an imprudent manner may lead to reduced share prices.

Sometimes the market takes an overly pessimistic view of the corporation's prospects. Under such circumstances, the board of directors may decide that having the corporation purchase its own shares makes good business sense. As an example, the corporation can invest $10 in a new machine that will make a $1 profit every year (a 10% return on investment). Due to some brokerage house sell recommendations, the stock, which earns $2 per share, has fallen to $10. The corporation has $100 spare cash on hand. The directors decide to buy back ten shares of stock, rather than buy ten machines. To them, it looks as if the share buy back produces a 20% return. Of course, the corporation does not really earn a return on shares that it buys back, but shareholders will definitely gain from the transaction. Assume that the corporation has 100 shares outstanding before a transaction takes place. Here is how the two choices compare:

	Invest in machine	Buy back stock
Net income before decision	$200	$200
Extra income from investment in 10 machines	10	—
Net income after decision	210	200
Shares outstanding	100	90
Earnings per share	$2.10	$2.22

Purchasing the shares, in this case, can serve two purposes. First, buying a large amount of stock at the time when many people want to sell it will help to stabilize the stock price, which might calm down potential sellers and allow the stock to recover in price. Second, by investing in the stock instead of the machines, the corporation raises earnings per share to a higher level than would have been the case otherwise, shareholders now see more money coming in per share, and that may cause buyers to pay more for the stock. (We assume that the share buy back does not, in some way, make the business riskier. Some share buy backs might take needed equity money out of the business, which could hurt the business in the long run.)

Directors could influence share price through dividend policy as well. Financial theorists would argue against that possibility. According to M & M, risk level inherent in the business determines the appropriate price for a given level of earnings. Changing the dividend does not affect the risk level, so it should not affect the price of the stock — not in theory, anyway. Recently, however, an influential group of financial analysts have examined almost two centuries of corporate data. They concluded that dividends have provided the bulk of the profits earned by investors, and that corporations do a poor job of reinvesting the profits that they keep in the business rather than pay out as dividends.[6] If that conclusion is correct, then shareholders might have good reason to pay more for stocks in companies that pay out more of the earnings as dividends.

Other Equity Risks

Some holding companies operate their various businesses as if they owned a portfolio of shares in those businesses. In order to get maximum attention for the separate businesses, and to get market valuations for the parts, they may have sold a portion of those businesses to the public, so markets exist for the stocks of the affiliated corporations. The partial ownership game has advantages and disadvantages. It allows investors to buy the part of the business that they like best, and pay an appropriate price for it. It provides market signals to the managers of the affiliates as to how well they are doing. It gives the affiliates the ability to make acquisitions using their own stock. The arrangement also creates the potential for conflicts of interest between the public minority shareholders of the affiliate and the parent company management, because the parent has the power to prevent the affiliate from doing things that might benefit the affiliate but hurt the parent, and the minority shareholders of the affiliate might object to arrangements between affiliate and parent that benefit the parent more than the affiliate. In addition, problems at an affiliate that affect the affiliate's stock price might affect the parent's stock price as well. Furthermore, the market has a tendency to mark down the value of a holding company to a level below the sum of the market values of its affiliates. That discount will, eventually, cause the holding company management to want to buy in the public shares in the affiliates, which will present problems of valuing those shares for the transaction, because the controlling shareholder (the holding company) would like to pay as little as possible to buy the positions of the minority shareholders.

These problems tell us why most corporations do not hold portfolios of stocks, or run affiliates as portfolio companies. But the corporations do run huge portfolios of stocks and bonds in their pension funds, and how those funds invest, and how the market rises or falls, may make an enormous difference to the corporation financially. Some corporations, in an attempt to reduce the contributions they would have to make to the pension fund, encouraged the pension fund managers to invest aggressively, that is take big risks in order to earn high returns. They figured that if the fund earned high returns on investment, that would reduce the need for the corporation to put money into the fund to assure that it could pay the pensions. Such a policy worked for a while, but when the stock market declined, the pension funds that had emphasized speculative stocks in their portfolios fell substantially, and the corporations had to put even more money into the funds so that they could meet future pension obligations.[7]

That, in turn, brings up the peculiar way that accountants measure the shortfall. First, they want to calculate the present value of the contributions that the corporation will have to make over time to fully fund the pensions. In other words, they want to determine how much money the corporation would have to set aside right now, and invest at current rates of interest, in order to pay the pension fund, when required, to make sure that it has enough money in it to meet obligations. That number goes up when interest rates decline and goes down when interest rates increase, so the number is, pretty much, beyond the control of the corporation or its board of directors. Second, the corporation has to estimate the return it expects the pension fund to earn on its investments, in order to estimate how much extra money the fund needs to pay its obligations. This estimate requires attention. Corporations that do not have money to put into the fund, or would rather not contribute to the fund, assert that the fund's investments will produce high returns, so the corporation will not have to contribute much to the fund. Yet, an avalanche of recent studies indicates that investors have an overly optimistic view of the returns produced in the market.[8] Some corporations have decided to bet on a rising stock market to bail them out from a pension deficiency. Given the size of some pension fund shortfalls, that involves taking a big equity market risk. Unfortunately, the discussion of these issues is relegated to the footnotes of the financial statements.

As a final point, when the stock market loses confidence in a firm, and its stock slides, outside investors and bankers start to view the firm as a target for takeover, a situation which makes it difficult for the firm to retain staff, make business deals, or take the measures necessary to reverse its fortunes and reverse the slide in the stock price. Equity risk takes many forms.

Conclusion

Corporations have to live with the fact that stock prices go up and down, sometimes for reasons that have nothing to do with the fortunes of the particular firm. They can, however, take steps to avoid or mitigate some equity risks, and they need to understand the risks that they cannot manage in any way.

Notes

[1]For a full (but nontechnical) discussion of the topic, *see* Leonard S. Hyman, Andrew S. Hyman and Robert C. Hyman, *America's Electric Utilities: Past, Present and Future*, Eighth Edition (Vienna, VA: Public Utilities Reports, 2005), Chapter 25.

[2]For a brief summary of M & M, *see* Richard A. Brealey and Stewart C. Myers, *Principles of Corporate Finance* (NY: McGraw-Hill, 1988), esp. pp. 400-401.

[3]**Chapter 10** discusses the inverse relationship between interest rates and bond prices. As interest rates fall, bond prices tend to rise, and when interest rates rise, bond prices tend to fall.

[4]Leonard S. Hyman, "Investing in the 'Plain Vanilla' Utility," *Energy Law Journal*. Vol. 24, No. 1, 2003, p. 1.

[5]This principle of diversification is discussed in **Chapter 5.**

[6]Robert D. Arnott and Peter L. Bernstein. "What Risk Premium is 'Normal'?" *Financial Analysts Journal*, March/April 2002, p. 64.

[7]Admittedly these pension funds could have hedged these risks by using equity index futures or options, or individual equity options, to cushion a fall in either the total portfolio or individual equities. A portfolio manager could sell a short futures, or buy a long put, on a stock index to hedge a portfolio from a drop in the overall stock markets. In addition, an investor could buy a long put on an individual stock to protect against the fall in price of an individual equity.

[8]Robert D. Arnott and Peter L. Bernstein, *loc. cit.*

Credit Risk

It's hard to run a business when you can't get paid for what you sell. On the other side of the coin, what happens when you can't borrow money because your creditors consider you a deadbeat? Ultimately this is what credit risk boils down to — the risk that you won't get paid or won't be able to borrow money or do business based on the creditworthiness of your counterparties or your own organization. This risk is fundamental to all businesses — not just energy. Energy markets cannot function without creditworthy participants. This became obvious in 2002, when the over-the-counter energy markets imploded as major players in the market were revealed as less creditworthy than believed. This unraveling started with the collapse of Enron in the fall of 2001, followed by the departure of Aquila and El Paso from energy trading, and then the bankruptcy of Mirant, which had been spun off from Southern Company to engage in power marketing.

Credit Policy Starts at the Top

Credit policy needs to be set at the top. This stems from the concept of risk appetite discussed in **Chapter 4: Risk Management Starts at the Top.** Given that the firm's health depends on getting paid, and getting what it pays for, the board of directors should discuss, analyze, and set credit policy and credit risk limits for management to implement. Credit policies will determine with whom the firm does business, and in what markets it participates.

Since over-the-counter markets spawned credit problems in the energy markets, most notably the 1998 Midwest power spikes where parties failed to obtain and deliver energy, and the collapse of the merchant energy markets following ratings downgrades in 2001 and 2002, the question of how and where to trade needs to be carefully considered. It is important to remember that due to the nature of their operation, and their clearing and margining processes (as discussed in **Chapter 5: Shifting Risk with Derivatives: The Building Blocks**) the regulated energy futures and options markets have not experienced these disruptive credit events. These events, outside the regulated markets, however, have not just affected the trading operations of firms but also affected the creditworthiness of parent firms and their cost of debt financing and in certain cases had dramatic impacts — notably negative — on stock prices. This is more than just a trading issue, but an issue that determines the health and survival of the firm.

Credit policy involves decisions about choosing those with whom the firm will do business and decisions that the firm makes about its own financing, which will affect its own creditworthiness and ability to access capital markets. Those decisions on financial matters affect the firm's credit rating and cost of borrowing money. In addition, items such as levels of working capital and other measures of liquidity will determine when and if the firm needs to access capital markets. For example, a firm that does a poor job of managing its receivables (relative to its peers) may have to seek short term financing more frequently, which may reduce profitability and simultaneously diminish creditworthiness.

Principles of Credit Policy[1]

The decision to grant credit involves five steps:

> 1. *Establish normal terms of sale* — This involves setting the schedule for payments, and discounts for early payment. The terms can depend on standards within an industry, as well as whether the deal is done on an organized exchange or through a clearinghouse, in which case the clearinghouse will set the terms of sale for each party. The terms process usually requires some form of upfront payment, such as margin, or a discount for early payments. When establishing terms of sales, do not engage in price discrimination, or its offshoot, credit discrimination, which could violate the Robinson-Patman Act. In designing terms of sale, legal counsel should be involved, to avoid creating legal risk when attempting to avoid credit risk.

> 2. *Determine the form of contract that will cover the sale* — Different industries often have different contractual arrangements. For example, in some cases a firm can sell the obligations of its debtors (such as a promissory note) at a discount to another party, which will seek to collect the payment from the debtor. A firm

needs to know what can be done with its contracts before it enters into them.

3. *Assess each customer or counterparty's creditworthiness* — Ways of assessing credit risk are analyzed later in this chapter in the section entitled **Measuring Credit Risk.** The firm will need to select the appropriate measures and use them to select counterparties and their respective credit limits.

4. *Decide to grant credit* — The goal of credit management is to ensure profitability, not to turn away customers. There needs to be a balance between the two — which the firm needs to decide at its upper levels. The decision to grant credit depends on the answer to a simple question: Is the expected profit from granting credit greater than the expected profit from not granting credit, taking into account the risk involved? Another related matter is that if the cost of investigating credit is greater than the expected loss from nonpayment, then a costly credit check is not worth it. When making credit decisions, keep in mind three factors. First, credit management is designed to enable the firm to be profitable. Second, focus efforts on those accounts with great danger of nonpayment. Third, factor in the possibility of repeat business into credit decisions — there is a trade-off between a strict credit policy and turning away repeat customers through an interpretation that may be too strict. Ultimately, this decision is a matter of judgement.

5. *Collect on payments* — Establish a balance between keeping on good terms with good customers, who may periodically pay late, and being firm with consistently delinquent payers. Creditors may wish to shift their credit risk by selling their debts — at a price (a discount to the debt's face value) — to factors who specialize in debt collection. In addition, credit insurance or credit derivatives may prove useful as ways of assuring that a firm can minimize its losses from uncollectable debts. Trading through a clearinghouse removes many of the collection worries a firm faces.

Monitoring

Once credit policy is set, monitor it. Firms should lay out credit policies clearly and enforce them. Traders make money by making deals, and they chafe at limits, such as with whom they can do business. Thus, monitoring traders' actions and their counterparties needs to be a major part of a risk management and oversight operation. Traders make deals by risking the firm's money, not their own, so this oversight is fully justified. If they don't like it they are free to leave and set up shop and risk their own money on making deals and making (or losing) their own money. Until that point, they are subject to the firm's rules and regulations. The firm (not the traders) will select those counterparties based on their credit risk.

Monitoring also covers how contracts are executed. Energy trades in over-the-counter products can create tremendous credit risks. It is advisable to lay down ground rules that state, for example, that deals can only be made when accompanied by contracts that set out performance standards. Allowing traders to enter into contracts that have not been approved could open the company up to unforeseen credit risks. In addition to providing set credit standards, it is also necessary to provide oversight and monitoring of the contracts and credit agreements between parties before they trade.

Company credit policies must furnish guidelines on how to set up credit limits based on quantitative and qualitative analysis of the firm's total credit portfolio, its counterparties, and credit costs. These policies should lay out procedures on how to authorize credit levels and how to report credit limit violations, as well as disciplinary action for violation of credit limits.

Trading without executed contracts is not advisable. These contracts should contain provisions that allow for margining of daily mark-to-market trading, as well as account receivables. In addition, contracts should allow for changes in credit limits as market conditions change, especially as they worsen.

In addition, firms must monitor credit risk to adjust for changing market conditions. Thresholds need to be set that call attention to credit events at all levels of the firm, in order to insure appropriate action is taken, such as adjustment of reserves, or limitations on who the firm can trade with, or the types of transactions allowed — basically a new look at a counterparty — as if starting from scratch.

Procedures outlining authorization levels for credit limits should be included in company policies, in addition to reporting procedures for credit limit violations.[2]

Measuring Credit Risk[3]

Effective credit risk management requires measures that assess risk. Certain accounting measures are indicative of credit and related risks and are used in determining credit ratings.

Leverage Ratios

Leverage ratios give an indication of a company's ability to cover its debt payments.

Debt Ratio — Ratio of Long-Term Debt to Long-Term Capital.

$$\text{Debt Ratio} = \frac{\text{Long-Term Debt} + \text{Value of Leases}}{\text{Long-Term Debt} + \text{Value of Leases} + \text{Equity}}$$

Creditors will compare the firm to others within the industry to assess the firm's risk posed by its debt level.

Times Interest Earned — Measures the ability of a company to cover its debt payments from earnings available to pay interest charges. (EBIT means Earnings Before Interest and Taxes.)

$$\text{Times Interest Earned} = \frac{\text{EBIT} + \text{Depreciation}}{\text{Interest}}$$

A higher number is an assurance of greater ability to repay debt.

Liquidity Ratios

Liquidity ratios measure the ability of a company to produce enough cash to repay debts in the short term.

Net Working Capital to Total Assets — Working Capital is the difference between current assets and current liabilities — cash and assets the firm can easily turn into cash minus payments that it must make in the short term (with the short term usually considered less than one year).

$$\frac{\text{Net Working Capital}}{\text{Total Assets}} \quad = \quad \frac{\text{Current Assets} - \text{Current Liabilities}}{\text{Total Assets}}$$

A higher ratio points to greater liquidity.

Current Ratio — This ratio is determined by dividing current assets by current liabilities. A ratio above two is usually desirable, although numbers vary by industry.

$$\text{Current Ratio} \quad = \quad \frac{\text{Current Assets}}{\text{Current Liabilities}}$$

Quick (Acid Test) Ratio — This focuses more on current assets that are closer to cash.

$$\text{Quick Ratio} \quad = \quad \frac{\text{Cash} + \text{Marketable Securities} + \text{Receivables}}{\text{Current Liabilities}}$$

Once again a higher ratio indicates a more liquid organization.

Cash Ratio — Looks at most liquid assets.

$$\text{Cash Ratio} \quad = \quad \frac{\text{Cash} + \text{Marketable Securities}}{\text{Current Liabilities}}$$

A higher ratio indicates a more liquid organization.

Interval Measure — Measures how long the current assets will last, assuming that expenditures continue at the existing rate. The higher the number, the longer the firm can hold out.

$$\text{Interval Measure} = \frac{\text{Current Assets}}{\text{Average Daily Expenses}} = \text{Days of Cash on Hand}$$

Accounts Receivable Turnover — Measures how many times in a year the firm has turned its accounts receivable into cash. A higher ratio implies a firm that is more efficient in turning its accounts receivable into cash.

$$\text{Accounts Receivable Turnover} = \frac{\text{Sales on Account}}{\text{Average Accounts Receivable Balance}}$$

Average Collection Period — The average number of days it takes for a firm to collect on an account. A shorter average collection period indicates a firm that is more efficient in turning its accounts receivable into cash.

$$\text{Average Collection Period} = \frac{365 \text{ days}}{\text{Accounts Receivable Turnover}}$$

These ratios are starting points. Ratios also exist for profitability measures such as the Return on Equity, but the measures discussed above are more basic for credit risk. In addition, credit analysis has a subjective element, and it should include a look at overall industry trends, to provide a holistic view of the credit environment that a company and its counterparties inhabit.

There are three primary approaches to measuring credit risk. One of the most recent approaches, which is beyond the scope of this book, is a model based on the work of Nobel laureate Robert Merton. It attempts to predict the probability of default based on its equity price, and liability structure, based on the assumption that a firm's equity is equivalent to a call option on the firm's assets.[4]

The second, and most popular approach is that traditionally practiced by ratings agencies, such as Standard & Poor's and Moody's. These ratings agencies do an exhaustive analysis of a company's financials and rate these companies as to their estimated creditworthiness. Table 12-1 shows comparative credit ratings for Standard & Poor's and Moody's. The ratings help determine the price that the borrower will pay for its loan (the interest rate). These ratings, although based on quantitative measures, do have subjective aspects, and are often subject to outside influence.[5] Credit rating agencies are paid by companies to provide a rating for a bond issuance or for other credit purposes. The rating agencies are supposed to do an exhaustive analysis and come to an objective rating. Yet, credit ratings for Enron were at investment grade until shortly before its bankruptcy and Pacific Gas & Electric had the highest credit ratings from the rating agencies until shortly before its bankruptcy.[6]

The third approach takes a more actuarial view of factors that appear to discriminate between companies that go into bankruptcy and those that do not. This approach is based on the work of Professor Edward Altman of New York University, who developed the Z-score approach, which assesses five factors that are likely predictors of bankruptcy.

Those factors are:

1) Working Capital/Total Assets.

2) Retained Earnings/Total Assets.

3) Earnings before Interest and Taxes (EBIT)/Total Assets.

4) Market Value of Equity/Book Value of Total Liabilities.

5) Sales/Total Assets.[7]

The formula is expressed as follows for non-manufacturing firms:

$$Z = 1.2X_1 + 1.4X_2 + 3.3X_3 + 0.6X_4 + 1.0X_5$$

Where:

X_1 = Working Capital/Total Assets

X_2 = Retained Earnings/Total Assets

Table 12-1
Credit Ratings

S&P	Comment	Moody's	Comment	Grade
AAA	Extremely Strong/Highest Rating	Aaa	Best Quality/Highest Rating	Investment Grade
AA	Very Strong	Aa	High Quality	Investment Grade
A	Strong	A	Favorable	Investment Grade
BBB	Adequate	Baa	Medium–Grade	Investment Grade
BB	Less Vulnerable	Ba	Speculative	Speculative Grade
B	More Vulnerable	B	Undesirable as an investment	Speculative Grade
CCC-CC	Currently Vulnerable — Currently Highly Vulnerable	Caa	Very Poor	Speculative Grade
C	Bankruptcy Petition or Equivalent Filed But Payments Continue	Ca	Highly Speculative/In Default	Speculative Grade
D	Default/Bankrupt/Lowest Rating	C	Lowest Rating	Speculative Grade

S&P Ratings can be modified by + and - for higher and lower rankings within a category

Moody's Ratings can be modified by an suffix of 1 to 3, with 1 as high, 2 as medium, and 3 as low.

Source: S&P Ratings from Standard & Poor's Bond Guide. (New York: August 2005.) p. 5.

Moody's Ratings from Mergent Bond Manual. (New York: July 2005). pp. 3–4.

X_3 = Earnings before Interest and Taxes (EBIT)/Total Assets

X_4 = Market Value of Equity/Book Value of Total Liabilities

X_5 = Sales/Assets

Z-scores less than 1.81 are a strong indicator of imminent bankruptcy in one year, while Z-scores between 1.81 and 2.675 are considered to be in a gray area or ignorance zone.[8] Enron had a Z-score of 2.46 based on its year 2000 10-K form.[9] Thus, Enron creditors had reason to be wary — even when using Enron's numbers, which are now known to be misleading. For those who wonder about the susceptibility of these formulas to manipulation, any tendency to overstate assets, would actually reduce many of the ratios, and lower the Z-score.

Avoid Risk

The only way to avoid credit risk is to not buy or sell anything, a formula that would kill any business. However, a company can choose to avoid certain credit risks by staying away from those organizations that have bad records of meeting their credit obligations, or are notorious for using contractual arguments, notably *force majeure* clauses, to wiggle out of deals.

There may be a reason someone can offer a deal that seems too good to be true: they can't or won't pay or deliver. Although these credit events could theoretically be factored into a model that shows the cost of credit, at some point it may just be simpler to set up a blacklist of people or organizations with whom the firm does no business. Period. Yes, review the list from time-to-time as conditions change, but in the interim, the staff must adhere to the blacklist, or the firm's policy decisions become irrelevant. Individuals need to be monitored to assure that they avoid dealing with the forbidden parties.

In addition to monitoring people, it may be wise to avoid certain types of trading venues or deals. For example, a company could choose not to trade over-the-counter or do deals without contracts in place. The structuring of deals can affect recoverability of an investment, and these factors that affect the creditworthiness of a transaction need to be factored in.

Bear the Risk

It seems inevitable that at some point an organization will actually have to bear credit risk. This must be understood from the start. After all, allowances for doubtful accounts are part of standardized accounting procedure. As with other risks, it is one thing to bear risk through a conscious decision, and another to bear credit risk through an oversight, or because of lack of adherence to credit policy.

Consider a board that decides not do business with counterparties that have a credit rating of less than BBB as defined by Standard and Poor's. One employee, however, decides that a counterparty will pay him, even though its credit rating is below BBB. He makes a transaction. He has made the company bear risk through his own actions — a decision that was not part of company policy. If this kind of behavior is tolerated, then the firm will bear far more credit risk than it planned.

In addition, the type of contract and instruments that the firm uses will determine the type of risk that the firm chooses to bear. For example, when buying or selling a futures contract from a regulated exchange, the firm faces very little credit risk because the clearinghouses have a strong financial profile and the margining system makes the costs transparent and obvious, and prevents the buildup of a big credit problem. The clearing mechanism assures users of these contracts that they face less risk of not getting paid. However, the OTC markets do not have these guarantees, and by entering them companies choose to bear a higher degree of risk than on the regulated futures and options exchanges.

Reduce the Hazard

Reducing the hazard of adverse credit events begins at the top, with the setting of credit policy. Ultimately, the risk of an adverse credit event is a function of whom a company trades with and the way that transactions are structured. Those decisions need to be made at the top in a clear and decisive manner and enforced strictly. Establishment of these policies sets an upper limit on the risks the company is willing to tolerate.

Accurate and timely measuring of credit risk lies at the heart of reducing credit risk, because knowledge of the riskiness of counterparties, the nature of credit agreements, and the exposure of the credit portfolio permits managers to understand their credit risk and take steps that can reduce the chances of losses.

One measure of risk is **Credit Value at Risk**, which is explained in **Appendix B: Common Risk Terminology and Important Measures.** However, given the possible weakness of the assumptions that underlie the theory, it should be used only in conjunction with other risk measures. Periodically, credit portfolios should be stress tested to see what could happen under extreme circumstances — such as the credit crunch that hit the merchant power markets in 2002. Then the company can test what may happen to its own financials if a number of counterparties can't make good on their obligations. Also, by seeing how these failures impact the company's own financials, and credit rating, the firm can see if failures by others in the markets may adversely affect its credit rating and hinder its ability to transact in the market. This iterative process could indicate the possibility of downward credit spirals and credit crunches for which companies must prepare.

Factors to consider in setting policies to reduce the hazards of adverse credit events include:

1. *Counterparty Selection* — Counterparties need to be screened to assure that they meet the creditworthiness standards established by the board. These standards can be based on credit ratings, such as those determined by the major credit rating agencies or other rating processes based on Merton models, measures of credit risk as determined by looking at credit spreads, or other measures of creditworthiness such as Altman's Z Scores. It may be simplistic, but a board could start a hazard reduction policy by setting minimum standards for trading partners, and making sure that those policies are followed, otherwise the hazard reduction effort will be for naught.

2. *Credit Limits* — In certain transactions, the firm may extend credit to counterparties. Limits need to be set on how much credit to offer counterparties based on their risk levels. Again, although the board may not set exact risk levels, it should make sure it approves these levels, giving an imprimatur of officialdom, and make clear to those on trading desks that there is no ambiguity in these limits, and they are to be followed or the vio-

lators will face dismissal from the organization. While this may seem extreme, can the firm afford having its finances put on the line so some trader can make a risky deal that may or may not pay off? At least by setting credit limits, in the event of an adverse credit event, the firm can limit how much it can lose, although the loss may not be as easy to define as with a premium paid out when buying a put or call option.

3. *Collateralization* — Collateralization is an old form of credit risk management. Collateral is something that a debtor is prepared to give up to a creditor in the event he can't pay his debts. It can be set as part of a contractual process. A simple example of collateralization involves the process of taking out a mortgage loan to buy a home. If the homeowner fails to pay the mortgage, the bank will take possession of the home and resell it in an attempt to recover its loss.

4. *Where You Trade* — The venue that a company uses to transact its business can greatly influence its credit risk. Basically, the risk of loss from a credit event on an organized, regulated exchange such as the NYMEX or CME is negligible. The same cannot be said for the over-the-counter markets, where credit risks range from small to large, and companies must constantly monitor their counterparties' credit positions. Contrast this with the regulated exchanges, where the cost of credit is made explicit through the margining and clearing system, where credit exposures are accounted for on a day-to-day basis, which prevents credit exposures from getting so large that they can not be managed.

By making trades through a regulated exchange, or having trades cleared through a clearing organization related to an exchange (such as NYMEX's Clearport^{sm} program), a company can significantly reduce its chances of a credit related loss, and may be able to reduce its time and effort required to monitor the credit ratings of counterparties and total credit exposures, because that job is handled by the clearing organization. When using one of these clearing systems, then, the company lets the clearing organization worry about the credit risk, so the company can focus on its business.

5. *Structuring of Credit Agreements* — Before setting up bilateral deals (or any deals) it is useful to have knowledgeable counsel

either set up or review contracts or bond agreements to assure that the conditions are most favorable for the firm, and to be aware of covenants within agreements that could affect the ability of the firm to collect on its agreements, or in the case of a purchaser, to install provisions that provide the maximum protections if it defaults.

A prime example of provisions to be wary of are ratings triggers, which are provisions within agreements (as in bond covenants) that are activated when an organization's credit rating falls beneath a threshold. For example, say a company has a loan with a bank that it is going to pay off over two years. However, a provision within the loan says that if the company's credit rating falls below investment grade during the term of the loan, then the bank has the right to demand immediate repayment of both the principal and interest on the loan. Thus, the company's structure of credit agreements can affect its credit risk, and this needs to be factored into strategies for reducing credit risk. It is not all about mathematical models — sound legal advice plays an important role in reducing the chances of losses from adverse credit events.

Reduce the Loss

The key to loss reduction lies in careful monitoring of credit portfolios, and an ability to act quickly to reduce losses before events get out of hand.

Monitoring

The Committee of Chief Risk Officers has suggestions on monitoring the creditworthiness of counterparties in deals, with these ten steps.

1. Monitor at all levels of the organization — management, operational, and analyst.

2. Ensure that those within the company fully understand the creditworthiness of the counterparty.

3. Monitor compliance with provisions of contracts.

4. Identify delinquent payers and review and classify potential problems regularly.

5. Correct problems once they occur — don't wait or maybe the money won't be there. It's hard to collect from a bankrupt organization.

6. Monitor the makeup and quality of the credit portfolio and identify concentrated risks.

7. Determine the adequacy of the firm's reserves for the risk level of the credit portfolio.

8. Consider the risks from low probability but high cost default events as well as from smaller events with smaller costs but higher default probabilities. The use of models based on the bell curve may understate the risk of those low probability, high cost events.[10]

9. Identify correlated risks — such as correlations between market risks and the default risks of counterparties. (For example, how could a rapid fall in the price of gas affect the ability of a gas producer to pay its bills?)

10. Consider what could happen to uncorrelated risks if they became correlated under extreme market stresses.[11]

IT Systems and Data Feeds

The company that commits to monitoring credit must make the financial and operational commitment to the information technology (IT) systems and data feeds necessary to support a credit monitoring operation. Given that the quality of credit operations can determine the success or failure of trading operations, this is no place to skimp on vital controls. When dealing with a large number of counterparties and rapidly changing markets, the credit picture can change rapidly. A lack of computing firepower and timely price data allows traders to make trades that violate the company's credit policies, inadvertently, because the positions have not been updated.

Be Prepared to Act Fast

Credit crunches happen quickly. A firm needs to have a plan in place to deal with volatile markets before disasters happen. For example, what happens when a counterparty's credit rating changes, yet there are still outstanding deals with that counterparty? Should they be un-

169

wound immediately, settled gradually, or just monitored? The firm will need to decide how it wishes to act, and have policies and procedures in place to prevent events from spiraling out of hand.

Shift the Risk

Credit Derivatives

Just as with energy price, interest rates, foreign exchange, and weather conditions, derivatives exist to shift credit risk from one party to another. There are many forms of credit derivatives that have relevance to the activities of energy companies. One of the most common is the credit default swap.[12]

Credit Default Swaps

A Credit Default Swap is a bilateral financial contract. The purchaser of the contract pays a fee to insure, in the event that a selected credit event happens (such as a default), that the seller of the protection pays a fixed amount to the buyer. The payment on the swap is designed to counter the loss from the default or specified credit event.[13] For example, a company is concerned that a counterparty may default on a deal. It can go to the credit markets, buy a credit default swap on that counterparty, and the counterparty need not be informed of the deal. The purchaser typically pays a number of basis points per year to obtain the credit protection.

Clearing

The Committee of Chief Risk Officers, made up of chief risk officers from many energy companies, sees the establishment of third party clearing of energy trades as the most effective way to manage credit risks in the over-the-counter energy markets. (The principle behind clearing was discussed in **Chapter 5: Shifting Risk with Derivatives: The Building Blocks.**) A *clearinghouse* is:

> An agency or separate corporation of a futures exchange that is responsible for settling trading accounts, clearing trades, collecting and maintaining margin monies, regulating delivery, and reporting trading data. Clearinghouses act as third parties to all futures and options contracts — acting as a buyer to every clearing member seller and a seller to every clearing member buyer.[14]

Thanks to the clearinghouse, individual buyers and sellers do not have to know the creditworthiness of their opposite numbers in a sale.

The beauty of a clearing system is that the clearinghouse bears the financial risk of nonpayment by parties to a deal. Of course, the clearinghouse can not guarantee the actual delivery of the energy products, but it can assure that a seller of power will receive payment for the power that it delivers. This clearing mechanism is an advantage of exchange traded derivative products over products sold over-the-counter, where the resolution of credit problems is left to the two parties or the courts, which can be time consuming and often unfulfilling. In addition, the clearinghouses associated with exchanges have far superior credit ratings and histories than participants in over-the-counter energy markets.

However, these advantages of regulated markets can be extended to the over-the-counter energy markets through the ability of over-the-counter parties to use the clearinghouses of the NYMEX and other independent clearing organizations for over-the-counter transactions. NYMEX ClearPort^{sm} is an internet based application that allows energy traders to clear bilateral energy deals through the NYMEX's clearinghouse, regardless of where the trades were made. The system allows for clearing of a number of products, including natural gas basis swap futures, Henry Hub natural gas, and electrical futures (NYISO Zones A,G, and J and PJM) that can be cash settled or require physical settlement (PJM, Palo Verde, and Mid Columbia).

To use the ClearPort^{sm} system a user must set up an account with a clearing member of the NYMEX. In order for the the exchange to clear the trades, each side has to meet the credit limits for the respective clearing member. This is analogous to the margin requirements that exchanges require on accounts that are mark-to-market, as described in **Chapter 5: Shifting Risk with Derivatives: The Building Blocks**.

The advantage of using a clearinghouse is that the company can focus more on the execution of trades, and be assured of the creditworthiness of its counterparties, which can expand the range of parties to trade with and may provide access to better priced products and deals. The energy company can focus on its business with less need for resources to examine the credit nature of each transaction and trading partner. The clearinghouse does that work. Admittedly there are costs such as clearing fees. In addition, margins may be required, and the mark-to-market nature of the clearinghouse operation may have an effect on cash flows as was detailed in **Chapter 5: Shifting Risk with Derivatives: The Building Blocks.** Still, this cost is upfront and transparent — the company knows what credit costs. This contrasts with the opaque costs that could be posed by the failure of counterparties to make good on deals, as happened in the Midwest power spikes of 1998, when power marketers failed to deliver goods, and creditors were not made whole.

Ultimately, the board of directors and senior management of a firm will need to decide what kind of credit operation they desire and whether clearing is superior and better meets the needs of the organization, rather than fretting about the creditworthiness of counterparties. This decision needs to be thought through and the costs considered. The costs of clearing trades through a clearinghouse must be compared with the savings from greater certainty about credit operations and the need to devote fewer resources to credit operations, by outsourcing that operation to an organization with solid clearing operations and a very low probability of default.

Reduce the Risk

Credit risk is a function of exposure to risk. If trading is only with one party, all credit risk is a function of that party's credit risk. It may be beneficial to explore how to reduce that credit risk through diversification of counterparties. The clearinghouse is highly creditworthy because of the large number of parties that make it up, and because they trade in more than energy markets. That way, a default by one party may not be disastrous, because the other counterparties may be able to pay their bills. The need to reduce risk is a good reason to encourage all sorts of players (even speculators), to enter the energy markets. This is because the credit risk profile of a bank, for instance, may not be correlated with the credit risk profile of a power trader. It may be possible to set up a portfolio of counterparties with non correlated credit profiles that may serve to reduce risk in the portfolio structure developed by Markowitz. Note that in the 2002 energy merchant credit crunch, the power traders saw their credit ratings crater together. Traders backed by financial institutions would have had the ability to withstand those shocks. Their capital base is diversified, and their credit standing is derived from a broad financial base, not an exposure to one industry alone.

Conclusion

Credit crunches in 2001 and 2002 made energy companies acutely aware of the credit risks they face in the markets that grew rapidly during the restructuring of the energy business in the late 1990s and early 2000s. The rapid rise of the markets, and the view that energy, especially electricity, was *different* allowed market participants to neglect long established business practices, such as clearing of trades designed to minimize credit risk. Many of the new entrants to the energy markets came from regulated markets, where if some customers didn't pay, the regulator would allow the costs to be borne (socialized) by all customers, so the utility did not need to scrutinize credit risk. It's time for energy companies to stop focusing on what makes them different from other businesses, and to start focusing on what they have in common — notably a desire to make a profit and get paid for their services — which is hard to do when credit risk is not managed.

Notes

[1] After Richard A. Brealey and Stewart C. Myers, *Principles of Corporate Finance*, Third Edition (New York: McGraw Hill Publishing Company, 1988). Chapter 30: Credit Management.

[2] After, Committee of Chief Risk Officers. *Introduction and Executive Summaries of CCRO Recommendations*, Volume 1 of 6, 19 November 2002, pp. 12-13.

[3] Richard A. Brealey and Stewart C. Myers. *Principles of Corporate Finance*, Third Edition (New York: McGraw Hill Publishing, 1988), pp. 652-654.

[4] Phillipe Jorion, *Value at Risk: The New Benchmark for Managing Financial Risk*, Second Edition (New York: McGraw Hill, 2001); J.P. Morgan, *The J.P. Morgan Guide to Credit Derivatives* (London: Risk Publications, 1999), p. 37. Given the complexity of these models, and the difficulty of interpreting their efficacy, these models are not highlighted in this book. Bharath, Sreedhar T. and Shumway, Tyler, "Forecasting Default with the KMV-Merton Model" (December 17, 2004). Available on the World Wide Web at: *http://ssrn.com/abstract=637342*

[5] Ratings agencies were influenced by investment banks to not downgrade Enron when it was clearly in the midst of troubles, because of how it might affect their investments and relationships. Frank Partnoy, *Infectious Greed: How Deceit and Risk Corrupted the Financial Markets* (New York: Times Books, 2003), p. 385.

[6] *Ibid.*

[7] Edward I. Altman, *Predicting Financial Distress of Companies: Revisiting the Z-Score and Zeta Models*, July 2000. Available on the World Wide Web at: *http://pages.stern.nyu.edu/~ealtman/Z-scores.pdf*

The analysis was originally developed based on an analysis of manufacturing firms. Altman also developed two other models for privately held manufacturing firms (Z') and privately held non-manufacturing firms (Z"). The formula for Z' is: $Z' = 0.717X_1 + 0.847X_2 + 3.107X_3 + 0.420X_4 + 0.998X_5$ and the formula for Z" is: $Z" = 6.56X_1 + 3.26X_2 + 6.72X_3 + 1.05X_4$. Book value of equity is substituted for market value of equity in the X_4 calculation. In the Z" model the X_5 is dropped to remove the potential industry effect. If Enron was a privately held non-manufacturing firm, with the Z" model it had a Z" score of 0.84 based on its year 2000 10-K form, which would have put it in the strong indicator of imminent bankruptcy category.

[8]Nikolai Chuvakhin and L. Wayne Gertmeninan, "Predicting Bankruptcy in the WorldCom Age," *Graziado Business Report*, Volume 6, No. 1, 2003. Available on the World Wide Web at: *http://gbr.pepperdine.edu/031/print_bankruptcy.html.*; Enron 2000 10-K.

[9]Here are the figures used in the calculations for Enron:

1) Working Capital = $1,975 Million.

2) Total Assets = $65,503 Million

3) Retained Earnings = $3,226 Million

4) EBIT = $2,482 Million

5) Market Value of Equity = $62,433 Million

6) Book Value of Equity = $11,470 Million

7) Book Value of Liabilities = $54,033 Million

8) Total Sales = $100,789 Million

Source: Enron, *Enron Annual Report 2000*, pp. 31-33. Available on the World Wide Web at: *http://www.enron.com/corp/investors/annuals/2000/.*

[10]Benoit Mandelbrot and Richard L. Hudson, *The (Mis)behavior of Markets: A Fractal View of Risk, Ruin, and Reward* (New York: Basic Books. 2004). *See* chapters 3,4, and 5.

[11]After Committee of Chief Risk Officers: Credit Risk Management Working Group. *White Paper, Volume 4 of 6, Credit Risk Management*, 19 November 2002, p. 17.

[12]Other types of credit derivatives include Total Return Swaps, credit options, and credit insurance. A detailed discussion of these instruments is beyond the scope of the book. For swaps and options, the principle basically is to create a product that is designed to reduce credit risk. For example, company A is selling to Company B. A is concerned that if B's credit rating falls, it will receive less revenue, or none at all. It desires to have an instrument that will increase in value and provide a gain that will counteract the loss from B's failure to pay. Another type of credit derivative called a collateralized default obligation is made when a financial organization sells debt to a

special purpose entity and then splits the debt into pieces by issuing securities that are linked to each piece of the debt. Given that some of these instruments are known as "toxic waste" in the financial sector, these instruments should be regarded with caution and probably avoided in looking at credit risk management. Credit insurance involves paying for insurance with an insurance company. Source for Credit Derivatives: Frank Partnoy, *op. cit.*, p. 387. Source for Credit Insurance: Brealey and Myers, *op. cit.*, pp. 738-739.

[13]Examples of credit events include:

- Failure to meet payment obligations when they are due

- Bankruptcy

- Repudiation

- A material adverse restructuring of debt

Source: *The J.P. Morgan Guide to Credit Derivatives* (London: Risk Publications, 1999), p. 14.

[14]Chicago Board of Trade: *Glossary.* Available on the World Wide Web at: *http:// www.cbot.com/cbot/pub/page/0,3181,1059,00.html.* Definition for **Clearinghouse**.

Advantages and Disadvantages of Various Trading Venues

Introduction

The decision to shift risk using derivatives requires management to ask an important question: Where to trade — on a regulated exchange or over-the-counter? The question is important because the choice will affect the credit risk, liquidity risk, and fraud risk of the transactions. Choosing an exchange is an essential risk management decision, because the venue determines the risk universe that the company inhabits when executing corporate risk management strategy.

Advantages of Regulated Exchanges

Regulated commodity exchanges are defined by the following elements: market regulation as self-regulatory organizations, standardized futures and options contracts, price transparency, and the exchange clearing function, which ensures financial trade performance. These elements are the primary advantages of the regulated exchanges compared with their over-the-counter competitors.

Regulation

In the United States of America, futures and commodity options are regulated by the Commodity Futures Trading Commission (CFTC), an independent federal agency created by Congress in 1974, self-regulatory organizations (exchanges), and the National Futures Association. The CFTC administers the Commodity Exchange Act of 1936, which is the primary legislative authority for U.S. exchange-traded futures and options contracts.[1]

Swaps and CFTC Regulation

Due to legal and commercial uncertainty, the CFTC, in 1989, issued a Swaps Policy Statement that sought to provide market participants with regulatory certainty regarding the jurisdiction of the CFTC. The statement concluded that qualifying swaps were not regulated futures contracts and thus not subject to CFTC jurisdiction. This policy statement encouraged the swaps industry to return to the U.S. from overseas, where operations had moved due to concerns related to potential CFTC regulation. To further support this position, Congress enacted the Futures Trading Practices Act (FTPA) that provided the CFTC with authority to exempt swaps from futures market regulation. The CFTC implemented the FTPA in 1993 and exempted swaps from the oversight provisions of the Commodity Exchange Act, barring market manipulation.[2]

Standardized Contracts

All futures and options contracts offered by regulated exchanges are highly standardized regarding contract terms and conditions. This standardization is necessary in order to develop market liquidity as only month and price are negotiated in the contract execution process. The standardized terms and conditions imbedded in exchange futures and options contracts reflect the commercial standards in the underlying cash market industries. In addition to cash market requirements, exchange futures and options contract terms and conditions also reflect regulatory requirements of the Commodity Futures Trading Commission.

Price Transparency

Price transparency is an integral value of regulated exchange trading. Regulated exchanges provide a neutral trading environment where futures and options contracts are traded anonymously in open and competitive continuous auctions. Floor-based trading is conducted by open-outcry auction in which traders verbally indicate prices and quantities to buy and sell. Prices related to open outcry trading are instantly communicated to data vendors that widely disseminate the price information. In addition to price, volume and **open interest** (total outstanding contracts) levels are also provided publicly. Exchange electronic trading systems also provide real-time price discovery through screen access and dissemination by data vendors. Wide availability of price, volume, and open interest statistics related to exchange traded contracts enables efficient decision-making by all sectors affected by commodity pricing.

Exchange Clearing Function

A key element in the operation of regulated exchanges is the clearing function, which ensures financial performance of all exchange trades. Following the execution of a trade, the exchange clearing house becomes the buyer to every seller, and the seller to every buyer, through its primary relationships with exchange clearing members. All exchange trades are financially guaranteed by exchange clearing members. Clearing member financial requirements, and operation of initial and variation margin processes, protect the financial integrity of the exchange clearing house. All positions held by clearing members are collateralized by the clearing house through the collection of original margin and variation margin while the clearing house carries the position. The operation of variation margin collection is based on a daily settlement system, that insures that all positions in the exchange clearing house reflect daily changes in commodity value. Additionally, regulated exchanges employ guarantee funds and insurance default protection policies, which provide further financial performance certainty of exchange contracts.

Credit Risk Management

Credit risk management is a valuable economic function of regulated exchanges. Following exchange trade execution, commercial participants shift counterparty risk to the exchange clearing house. The efficient transfer of credit risk through the operation of the clearing function enables trade participants to access a larger population of trading participants due to reduced counterparty credit concerns. This transfer of credit risk is of paramount significance due to pervasive credit-related concerns in the energy merchant sector.

Market Efficiency

Exchange clearing promotes market efficiency through reduced bilateral credit costs and lower collateral requirements due to position netting. Counterparty positions in related exchange markets are subject to uniform margining. The margining process calculates margins on a net basis: that is the net difference between long and short positions of exchange clearing members. Additionally, margin reduction credits are typically provided on **intercommodity spread** transactions involving related contract markets. The original margin discount is based on the correlation relationship between the related commodities.

Disadvantages of Regulated Exchanges

For some, the perceived advantages of exchange traded derivatives may not appear as advantages. The standardization of contracts, while increasing liquidity, may make it more difficult to hedge because of basis risk. However, lower levels of liquidity, and lesser trading volumes, may in turn create wider bid-ask spreads that could increase the cost of doing business outside of an exchange. In addition, the level of regulatory oversight, and the infrastructure needed to provide that oversight, may make trading on a regulated exchange more expensive than on a less-regulated or over-the-counter exchange. Still, that lower price comes with a tradeoff — a greater chance of fraudulent behavior and default by a counterparty.

In the past, over-the-counter markets were often seen as faster to market than regulated exchanges, given that there were fewer (if any) regulatory hoops necessary to jump through to get a new product trading. However, the overhaul of commodities regulation in recent years has increased the speed that new products come to market, so this is less of a disadvantage. And, the fact that the regulated markets have outlasted some of those operations that were perceived as a threat, such as Enron Online, says something for the viability of the regulated exchange model, and the service these exchanges provide to their customers.

Important Exchanges for the Utility Sector

New York Mercantile Exchange

Founded in 1872 as the Butter and Cheese Exchange, the New York Mercantile Exchange (NYMEX) is the largest energy futures and options exchange in the world. Volume at the exchange in 2005 totaled over 215 million contracts, an all time record, and 27% over 2004. NYMEX consists of two divisions: the NYMEX Division with trading in crude oil, natural gas, heating oil, unleaded gasoline, platinum, and palladium, and the COMEX Division with trading in gold, silver, copper, and aluminum. The 2005 total includes 39.3 million energy futures and options contracts cleared through NYMEX ClearPort^{sm}, an increase of 175% over 2004. ClearPort^{sm} is the NYMEX internet-based trading and clearing platform that includes over 200 futures and options contracts. This platform currently includes 42 electricity contracts that accounted for over 197,000 cleared contracts in 2004. The following electricity markets are served by ClearPort^sm: PJM Western Hub, PJM NI Hub, PJM AEP-Dayton NYISO Zones A, G and J, SO New England's Internal Hub, and Hubs established by the Midwest Independent System Operator. NYMEX also offers electricity futures contracts based on the Dow Jones western electricity price indices. NYMEX developed ClearPort^sm to transfer bilateral over-the counter energy contracts market credit risk to the NYMEX clearing house. The NYMEX clearing house is wholly owned and operated by NYMEX and has over $14 billion in deposits.

IntercontinentalExchange (ICE)

IntercontinentalExchange (ICE) is a leading online marketplace for global commodity trading, primarily of electricity, natural gas, crude oil, refined petroleum products, precious metals, and weather and emission credits. A group of financial and energy firms formed ICE in 2000. Headquartered in Atlanta, ICE also has regional offices in Calgary, Chicago, Houston, London, New York, and Singapore.

ICE also owns ICE Futures, formerly the International Petroleum Exchange (IPE), a leading European energy futures and options platform. On 7 April 2005, the IPE closed its floor trading rings and converted to all-electronic trading as of 8 April 2005. From the inception of the IPE until the floor closure, the IPE's futures and options contracts were traded in pits on the exchange floor using the open outcry system. The IPE launched its first contract, Gas Oil futures, in 1981 with the Brent Crude futures following in 1988.

The ICE Data group provides real-time market data reports, and the company's eConfirm platform provides electronic trade confirmations. ICE offers real-time over-the-counter (OTC) clearing and credit and risk management services. Clearing functions are provided by LCH.Clearnet, as the ICE does not own or operate a clearing house.[3]

During the year ended December 31, 2005, 42.1 million contracts were traded in the Company's futures markets, and 47.9 million contracts were traded in its OTC business segment.

Chicago Board of Trade

Established in 1848, the Chicago Board of Trade (CBOT) is a leading futures and options commodity exchange. Volume at the exchange in 2005 totaled over 674 million contracts, its fourth consecutive annual record. Electronic trading volume accounted for 65% of the 2005 total. In its early history, the CBOT traded only agricultural commodities such as corn, wheat, oats, and soybeans. Futures contracts at the exchange evolved over the years to include non-storable agricultural commodities and non-agricultural products, such as gold and silver. Since the introduction of financial futures, trading has been implemented in many financial instruments, including U.S. Treasury bonds and notes, stock indexes, and swaps. CBOT trading takes place through floor-based open-outcry and by electronic trading, which was launched in 1994. CBOT does not own a clearing house and previously used the Board of Trade Clearing Corporation (now the Clearing Corporation) as its provider of clearing services. In 2003, CBOT ended its relationship with the Clearing Corporation and negotiated an agreement with the Chicago Mercantile Exchange (CME) to use the CME clearing house to clear all CBOT contracts.

Chicago Mercantile Exchange

Founded in 1898 as the Chicago Butter and Egg Board, the Chicago Mercantile Exchange (CME) is the largest futures exchange in the United States. CME Volume in 2005 totaled more than one billion contracts, the sixth consecutive annual record. Electronic trading accounted for 70% of the annual total. CME futures and options contracts are segmented into the following areas: interest rates, stock indexes, foreign exchange, and agricultural commodities. The CME Eurodollar futures contract is the most actively traded interest rate futures contract in the world. Two forums are available for trading CME products, open-outcry trading and the CME Globex® electronic trading platform. In December 2002, CME became the first publicly traded U.S. financial exchange when its common stock began trading on the New York Stock Exchange. CME owns and operates its clearing house and in 2003 agreed to provide clearing services to the CBOT.

Over-the-Counter

The over-the-counter (OTC) market refers to trading venues outside of regulated exchanges. Historically, the OTC market has been operated by OTC voice brokers, who match customer orders for various energy commodities. Electronic brokers, such as the IntercontinentalExchange, also facilitate OTC transactions. Following the financial collapse of Enron and other energy merchants, credit concerns related to OTC matched counter-parties reduced OTC market activity in the energy sector.

Clearing services, such as NYMEX ClearPort^{sm} through its wholly-owned clearing house and ICE Clearing through LCH-Clearnet, have enabled the recovery of OTC energy market activity through counter-party credit mitigation.

Conclusion

The firm's appetite for risk must be the prime factor when choosing a trading venue. Consequently, the Board and Top Management need to decide where to trade, otherwise the firm's traders will make the decision — and they'll make their decision based on personal compensation from trading, not the company's risk appetite. Where a firm trades determines the risks it faces as it executes a firm's trading or risk management strategies.

Notes

[1]**Chapter 16** covers regulation in depth.

[2]Code of Federal Regulations, **Title 17: Commodity and Securities Exchanges. PART 35 — EXEMPTION OF SWAP AGREEMENTS §35.2 Exemption.**

[3]LCH.Clearnet is a European clearing house.

Operational Risk

What can go wrong? The generator fails to operate just when demand is highest, and the company has to buy replacement power at astronomical prices. Coal barges cannot deliver fuel due to ice flows on the river. An explosion on the pipeline cuts off delivery of natural gas. Storms damage power lines. Hot weather pushes demand above the capability of the network to deliver. Difficulties at a nuclear facility halfway around the world cause American regulators to require expensive modifications of domestic nuclear facilities.

Environmental rule changes force utilities to seek new fuels or add equipment to existing power stations. Declining deliverability from existing natural gas wells reduces the security of gas supplies.

Often, operational risks intertwine with financial risks. Nuclear power plants probably operate more reliably than coal fired plants, but malfunctions at the nuclear plants can create financial havoc because the nuclear plant is so large in relation to its owner's assets or output. Unexpectedly poor demand leaves the energy company with the bills paid to secure supply (an operating decision), but without the revenues to pay the bills (the financial consequence). Recently, utilities that have contracted for power (an operational decision) have argued that those contracts are no different than debt, so regulators should take that imputed debt into account when deciding on the risk level and required return on equity of the purchasing utility.

Selecting the technologies for operations involves risk, too. During the 1960s and 1970s, the electric utilities opted for the wrong generating technologies.[1] Today, every decision to choose a particular fuel, or type of generator, or metering device not only involves the risk that something new will do the job better but also that a competitor might utilize the new device, whereas, before, the utility had a monopoly on the market and could prevent the introduction of new devices until the old ones had been paid for. Furthermore, the introduction of new tech-

185

nologies could affect the value of location, as well, thereby changing the economics of even the most modern facilities.

Managing operational risk involves more than making sure that the engineers pay attention to the instruments in front of them. Executives, regulators and directors have to pay attention, as well.

Defining the Problem

Academics and risk managers seem to take a static view of operational risk, sort of declaring, "It happens and there's not much that you can do about it," which calls into doubt the value of attempting to prevent or mitigate the risk. Emery and Finnerty define business risk as:

> The inherent or fundamental risk of a business, without regard to *financial risk* . . . *The nondiversifiable risk* of the business. Also called operating risk.[2]

And, nondiversifiable risk is:

> Risk that cannot be eliminated by diversification.[3]

Eugene F. Brigham defined business risk as:

> The basic risk inherent in a firm's operations. Business risk plus financial risk resulting from the use of debt equals total corporate risk.[4]

The last definition helps, because it seems to say that risk managers that cannot limit operating risk could try to compensate for that weakness by reducing financial risk.

Yet, we know that some firms manage to operate in a manner that minimizes the problems suffered by them compared to other firms in the same line of business using similar equipment, and some firms, through foresight (or sheer luck) avoid the problems altogether. Narrowing the definition of operating risk to something unavoidable trivializes the issue, and gives all parties an easy excuse for doing nothing.

The firm, however, could reduce operating risk if it reexamined how it made major decisions in the first place. In the words of Warren Buffett, "We think that the best way to minimize risk is to *think*."[5]

Making Decisions that Determine Risk

Let us begin with the decision making process. The firm, usually, decides to do or not do something based on a discounted cash flow (DCF) analysis, or variants thereof. In most basic terms, it wants to know how much cash that it will collect over time as a result of a particular decision, as opposed to the cash that it will have to lay out to implement the decision. To determine the answer, the firm applies the DCF analysis as follows. It estimates the flow of cash returns over the life of the particular project, and then determines the present value of those flows using an appropriate discount rate that, supposedly, reflects the risk inherent in the decision.[6] It then compares the present value of the receipts to the cash investment needed to implement the idea. Obviously, the estimated value of the receipts had better equal or exceed the investment, or the decision to go ahead would make no sense, one would think.

Setting aside three serious questions —whether the firm has correctly calculated the original cost of the investment, whether the firm has accurately estimated the receipts from the investment, and whether the firm has used the appropriate discount rate —the DCF approach suffers from another flaw. According to Chance and Peterson:

> Although this approach is generally well accepted, in many instances the DCF approach does not capture the realistic valuation of an investment. Many investments in real assets have opportunities, such as abandonment, expansion, and deferment that might alter the investment's future cash flows and thus its value.[7]

For example, a firm decides to build a power plant. It can invest extra money in equipment that permits the facility to burn a second fuel. No other power plants in the region can burn a second fuel, and their old equipment will not permit modification to do so. The firm decides not to install the additional equipment because the added investment reduces the DCF return earned. The analysis, however, does not take account of the fact that the equipment gives the firm the option to burn another fuel when nobody else in the area can do so. It could offer more reliable service to customers, which would have some value in the market place. The firm could not calculate potential revenues from such advantages, but it does have the flexibility to offer what others cannot, and the option to do so must have some value. The extra equipment reduces operating risk, because the firm can switch to another fuel if supply of primary fuel were interrupted or its price rose dramatically, and it offers the firm the opportunity to offer what competitors cannot.

Why might the firm make a wrong decision? First, if a regulated utility, the regulator might deem the extra investment imprudent, not allowing the utility to earn a return on it. Second, if the regulated utility has in place a fuel or purchased power adjustment clause, it can pass on to consumers all the extra cost of the fuel interruption, the high costs of the primary fuel and the need to buy replacement power. So why bother taking precautionary measures that would obviate an obvious operating risk? Neither the utility nor the regulator gives the real risk taker, the consumer, a voice in the decision. In a sense, the operating risk never becomes a business risk to the utility. An unregulated generator might make a different decision. That generator has no obligation to provide reliable service. It should make the decision based on whether the value of that option to burn a second fuel has greater value than the cost of the additional investment.

In sum, the firm can create or reduce operating risks, in advance, through its investment in the decision making process.

Real Operating Risks

Rivers do freeze up, preventing deliveries of coal by barge. Coal piles freeze up, too, making it difficult to use the coal. Low water levels due to drought not only reduce production of hydroelectric power, but also prevent deliveries of fuel by barge and reduce the output of power stations that must utilize water in the production process. Electricity demand during scorchingly hot weather may damage the distribution network, leading to outages and health emergencies. Unusually hot or cold weather, which affects sales, adds to the variability of earnings and, as a result, to the cost of capital of the energy company. Violent storms take down power lines, force closure of offshore gas production facilities and cause service interruptions. It does not take genius to foresee the recurrence of such events, but it does take money to put into place or maintain assets that prevent or mitigate those occurrences. Given the possibility that global climate change includes the possibility of more severe storm conditions, energy companies might face greater operating risks of these types in the future. Where they cannot take preventive steps or sign up an adequate amount of insurance, they might have to look for financial derivatives that trade in a way that offsets some of the costs of the operating events. Or they can do what they do now: let the customer foot the bill or incur the inconvenience.

The nuclear arena presents operating risks that translate into financial risks. The Federal government has limited the liability of nuclear plant operators from a major nuclear disaster through the Price-Anderson Act, but not the financial consequences of nuclear malfunctions on the nuclear operators, such as the losses when a plant is unable to provide power. The nuclear operation often accounts for a significant part of the utility's assets and its output. Any unusual difficulty at a nuclear facility usually has a serious impact on profitability and production. Furthermore, a nuclear malfunction elsewhere may cause regulators to order expensive modifications in plant or in operating procedures. Thus operating risk extends to the risk of what others do. Yet, the average nuclear plant runs reliably, possibly more reliably than the average coal fired power plant. The business risk of the nuclear operation lies in the enormous size of the nuclear facility in relation to the owner utility, which has, in effect, put too many eggs in one basket. The owner needs to reduce financial risk of concentrated ownership rather than the operating risk inherent in the nuclear facility. The solution may lie in selling ownership shares to other utilities, or putting nuclear ownership in huge companies that have many nuclear facilities.

Fuel costs and availability present major business risks. Merchant generators have tended to rush like lemmings to the same fuel at the same place and time: the cheapest, most available fuel of the moment — natural gas during the last generation building binge. Did they consider the collective impact of those individual decisions on fuel price or deliverability? (For that matter, did the organizations that pick power plants for dispatch consider the risk of a nondiversified fuel supply to the consumers in the region?) Generators take steps to protect themselves from swings in fuel prices, either by signing contracts to purchase fuel at given prices for given periods of time, or by hedging

189

price risks on the commodities markets, to the extent possible. They might buy fuel reserves in the ground, too, hoping that prices received for the power they produce tracks the prices paid by the generators for fuel that goes into their power plants. Those measures, however, do not deal with supply shortfalls caused by pipeline accidents, declines in deliverability from gas wells, miners' strikes or international incidents. Nor do they take into account the possibility that significant changes in the pricing of other fuels could affect the competitiveness of electricity produced by burning a particular fuel. If the energy firms cannot build in enough flexibility to prepare for such eventualities, or devise financial mitigation techniques, then the investment decision must take into account the risks, meaning a higher discount rate for the DCF formula.

Energy sales depend on the ups and downs of the economy as well as from changes in weather conditions. As noted above, extreme weather conditions also affect operating expenses and the ability to produce and deliver energy. Due to the fixed nature of a large part of the energy provider's expenses, a small percentage change in sales can make a profound impact on profits. Most regulatory agencies do not allow for after-the-fact adjustments to cover revenue shortfalls that prevent the utility from earning the allowed return. Most regulatory agencies, during rate cases, adjust results for weather using long term averages that may no longer reflect actual conditions. Earnings variability caused by uncertain sales may disturb shareholders and raise the cost of capital to the utility. A few utilities have taken steps to mitigate the instability by means of the use of weather derivatives, but few, if any, have considered the use of derivatives that might provide protection against sales swings peculiar to their region. (As a simple example, the energy provider sells a large part of its output to a lead mine. Its other customers depend on the mine for employment. The lead business has sharp ups and downs. Perhaps the energy provider should find a financial instrument that rises in value when lead prices decline and declines when lead prices rise. Doing so would protect the company from sharp declines in revenue, although it would also take some of the profit away when sales rose. Or, it might use the financial instrument strategy only after a prolonged rise in prices and economic activity, on the theory that a decline in lead prices from a high point could do severe damage to the local economy, and the purpose of the financial strategy is to protect against the risk of a severe fall. The problem with trying to time the market, as opposed to protecting against extremes, is that the firm starts to get into commodity speculation as opposed to the risk management business.)

Due to energy's central role in the economy and society, as well as the obtrusive nature of its facilities, public policy risks (such as environmentalism, national security and terrorism) must play a role in the evaluation of operational risks. New environmental regulations could affect the profitability of power stations by requiring changes of fuel or reduction of pollutant output. Industry planners should take into account the possibility that the United States will have to take action in regard to greenhouse gases, and that action will target the energy industry above all others. When wildlife experts declare that windmills kill bats, should anyone be surprised? Poor tree trimming practices supposedly led to a major blackout that cost the economy billions of dollars. When will planners spend more time considering how complicated systems fail? Given both terrorist threats and dependence on unfriendly foreign nations for fuel supply, energy purveyors should make preparations for attacks and fuel disruptions a standard part of doing business. The politically incorrect question is whether — in addition to the measures to protect employees and customers that any self-respecting enterprise should take — there exist financial vehicles that would provide financial compensation in case of disaster beyond the usual insurance.

The electric and gas industries spend pathetically small sums on research and development. The industries tend to depreciate assets over decades, thereby indicating their lack of concern that technological change could obsolete their plant and equipment, or disturb their holds on the market. Perhaps nobody can project the future, but Peter F. Drucker advised:

> Any attempts to base today's actions and commitments on *predictions of future events* is futile. The best we can hope to do is to anticipate *future effects of events* which have irrevocably happened.[8]

As examples, superconducting cable and devices could ease congestion on the network. Hybrid or fuel cell vehicles could operate as portable generators plugged into the grid at key locations. Either development could destroy the profitability of many generating plants, erase the rationale for the transmission pricing system being implemented by the Federal Energy Regulatory Commission, and improve the reliability of the network. Superconducting cables, fuel cells and hybrid vehicles already exist. At what point does anyone admit the existence of risk to the existing business or to the market model from the application of already existing technologies? Years of monopolization of the market, regulatory reluctance to face change, and minimal interest in R & D may leave the electric and gas industries vulnerable to technological change because they never think about such changes enough to devise risk mitigating strategies.

Conclusion

Energy firms (and their customers) can take preventive measures, that is instituting procedures or making investments that reduce the risk that events will take place. They can search for financial instruments that mitigate the financial damages caused by such events, ranging from insurance to financial derivatives. They have to balance the costs of such measures against the risks, though.

Probably, the first step involves not buying protection but determining what are the risks. Doing so may require the construction of scenarios for operational and business risks, probably with the help of those who do not subscribe to the usual groupthink that pervades large, slow moving bureaucratic organizations and consensus-driven trade groups, with the scenarios delivered directly to directors and other decision makers, without suppression by those who do not like the outcomes.

After that, the decision makers can decide the need for risk management measures, their feasibility, and, possibly, the need to take directions that avoid the risks altogether. In the end, though, rather than devising formulas that delight the academic, decision makers will have to do what they get paid for, think.

Notes

[1]Leonard S. Hyman, Andrew S. Hyman, and Robert C. Hyman, *America's Electric Utilities: Past, Present, and Future*, Eighth Edition (Vienna, Va: Public Utilities Reports, 2005), Chapter 19.

[2]Douglas R. Emery and John D. Finnerty, *Principles of Finance* (St. Paul: West Publishing, 1991), p. G 5.

[3]*Op. cit.*, p. G 16.

[4]Eugene F. Brigham, *Financial Management Theory and Practice* (Chicago: Dryden Press, 1982), p. 856.

[5]Berkshire Hathaway's Warren Buffett and Wesco Financial's Charlie Munger, "Asset Allocation is Pure Nonsense: The Best Way to Minimize Risk is to *Think*." *Outstanding Investor Digest*, Vol. XIX, Numbers 3 & 4, Dec. 31, 2004, p.32.

[6]The concept of present value is discussed in **Chapter 10.**

[7]Don M. Chance, CFA, and Pamela P. Peterson, CFA, *Real Options and Investment Valuation* (Charlottesville, VA: Research Foundation of the Association for Investment Management and Research, July 2002), p. 1.

[8]Peter Drucker, *Managing for Results: Economic Tasks and Risk Taking Decisions* (New York: Harper & Row, Publishers, 1964), p. 173.

Fraud

Introduction

During the 1990s, suspect business practices such as wash trading, deceptive bookkeeping, and cronyism in the boardroom, brought the energy business into disrepute, and severely damaged the image of the once reliable and trustworthy utility. This fall from grace had more than just moral ramifications — it caused investors to shun the industry and it closed the door to needed capital. It was disruptive not only to capital markets but to all it touched — damaging communities, spawning joblessness, and disrupting energy markets.

This chapter provides an overview of fraudulent financial reporting, and how a company can confront it. It begins by defining fraud in the business context, because this chapter focuses on one element — management fraud. Then the chapter examines common frauds and how they start. Next, the characteristics of common methods of fraudulent financial reporting that have occurred in the past few years are highlighted to point out how fraud happens in the financial statements. To deal with fraud it helps to have models that explain fraud — and can be used to weed it out. With a foundation of understanding what fraud is, the next point of learning is to use models that explain fraud to gain insight into the players and their methods. Most models look at how the interplay of a corporate environment, actors, incentives, and ethics encourage or discourage fraudulent behavior in a corporation.

Once the typical shenanigans are known, it is easier to understand who the perpetrators are, and the environments that permit fraudulent financial reporting. With this knowledge, it is possible to help plan out the governance strategies to counter financial fraud. Fighting financial fraud depends on the work of these six forces: The board, the audit committee, management, internal auditors, external auditors, and outside regulators.

Ultimately, management is the most responsible for producing reliable financial reporting and developing the internal control structure to produce reliable financial reports and to guide the company in an honest and productive manner. If CEOs are to receive the extremely lucrative pay packages that have become common in the past few years, then that salary and position necessitates a responsibility for the quality of financial reporting that the company engages in and the internal controls instituted at the company.

What is Fraud?

What does fraud mean in a business setting? According to Jack C. Robertson:

> *Fraud* consists of knowingly making material misrepresentations of fact, with the intent of inducing someone to believe the falsehood and act upon it and, thus, suffer a loss or damage. This definition encompasses all the varieties by which people can lie, cheat, steal, and dupe other people.[1]

Fraud comes in many varieties:

> *Employee fraud* — "the use of fraudulent means to take money or other property from an employer."[2]

> *Embezzlement* — "employees' or nonemployees' wrongfully taking money or property entrusted to their care."[3]

> *Larceny* — "simple theft."[4]

> *Defalcation* — "another name for employee fraud, embezzlement, and larceny."[5]

As defined by Elliott and Willingham, *Management fraud* is a major subcategory of fraud, "that injures investors and creditors through materially misleading financial statements. . . The class of perpetrators is management; the class of victims is investors and creditors; and the instrument of perpetration is financial statements."[6]

The National Commission on Fraudulent Financial Reporting divides management fraud into: *Fraudulent financial reporting* — "intentional or reckless conduct, whether [by] act or omission, that results in materially misleading financial statements."[7]

> *Errors* — "unintentional misstatements or omissions in financial statements."[8]

Irregularities — "intentional misstatements or omissions in financial statements."[9]

Rezaee defines *Financial statement fraud* as — "a deliberate attempt . . . to deceive or mislead users of published financial statements . . . by preparing and disseminating materially misstated financial statements."[10] Fraudulent statements are not only misstated — they are plain misleading.

Management Fraud[11]

While the perpetrators of fraudulent financial reporting use many different means, the effect of their actions is almost always to inflate or "smooth" earnings or to overstate the company's assets. Other means include concealing potential risks through lack of disclosure of risk factors or financial triggers. Beasley, Carcello, and Hermanson, in their study of fraud argue that:

. . . fraudulent financial reporting usually does not begin with an overt intentional act to distort the financial statements. In many cases, fraudulent financial reporting is the culmination of a series of acts designed to respond to operational difficulties. Initially, the activities may not be fraudulent, but in time they may become increasingly questionable. When the tone set by top management permits or encourages such activities, eventually the result may be fraudulent financial reporting.

Many of the frauds began with misstatements of interim financial statements that were continued in annual financial statement filings.[12]

Beasley, Carcello, and Hermanson determined that:

. . . the two most common techniques used to fraudulently misstate financial statement information involved improper revenue recognition techniques to overstate revenues and improper techniques to overstate assets.[13]

Revenue overstatement techniques include:

• *Fictitious Sales* — No goods are shipped to customers. To cover up such a fraud, employees falsify inventory and shipping records and invoices. Sometimes a company records sales shipped to another company location — or even a warehouse rented for the purpose. In other cases companies pretend to ship goods as if a sale occurred and hide the inventory from auditors.

• *Premature revenue recognition* — Recognizing revenues from a sale after an order is made, but before the goods are shipped. This is often done near the end of a reporting period to make the period's financial books look better.

• *Conditional sales* — Revenues are recorded from sales even though the sale involves contingencies that are unresolved, or sales terms are amended so the customer need not keep the merchandise he bought.

• *Extending sales cutoffs* — Holding the books open at the end of an accounting period to record sales from the next accounting period to make sales records look better for the period that ended.

• *Improper use of the percentage of completion method* — Overstating revenues by increasing the percentage of completion for projects that are underway. The percentage of completion method is used for accounting for revenues from large capital projects.

• *Unauthorized shipments* — Revenues are overstated by shipping goods never ordered by the customer, or by shipping defective products and recording revenues at full, rather than discounted, prices.

• *Consignment sales* — Revenues are recorded for goods placed on consignment with customers or those shipped on a trial basis to customers.[14]

• *Mark-to-market accounting* — According to Mark Bell, a retired PricewaterhouseCoopers audit partner who had extensive experience auditing major U.S. utility clients, a major revenue recognition issue was aggressive or improper application of mark-to-market accounting. While mark-to-market accounting is relatively straightforward in futures markets, it is not so simple in dealing with many of the contracts in the energy markets — notably contracts that are not traded on organized exchanges — but those traded over the counter — often under the provisions of long term contracts. The contracts are often marked-to-model, and with revenues determined by the output of a financial model that is subject to manipulation. In addition, the electric markets are often immature and illiquid, so it can be hard to value a contract over its life, when there is not a clear benchmark with which to compare it. Remember, the mark-to-market value of a futures contract is based on the value of an **underlying** that trades in a transparent, observable market — such as a stock price on an open market. That transparency does not exist in electric markets.[15]

In some cases, the external auditors didn't detect the fraud because employees falsified confirmations of the sales or influenced third parties to alter the confirmations.[16]

Overstating Assets

In Beasley, Carcello, and Hermanson's report, the most misstated assets were inventory and accounts receivable. Other misstated assets were cash, investments, patents, and valuations of oil, gas, and mineral reserves.[17] Misstatements of assets usually revolve around:

• Understating allowances for receivables.

• Inflating the value of existing assets by valuing them at the higher of market, not cost values (when the market value is higher).

• Recording nonexistent assets.[18]

Off-Balance Sheet Items and Related Party Transactions

Two areas that helped bring Enron down were its accounting treatment of off-balance sheet items and its concealment of related party transactions, covered extensively in Kurt Eichenwald's book, *A Conspiracy of Fools.* Enron took assets off its balance sheet for the purpose of the financial statements, while creating large future liabilities, due to their structuring.[19] In addition, these entities were managed by the Chief Financial Officer, Andrew Fastow, although his involvement was not specified in the annual report — it was simply stated that a senior officer was involved in these transactions.[20] Fastow convinced the board that it was better to have assets sold to a group controlled by its chief financial officer and backed by Enron assets rather than to an outside (as in no connection with Enron) group.[21] This conflict of interest was approved by Enron's board, apparently under the impression that Fastow would spend only a modest amount of time on the deals and receive minimal financial benefits, and that the limited partners had no relation to Enron — a condition for the off balance sheet treatment, according to accounting rules that existed at that time.[22] The problem was that the many of the limited partners were Enron employees, their families, friends and domestic partners.[23]

In the end, these off balance sheet entities became Fastow's focus at work — not Enron.[24] He even used Enron resources and employees to run the entities.[25] When Enron was doing deals with the entities, Fastow had influence over the compensation of those who were negotiating on behalf of Enron and he pressured them to do deals that benefited his entities to the disadvantage of Enron, to which he had a fiduciary responsibility — a clear conflict of interest.[26]

Enron's troubles (which started with the resignation of CEO Jeff Skilling) accelerated once it was discovered that Andrew Fastow was the related party behind the entities, and that the limited partners were not unrelated to Enron. This meant that the partnerships were invalid as a mechanism to keep the liabilities off the books, which meant the liabilities came back on the books, and earnings had to be restated, because the financial statements did not accurately depict the firm's finances.[27] These disclosures proved fatal to Enron, because Enron's creditors refused to deal with it — a deathblow to a trading firm that relies on its creditworthiness to transact deals in the over-the-counter energy markets.[28]

How can Fraud be Explained?

The CRIME model developed by Zabihollah Rezaee categorizes management fraud by these elements:

C = Cooks

R = Recipes

I = Incentives

M = Monitoring

E = End Results

Cooks

Cooks instigate frauds. Usually they are top management enabled by weak boards of directors that may consist of many insiders.[29]

Recipes

The most common recipes are overstating revenues and assets. Another, less common, recipe is understating liabilities.[30] In addition, according to Mark Bell, another major recipe is failing to properly disclose significant risks, such as trigger events that are part of debt covenants, such as a drop in a credit rating, that could lead to acceleration of debt payments, or invoke contract provisions that require a company to put cash up to keep on doing business.

Incentives

Incentives for manipulating financial statements include:

• Enabling a firm to meet the investment community's expectations

• Obtaining access to capital markets and related financing.[31]

• Enrichment of top executives — this may be the biggest incentive of all.[32]

Monitoring

The quality of the monitoring of a firm's operations affects the likelihood of fraud. Management needs to create a strong internal control culture, with vigorous internal and external audit functions. Companies with less financial stress have less incentive to engage in fraudulent financial reporting.

These factors create environments in which fraud flourishes:

• Boards and audit committees that are not vigilant.

• Weak internal controls.

• No internal audit function — or a weak one.

• Weak external auditor.

201

• Unusual and complex transactions.

• Financial estimates by management that require substantial discretion and judgement.[33]

• Rich and improperly designed incentive plans.[34]

End Results

The end results of fraudulent financial reporting involve more than misstated books. They include loss of value in the market, bankruptcy and criminal charges.[35] The sad or unfortunate element is that this fraud obfuscates business problems that if dealt with earlier could have enabled the company to minimize losses or avoid the extreme consequences that resulted from the fraud.[36]

How can a Company be Assessed to See if Fraud is Likely?

One model that assesses a corporate environment for the likelihood of fraud is Rezaee's 3Cs model of Conditions, Corporate Structure, and Choice.[37]

Conditions

This model starts with a look at whether conditions are favorable for the promotion of fraud. Does the general environment encourage fraud? Certain industries seem to follow similar patterns — for example incidents of wash trading or gaming of markets (*e.g.* California) seemed to spread across the energy industry.[38] It may be a case of follow the leader or shared norms.[39] Is there pressure to make the numbers and the ability to make those numbers through fraud?

Conditions that may create an impetus for fraud include:

• Ineffective board(s).

• Weak audit committee.

• Dominant/unaccountable management.[40]

• Inadequate review of executives or disclosure.

• Material related party transactions.

- No/weak internal audit function.

- Poor credit rating.

- Bad economic conditions.

- Inadequate cash flow.

- Restrictive contractual covenants.

- Dependent on a few customers.[41]

- Highly leveraged/risk transactions.[42]

Corporate Culture

Corporate Culture — does it provide the opportunity and motivation to commit fraud? The nature of corporate governance can influence the possibility of management fraud. A company or group that is very cohesive and insulates itself from the outside world (including the outside world's *mores*) is more likely to engage in fraudulent behavior.

Too often, top management is looking out for itself. Compensation committees need to design mechanisms that encourage managers to align themselves with shareholders, but not to manipulate the numbers that are used to determine their compensation. The overwhelming fact is that top management is responsible for most fraudulent financial reporting.[43]

When a company ventures outside of its core competency without adequate infrastructure or expertise, the firm can increase the chances of fraudulent behavior.[44] The lack of infrastructure can lead to a lack of adequate internal control. This is often exacerbated by a lemming like rush that companies make by all deciding to go into a new business — and this sense of urgency — as in, "we need to get there first" — may inhibit a focus on control. For example, Enron ventured out of its area of expertise by getting into the broadband business — it did not have the adequate infrastructure or expertise to handle that business, and the business was plagued by illegalities. In another case, with the restructuring of the utility business, there was a great rush to get into energy trading — whether a firm had a justification for going into that business or not. It was seen as a hot business and a way to make a lot of money as well as boost the stock price. Unfortunately, utilities often did not build up the infrastructure and risk management expertise to get into trading. A few years after there was a rush to get into trading, there was a mass exodus from proprietary trading after trading units cratered and were investigated by regulatory authorities such as the Commodities Futures Trading Commission and fined for their behavior.

Choice

Choice looks at the choices of accounting principles that management selects — and whether it chooses to engage in aggressive accounting that may cross over the line into fraudulent accounting. The accounting options a firm chooses indicate its proclivity towards aggressive accounting and the potential to engage in fraudulent behavior. This behavior is encouraged by the company's application of accounting principles. According to Mark Bell, firms that are engaged in rules based accounting are more likely to engage in improper accounting than principles based firms.[45]

Who are the Likely Perpetrators?

The most common perpetrators of financial statement fraud are usually the company's top management — notably the CEO and CFO. In fact, according to the Treadway Commission, the SEC cited top management — CEO, President, and CFO as being involved in 66 percent of cases against public companies.[46]

Fraudsters are not always easy to spot within firms. They typically have characteristics that make them look like upstanding citizens such as:

- Married.

- Education beyond high school.

- Church members.

- Wide range in age — from teenagers to over 60.

- Short to long term employees.

- Unlikely to be divorced.

- No arrest record.

- Social conformists.[47]

How can an Individual's Risk of Committing Fraud be Assessed?

The likelihood of an individual committing fraud depends on motivation, opportunity, and lack of integrity within the organization.

Motive

"A motive is some kind of pressure experienced by a person and believed unshareable with friends and confidants."[48] Some motives that can push usually honest people over the edge to commit fraud are:[49]

- "Getting back" at the company for some perceived or actual wrong.

- Greed.

- Ego gratification.

- A feeling of being above the law.

Any number of factors can encourage an individual to commit fraud. When attempting to assess the risk of fraudulent reporting, managers need to consider the question, "Why do good people do bad things?" This may help managers elucidate the factors that lead to fraudulent behavior and help stop this behavior.

Beasley, Carcello and Hermanson found the most common reasons for committing business fraud were to:

- Make the financial reports look better.

- Boost the stock price.

- Cover up misappropriation of assets.

- Maintain or obtain a stock exchange listing.[50]

Rezaee gave these reasons why managements manipulate their books:

- Obtain credit and/or capital.

- Conceal performance deficiencies.

- Hide improper transactions.

• Temporarily resolve financial difficulties.

• Management's compensation packages.

• It enhances the value of management's personal stock holdings.

• It helps the management get promoted or keep a job.[51] This is often common in decentralized organizations with divisional and branch managers.

Many companies manage earnings to meet the expectations of Wall Street, which is obsessed with the quarterly earnings of companies. Firms are often punished when they don't make their "number" in their quarterly reports. This can affect options based compensation for senior executives. One definition of earnings management is, "purposeful intervention in the external financial reporting process with the intent of obtaining some private gain."[52]

Opportunity

"An opportunity is an open door for solving the unshareable problem in secret by violating a trust."[53] Opportunities to commit financial statement fraud arise because of ineffective and irresponsible corporate governance.[54] It is easier to engage in fraudulent financial reporting when the fraud is easy to commit and detection is unlikely. Opportunities for fraud are more apparent when:

• The board and audit committee are not vigilant in overseeing financial reporting.

• Weak internal accounting controls exist. Controls can be overwhelmed by a rapid increase in sales, acquisition of new entities, and entry into a new business line.

• Infrequent or complicated transactions such as mergers and acquisitions or closing an operation are taking place.

• Making accounting estimates which allow significant subjective judgement by management, such as reserve accounts.

• Internal audit operations are ineffective due to insufficient or inadequate staffing or limited scope of coverage.[55]

Integrity

"Unimpeachable integrity is the ability to act in accordance with the highest moral and ethical values at all times."[56] The level of integrity is very important when a company is faced with situations when accounting principles for certain transactions do not exist, are undergoing evolution, or are open to differing interpretations, because these situations create opportunities for financial fraud in the choice of accounting procedures.[57]

Managers with higher integrity will likely choose more conservative accounting procedures.

What are Organizational Characteristics of Fraudulent Companies?

Organizational factors that encourage fraudulent financial reporting include:

- Autocratic leadership and poor ethical guidance.

- Complex rules, regulations, and policies that may present vague lines between right and wrong.

- Unrealistic financial targets.

- Insufficient internal controls, especially organizations undergoing rapid change.

- Highly autonomous divisions.

- Deficient internal audit operation.

- Weak boards of directors and audit committees.[58]

- Lack of financial competence.

- Lack of training on ethics — which shows that firms do not value ethics.[59]

These organizational factors may induce individuals to engage in deceptive financial reporting. An individual's perception of right and wrong can be affected by the ethical atmosphere in the workplace. Individuals may rationalize fraudulent financial reporting as a way to fit in and be part of the corporate team. At other times, individuals may be involved in deceptive financial reporting due to ignorance. Given the complexity of accounting rules, sales and marketing personnel may not know they are violating GAAP when they record undelivered goods as sales.[60]

The opportunities to commit fraudulent financial reporting are increased by weak governance. There are a number of indicators of weak governance. These include:

> • Insiders on the board of directors. The board is supposed to be responsible to the shareholders for oversight of the company. If management or those who benefit from relations with the company are on the board, they can not independently represent shareholders. Some governance experts, including Dennis Chookaszian, accountant, former Chairman and CEO of CNA Insurance, and noted authority on management fraud and internal controls, state the contrary view. They believe that insiders are valuable board members, as long as there are a sufficient number of outside board members, because having the insiders can promote better understanding of the company's operations.[61]

> • Founder as CEO. A founder may tend to view the company as his — even if he does not have 51% control of the stock. These types of CEOs may view the firm as their own — and use the company as a personal piggy bank.

> • No audit committee. With the introduction of the Sarbanes-Oxley Act, all NYSE, AMEX, and NASDAQ listed stocks need to have audit committees.

Beasley, Carcello, and Hermanson, in their study, discern characteristics of fraudulent companies, managements, and boards.

Characteristics of Fraudulent Companies

Many companies were under severe strain before the fraud took place. These financial conditions may have motivated the fraudulent behavior.

Characteristics of the Control Environment (Top Management and Board)

• Fraud went to the top of organizations. In 72% of the instances, the SEC named the CEO as being part of the fraud, and in 43% of the cases the CFO was named. *In toto*, in 83% of the cases the SEC named either the CEO or CFO as being associated with financial statement fraud.[62]

• These companies had weak audit committees, which rarely met and were dominated by company insiders and those with close ties to the company. Most audit committee members were not certified accountants or had not worked in accounting or finance.[63]

Characteristics of the Board

The company's founder and board members owned a major share of the company.[64] In addition these boards were dominated by insiders and grey directors (outsiders with special ties to company management) who had significant ownership stakes in the firms and little experience serving on other boards.[65] In almost 40% of the companies involved, family relationships existed between directors and/or officers. In over 20% of the cases officers held incompatible job functions, such as CEO **and** CFO.[66]

What are Internal Controls? What Can They do?

Internal controls refer to controls over operational tasks (such as production and maintenance), controls over financial reporting, and compliance with laws and regulations. Controls over financial reporting are more than just internal accounting controls.

The corporate control environment is the climate in which the internal accounting controls are instituted and financial statements are prepared. This environment reflects the company's approach to financial reporting. A company that supports honest financial reporting will generate a stronger control environment than one that encourages individuals to play games with accounting rules and cross over into the realm of aggressive accounting.

One place to start building internal controls is through a written code of corporate conduct and let all employees know what will and will not be tolerated. In fact, Section 406 of the Sarbanes-Oxley Act of 2002 requires issuers of securities to disclose if they have adopted a code of ethics for senior financial officers — and to explain why if they haven't.[67] Of course, if the code is not enforced — especially for top management — it will not be respected by anyone else.[68] For this reason, there needs to be follow up with adequate ethics training to insure that all employees are aware of the code and the company's commitment to it.

In addition, a system, independent of top management, needs to be set up to allow employees to voice complaints or express concerns about unethical behavior, and be assured that these concerns are followed up on with action from on high — and when necessary the board may need to discipline or dismiss top management based on these findings.[69]

Internal Control

Section 404 of the Sarbanes-Oxley Act of 2002 has forced companies to focus on their internal controls, which has created a great deal of work in this area. First, though, what is internal control? According to The Committee of Sponsoring Organizations of the Treadway Commission, internal control is:

> A process, effected by an entity's board of directors, management and other personnel, designed to provide reasonable assurance regarding the achievement of objectives in the following categories:
>
> • Effectiveness and efficiency of operations
>
> • Reliability of financial reporting
>
> • Compliance with applicable laws and regulations[70]

The Sarbanes-Oxley Act is quite broad in its requirements relating to internal control:

> **SEC. 404. MANAGEMENT ASSESSMENT OF INTERNAL CONTROLS.**
>
> (a) RULES REQUIRED. — The [Securities and Exchange] Commission shall prescribe rules requiring each annual report required by section 13(a) or 15(d) of the Securities Exchange Act of 1934 (15 U.S.C. 78m or 78o(d)) to contain an internal control report, which shall —

(1) state the responsibility of management for establishing and maintaining an adequate internal control structure and procedures for financial reporting; and

(2) contain an assessment, as of the end of the most recent fiscal year of the issuer, of the effectiveness of the internal control structure and procedures of the issuer. An attestation made under this subsection shall be made in accordance with the standards for attestation engagements issued or adopted by the [Public Company Accounting Oversight] Board. Any such attestation shall not be the subject of a separate engagement.[71]

SEC Rules on Internal Controls

The SEC's rules related to Section 404 provide a narrow description of what internal controls are considered for the sake of the act. The SEC provides this definition of *internal control over financial reporting:*

A process designed by, or under the supervision of, the company's principal executive and principal financial officers, or persons performing similar functions, and effected by the company's board of directors, management, and other personnel, to provide reasonable assurance regarding the reliability of financial reporting and the preparation of financial statements for external purposes in accordance with generally accepted accounting principles and includes those policies and procedures that:

(1) Pertain to the maintenance of records that, in reasonable detail, accurately and fairly reflect the transactions and dispositions of the assets of the company;

(2) Provide reasonable assurance that transactions are recorded as necessary to permit preparation of financial statements in accordance with generally accepted accounting principles, and that receipts and expenditures of the company are being made only in accordance with authorizations of management and directors of the company; and

(3) Provide reasonable assurance regarding prevention or timely detection of unauthorized acquisition, use or disposition of the company's assets that could have a material effect on the financial statements.[72]

The SEC requires the company to issue, "A statement identifying the framework used by management to conduct the required evaluation of the effectiveness of of the company's internal control over financial reporting."[73] Although the SEC does not require the use of the COSO framework, specifically it notes that, "The COSO framework satisfies our criteria and may be used as an evaluation framework for purposes of management's annual internal control evaluation and disclosure requirements."[74] Management needs to apply the COSO framework, because while the SEC presents the framework as one possible framework for internal control, the Public Accounting Oversight Board (PCAOB), in its standards on *auditing* of management's assessment of internal controls, states: "the COSO report *Internal Control — Integrated Framework* . . . provides a suitable and available framework for purposes of management's assessment. For that reason, the performance and reporting directions in this standard are based on the COSO framework."[75]

Managers who wish to prepare their controls, and get ready for the audit, are well advised to consult the framework and the PCAOB's standards for evaluating management's assessment of internal controls.

While these rules need to be complied with to meet the needs of the Act, internal control is more than about meeting SEC requirements. It is a process that allows a company to better manage itself — and help meet its goals. Although the SEC definition needs to be followed in order to comply with the Sarbanes-Oxley Act, the COSO approach creates an internal control process that goes beyond mere compliance with the law, to build a process within a business (not just an add-on) that can better manage the organization.

Internal Control with the COSO Framework

Internal control goes beyond the relatively narrow definition used in the Sarbanes-Oxley rules. Management needs to develop a system of internal controls based on the COSO Framework, discussed in the report, *Internal Control — Integrated Framework.*[76] As seen in Figure 15-1, the COSO cube, the framework is based on the five components of internal control (Control Environment, Risk Assessment, Control Activities, Information and Communications, and Monitoring that are necessary to achieve the three objectives of internal control:

- Effectiveness and efficiency of operations

- Reliability of financial reporting

- Compliance with applicable laws and regulations

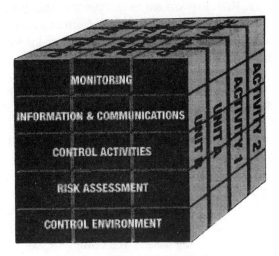

Figure 15-1: COSO Cube

Source: Institute of Internal Auditors, *Tone at the Top*: Issue 28, Nov. 2005.

The five components are applied to the three objectives of control across the enterprise. At a minimum the components need to be effectively implemented across all objectives at all levels of the firm to assure a *de minimis* level of internal control.[77]

The five components of good internal control are:

1. *Control Environment* — The tone set at the top creates an atmosphere that will determine the effectiveness of the controls — if they are a priority of the board and management, and management abides by them, there is greater chance of creating effective internal controls. The control environment is a function of employees' integrity, ethics, competence; management's *modus operandi* and attention to its people, and the attention and direction from the board.[78]

2. *Risk Assessment* — The reader of this book is fully aware that an entity faces all sorts of risks from inside and outside of the company. Needless to say, these risks need to be carefully assessed. However, before risks can be assessed, the firm needs to clearly set its objectives regarding operational goals, financial reporting, and compliance with laws and regulations. Then it is able to assess the risks that could prevent achievement of those objectives. Risk assessment is the process that leads to identifying and analyzing the risks that could affect achieving the objectives, which can guide how to manage the risks. Provisions need to be made for risks that come with change.[79]

3. *Control Activities* — Policies and procedures put in place to make sure that management edicts are carried out within the organization. These control activities are designed to assure that the organization takes the necessary steps to manage the risks that could affect the achievement of the company's objectives. Control activities need to function throughout the company, at all levels to assure that the company is focused on its objectives and minimizing risks that they are not achieved. Control activities range from reviewing operating performance, policies for authorizing funds, protecting assets, and complying with laws and regulations.

4. *Information and Communication* — Internal control depends on information and communication. The company needs to identify, capture, and communicate in a timely manner the information that is needed to create reports on operating performance, financials, and compliance with laws and regulations — the three objectives of internal control. The information required to operate and control the business, is generated not only from within, but also from outside the company. (Outside information that affects business decisions could include changes in fuel prices, or financial reporting regulations, or changes in law that affect the firm).

This objective requires more than just capturing information. Control also depends on how a information flows throughout the organization.

Effective communication means that information flows up, down, and around the organization. The message from the top needs to get out that control activities and responsibilities are serious business. Management needs to reinforce that message through behavior, not words, that reinforces the message of the importance of internal control. Employees need to be trained on their role in the internal control system, and the importance of their responsibilities in the organization. Additionally, information from the organization needs to flow up to top management, so gaps in control can be identified. This includes provisions for a whistleblowing program. In addition, the firm needs to hear from outside parties, as a way of exercising internal control. (For example a company would want to hear from its customers if the customer were receiving a large amount of unordered goods — a sign of a possible revenue recognition fraud.)

5. *Monitoring* — It is one thing to actually have the controls in place — on paper — and another to make sure that they are actually working.[80] Thus, internal controls require monitoring to measure the system's quality. Monitoring internal controls can be through ongoing monitoring, separate evaluations, or a combination of the two methods. Ongoing monitoring takes place over the normal course of operations, consisting of regular management and supervisory activities that are part of employees' normal duties. The range and frequency of separate evaluations (such as internal and external audits) depend on the risk of control failure and the potential impact of the failure. Deficiencies in internal control should be reported to the managers of the operation, and to the level of management one step above. Serious matters need to go to top managers or the board, depending on the situation and who is involved.

Conclusions about Management and Fraud

1. Fraud is more common when management has a lax attitude towards internal controls.

2. Lax attitudes encourage unethical behavior.

3. Organizations with lax attitudes toward internal controls show more warning signs of fraud (red flags).[81]

Setting the Tone at the Top

The tone at the top, set by the board of directors and management, can create an environment that discourages fraudulent financial reporting, and makes it more likely to be detected, if it does occur. In fact the tone at the top — if it favors honest reporting may be the most important factor in creating honest financials.[82] The Treadway Commission recommended three steps for setting the tone at the top:

1. Identify and understand the factors that can lead to fraudulent financial reporting, including factors unique to the company.

2. Assess the risk of fraudulent financial reporting that these factors create within the company.

3. Design and implement internal controls that will provide reasonable assurance that fraudulent financial reporting will be prevented or detected.[83]

What Environmental Factors Influence the Probability of Fraud? How?

Many frauds are driven by a need to create financial reports that will make it easier to sell stock or debt — especially to increase the cash received from offerings. In addition, reports may be manipulated to avoid the triggering of restrictive debt covenants or to cover up poor performance. Preventing fraud depends on understanding these incentives, and trying to minimize them.

Unrealistic budgets also place pressures on managers — especially when they involve arbitrarily determined numbers delivered from the top, and bonus plans for employees that are based on short term economic performance, especially when a bonus is a large portion of an individual's compensation.[84]

Conditions Associated with Fraudulent Financial Reporting

There are a number of environmental factors associated with fraudulent financial reporting.

• Internal controls are weak.

• Management is dominated by an individual or small group of executives.

• Aggressive and domineering management emphasizes earnings projections.

• The company is a laggard in profitability in its industry.

• The company is decentralized with little monitoring.

• The auditors have expressed doubts about the company as a going concern.

• The company has many complex accounting and financial reporting issues.

• The company has related-party transactions that are out-of-the-ordinary and significant in size.

• Management engages in many disputes with auditors.[85]

What are the Basics of a Fraud Fighting Program?

All right, where can a company start? The prevention, detection, and correction model provides a good start. Then it is down to governance.

Here is an outline of the ingredients for a fraud fighting program:

Prevention:

• Good corporate governance.

• Vigilant and competent board.

• Vigilant and competent audit committee.

• Diligent and competent management.

• Effective internal audit function.

Detection:

• Adequate/effective internal controls.

• Independent legal counsel with strong sense of fiduciary responsibility to shareholders.[86]

• Alert, skeptical external auditors.

• External regulatory oversight.

Correction:

- Restate current year fraudulent financials.

- Do same for previous years.

- Deal with the interaction of motivation and opportunity that lead to the fraud.

- Set up strategies to restore confidence in reports.[87]

The Six-Legged Stool — Corporate Governance to Counteract Fraudulent Financial Reporting

Rezaee argues that quality financial reporting rests on a stool made up of six legs: the Board of Directors, the Audit Committee, Management, Internal Audit, External Audit and Governing Bodies.

Board of Directors

The board of directors has an explicit function in a firm as the designated representatives of the shareholders — the owners of the firm.

Directors have oversight responsibility for the firm's financial health. Their job is to increase shareholder value by minimizing the expropriation of wealth via financial statement fraud.[88] According to Rezaee, they need to also:

- Represent investors.

- Safeguard investors' capital.

- Approve management decisions.

- Assess management performance.

- Monitor management and design compensation policies that discourage excessive risk taking and align executives with shareholders' interests. Option compensation does not align executives with shareholders' interests because option holders, who have no invested cash at risk, benefit from stock price rises, but are not hurt when prices fall.

- Oversee audit effectiveness.

- Assure integrity, reliability, and quality of financial reporting.

- Select/evaluate and replace CEO.

- Review and approve strategy and financial decisions.[89]

- Advise management on major issues.

- Oversee:

    - Internal Controls.

    - Risk Management.

    - Compliance.

- Nominate Directors and insure good governance.[90]

Guidelines for Improving Professionalism of Board Members

Given that the market values outsiders on boards, perhaps the market will also value boards that are highly professional in their approach to their responsibilities. The National Association of Corporate Directors in its 1999 Board Guidelines offered some suggestions for board members on how to do a good job:

- Board members should be actively involved in board matters — not just passive observers.

- Members should limit service to a few boards — it takes a lot of time and work to be an effective board member.

- Board members need to immerse themselves in the industry and understand what is happening.

- Board members must be able to read a balance sheet and understand financial ratios.

- Own a significant equity position — board members who have a significant monetary interest in the firm are likely to pay careful attention to governance matters.[91]

Other findings from accounting literature on key aspects of board governance point the path toward better governance.

- CEO's may try to influence board members through perks, including excessive compensation.

• Dual leadership (separate CEO and Chairman) is better. The CEO as chairman of the board is to be avoided because it puts the board in the uncomfortable position of managing one of their own members. One danger arises when the CEO is the Chairman of the Board, and he attempts to use the power of his position to pressure board members on decisions, because he "knows better" or has packed the board with his friends and will not incur much opposition. Dennis Chookaszian, holds the contrary viewpoint that the CEO as chairman is satisfactory, provided that the company has appointed a lead director, as discussed below in the *Guidelines for Improving Professionalism of Board Members.*[92]

• The board, not the management, needs to nominate new directors.

• Boards need outside directors with significant tenure, as they provide better oversight and appear to be more questioning of management.[93] Outside directors are valuable because they offer an independent voice on the firm's operations and are not captive of management. The significant tenure can make a difference because these directors will have more knowledge of the firm and are often willing to confront management. Boards need to be aware of grey directors — these directors may not be employees, but have close ties with the management.

• Smaller boards. Large boards can often lead to inertia and groupthink — and the ability of members to coast along on the work of others. A small board makes the failings of members obvious early on — and requires members to work and pay attention lest they be exposed as lazy or incompetent.

In addition, Beasley, Carcello, and Hermanson noted the dangers that stem from family ties within companies:

Investors should be aware of the possible complications arising from family relationships and from individuals (founders, CEO/board chairs, etc.) who hold significant power or incompatible job functions.[94]

They also found that:

"The CEO and board Chair were the same person in 66 percent of the cases [of fraudulent financial reporting cited in AAER's between 1987 and 1997]. The board Chair was a non-company executive in 16 percent of cases. The company founder and the current CEO were the same person or the original CEO/President was still in place in 45 percent of the companies."[95]

Boards need to pay very close attention to the incentive packages offered to senior executives at merger and acquisition time. If the CEO or other executive has structured an extremely generous payout that depends on the completion of a merger or acquisition, it would not help the executive if something negative in the financials came up that could scuttle the merger and resultant payout. Boards need to very carefully consider the financial motivations of managers that may push for a merger or acquisition — as it is possible their interests are not aligned with those of the shareholders. One way for boards to decrease the possibility of fraud around buyout time is to make sure the deal is not contingent on perks for managers, but simply shareholder interests. At least this will help frame the decision around shareholders and not managers and may reduce pressure from management to engage in questionable acquisitions or ventures.

Code of Conduct

Creating a corporate code of conduct helps create an environment that discourages management fraud. The code clarifies the company's commitment to doing business in an ethical and lawful manner. If desired, codes can specify prohibited acts and steps to take when violations are found.[96] Ideally, a code should create open channels of communication that allow an employee to bring suspected fraud to management's attention without fear of reprisals.[97] The audit committee should regularly review management's compliance with the code and management's programs to insure that the code is enforced throughout the firm. This is essential, because without a strong commitment from boards and management to abide by the codes, they are not helpful.[98]

In addition, the company needs to make a strong commitment to ethics training and follow up on its commitment to ethics. Putting together a corporate code of conduct is not that difficult — living by it is another matter. That is why ethics training is important — to make all employees aware of the firm's ethical policies — which in addition to pointing out what not to do, also needs to teach employees how to communicate ethical concerns so they are heard on top. The firm needs to set up a whistleblowing process independent of management that reports directly to the board.[99]

<u>Early Warning Signals</u>

An authority on boards, Douglas Enns, cautions boards against the belief that detailed reviews of internal controls and enterprise risk management systems will lead to clear manifestations of early warnings of control problems. This arises because boards will not see the signals unless they are looking for them, and important signals come from changes in the behavior of executives. Boards, because of their distance from day-to-day activities may spot problems that management may not spot. The directors, according to Enns, need to be fully on board to look for potential problems and be prepared to act on them.

Boards and management could benefit, according to Enns in setting aside time to go over potential early warning signals of problems, and putting mechanisms in place to deal with these problems if they materialize.

What should board members look for? Board members must be aware that companies usually don't go bankrupt or perform poorly without warning signs. These signs could include problems with customers, engaging in the revenue recognition tricks highlighted above, and deterioration in turnover of receivables among others. If the top management does not seem to be aware of these matters or of emerging threats and competitors, then the board has signs that it needs to investigate further.

If directors have concerns about the company's course, then they need to bring them up with management and with other board members. Otherwise, holding off could allow events to materialize that would have far worse consequences than upsetting the management or other board members.[100]

Audit Committee

The audit committee is in a strong position to make sure that the systems are in place to prevent, uncover, and disclose fraudulent financial reporting.[101] Active audit committees make fraud less likely. In order to do this, audit committees should meet frequently. In addition, an audit committee needs:

(1) to be informed and vigilant,

(2) to have its duties and responsibilities set forth in a written charter, and

(3) to be given resources and authority adequate to discharge its responsibilities.[102]

Audit committees must review the company's assessment of the risk of fraudulent financial reporting and insure that the management has processes in place to deal with these risks and comply with the code of conduct. The committee should have direct and unobstructed access to the internal auditor and vice versa.[103] The internal auditor should be responsible to the audit committee — and management should not be able to interfere with that relationship.

Pay Attention to End of Period Financials

Since misstatements often occur at or near the end of a fiscal period, in order to make that period look better than it was, the audit committee needs to make careful consideration of and testing of internal controls related to transaction cutoff dates and asset valuation.[104]

Sarbanes-Oxley Requirements for the Audit Committee

Section 301 of the Sarbanes-Oxley Act of 2002 prohibits the national securities exchanges (primarily the NYSE, AMEX, and Nasdaq) from listing the security of any company that does not comply with audit committee provisions of the Sarbanes Oxley Act.[105] These are the key criteria for compliance:

- Audit committee members must be independent. That means audit committee members can't receive compensation other than for serving on the board. A company's employees can't serve on its audit committee. Employees of corporate affiliates are also prohibited from serving on the audit committee.

- The audit committee is responsible for appointing, paying, retaining and overseeing the external auditor's work. The external auditors must report directly to the audit committee.

- The audit committee must have authority and funds to hire and engage independent advisors and consultants, including legal counsel, when necessary to perform its duties. Each company will be required to provide funding, as determined by the audit committee, to pay the external auditors, outside consultants, advisors, and counsel. In addition, the company is required to pay the administrative expenses of the audit committee which are necessary for it to do its job.

• The audit committee has to establish procedures for resolving complaints about financial reporting matters, including confidential and anonymous submission of complaints by employees (whistleblowing).[106]

While the SEC's regulations for audit committees from the Sarbanes-Oxley Act specify the basic requirements audit committees need to meet, they only represent the beginning. These suggestions will help the committee go beyond those basic requirements:

• *Composition, Size, and Term of Appointment* — Not less than three independent directors, with accounting and financial backgrounds. Keep the committee small to encourage active participation. It is advisable to have staggered terms to allow for continuity — yet also to allow fresh ideas to percolate.

• *Meetings* — The committee needs to meet regularly, with special meetings called as needed. Meetings with the external accountant and internal auditor should be private — *i.e.* no managers present.

• *Reporting to the Board of Directors* — The committee should report regularly to the full board after each meeting.

• *Expand Knowledge of Company Operations* — A better informed audit committee will be more effective. It can get that way by systematically reviewing the company's financials.

• *Company Counsel* — The committee should meet regularly with the general counsel, and outside counsel when needed, to discuss legal matters that may have a major effect on the financial statements.

• *Audit Plans* — The committee should review the audit plans of the chief internal accountant and external accountant with each of them to ensure coordination of efforts. The committee needs to determine if the proposed audit scope will enable detection of fraud or weak internal controls.

• *Electronic Data Processing* — The committee needs to work with internal and external accountants to have them review the company's electronic data processing procedures and controls, and inquire about how to institute security systems to protect against computer fraud.

• *Areas Requiring Special Attention* — The committee should make sure that the external and internal accountants bring unusual matters to its attention.[107]

• *Designating a Chief Ethics Officer* — Creating a Chief Ethics Officer is a good way to establish the tone at the top — provided this office is not just window dressing. The Chief Ethics Officer should be responsible for investigating ethical problems at the firm — including those of fraudulent financial reporting that are brought to his attention via a communication route, such as a hotline, that top management does not control or access. The Chief Ethics Officer needs to report to the audit committee (or board if necessary) concerning violations of the company's ethical practices, charter, or laws or regulations. This allows those lower down in the firm, who may be aware of misdeeds, to get the word to the top. This role could be handled by the general counsel or a branch of his office.[108]

The Job of the Audit Committee

The members of the audit committee need to:

1. Monitor the audit process.

2. Make sure that management understands that the audit committee will not tolerate fraudulent financial reporting.

3. Review management's interaction with the internal auditor.

4. Have candid discussions with management, the internal auditor, and external auditor on issues of judgement and quality in the financial reporting process.

5. Be diligent and knowledgeable.

6. Evaluate management's assessment of the possibility of fraud and its impact on the company.

7. Evaluate internal control practices, especially the tone at the top.

8. Evaluate the internal auditor's testing of fraud controls and review the auditor's findings.

9. Assure that internal audit has a direct link to the audit committee.

10. Assure that internal audit has resources that it needs.

11. Make sure that financial statements have been tested with computerized fraud tools.

12. Make sure the firm has installed fraud sentinels on its computer systems.

13. Furnish a report in the proxy.[109]

Audit Committee Charter

The charter of the audit committee should specify:

1. The committee's role, authority, and responsibilities.

2. The composition of the committee.

3. The frequency of meetings.

4. That the external auditor is accountable to the board and audit committee — not to management.

5. That the external auditor is independent of the firm.

Management

Management bears ultimate responsibility for financial reporting to create financial statements that are in accordance with GAAP and free of material error and fraud. It is accountable to investors and creditors for the quality of the statements it produces. The top management, starting with the CEO, sets the tone at the top and shapes the financial reporting environment. Therefore, the task of reducing the risk of fraud starts with management.[110]

Who Makes up Management?

Management consists of "any owner or employee who is able to create a distortion of the financial statements, either because of an absence of internal accounting controls or circumvention of such controls."[111]

What is Management's Responsibility to Shareholders?

With respect to fraud, management has the fiduciary responsibility to manage on behalf of shareholders' interests not management's interests.[112] To do this, management needs, at the very least, to:

1. Identify and assess conditions that lead to fraud.

2. Assess and manage the risk of fraud.

3. Follow GAAP accounting.

4. Provide full and fair disclosure of financial and non financial information.[113]

5. Develop, implement, and maintain internal controls.

6. Obey laws and regulations.

7. Record transactions in accordance with accounting policies and regulations.

8. Safeguard assets.

9. Make records available to external auditors and cooperate with their audit.

10. Ensure that financial statements are free of material misstatements from errors and fraud.[114]

Motives and Incentives for Management

A number of factors contribute to management fraud. The motives for management fraud start with pressures, both external and internal, on management.[115] External pressures exist for a company to make its numbers in order to meet Wall Street's demands. These pressures create a motive for executives to try to meet or beat earnings forecasts in order to maintain the value of the company's stock — and eventually to help the price rise. When it is not possible to meet the numbers, whether for internal or external reasons — the possibility of fraudulent financial reporting increases. The result depends on whether the corporate environment is conducive to fraud (provides opportunities) and the integrity of those involved making the decisions.

Management is likely to cross the line into fraudulent reporting when:

1. The line is vague.

2. The perceived benefits of engaging in fraudulent reporting exceed the costs.

3. Management has a tendency towards excessive risk.

4. Management has reasons involving personal satisfaction/self image.[116]

Gamesmanship

Management invites fraudulent financial reporting when it engages in gamesmanship, which consists of pushing accounting rules to the limit and engaging in aggressive and questionable choice of accounting principles. In the energy industry, this has shown up in the abuse of mark-to-market accounting and improper application of off-balance sheet transactions.[117] Common gamesmanship actions include:

1. Overstating restructuring charges — create reserves now to make future earnings look better.

2. Using acquisition accounting to overstate future earnings.

3. Smoothing earnings — manipulating timing of recognition of charges — such as loan losses/sales returns.

4. Revenue recognition — before completion of sales or when still reversible by customers.

5. Overstated revenues/assets.

6. Deferring expenses — which creates an appearance of growth.[118]

Gamesmanship is best deterred by vigilant board oversight on accounting issues and a conservative approach to labeling items as material in reporting — that is being more likely to mention items in reports than to hide them from disclosure.[119]

<u>Management and Sarbanes-Oxley</u>

As mentioned in the Section on Internal Control above, the Sarbanes-Oxley Act's Section 404 requires management to state its responsibility for establishing and maintaining adequate internal controls for financial reporting as well as an assessment of the effectiveness. In addition, management, at the end of the fiscal year, needs to provide an assessment of the effectiveness of the internal control structures and procedures.[120]

Section 302 of the Sarbanes-Oxley Act has significant implications for management as it requires management, including the chief executive and financial officers to make quarterly and annual certifications with respect to the firm's internal controls over annual reporting.[121] The Public Company Accounting Oversight Board outlines what is required:

• A statement that the certifying officers are responsible for establishing and maintaining internal control over financial reporting;

• A statement that the certifying officers have designed such internal control over financial reporting, or caused such internal control over financial reporting to be designed under their supervision, to provide reasonable assurance regarding the reliability of financial reporting and the preparation of financial statements for external purposes in accordance with generally accepted accounting principles; and

• A statement that the report discloses any changes in the company's internal control over financial reporting that occurred during the most recent fiscal quarter (the company's fourth fiscal quarter in the case of an annual report) that have materially affected, or are reasonably likely to materially affect, the company's internal control over financial reporting.[122]

Section 906 requires CEO's and CFO's to certify that their financial reports provide a fair representation, "in all material respects, [of] the financial condition and results of operations of the issuer." Criminal penalties that include fines of up to $5,000,000 and up to 20 years in jail apply for false certification.[123]

It is important to note that Section 302 relies on the general criminal penalties associated with violations of the Securities Exchange Act, while Section 906 has specific criminal penalties for violation of its sections.[124]

One result of all these requirements for certifications is that those who face potential prison time (the top management) for miscertifications, are now requiring certifications for those below them, under the premise that they help to insure control at lower levels of the organization. Dennis Chookaszian regards subcertification as one of the most important factors in development of sound internal controls and preventing fraud.[125] Others see subcertifications as a way for executives to pass the buck, but the reality is that the Act does not refer to subcertifications and legal consensus is that these subcertifications cannot substitute for due diligence by management and knowledge of corporate affairs by CEO's and CFO's.[126]

Internal Audit

Internal auditors are a vital force in evaluating whether the firm is meeting its objectives related to operations, financial reporting, and compliance with laws and regulations. Internal auditors are well positioned to deter fraud. To do so, they need to:

1. Be sheltered from any management attempt to pressure them.

2. Have a direct line to, and regular contact with, the audit committee.

3. Work with the external auditor, accounting staff, and top management on quality of corporate reporting.

4. Report findings on fraud to the audit committee.

5. Be able to go higher, if the audit committee does not respond, possibly to the full board, or even regulatory agencies and shareholders.

6. Assess adequacy of internal controls.

7. Evaluate quality of quarterly statements.[127]

External Auditor

The external auditor's work is supposed to reduce information risk — notably the risk that the financial statements do not provide an accurate portrayal of the company's fiscal health.

> "The independent public accountant who audits the financial statements of a public company also has a public obligation. As the U.S. Supreme Court has recognized, when the independent public accountant opines on a public company's financial statements, he assumes a public responsibility that transcends the contractual relationship with his client. The independent public accountant's responsibility extends to the corporation's stockholders, creditors, customers, and the rest of the investing public. The regulations and standards for auditing public companies must be adequate to safeguard that public trust and auditors must adhere to those standards."[128]

The external auditor is hired by the company to provide investors and creditors with reasonable assurance that the financial statements are not misstated, that is a reasonable assurance that the statements are free of material errors, irregularities, and fraud. The audit does not provide an absolute assurance that the statements are free of fraud.[129]

Auditors are supposed to be independent, objective, and ethical in their work.[130]

When planning an audit, the external auditor assesses the likelihood of fraud at the organization undergoing an audit, which influences the types of procedures that are used — and the level of scrutiny focused on the auditee. The management, industry, and operating factors studied by auditors are also useful indicators for board members and investors to consider in analyzing governance. Management factors to consider include:

• Performance based compensation — managers may attempt to manage earnings to encourage the stock of a company to move in ways that benefit them financially — and the compensation scheme may encourage them to engage in risky decisions for the firm or engage in fraudulent behavior.

• Stock price pressures.

• Authoritarian management without oversight by Board of Directors.

• Management does not correct known violations in financial statements.[131]

• Disregard for regulators and regulations.

• Earnings minimization for tax purposes.

• Poor communication of values and ethics throughout the organization.

• Aggressive targets.

• High turnover amongst upper management, general counsel, and board.

• Management employs — and keeps on staff — low quality or incompetent accounting, IT, and internal audit staff.

• Pressures auditors to conform to management's views.

• Restricts auditors access to needed materials.

• Management influences the scope of the audit.

• Past record of securities laws violations or allegations of fraudulent financial reporting.[132]

Industry and operating factors that highlight the need for close scrutiny include:

• A highly competitive industry (often with high degrees of market saturation) accompanied by declining margins.[133]

• The firm's revenues are up but cash flows do not match the increase.

• Complex or unusual transactions, especially ones at year-end, that may emphasize substance over form.

• Accounts located in offshore tax havens with little business purpose for having them there.

• Rapid growth compared to the industry as a whole.

• Bankruptcy or takeover threats.

• Bad corporate finances and management personally guarantees the corporate debt.[134]

The External Auditor and Sarbanes-Oxley's Section 404

Section 404 of the Sarbanes-Oxley Act of 2002 requires a firm's external auditor to express an opinion on the management's assessment of the effectiveness of the company's internal control over financial reporting. It is useful for boards and managers to have an outline of what the auditor will be looking for. The auditor is to determine whether he has *reasonable assurance* to attest whether the company has maintained, "in all material respects, effective internal control over financial reporting as of the date specified in management's assessment."[135] According to the PCAOB:

> Maintaining effective internal control over financial reporting means that no material weaknesses exist; therefore, the objective of the audit of internal control over financial reporting is to obtain reasonable assurance that no material weaknesses exist as of the date specified in management's assessment.[136]

In order to obtain this *reasonable assurance* the auditor needs to evaluate management's assessments and evaluate evidence as to whether the internal controls over financial reporting were properly designed and effective in operation.[137]

What Leads to an Unqualified Opinion under Section 404?

According to the PCAOB, an auditor can issue an unqualified opinion on a company's internal controls only if the auditor has identified no material weaknesses, and the client has not restricted the scope of the auditor's work.[138] A material weakness requires the auditor to issue an adverse opinion, and a scope restriction requires the auditor to issue either a qualified opinion or a disclaimer of an opinion, depending on the limitation.[139] A company does not want an adverse, qualified opinion, or a disclaimer of opinion, as those opinions will not be viewed favorably by the investment community or creditors.

Here are circumstances that are regarded as significant deficiencies and strong indicators that material weaknesses exist in internal control over financial reporting:

• Restatement of previously issued financial statements to reflect the correction of a misstatement.

Note: The correction of a misstatement includes misstatements due to error or fraud; it does not include restatements to reflect a change in accounting principle to comply with a new accounting principle or a voluntary change from one generally accepted accounting principle to another generally accepted accounting principle.

• Identification by the auditor of a material misstatement in financial statements in the current period that was not initially identified by the company's internal control over financial reporting. (This is a strong indicator of a material weakness even if management subsequently corrects the misstatement.)

• Oversight of the company's external financial reporting and internal control over financial reporting by the company's audit committee is ineffective . . .

• The internal audit function or the risk assessment function is ineffective at a company for which such a function needs to be effective for the company to have an effective monitoring or risk assessment component, such as for very large or highly complex companies . . .

• For complex entities in highly regulated industries, an ineffective regulatory compliance function. This relates solely to those aspects of the ineffective regulatory compliance function in which associated violations of laws and regulations could have a material effect on the reliability of financial reporting.

• Identification of fraud of any magnitude on the part of senior management . . .

• Significant deficiencies that have been communicated to management and the audit committee remain uncorrected after some reasonable period of time.

• An ineffective control environment.[140]

What can a Client Expect from an Audit?

Auditors probably can't detect all fraud. It is especially difficult for an external auditor to detect fraud that is based on collusion between management and other parties that the auditor does not suspect of being duplicitous.[141] Also, there is a point where the marginal cost of expanding the audit may exceed the marginal benefits of fraud detection. Admittedly, it may be difficult to determine this line in a formulaic manner. Clients need to know that, with the onset of Sarbanes-Oxley and its requirements for close scrutiny by auditors of internal controls, as prescribed under Section 404 of the act, auditors have a heightened responsibility to look for fraud in a company.

With the collapse of Arthur Andersen, there are limited choices for audit clients in selection of corporate auditors. In some cases, due to the new Sarbanes-Oxley requirements, one or more of the large firms may not qualify as independent for auditing purposes, which is a less than ideal situation for the auditing profession and its clients.[142]

The Regulators/Standard Setters

Given that the goal of this book is to assist boards and managers to meet current standards, this is not the place to propose policy changes. The main point is that companies need to comply with laws and regulations — a sign of good governance. There has been a trend in the past several decades of setting up rules based accounting standards. The standard setters and regulators need to develop an accounting model that is less rules based and more principles based. The rules have become so complicated, often contradictory, it makes it difficult for companies engaged in complex transactions to be assured that their accounting is correct. Often there aren't bright lines in accounting rules, which can lead to situations that require the exercise of judgement, which varies among accounting firms. Contrary to public perception, accounting is more art than science.[143]

The Risk Framework

The framework used in earlier chapters to analyze risk can also provide some insights into how to deal with fraud.

Avoid the Risk

As with other business risks, it is not possible to avoid the risk of fraud in a large business, as the complex interaction of motives, opportunity, and integrity will inevitably lead to a mix that leads to fraud's occurrence. But just because fraud it not avoidable, does not mean that companies can not take steps to minimize the chances of it happening or to take actions to pursue and prosecute those who commit fraud.

Bear the Risk

Ultimately a company must be prepared to bear the risk of fraud occurring. The extent to which it bears the risk of fraud depends on the steps it takes to deter fraud.

Reduce the Hazard

Reducing the chance of fraud involves a careful attention to fraud prevention, as discussed above. In addition, care needs to be taken in design of trading operations and providing for their oversight. The chance of loss increases with increased disregard for the conditions that encourage fraud to flourish, as well as ignoring warning signs of fraud (red flags), and refusing to aggressively pursue fraud when it is suspected.

Normal turnover in departments also may help expose fraud, because as new people come in, they may question practices that have existed for some time at the company and may not be appropriate. In addition, bringing people together on task forces to do work on specific projects may expose elements of deviance as people rush into a new position and fail to cover up the fraudulent activities they left behind.[144]

Reduce the Loss

The moment an organization suspects fraud, that is the time to act to reduce the loss. Investigations of fraud can be complex matters. The expertise may not exist within the organization. Even the firm's audit partner may not have the expertise. When fraud is suspected that is the time to bring in investigators with expertise, such as Certified Fraud Examiners (the detectives of the financial world) and experienced legal counsel (internal or external, depending on experience), who are trained to ferret out fraud and specialize in looking at and for irregularities that point to fraudulent operations.[145] The investigators need to report their findings to the audit committee and external counsel.

When a company fails to act — or maybe simply dismisses a suspect employee without an investigation — the firm sends a message that it will not pursue fraud aggressively.

Conclusion

When Enron collapsed in 2001 and the rest of the merchant sector came crashing down, many in the media and government sought to find simple explanations for the onslaught of the fraud — they blamed it on dishonest dealings by Enron senior staff and incompetence at Arthur Andersen (Enron's auditor). This was a great oversimplification of the situation, and makes it appear that to create good control systems we just need honest accountants and heavy prison terms for senior executives. In reality, Enron was brought down by the actions of both honest and dishonest people. The board of directors of Enron approved deals that involved conflicts of interest and entry into money losing businesses where Enron did not have expertise or failed to implement adequate risk management. In short, a series of bad investments, made with the board's approval, were hidden from view through off-balance sheet financing by Enron's chief financial officer, in a clear conflict of interest that an independent, financially knowledgeable board would have stopped in its tracks.

The pressures to make businesses work, when there may not have been a way to do so, often lead managers to manipulate the numbers.

While all the procedures and processes are very important to reducing fraud and its impact, they are no substitute for the integrity of senior management and its management team. As the Treadway Commission has pointed out, the integrity of a firm is a function of the tone at the top.

Notes

[1]Jack C. Robertson: *Auditing*, Eighth Edition (Chicago: Irwin, 1996), p. 292. Italics added.

[2]*Ibid.*

[3]*Ibid.*

[4]*Ibid.*

[5]Robertson, *op., cit.*, p. 293.

[6]Robert K. Elliott and John J. Willingham. *Management Fraud: Detection and Deterrence* (New York: Petrocelli Books, 1980), p. 4.

[7]National Commission on Fraudulent Financial Reporting. *Report of the National Commission on Fraudulent Financial Reporting*, 1987, p. 2. Available on the World Wide Web at: *http://www.coso.org/ncffr.pdf*

[8]*Ibid.*

[9]*Ibid.*

[10]Zabihollah Rezaee. *Financial Statement Fraud: Prevention and Detection* (New York: John Wiley & Sons, Inc., 2002), p. 44.

[11]One of the most comprehensive studies of fraud in recent years was based on instances of fraudulent financial reporting investigated by the Securities and Exchange Commission from 1987 to 1997. The report, *Fraudulent Financial Reporting: 1987-1997: An Analysis of U.S. Public Companies* analyzes frauds that were first reported by the SEC in Accounting and Auditing Enforcement Releases issues from 1987 to 1997. The report was sponsored by the Committee of Sponsoring Organizations of the Treadway Commission (COSO), the same organization that issued the 1987 *Report of the National Commission on Fraudulent Financial Reporting.* COSO is made up of the American Accounting Association (AAA), American Institute of Certified Public Accountants (AICPA), Financial Executives Institute (FEI), Institute of Management Accountants (IMA), and the Institute of Internal Auditors (IIA). The report's full citation is: Mark S. Beasley, Joseph V. Carcello, and Dana R. Hermanson. *Fraudulent Financial Reporting: 1987-1997: An Analysis of U.S. Public Companies*, Committee of Sponsoring Organizations of the Treadway Commission, 1999. Available on the World Wide Web at: *http://www.coso.org/publications/FFR_1987_1997.pdf*

[12]Mark S. Beasley, Joseph V. Carcello, and Dana R. Hermanson, *Fraudulent Financial Reporting: 1987-1997: An Analysis of U.S. Public Companies*, Committee of Sponsoring Organizations of the Treadway Commission, p. 30.

[13]Beasley, *et al., op. cit.*, pp. 30-31. 50% of the frauds involved revenue recognition; 50% involved overstating assets; 18% involved understating liabilities; 12% involved misappropriation of assets.

[14]Beasley, *et al., op. cit.*, pp. 32-33.

[15]This based on a conversation with Mark Bell, a retired PricewaterhouseCoopers audit partner who had extensive experience auditing major U.S. utility clients, 4 January 2006.

[16]*Ibid.*

[17]Beasley. *et al., op. cit.*, p. 34.

[18]Beasley *et al., op. cit.*, p. 33.

[19]Kurt Eichenwald. *Conspiracy of Fools: a True Story.* (New York: Broadway Books, 2005), p. 430.

[20]Enron Corporation: *Enron Annual Report 2000.* The text of the disclosure on page 50 of the Annual Report read: "In 2000 and 1999, Enron entered into transactions with limited partnerships (the Related Party) whose general partner's managing member is a senior officer of Enron. The limited partners of the Related Party are unrelated to Enron. Management believes that the terms of the transactions with the Related Party were reasonable compared to those which could have been negotiated with unrelated third parties."

[21]Kurt Eichenwald, *op. cit.*, pp. 249-250; 325.

[22]William C. Powers, Jr., Chair, Raymond S. Troubh, and Herbert S. Winokur, Jr., *Report of Investigation by the Special Investigative Committee of the Board of Directors of Enron Corp.*, p. 163. Available on the World Wide Web at: *http://images.chron. com/content/news/photos/02/02/03/enron-powersreport.pdf*

[23]William C. Powers, Jr., Chair, Raymond S. Troubh, and Herbert S. Winokur, Jr., *op. cit.*, pp. 18, 48, and 92.

[24]Kurt Eichenwald, *op. cit.*, p. 456.

[25]Kurt Eichenwald, *op. cit.*, p. 331.

[26]Kurt Eichenwald, *op. cit.*, pp. 310-311; p. 328.

[27]Kurt Eichenwald, *op. cit.*, p. 598.

[28]Kurt Eichenwald, *op. cit.*, pp. 625-626; 631.

[29]Rezaee, *op. cit.*, p. 46.

[30]Rezaee, *op. cit.*, p. 51.

[31]Rezaee, *op. cit.*, p. 56.

[32]Conversation with Mark Bell.

[33]Rezaee, *op. cit.*, pp. 57-58.

[34]Conversation with Mark Bell.

[35]Rezaee, *op. cit.*, pp. 59-61.

[36]Conversation with Mark Bell.

[37]Rezaee, *op. cit.*, p. 70.

[38]The dealings that created problems in the California power markets arose through the design of the markets that created economic incentives to trade in ways that helped bring about the California power crisis. While this does not excuse companies choosing to break laws, the market design created motives (to make money) and opportunities (the market rules) that allowed market manipulation. With two of the three prerequisites for fraud (motive, opportunity) this leaves only integrity to constrain bad behavior. Some may argue that in extreme cases, wash trading could be used to test market prices and gauge the market's reaction to a potential deal. However, the abuse of the methods by traders — and firms — should make a company wary about allowing the practice. The fact that wash trading is felonious behavior on a regulated exchange, such as the Chicago Mercantile Exchange, may indicate that markets can survive and prosper without this sort of behavior.

[39]Rezaee, *op. cit.*, p. 74.

[40]With **dominant** being the key word, according to Mark Bell.

[41]Rezaee, *op. cit.*, p. 71. The dependency on a few customers was characteristic of the merchant energy business — which was the sector of the utility business that melted the most in the early 2000s.

[42]Conversation with Mark Bell, 4 January 2006.

[43]Rezaee, *op. cit.*, p. 76.

[44]Conversation with Mark Bell, 4 January 2006.

[45]Conversation with Mark Bell, 4 January 2006.

[46]National Commission on Fraudulent Financial Reporting, *op. cit.*, pp. 12-13

[47]Robertson, *op. cit.*, p. 294.

[48]Robertson, *op. cit.*, p. 301.

[49]When dealing with defalcation, monetary needs may drive fraudulent behavior — such as a need to pay hospital bills or gambling debts. With management fraud, however, this is not a major factor.

[50]Beasley, *et al.*, *op. cit.*, p. 21.

[51]Rezaee, *op. cit.*, p. 45.

[52]Rezaee, *op. cit.*, p. 35.

[53]Robertson, *op. cit.*, p. 301.

[54]Rezaee, *op. cit.*, p. 44.

[55]National Commission on Fraudulent Financial Reporting, *op. cit.*, p. 24.

[56]Robertson, *op. cit.*, p. 302.

[57]National Commission on Fraudulent Financial Reporting, *loc. cit.*

[58]National Commission on Fraudulent Financial Reporting, *op. cit.*, p. 40.

[59]The last two factors were from a conversation with Mark Bell on 4 January 2006.

[60]National Commission on Fraudulent Financial Reporting, *op. cit.*, p. 97.

[61]E-mail from Dennis Chookaszian, 7 January 2006.

[62]Beasley, *et al., op. cit.*, p. 5.

[63]Beasley, *et al., op. cit.*, pp. 1 and 5.

[64]Beasley, *et al., op. cit.*, p. 1.

[65]Beasley, *et al., op. cit.*, p. 6.

[66]*Ibid.*

[67]Here is the relevant section from the Sarbanes-Oxley Act of 2002: **SEC. 406. CODE OF ETHICS FOR SENIOR FINANCIAL OFFICERS.**

> (a) *CODE OF ETHICS DISCLOSURE.* — The Commission shall issue rules to require each issuer, together with periodic reports required pursuant to section 13 (a) or 15 (d) of the Securities Exchange Act of 1934, to disclose whether or not, and if not, the reason therefor, such issuer has adopted a code of ethics for senior financial officers, applicable to its principal financial officer and comptroller or principal accounting officer, or persons performing similar functions.
>
> (b) *CHANGES IN CODES OF ETHICS.* — The Commission shall revise its regulations concerning matters requiring prompt disclosure on Form 8-K (or any successor thereto) to require the immediate disclosure, by means of the filing of such form, dissemination by the Internet or by other electronic means, by any issuer of any change in or waiver of the code of ethics for senior financial officers.
>
> (c) *DEFINITION.* — In this section, the term "code of ethics" means such standards as are reasonably necessary to promote—
>
>> (1) honest and ethical conduct, including the ethical handling of actual or apparent conflicts of interest between personal and professional relationships;
>>
>> (2) full, fair, accurate, timely, and understandable disclosure in the periodic reports required to be filed by the issuer; and
>>
>> (3) compliance with applicable governmental rules and regulations.

[68]National Commission on Fraudulent Financial Reporting, *op. cit.*, pp. 33-34.

[69]This need to discipline or dismiss top managers is made easier if the board is not made up of friends of the executives, given that the board members have a fiduciary responsibility to the shareholders — not a responsibility to keep an unethical executive on the company payroll.

[70]Committee of Sponsoring Organizations of the Treadway Commission. "COSO Definition of Internal Control." Available on the World Wide Web at: *http://www. coso.org/key.htm.*

[71]Sarbanes-Oxley Act of 2002. Public Law 107-24. Section 404, Management Assessment of Internal Controls, 116 Stat 789. Available on the World Wide Web at: *http://www.sec.gov/about/ laws/soa2002.pdf.*

[72]U.S. Securities and Exchange Commission. Management's Reports on Internal Control Over Financial Reporting and Certification of Disclosure in Exchange Act Periodic Reports (Release Nos. 33-8238; 34-47986; IC-26068; June 5, 2003). PART 240 — GENERAL RULES AND REGULATIONS, SECURITIES EXCHANGE ACT OF 1934. §240.13a-15 Controls and procedures. Paragraph f. Available on the World Wide Web at: *http://www.sec. gov/rules/final/33-8238.htm.*

[73]U.S. Securities and Exchange Commission. Management's Reports on Internal Control Over Financial Reporting and Certification of Disclosure in Exchange Act Periodic Reports (Release Nos. 33-8238; 34-47986; IC-26068; June 5, 2003). Section IV. PAPERWORK REDUCTION ACT. Subsection B. Summary of the Final Rules. Available on the World Wide Web at: *http://www.sec.gov/rules/final/33-8238.htm.*

[74]Securities and Exchange Commission, *op. cit.,* Section II. DISCUSSION OF AMENDMENTS IMPLEMENTING SECTION 404. Subsection B. Management's Annual Assessment of, and Report on, the Company's Internal Control over Financial Reporting, Paragraph 3. Final Rules, Sub Paragraph a, Evaluation of Internal Control over Financial Reporting.

[75]Public Company Accounting Oversight Board. *Auditing Standard No. 2 — An Audit of Internal Control Over Financial Reporting Performed in Conjunction with An Audit of Financial Statements,* p. 150. Available on the World Wide Web at: *http://www. pcaob.org/Rules/Rules_of_the_Board/Auditing_Standard_2.pdf.*

[76]COSO. "Internal Control — Integrated Framework Executive Summary." Available on the World Wide Web at: *http://www.coso.org/publications/executive_summary_ integrated_framework.htm.*

[77]COSO has recently released an Enterprise Risk Management Framework that is similar to the Internal Control Framework although it has added another objective (Strategic Goals) and three other components: Objective Setting, Event Identification, and Risk Response. This framework could prove useful to boards that wish to create a systematic approach to Enterprise Risk Management. The approach is actually similar to a number of the approaches discussed in this book. In addition, the tools that are developed to deal with specific risks elucidated throughout this book serve as effective methods for handling the Risk Response component within the ERM framework.

Available on the World Wide Web at: *http://www.coso.org/Publications/ERM/ COSO_ERM_ExecutiveSummary.pdf.*

[78]COSO. "Internal Control — Integrated Framework." *Executive Summary.* Available on the World Wide Web at: *http://www.coso.org/publications/executive_summary_integrated_framework.htm.*

[79]*Ibid.*

[80]Rezaee, *op. cit.*, pp. 194-196.

[81]Rezaee, *op. cit.*, p. 200.

[82]National Commission on Fraudulent Financial Reporting, *op. cit.*, pp. 31-32.

[83]National Commission on Fraudulent Financial Reporting, *op. cit.*, pp. 32-33.

[84]National Commission on Fraudulent Financial Reporting, *op. cit.*, pp. 23-24.

[85]Robertson, *op. cit.*, p. 308.

[86]In the case of in-house legal counsel, it needs to be made clear that the legal counsel's role is to protect the firm and its shareholders, *not the management.* In house counsel is the company's counsel, not the CEO's. Perhaps legal counsel needs to report to the audit committee or a committee of directors who are independent of the company (as is the case for the audit committee under the Sarbanes-Oxley rules).

[87]Rezaee, *op. cit.*, p. 79.

[88]Rezaee, *op. cit.*, p. 142.

[89]"Boards serve as a management control when their authorization is required for the execution of a transaction. In formulating authorization policies, boards must determine the dollar amount of the transactions they wish to approve on a regular basis. The dollar threshold may vary according to the types of transactions." Source: Elliott and Willingham, *op. cit.*, p. 52.

[90]Rezaee, *op. cit.*, pp. 141-144.

[91]Rezaee, *op. cit.*, pp. 144-145.

[92]Based on e-mail from Dennis Chookaszian, 7 January 2006. Other governance experts also hold this view.

Here, for example is the role of the lead director for Ameren Corporation. This reference here is for illustration. "The Board of Directors will schedule regular executive sessions where non-management directors (*i.e.*, directors who are not Company officers but who do not otherwise have to qualify as 'independent' directors) meet without management participation. The Nominating and Corporate Governance Committee of the Board of Directors shall select an independent director to preside or lead at each executive session (which selection shall be ratified by vote of the non-management directors of the Board of Directors) (the 'Lead Director'). The Board of Directors will establish methods by which interested parties may communicate directly with the Lead Director or with the non-management directors of the Board of Directors as a group and cause such methods to be disclosed in accordance with the applicable law and the rules of the NYSE.

The authority, duties and responsibilities of the Lead Director are as follows: convene and chair meetings of the non-management directors in executive session on a quarterly basis and more often if needed; convene and chair meetings of the independent directors in executive session on an annual basis and more often if needed; preside at all meetings of the Board at which the Chairman is not present, including executive sessions of the non-management directors and independent directors; regularly poll the non-management directors for advice on agenda items for meetings of the Board; serve as a liaison between the Chairman and Chief Executive Officer (the 'Chairman and CEO') and the non-management directors; collaborate with the Chairman and CEO in developing the agenda for meetings of the Board and approve such agendas; approve information that is sent to the Board; collaborate with the Chairman and the CEO and the chairpersons of the standing committees in developing and managing the schedule of meetings of the Board and approve such schedules; collaborate with the Chairman and CEO in developing the budget of the Board; and if requested by major shareholders, ensure that he or she is available for consultation and direct communication. In performing the duties described above, the Lead Director is expected to consult with the chairs of the appropriate Board committees and solicit their participation. The Lead Director shall also perform such other duties as may be assigned to the Lead Director by the Company's By-Laws or the Board." Source: *http://www.ameren.com/ Investors/ADC_IV_Corp_Gov_Guidelines.asp.*

[93]Rezaee, *op. cit.*, pp. 146-151.

[94]Beasley, *et al., op. cit.*, p. 9.

[95]Beasley, *et al., op. cit.*, p. 26.

[96]Elliott and Willingham, *op. cit.*, p. 52.

[97]National Commission on Fraudulent Financial Reporting, *op. cit.*, pp. 35-36.

[98]Enron had code of conduct that was over 60 pages, yet it was suspended to allow the company's CFO, Andrew Fastow, to do business with Enron running a separate entity that wound up compensating him far more than Enron did and eventually led to the firm's demise. Source: Lynn Brewer, "Confessions of an Enron Executive." *http:// www.sas.com/news/sascom/2004q2/column_guest.html.*

[99]Conversation with Mark Bell, 4 January 2006.

[100]Douglas Enns, *Directors and Boards E-Briefing*, December 2005, Volume II, No. 12.

[101]National Commission on Fraudulent Financial Reporting, *op. cit.*, p. 100.

[102]National Commission on Fraudulent Financial Reporting, *op. cit.*, p. 182.

[103] *Ibid.*

[104] Beasley, *et al., op. cit.*, p. 9.

[105] Goodwin Proctor LLP. *Goodwin Proctor Public Company Advisory: Recent developments governing public companies and their officers, directors and investors.* "SEC Adopts Final Rules Requiring Listing Standards for Audit Committee Independence and Powers." April 30, 2003, p. 1. Available on the World Wide Web at: *http://www.goodwinprocter.com/publications/PC_AudComRules_4_30_03.pdf*

[106] *Ibid.*

[107] National Commission on Fraudulent Financial Reporting, *op. cit.*, pp. 182-183.

[108] Conversation with Mark Bell, 4 January 2006.

[109] Rezaee, *op. cit.*, p. 178.

[110] National Commission on Fraudulent Financial Reporting, *op. cit.*, p. 6.

[111] Elliott and Willingham, *op. cit.*, p. 97.

[112] Conversation with Mark Bell, 4 January 2006.

[113] Conversation with Mark Bell, 4 January 2006.

[114] Rezaee, *op. cit.*, pp. 182-183.

[115] Rezaee, *op. cit.*, p. 184.

[116] Rezaee, *op. cit.*, p. 183.

[117] Conversation with Mark Bell, 4 January 2006.

[118] Rezaee, *op. cit.*, p. 187.

[119] Rezaee, *op. cit.*, pp. 189-190.

[120] Sarbanes-Oxley Act of 2002. Public Law 107-24, Section 404, Management Assessment of Internal Controls. The Public Company Accounting Oversight Board has stated what management needs to do — and what the external auditor needs to evaluate in considering the management's assessment of internal controls:

"For the auditor to satisfactorily complete an audit of internal control over financial reporting, management must do the following:

a. Accept responsibility for the effectiveness of the company's internal control over financial reporting;

b. Evaluate the effectiveness of the company's internal control over financial reporting using suitable control criteria;

c. Support its evaluation with sufficient evidence, including documentation; and

d. Present a written assessment of the effectiveness of the company's internal control over financial reporting as of the end of the company's most recent fiscal year." Source: Public Company Accounting Oversight Board, *op. cit.*, p. 152.

[121]Public Company Accounting Oversight Board, *op. cit.*, p. 147.

[122]Public Company Accounting Oversight Board, *op. cit.*, p. 211.

[123]Sarbanes-Oxley Act of 2002. Public Law 107-204, Section 906.

[124]Protiviti, *Guide to the Sarbanes-Oxley Act: Internal Control Reporting Requirements. Frequently Asked Questions Regarding Section 404*, 2003. Available on the World Wide Web at: *http://www.protiviti.com*

[125]E-mail correspondence with Dennis Chookaszian, 7 January 2006.

[126]Stephen D. Poss, "Please Sign Here"— Preparing For Those CEO/CFO Certifications". Available on the World Wide Web at: *http://www.goodwinprocter.com/publications/poss_s_5_04.pdf*

[127]Rezaee, *op. cit.*, pp. 205-206.

[128]National Commission on Fraudulent Financial Reporting, *op. cit.*, p. 5.

[129]Rezaee, *op. cit.*, p. 218.

[130]The PCAOB offers guidance on independence: Independence. The applicable requirements of independence are largely predicated on four basic principles: (1) an auditor must not act as management or as an employee of the audit client, (2) an auditor must not audit his or her own work, (3) an auditor must not serve in a position of being an advocate for his or her client, and (4) an auditor must not have mutual or conflicting interests with his or her audit client. . . . If the auditor were to design or implement controls, that situation would place the auditor in a management role and result in the auditor auditing his or her own work. These requirements, however, do not preclude the auditor from making substantive recommendations as to how management may improve the design or operation of the company's internal controls as a by-product of an audit. Public Company Accounting Oversight Board, *op. cit.*, p. 156.

[131]This is discussed in the section entitled **What are the Basics of a Fraud Fighting Program?**

[132]Rezaee, *op. cit.*, pp. 240-241.

[133]Rezaee, *op. cit.*, p. 241.

[134]*Ibid.*

[135]Public Company Accounting Oversight Board, *op. cit.*, p. 146.

[136]*Ibid.*

[137]*Ibid.* According to the PCAOB, "Reasonable assurance includes the understanding that there is a remote likelihood that material misstatements will not be prevented or detected on a timely basis. Although not absolute assurance, reasonable assurance is, nevertheless, a high level of assurance." (Public Company Accounting Oversight Board, *op. cit.*, p. 151.)

[138]Public Company Accounting Oversight Board, *op. cit.*, p. 188.

[139]*Ibid.*

[140]Public Company Accounting Oversight Board, *op. cit.*, pp. 191-192.

[141]American Institute of Certified Public Accountants, Reprint of Chapter 4 from *Report, Conclusions, and Recommendations* by the Commission on Auditors' Responsibilities. In Elliott and Willingham, *op. cit.*, p. 271.

[142]Conversation with Mark Bell, 4 January 2006.

[143]Mark Bell, Conversation, 4 January 2006.

[144]Jack Katz, "Concerted Ignorance: The Social Psychology of Cover-up," in Elliot and Willingham, *op. cit.*, p. 168. Bringing suspected fraudsters onto a task force at short notice may then be a way to investigate whether fraudulent activities were taking place at the post prior to joining the task force.

[145]In addition, it is probably wise to involve some legal counsel to assure that an investigation can produce evidence that can be used in court should the company desire to prosecute the fraudsters. Unfortunately, the firm may have difficulty obtaining help from local law enforcement because fraud prevention may not be a priority, or the local authorities may not have the right expertise to handle investigations.

Regulation

The average energy company in the United States operates under a plethora of regulatory jurisdictions, some of which are at odds with each other. Any one of them can institute or change rules in a way that affects a company's plans, ongoing strategy, finances and level of risk. Regulatory entities range from government agencies to voluntary committees. The following constitutes the major regulatory entities that have influence over the risk levels of energy companies.

Federal Agencies

Federal regulatory agencies cover economic, operating and financial aspects of energy markets.

The **Commodities Futures Trading Commission** (CFTC) supervises commodities futures and options markets, guards against manipulation of those markets and against fraud. Energy trading activities that take place on organized exchanges fall within the purview of the CFTC. The proprietary trading activities that produced so many scandals took place in unregulated markets.

The Federal government has empowered the CFTC to police commodities markets — and its enforcement powers are designed to prevent the scandals that plagued the energy markets in the late 1990s and early 2000s. Many of the behaviors that energy traders engaged in would lead to prison time in the regulated commodity markets (the Energy Policy Act of 2005 now prohibits many of these activities in the energy market).

One way the CFTC regulates markets is by preventing dissemination of false or misleading market information.[1] Compare this to the behaviors of energy traders, who knowingly submitted incorrect price data to publishers of various energy price indices.

In addition, the Commodity Exchange Act, which the CFTC enforces, prohibits:

• Cheating or defrauding or attempting to cheat or defraud another person.

• Willfully making false reports, statements, or records.

• Willfully deceiving or attempting to deceive another person.[2]

This seems to be a good description of practices that prevailed in the unregulated energy markets in the late 1990s and the deceptive practices engaged in by energy traders at the time of the California power crisis.

Federal laws and CFTC regulations specifically prohibit wash trades (rigged or fictitious trades).[3] In 2002, it came to light that many energy traders were engaging in wash trades to raise their standings in league tables of energy traders. These behaviors lead to a loss of faith in energy markets, with bad financial consequences for their practitioners.

When it comes to enforcement, the CFTC can initiate actions that can lead to individuals or organizations losing trading privileges, fines, and restitution. In addition, the CFTC can also refer cases to the Justice Department for criminal prosecution of not only the Commodity Exchange Act, but also for violation of federal criminal statutes such as mail fraud, wire fraud, and conspiracy.

The **Environmental Protection Administration** (EPA) enforces regulations that protect the environment. The two laws most likely to affect the energy industry are the Clean Water and the Clean Air Acts. Power plants are major users of water and major producers of air pollutants. Changes in the rules or in enforcement procedures affect operating expenses, need for capital expenditures on pollution control equipment and even whether a plant can operate.

The **Federal Energy Regulatory Commission** (FERC) regulates wholesale and interstate gas and electric markets, supervises the licensing of dams, and approves mergers. It decides whether markets qualify for market based or regulated pricing. It has attempted to exercise jurisdiction over contracts of companies in bankruptcy. "Subtitle G — Electricity Market Transparency, Enforcement, and Consumer Protection" of the Energy Policy Act of 2005 prohibited the filing of false information and market manipulation and gave FERC enforcement powers over those activities. FERC has enormous power in the energy markets, and can use the power to withhold judgment in a particular matter to force compliance with other policies.

The **Nuclear Regulatory Commission** (NRC) supervises all aspects of nuclear operations, licensing and safety. It can order plant modifications and shutdowns. Inability or unwillingness to adhere to NRC instructions can lead to being put on a watch list, at the least, and severe economic penalties for failure to comply with direction.

The **Securities Exchange Commission** (SEC) supervises stock and bond exchanges, investment organizations that deal with the public, public offerings of stocks and bonds, issuance of information to investors, and accounting standards. It also enforced the Public Utility Holding Company Act of 1935, which regulated the formation and corporate organization of interstate natural gas and electric holding companies, until its repeal in 2005. In addition, the SEC enforces the Sarbanes-Oxley Act of 2002, which reformed corporate governance and set up procedures to prevent accounting fraud. The law places new burdens on executives and directors, requiring their verification of accounts, and threatening criminal penalties for noncompliance.

State Regulators

Every state has a state utility regulatory commission that supervises electric, gas, water and telephone utilities. The commissions set the prices charged by, and regulate the profitability of the regulated utilities, for services not considered wholesale or interstate commerce. They may control the ability of the utility to merge with or sell out to other entities, and may have to approve the siting of facilities, as well. Generally speaking, the state legislature sets the structure for the industry and the regulators enforce those rules. All regulators must comply with constitutional rulings that provide for a fair return on investment. State regulators probably control over 80% of the regulated revenue of the average utility. State regulators can, after hearings, alter previous rulings about levels of profitability, and they can declare previously made expenditures as imprudent, and therefore, not deserving of return on and return of investment.

Credit Rating Agencies

The **rating agencies** are private companies that rate the quality of bonds and other debt instruments issued by corporations and government agencies. Four credit rating agencies — Standard & Poor's, Moody's, Fitch and Dominion — have semi-official status as recognized rating agencies. The debt issuer pays the fees for the rating. While the law does not require that a corporation have a rating for its debt, many buyers of debt instruments will not — or cannot by law — buy securities that lack ratings or that have ratings below investment grade.[4] Furthermore, credit agreements may force the corporate issuer to take specified actions when the credit rating falls below a stated level, in order to protect the existing debt. Credit rating upgrades or downgrades — made either because of a change in the credit situation of the corporation or because the rating agency has changed its standards — can affect the ability of the corporation to raise money and what it pays for the borrowing. Some state regulators insist that the utility maintain a specified rating. Organizations must consider the risk that any action could precipitate a change in its credit rating, and weigh the cost of a loss in credit rating against any benefits expected from the action.

Nongovernmental Regulators and Standard Setters

Numerous nonprofit organizations, some with semi-official status set standards for the industry or evaluate industry operations in such key fields as nuclear operations and reliability. Although many of them claim that membership is voluntary, nonmembers might have a hard time explaining to their government regulators why they had not joined or abided by the rulings of the organizations.

The **Committee of Chief Risk Officers** (CCRO) is a voluntary organization of the chief risk officers of organizations that may account for about half of gas and electric transactions in the country. The CCRO makes studies to determine best practices for risk management, and works to develop common measures for risk management. The CCRO can make recommendations but not mandate practices. That said, ignoring the recommendations involves the risk that investors and others in the business might view the noncomplying corporation as less safe, which could increase its cost of doing business or deprive it of business from those who want to deal with a solid enterprise.

The **Financial Accounting Standards Board** (FASB) is a private organization that sets standards for financial accounting. The SEC recognizes the findings of the FASB, and all public accountants follow the FASB's findings. During the boom years of the 1990s, many companies looked for ways to deceive investors by exploiting loopholes in the accounting rules. Tightening the rules, which forces disclosures of policies, may force corporations to change financial policies, sometimes suddenly, and sometimes at inconvenient moments.

The **Institute of Nuclear Power Operations** (INPO) is a nonprofit, voluntary organization dedicated to promoting nuclear safety, reliability and excellence of operations. INPO evaluates operations, provides assistance, information and training to nuclear operators. Although INPO does not publicize the results of its evaluations, it is unlikely that any company would dare to ignore them.

The **National Futures Association** (NFA) is a self-regulatory organization. All firms and individuals doing business with the public in the futures markets must belong to the NFA, which sets and polices regulatory standards. NFA has the power to censure, suspend and fine those who do not follow the rules. Among other behaviors, NFA members and associates are prohibited from:

- Disseminating, or causing to be disseminated, false or misleading information, or a knowingly inaccurate report, that affects or tends to affect the price of any commodity that is the subject of a futures or options contract;[5]

- Engaging in manipulative acts or practices regarding the price of a futures or options contract;"[6]

The ranges of possible penalties for violation of NFA Rules include:

- Expulsion or suspension from membership or association with a member;

- Censure or reprimand

- A fine of up to $250,000 for each violation; and

- An order to cease and desist.[7]

Membership in the NFA is required to engage in futures and options business, so being thrown out of the organization means no more employment as a trader, or a prohibition on a firm engaging in the futures and options business. This is an effective way for an industry to police itself. Imagine if a power trader knew it couldn't engage in power trading if it committed fraud — this would be a strong deterrent to allowing questionable practices on a trading floor.[8]

The **North American Electric Reliability Council** (NERC) is a nonprofit, voluntary organization whose members deliver almost all electricity produced in the United States, Canada and parts of northern Mexico. NERC sets standards of operation designed to maintain or improve the reliability of the bulk power network. It monitors compliance with those standards. NERC, however, has no enforcement powers, although most energy firms would not want to have to explain why they do not comply with NERC rules. The Energy Policy Act of 2005 (Section 1211) authorizes an Electricity Reliability Organization (ERO) with enforcement powers, operating under FERC jurisdiction, which will presumably, take over the existing tasks of NERC.

The **North American Energy Standards Board** (NAESB) is a nonprofit organization dedicated to developing standards for the wholesale and retail electricity and gas markets. Without such standards, every transaction and interconnection with the network would require a newly written contract.

Regional Transmission Organizations

The **regional transmission organization** (RTO) is a nonprofit organization that, in some regions of the country, supervises the operation of the transmission lines, operates a regional power market, and oversees that market to assure that it remains competitive. The RTO does not operate for the benefit of any participant in the market, and those operating under the RTO's control take the risks of having assets under the control of an organization that has no fiduciary responsibility to the owner of the assets, and has no capital at risk when it makes decisions.

Organized Exchanges

The dictionary defines an **exchange** as, "a place where . . . merchants gather to transact business."[9] Eugene F. Brigham improved on that quaint definition when he wrote:

> There are basic types of security markets — the organized exchanges typified by the New York Stock Exchange, and the less

formal over-the-counter markets . . . The organized security exchanges are tangible, physical entities. Each of the larger ones occupies its own building, has specifically designated members, and has an elected governing body . . .[10]

That 20 year old definition tells part of the story. Now an organized exchange need not have a trading floor on which transactions take place. NASDAQ, for instance, transacts all business electronically, but has members, directors, and a set of rules by which the traders must abide. In addition, organized exchanges also have a mechanism to assure that the transaction that takes place is consummated (meaning that the seller delivers the good sold, and the buyer pays for it). That mechanism reduces the risk of trading, because neither buyer nor seller have to know each other or check on their respective reputations for honesty.

Organized exchanges operate under the jurisdiction of the SEC (stocks, equity options, and bonds) and the CFTC (commodities, futures, and options on futures). The exchanges enforce codes of conduct for members, decide the requirements for listing and delisting, and the terms of contracts traded on the exchanges.

Members that disregard exchange rules may be fined or banned from trading, thereby suffering major economic damage. Delisted companies may lose coverage in newspapers, and investors might take delisting as a sign of financial weakness or corporate hanky-panky, both of which could lead to serious consequences for the stock price. Termination of trading in a commodities contract could have serious consequences for firms that use that contract in the regular course of business to shift risk.

Conclusion

A large energy firm might fall under the jurisdiction of five or more governmental or semi-governmental regulators, plus face regulation of sorts from numerous industry organizations that set standards to which the energy industry "voluntarily" adheres. In one sense, all those oversight bodies must reduce risk, because they keep the spotlight on all activities. In another sense, however, their multiplicity increases the likelihood that the energy firm will trip up on one or another regulation, especially considering the possibility that two or more regulators have different ideas about what they want.

255

Notes

[1]Futures Industry Institute, *Guide to U.S. Futures Regulation* (Washington, D.C.: Futures Industry Institute, 1995), p. 2.

[2]*Ibid.*

[3]Futures Industry Institute, *op. cit.*, p. 3.

[4]Credit Ratings are discussed in **Chapter 12: Credit Risk.**

[5]This would prohibit the type of behavior that had companies disseminating false price information to publishers of energy price indices.

[6]Futures Industry Institute, *op. cit.*, p. 21.

[7]Futures Industry Institute, *op. cit.*, p. 25.

[8]This may be a good model for the CCRO to follow in policing energy traders.

[9]*Reader's Digest-Oxford Complete Wordfinder* (Pleasantville, NY: Reader's Digest, 1996), p. 502.

[10]Brigham, *op. cit.*, pp. 526-527.

Regulatory Risk

Regulation pervades the energy sector. Managers of energy firms must focus on regulation as much as any other aspect of doing business. Consumers of energy have to realize that, in many energy markets, what the regulator determines sets prices as much as, or even more than normal market forces, at least in the short run.[1]

Federal Regulatory Risks

In the case of regulatory agencies with policing powers, such as the **CFTC** and the **SEC**, risk management involves several approaches. First, the affected parties will lobby Congress to pass laws favorable to those doing the lobbying. That will circumscribe the activities of the regulators. Second, politically influential groups will lobby Congress or the government to exert pressure on the CFTC and SEC. Third, outside the lobbying and influence peddling arena, the best risk management involves the understanding that honesty is the best policy, trite as that advice sounds. (After all, what legitimate purpose is served by trying to skirt the law? Admittedly, fines may not amount to much, but loss of reputation can cost the corporation market value, and raise cost of capital.) After that, get a good lawyer.

Due to the manner of its administration of the **Public Utility Holding Company Act**, the SEC posed a risk to those who fell under its jurisdiction or who needed approval for merger activities. Repeal of the law in 2005 removed the need to devise elaborate structures to evade the intent of the Act, but it also created a new set of risks for energy companies, because it removed ownership rules that have protected certain energy companies from takeover attempts. Repeal, in addition, could create new risks and problems on the regulatory front. Some state regulators that do not have jurisdiction over mergers and finances of utilities have depended on the Act to limit extracurricular activities of utilities and prevent them from engaging in shaky financial procedures.

Sarbanes-Oxley compliance has become a major cost to corporations, large enough to discourage foreign corporations from listing their securities in the United States and encouraging some smaller American corporations to contemplate going private. In addition to costs, the law provides for criminal penalties for those who do not follow the law's strictures. It may discourage outsiders from taking directorships because of the new responsibilities placed on directors, too. Managing the risk requires scrupulous attention to the requirements of the law, because this is a law that focuses on processes. Attitude and corporate strategy will matter, too. For instance, the management that focuses on processes while looking for ways to evade the intent of the law continues to risk prosecution if the efforts lead to events that gain the attention of the government. As for corporate strategy, running a simplified business — both operationally and financially — may reduce the risks more than the elaborate processes, because officers and directors will actually be able to understand what is going on.

Dealing with the **NRC** presents little or no opportunity for maneuver. The agency enforces technical safety rules — nobody wants to contemplate an accident — and the agency can shut down an asset whose closure can have enormous impact on the finances of the owner and the availability of electricity in a market. One rarely hears about court orders holding up NRC safety decisions. The owner has to establish its trustworthiness in the eyes of the NRC, and not lose that confidence, no matter the cost in terms of operating or capital expenses, unless it is willing to close the plant permanently. (Even then, it remains under NRC jurisdiction until the facility is removed.) That said, the NRC may show flexibility about timing of events, if it finds no safety threats to the public, and it is not a crusading or antinuclear organization. On the whole, given the importance of nuclear assets to their owners and the powers of the NRC, the best risk management policy (maybe the only viable policy) is to run the facilities in the most efficient, open, and safe manner and adhere to NRC directives, even if the financial officers of the corporation take exception about the costs. The cost of an imposed outage could exceed any savings extracted by the bean counters.

The **EPA** seems susceptible to lobbying and political pressure, and litigants can and do delay actions through lawsuits. Energy firms with little enthusiasm for environmental protection may gamble that they can prevent or delay EPA action. They take the risk that the EPA, at some time in the future, may move back into a strict enforcement mode, or the courts will require enforcement, leaving them in a shaky business position due to lack of preparation for the environmental protection activities. As an alternative, other energy firms have attempted to develop trials of environmental protection mechanisms that accomplish goals more efficiently than through the methods that the EPA might propose, and these trials have measures to deal with pollutants not yet on the EPA's enforcement schedule, such as greenhouse gases.

Of all Federal regulatory agencies, **FERC** seems the most traditional, in the sense that it concerns itself with rate base, rate of return and "just and reasonable" rates, and the comments made below in the discussion of state regulatory risks also apply to the FERC jurisdiction. Since the passage of the Energy Policy Act of 1992, though, FERC has become an agency with an agenda: to promote competitiveness in wholesale power markets. FERC has interpreted that charge to mean reducing the market power of incumbents (usually the old utilities). FERC has jurisdictional authority over mergers and acquisitions, wholesale transactions, and the activities of RTOs, which gives it the ability to accomplish its goals directly or indirectly. FERC may not be able to order a utility to take action A, but it could withhold authority for the utility to undertake action B until the utility "voluntarily" decides to undertake action A. Thus utilities that have to ask FERC for approval for anything risk putting more on the table than they may wish. Reducing regulatory risk from FERC may mean trying to stay away from FERC altogether, not an easy path given the nature of FERC's authority.[2] Some utilities have resorted to strong political pressure and court appeals of FERC decisions to bring about desired results, but they still may have difficulty escaping FERC jurisdiction.

State Regulation

On one hand, **state regulation** limits exposure to competition, which reduces risk to energy companies, although it also reduces the options available to consumers. On the other hand, the existence and activities of the regulators create another set of risks, each of which requires management, among which are:

1. *Turnover and lack of experience at regulatory agencies* — Dealing with this problem requires frequent contacts and educational efforts, but it also provides an opportunity to introduce new ideas. The long period without rate cases, just ended, has

left both regulators and utilities with few experienced rate case experts, which might slow regulation during a new learning process.

2. *Political pressures on regulators* — These activities subvert the semi-judicial nature of regulation, but if one party plays the other must play, as well.

3. *Pricing that does not reflect causation of costs* — An extremely unpopular topic, because it inevitably leads to discussions of time of day pricing and the need to pay for infrastructure investment via access charges rather than by volumetric charges. Avoidance of the topic, however, leads to subsidies for some users, which opens the way for "cherry pickers" to take the business of the subsidizing parties from the utility. The use of volumetric pricing to cover fixed costs reduces the certainty of payment (and raises cost of capital) for utilities. The avoidance of time of day pricing raises overall prices to consumers, and forces the utility to build unnecessary plant.

4. *Backward looking rate procedures* — Rate policy must try for procedures and concepts that make it likelier the utility can earn a reasonable return in reality rather than on paper.

5. *Cost of service regulation* — Often criticized by theorists, cost of service regulation tends to to curb innovation and efficiency. Consumers could seek regulation that focuses on pricing rather than profit, and rewards or penalizes for good or bad service, which would create a risk of bad management for utilities that could not adapt.

6. *Restructuring deals* — Deal making by stakeholders can produce restructuring that favors those with the best lawyers or biggest political clout. Be wary of deals so devised. Demand testing on a small scale before implementation. Remember California. The utilities got what they wanted. Too bad they did not know what to want.

7. *Nobody in charge* — In the fragmented supply chain created after restructuring, nobody has responsibility to control the total cost and reliability of the product or service offered to the consumer, which leaves all the suppliers at the mercy of any supplier that does not meet its responsibility. This is a fundamental risk

that cannot be managed until the regulators accept it, so its management requires a major regulatory effort.

8. *Contracts and risks* — Due to the apparent failure of the merchant model, suppliers want buyers to purchase service contracts before committing to build assets in order to reduce their risks. That shifts the risk onto the buying party (usually the local utility), which cannot force its customers to sign contracts that will back up the purchase contracts. Thus the utility may have to bear the risk of the contract, often without compensation for the risk. For that matter, where the customers do stick with the utility, they take the risk of the contract (ultimately), which reconstructs the old utility paradigm without the protections of regulation.

The semi-restructuring of the energy industry has gone forward with little thought to the new risks created or the old risks unaddressed. Those risks affect both the suppliers and the consumers.[3]

Credit Rating Agencies

Managing credit agency risk really means knowing what the agencies look at, meeting those standards, maintaining the corporation's financial ratios within the parameters necessary to keep the desired rating, and keeping the agencies informed.[4]

Occasionally, after a major review, the credit agency may change its standards, a move that tends to damage those corporations that fashioned their financial policies in a manner to meet the letter (but not the intent) of the credit standards. (Using off balance sheet debt in excess is an example of such a misleading strategy.) The damage to the corporate issuer comes in two forms. First, lower ratings should lead to higher interest rates, because greater risk requires higher return. (In truth though, the markets probably noticed the decline in quality before the credit agency acted, so the corporation already paid higher interest rates.) Second, lower ratings may trigger actions to restore credit quality or may force the corporation to pay off debt whose issuance was tied to maintaining a specific bond rating. If the corporation cannot undertake remedial action (such as reducing the loss), in time, it would default on its debt and go bankrupt. (The crash of the power generators followed the credit rating policy revisions that triggered downgradings.)

Managements of corporations like to issue press releases regretting the downgradings of their debt, with the implication that the credit rating agency just did not understand the situation. Owners of stock and bonds of corporations that collapsed after downgradings tend to blame the rating agencies for changing the rules in the middle of the game. But those are among the risks of investing, and the best risk management strategy remains to maintain conservative financial policies.

Nongovernmental Regulators and Standard Setters

The **nongovernnmental regulators and standard setters** vary from those that attempt to introduce uniformity to those that impose it. Most, however, encourage the active participation of those who will fall under the standards in setting the standards. Therefore, the best way to manage the risk of the standard is to participate in its writing. In some instances, those affected have resorted to political lobbying, as well.

The **CCRO** not only works in a voluntary fashion but the fact that half the energy suppliers in the United States do not belong indicates either a lack of interest in standards or the feeling on the part of nonmembers that they do not take sufficient risks to make membership worthwhile. Members can learn how to limit risk by examining best practices of others, by avoiding mistakes, and by working to codify rules that allow market participants to better judge risks, including risks caused by the activities of others. At some time in the future, following CCRO recommendations might constitute evidence of prudent risk management for directors, creditors, regulators and class action lawyers. Thus ignoring the CCRO might not just institutionalize poor practices but also have legal or governance consequences.

FASB, after extensive study, mandates accounting standards that public accountants must follow. Thus corporations that require public audits must follow the rules. The only risk management consists of the attempts to influence the standards before they are promulgated, either by testimony or by lobbying.[5] After that, prudent risk management means following the rules.

INPO membership gives nuclear operators the opportunity to find out what others do better, and inspections that provide a second opinion to operators. Given the enormous risk involved in nuclear operation, active membership in INPO should be viewed as a hazard reducing mechanism.

Basically, the NFA presents members with two choices: follow the rules or get out. So know the rules and follow them. Or get a good lawyer.

Passage of the Energy Policy Act of 2005 finally provides NERC (or its successor) with a legal underpinning for its practices. The organization works through committees and regional organizations. It has an engineering focus. It exerts peer pressure to bring about conformity. Suffering an operating breakdown after not following NERC procedures can cause great embarrassment and lead to major corrective expenditures, not to mention lawsuits. Post 2005, the Energy Reliability Organization (ERO) will have enforcement powers too. Unfortunately, restructuring has blurred (and, perhaps, erased) the line between reliability (under NERC's purview) and commercial needs (under RTO and FERC purview), and efforts to reduce reliability risks may increase commercial risks.

Standards set by NAESB will enable more entities to interconnect with the energy grids, with less likelihood that the interconnect arrangement or contract will require endless negotiation, which lowers the risk for those trying to break into the business, but also raises the risks for incumbents that would prefer to keep out the potential entrants. Given the interactive nature of the standard setting process, risk management means participation in the process to influence the results, and understanding the meaning of the results for one's standing in the market.

Regional Transmission Organizations

RTOs have numerous committees of participants, but due to the peculiar nature of their governance (independent directors not responsible to any market participants), limiting risk from RTO activity may require visits to FERC and the courts. Generation owners must realize that RTOs can take steps to open markets to more competition, determine the rules and costs of connection, and change these rules in a way that increases risk for some players. Transmission owners may have to put capital into projects not of their choosing, if required by the RTO. Consumers have to pay congestion charges and RTO charges, whether they benefit from RTO activities or not, and the RTO plays a major part in supervising reliability while consumers foot the bill for any failures. Given the lack of control and limited influence over the activities of the RTO, risk management for market participants may be limited to accurately assessing risks, and then requiring a compensatory return on investments.

Organized Exchanges

Organized exchanges have rules (endorsed by Federal regulators) that members and market participants must follow, so risk management, in a sense, entails knowing and following the rules, especially those regarding the need to provide relevant information to the public. Operating on the exchange, however, also requires knowledge of what the market instruments can and cannot do for risk management purposes. (As an example, the market may not provide an opportunity to hedge prices beyond a certain time period or may not handle the transaction in the volume required.) Managements of energy companies and others have to understand, as well, how their activities or announcements will affect public markets, prices and cost of capital. Risk management might, as well, involve taking mitigative actions on the markets, but that brings up the question of what constitutes market manipulation, and whether organizations simply have to learn to live with some unfavorable market movements.

Conclusion

Market participants have the greatest opportunity to manage risks during the formative periods of various standard setters and other regulatory organizations. Beyond that period, risk management can take the form of political or legal activity, but the most prudent route would be to follow the rules. And, if you would not want to tell your mother what you plan to do, don't do it.

Notes

[1]The agencies are described in **Chapter 16: Regulation and Government**, and their acronyms spelled out in full. Many agencies are better known by their acronyms rather than full names.

[2]This approach is a combination of the **Avoid the Risk** and **Reduce the Hazard** strategies discussed in **Chapter 2.**

[3]For a more complete explanation of issues, *see* Hyman, Hyman and Hyman, *America's Electric Utilities*, Eighth Edition (Public Utilities Reports, Inc., Vienna, Va., 2005); **Chapter 36**.

[4]**Chapter 12: Credit Risk** examines the criteria of these rating agencies.

[5]Clifford S. Asness, "Stock Options and the Lying Liars Who Don't Want to Expense Them," *Financial Analysts Journal*, July/August, 2004, p. 9.

Improving Energy Risk Management with Experimental Economics

A number of issues that face those in energy risk control and management deal not with process or "how to" problems, but address thornier and less tangible issues involving individual behaviors and preferences. These come up regularly in commodities and derivatives trading, and other risk management areas as well. A sampling might include:

- What instruments should the firm be allowed to trade?

- How can the firm "trade around the assets," and what will that do?

- Should traders' bonuses be based on returns, RaROC, or firm performance?

- Is there moral hazard in the credit, notional, and VaR limits on a firm's trading desks?

- How should risk limits be related to position limits, to motivate effective hedging?

- Should the traders' risk preferences match those of the Risk Committee or firm, and do they?

Sadly, the answers to these questions are unknown to most risk managers in energy and in many other industries. And the questions are not just conversation starters for the next energy risk conference, but are crucial to both maintaining adequate risk control and maximizing the return on scarce risk capital.

The reason these topics are different, and more difficult to address, is that they involve human behaviors as responses to external (*i.e.*, market or other human) stimuli. Dynamic and complex environments coupled with a high level of human behavioral impact, create environments in which outcomes are volatile and unpredictable. In these situations, standard management approaches to finding optimal organizational and procedural structures are rarely successful. Standard practice holds that management should institute a set of controls or procedures, and slowly adjust these in response to the outcomes. Unfortunately, because the risk management environment involves much randomness, a large number of outcomes are needed to confidently identify results of a given set of procedures or controls. Thus the trial and error process of making adjustments can take quite some time. During that time sub-optimal controls are in place, creating opportunities for significant adverse events. In order to avoid these costly outcomes, the typical approach also hinges on beginning with extremely conservative limits and procedures. And while this may limit some forms of downside risk, it can also severely limit the effectiveness of some hedging and profit making strategies. However, these subjects should also be susceptible to analysis using experimental methods, which can address these issues and reveal the underlying behavioral drivers in a safe, low cost environment.

Experimental methods have been proven exceptionally good at providing insights regarding the economic impact of rules, limits and procedures in competitive settings. In particular, rules governing market mechanisms and rules addressing those who participate in the markets can be readily explored and tuned to shape the resulting behaviors. By performing the "trial and error" tuning in a laboratory, the tremendous exposure to real-world adverse events is avoided and a much greater range of risk controls or strategies can be examined safely.

The Experimental Approach

Intuitively, it only makes sense that we should experiment with new things before implementing them, especially when the stakes and uncertainties are high. Almost everyone test drives an automobile before buying it, but it is much more difficult to try out RaROC incentives on a group of crude oil traders.

Experimental economics is a research technique that uses scientific testing to investigate human economic behavior. Much of the existing work in the field has been focused on areas such as how to design markets to make them more efficient, and why people rarely act completely in their own self-interest. At the core of this approach is the creation of a model of some economic situation — such as an auction or a stock market — that is used repeatedly by human subjects. This allows the research team to build up statistical data on human behaviors, and identify any behavioral shifts driven by incremental changes in the model. More formally, "Experimental Economics applies laboratory methods of inquiry to the study of motivated human interactive decision behavior in social contexts governed by explicit or implicit rules."[1]

To observe a typical economic experiment you might think you were watching a group of people working on computers in a set of office carrels. While manual experiments are also common, networked computers allow researchers to provide each subject with a very rich, closely controlled stream of information that can easily be duplicated. Modern experiments provide each subject with a carefully designed set of rules and data, and record how the subjects react and interact as new data are introduced. Key aspects of all experiments include control over many of the drivers of economic activity (market design, supply of goods, demand for goods, information flow, etc.) and salient rewards to motivate the agents or players.

Typically experiments are structured so that numerous groups will experience the exact same environment and information to give the researchers a sense of which aspects of their performance are driven by the market design or information, and which are idiosyncratic. Changing a single aspect of the market design or information and repeating the trading sessions with new groups can reveal important relationships that can otherwise only be imagined.

Hypothetical Example

An example might make this clearer. Let's say we have 10 players, each of whom uses a computer interface to an actively traded market for day-ahead and forward power contracts (not unlike the ICE interface).[2] Each player might also be given a schedule of planned output from a hypothetical power plant and the associated costs of production and startup. For the purposes of the experiment, trading might take place for two minutes, then close, and begin again with revised pricing. In this way, each two minute period would be a model of trading over a real-time day, and an entire month of trading could be simulated in under an hour. Each player would see the economic impact of his activity as it occurred, by incurring costs for production and receiving revenue for power sold. At the end of the simulated month the players would be paid in cash, with the amount corresponding to their net earnings.

With such an experimental environment in place, it is easy to track the variability in the value of each trader's positions or cash flows, the net profits, maximum exposure, or any other measurements of interest. A number of decision support issues could then be addressed, such as the impact of allowing trading in options. If five of the traders were permitted to buy options and five were permitted to buy or sell options, changes in their performance measures could be directly attributed to that change in the experiment's rules.

By altering a number of the permissions or experimental inputs, deep insights can be developed regarding the risky environment and the most effective ways of controlling those risks. In this example, it is possible that buying options is only cost effective when the power plants have some risk of failure, but selling options can be a low risk way to enhance returns. Or that options are never cost-effective unless power price volatility is high. Whatever the insights, the cost of the knowledge gained is significantly below that of the live trial and error approach.

In any case, the insights developed can be used to implement actual risk controls with a high level of confidence in the resulting behaviors and economic results. The sensitivity of the performance metrics to the procedural changes will also provide the risk management team with sorely needed guidance regarding the signs of pending problems with the risk control framework.

Alternatives to the Experimental Approach

As the hypothetical example shows, experimentation does require some preparation and time to construct a sufficiently detailed environment, run an adequate number of experiments, and assess the results. When faced with these dynamic behavioral issues in the past, several alternative approaches have been taken, including surveys, speculation, and econometrics.

The survey approach has long been a close cousin of the experimental approach, substituting a number of "what-if" questions to human participants for actual experimentation. As such, it is much faster and less resource-intensive than a series of laboratory experiments. Like experimentation, it also allows the use of "real" agents; such as surveying actual crude oil traders for issues addressing crude oil trading risk.

Surveys have a number of serious flaws, however, including the abstract nature of the "what-if" framework. It can be difficult, if not impossible, to put oneself in an imagined position, and give a reasoned response. It is also difficult for the surveyor to motivate the respondent to devote significant attention to the questions, and to provide unbiased answers. For many issues, the respondent may have no way of even knowing how he might behave. As a result, surveys are severely limited in the topics they can address and in the veracity of the results they can provide.

Speculation is commonly used to some extent, and will always have a role in decision making. In designing risk control measures, management will certainly envision the various personnel, the procedures and incentives in place, and speculate on likely outcomes. This intuitive process is useful as a sanity check on any new or changed rule, but suffers from a number of heuristic biases and is never a substitute for rigorous analysis.

Econometric techniques could provide any of the results or insights that might be available from experimental methods — if sufficient, appropriate historical data were available. Unfortunately changing market conditions and other factors can easily confound whatever data are available. To duplicate the data generated by 10 hours of results from the hypothetical experiment above would require information on the daily trades of 10 individuals over 10 months. But the experiment can also be repeated precisely (same market prices and information flow) with new agents or rules. Econometric methods are typically used to analyze the results of larger experimental programs. This fact provides an interesting view of the respective roles of the two methods: Econometrics are best used when there is a wealth of well understood, high quality data, and experimental methods are best used to generate those data when few exist.

Experiments, in a controlled environment, suffer none of these shortcomings and are significantly less expensive than a single major adverse event that might result from implementing non-optimal incentives, rules or procedures for many risk control issues.

Experimental Economics

The roots of economic experimentation extend at least as far back as the 1930's. At that time classroom experiments were occasionally conducted, focusing on the development of prices in simple competitive markets. The field remained little known, and largely academic, over the next 50 years, with the number of researchers beginning to grow slowly in the 1970's. The importance of the contribution this research has made, and the potential it holds, was brought to worldwide attention when part of the 2002 Nobel Prize in economics was awarded to Vernon L. Smith for his work in developing the field of experimental economics. Today, a significant number of universities and research foundations around the world operate experimental laboratories, both for academic and commercial research, and as a teaching method for undergraduate and graduate students.

While most of this research is performed in a laboratory, field experiments are also performed. These differ from laboratory experiments in that they are performed *in situ*, and this typically substitutes some loss of experimental control for an increase in contextual richness. One example would be the current examination of whether individual or group incentives are more effective in motivating achievement in elementary school students. In this case, the classroom serves as the experimental environment and the subjects are largely unaware of their role in the experimental program.[3]

Much of the academic and commercial research to date has focused on the design of markets. This work has sought to identify market rules that promote the most efficient forum for transactions and thus benefit all of the market participants. For complex markets, such as those for public goods, specialized auctions, and electric power markets, this research has already made significant contributions. Commercial enterprises have yet to fully exploit the power of this approach in solving some of the least tractable decision support problems, but there are significant instances in which it has been used.

One of these was the internal market for resources that was used to manage the scientific payloads comprising the Cassini project, currently orbiting Saturn's eponymous moon. Cassini project management needed to maximize the amount and quality of scientific information gathered during the spacecraft's journey, while subject to a number of budgetary and engineering constraints. The payloads consisted of 30 individual instruments or modules, each to be designed and built independently by organizations on four continents over a period of several years. In constructing these payloads, the design teams each made decisions and trade-offs regarding the cost, size, and mass of its modules, as well as their power consumption and data transmission requirements.

To ensure efficient trade-offs, the Cassini project management team established a market for these resources, in which the module design teams could dynamically trade resources and adjust their requirements as the payloads were designed and constructed. Because the project was truly a "once in a lifetime" opportunity to collect scientific data, an experimental approach was adopted for the design of the internal resource market. A model market was constructed in a computer laboratory environment, and three sets of market rules and mechanisms were tested. Those results guided the implementation of the resource market used on the Cassini project for the following three years, and thereby shaped the scientific instruments that are currently providing our first good look at this part of the solar system.[4]

With regard to risk management in the energy sector, two broad categories of issues might yield particularly useful results when approached with experimental methods; those involving risk management structures and those addressing individual risk preferences and decision making.

Risk Management Structure Issues

The set of procedures, rules and guidelines that form the typical risk control structure in firms facing energy commodity risk could be optimized or enhanced through a more rigorous design process. The experimental approach has the unique capability to support that design process with deep behavioral insights and robust analyses. Some key risk management questions that should be addressed using this framework include:

273

Limits. Budget limits could be compared to risk limits (notional vs. VaR limits) for a buyer's or trader's holdings. Many risk control structures currently use both, without fully understanding the incentive effects and interaction between the two constraints.

Incentives. Some organizations have adopted buyer or trader incentive compensation programs based on a risk-adjusted measure, such as earnings divided by variance or VaR. Much theoretical literature suggests this is preferable to incentives based on earnings alone, but the full impact of risk-adjusted incentives has never been explicitly tested. A clear goal of all risk control structures is to avoid incentives that create behavioral biases for taking on undue risk, and a full understanding of the effects of these compensation systems is crucial.

Speculation. The goals of the energy commodities transactions team might include native position[5] hedging, client-driven hedging, market-making, arbitrage, or pure speculation, all over multiple tenors. How these are defined, and the acceptable levels of each, can clearly impact the risk and expected returns of this team. Experimenting in a laboratory with different levels of speculation, or allocations of risk capital, can illuminate the risks associated with such changes, and identify the interaction of these changes with different control structures.

Assets. The existence of native physical assets (power plants, gas storage facilities, native load, etc.) is considered highly desirable by some traders, as a fulcrum for certain trading strategies. The extent to which individuals can take advantage of such assets, and whether they add or reduce overall risk or returns is not always clear. Limit setting and risk reporting in this environment are also impacted by the difficulty of reversing or closing the asset holdings. All of these considerations point to the importance of understanding the behavioral impacts of holding physical energy assets.

Privacy. Past experimental work has revealed that the level of anonymity can play a key role in human exchange environments. Awareness of other players' incentives, knowledge of counterparty (as opposed to exchange trading) and public performance records all impact the players' reputation and behavior. Each of these needs to be considered in the implementation of a risk control structure, and can only be fully explored via experimental methods.

Individual Issues

Most of the issues discussed above are focused on energy commodities transactions, and as such are heavily influenced by the market structure and its performance, such as its price volatility and liquidity.

A more fundamental set of issues centers on individual and group risk preferences. Risk limits and controls are mandated by executive management because while the acceptance of some risk is a crucial part of any business enterprise, risk capital is limited and high levels of risk have the potential to damage the firm. Traditionally, management sets risk limits and allocates capital based on what the Board of Directors, CFO, or Risk Committee, "feel comfortable with." Rigorous methods to discern what levels of risk are acceptable, or to examine differences in these risk preferences among the key personnel are not well known or utilized.

Academic research in economics and psychology regularly refers to individuals as "risk averse,"[6] and has reasoned that varying levels of risk aversion play a role in some of the broad differences in behaviors. Within the past decade, experimental techniques have been able to define robust measures of risk aversion or preference by examining the choices people make when offered a set of gambles of varying levels of risk. This laboratory method has opened a door in risk management that may provide tremendous insight and a means to the improved implementation of risk controls.

These techniques can provide clear, consistent, cogent quantification of the risk comfort levels for all of the individuals involved, especially Directors, Officers, Managers, and Traders. It could also be used to explore the risk comfort levels of various groups, such as the Risk Committee and the Board of Directors. Thus this approach makes it possible to begin aligning the allowable trading strategies, goals and limits with the actual preferences of the firm.

The impact of assigning risk control personnel and trading staff who are aware of their risk preferences relative to those of the organization to various tasks or functions (hedging, speculating, arbitrage, etc.) has not been fully explored. This is an area in which even a small experimental program is sure to offer benefits in terms of incentive alignment and risk control efficiency.

Experimentation: In the Laboratory or on the Balance Sheet

Much risk management and control requires judgment, and is crucially dependent on human agents to develop corporate strategies and put them into action. In the energy industry, the scale of investment and the volatility of the markets is such that relatively common market movements can effect windfall profits or financial devastation. The process of mitigating these risks is made more difficult by the potential failure of physical plant, market interdependency across a complex of commodities and instruments, and dynamics driven by low liquidity, regional effects and seasonal demands.

The goal of most energy risk management teams seems quite clear: to minimize the likelihood and severity of losses, while providing adequate risk capital to undertake sufficient risk for the organization to meet its financial objectives. All such organizations face choices regarding whether the proper management metrics involve cash flow, earnings or market value, and how capital adequacy is determined. In addition, due to the nature of the forward markets in the energy complex, there are a number of issues surrounding data adequacy and the modeling methods employed. But in the end, it will always be the risk management team's responsibility to maintain controls that allow executive management to sleep well. Typically those controls include many of the following:

> *Reporting* — The selection of reports produced daily, monthly or quarterly and the information they contain, such as VaR by book or region, exposure by counterparty, net position, etc.

> *Incentives* — The structure of the compensation plan for those in trading and risk, focusing on the basis for incentives, bonus limits, and joint vs. individual targets.

> *Authority* — Assignment of authorities regarding who is empowered to execute trades, and to close positions opened by others.

Active commodities — Approval of which commodities, delivery dates, and instruments (forwards, swaps, options, etc.) are available for active trading or hedging.

Goal setting — Identification of the long and short term objectives, such as expected rate of return, portfolio variance, performance relative to benchmarks, and utilization of risk capital.

Limits — Setting limits for individuals and groups regarding the maximum permissible levels of exposure or risk, using metrics such as VaR, notional value, net quantity, or variance.

Reserves — Allocation of economic capital to various sources of risk exposure to serve as reserves against losses incurred in the normal course of business.

Astonishingly, the impact of choices regarding any of these controls has never been rigorously explored in a scientific sense. This is certainly due in part to the paucity of tools for performing these analyses. The primary approach to optimizing these controls has always been to begin with very conservative choices, and to relax those constraints very gradually. That approach may have saved some (but not all) firms in the energy industry from severe financial setbacks, but it has certainly reduced their profitability as well.

Experimenting with a firm's risk controls, however carefully, is bound to have occasional impact on that firm's financial performance. Reporting material adverse effects to one's shareholders is an excruciating exercise at best, and doing so as a result of improper risk controls is inexcusable. Experimental methods can now be utilized in a laboratory, where shareholders are insulated from the impacts of adjusting risk controls and incentives through trial and error.

Notes

[1] Vernon Smith, "What is Experimental Economics." Available on the World Wide Web at: *http://gmu-ices.org/article.php/368.html*

[2] ICE stands for the IntercontinentalExchange, an electronically traded energy market.

[3] "Incentivising: An Intuitive Approach to Raising Achievement;" on-going research lead by Roland Fryer. Available on the World Wide Web at *http://post.economics.harvard.edu/faculty/fryer/projects.html.*

[4]John O. Ledyard, David Porter and Antonio Rangel, "Using Computerized Exchanges to solve an Allocation Problem in Project Management." *Journal of Organizational Computing*, 4(3) 271-296 (1994).

[5]"Native position" here refers to exposures that reflect a core component of a business' activity, that are required for ongoing operations. Examples would include the obligation to serve customer load for a utility, or to market natural gas for a production company.

[6]Charles A. Holt and Susan K. Laury, "Risk Aversion and Incentive Effects." *American Economic Review*, 1644-1655, December (2002).

IMPORTANT CONTRACTS: APPENDIX A

Relevant Contracts for Energy Companies and Utilities in the USA

Commodity	Exchange	Futures	Options	Months Traded	Contract Size	Tick Size & Value	Daily Futures Volume	Daily Options Volume	Source
Energy									
Light, sweet crude,	NYMEX	X	X	All months	1,000 U.S. bbl (42,000 gal)	$0.01/bbl=$10	200,315	43,610	Futures
Henry Hub Natural Gas	NYMEX	X	X	All months	10,000 MMBtu	$0.001/mmBtu	66,068	30,576	Futures
Heating Oil	NYMEX	X	X	All months	1,000 U.S. bbl (42,000 gal)	$0.0001/gal= $4.20	48,805	3031	Futures
Propane*	NYMEX	X	None	All months	1,000 U.S. bbl (42,000 gal)	$0.0001/gal= $4.20	74	—	NYMEX, CFTC
Unleaded Gasoline	NYMEX	X	X	All months	1,000 U.S. bbl (42,000 gal)	$0.0001/gal= $4.20	48,399	3,426	Futures
Brent Crude	IPE	X	X	All months	1,000 U.S. bbl	$0.01/bbl=$10	96,433	109	Futures
Gas Oil	IPE	X	X	All months	100 metric tons	$0.25/ton=$25.00	35,439	171	Futures

279

Weather

Commodity	Exchange	Futures	Options	Months Traded	Contract Size	Tick Size & Value	Daily Futures and Options Volume	Source
Atlanta CDD Monthly	CME	X	X	Apr, May, Jun, Jul, Aug, Sep, Oct	$20 × CDD Index	1 DD = $20.00	22	CME
Atlanta CDD Seasonal	CME	X	X	Cooling Season — May through Sep	$20 × CDD Index	1 DD = $20.00	2	CME
Atlanta HDD Monthly	CME	X	X	Oct, Nov, Dec, Jan, Feb, Mar, Apr	$20 × HDD Index	1 DD = $20.00	22	CME
Atlanta HDD Seasonal	CME	X	X	Heating Season — Nov through Mar	$20 × HDD Index	1 DD = $20.00	2	CME
Boston CDD Monthly	CME	X	X	Apr, May, Jun, Jul, Aug, Sep, Oct	$20 × CDD Index	1 DD = $20.00	18	CME
Boston CDD Seasonal	CME	X	X	Cooling Season — May through Sep	$20 × CDD Index	1 DD = $20.00	0	CME
Boston HDD Monthly	CME	X	X	Oct, Nov, Dec, Jan, Feb, Mar, Apr	$20 × HDD Index	1 DD = $20.00	8	CME
Boston HDD Seasonal	CME	X	X	Heating Season — Nov through Mar	$20 × HDD Index	1 DD = $20.00	0	CME
Chicago CDD Monthly	CME	X	X	Apr, May, Jun, Jul, Aug, Sep, Oct	$20 × CDD Index	1 DD = $20.00	21	CME
Chicago CDD Seasonal	CME	X	X	Cooling Season — May through Sep	$20 × CDD Index	1 DD = $20.00	10	CME
Chicago HDD Monthly	CME	X	X	Oct, Nov, Dec, Jan, Feb, Mar, Apr	$20 × HDD Index	1 DD = $20.00	32	CME
Chicago HDD Seasonal	CME	X	X	Heating Season — Nov	$20 × HDD Index	1 DD = $20.00	8	CME

Commodity	Exchange	Futures	Options	Months Traded	Contract Size	Tick Size & Value	Daily Futures and Options Volume	Source
Cincinnati CDD Monthly	CME	X	X	Apr, May, Jun, Jul, Aug, Sep, Oct	$20 × CDD Index	1 DD = $20.00	37	CME
Cincinnati CDD Seasonal	CME	X	X	Cooling Season — May through Sep	$20 × CDD Index	1 DD = $20.00	2	CME
Cincinnati HDD Monthly	CME	X	X	Oct, Nov, Dec, Jan, Feb, Mar, Apr	$20 × HDD Index	1 DD = $20.00	8	CME
Cincinnati HDD Seasonal	CME	X	X	Heating Season — Nov through Mar	$20 × HDD Index	1 DD = $20.00	2	CME
Dallas CDD Monthly	CME	X	X	Apr, May, Jun, Jul, Aug, Sep, Oct	$20 × CDD Index	1 DD = $20.00	18	CME
Dallas CDD Seasonal	CME	X	X	Cooling Season — May through Sep	$20 × CDD Index	1 DD = $20.00	4	CME
Dallas HDD Monthly	CME	X	X	Oct, Nov, Dec, Jan, Feb, Mar, Apr	$20 × HDD Index	1 DD = $20.00	11	CME
Dallas HDD Seasonal	CME	X	X	Heating Season — Nov through Mar	$20 × HDD Index	1 DD = $20.00	0	CME
Des Moines CDD Monthly	CME	X	X	Apr, May, Jun, Jul, Aug, Sep, Oct	$20 × CDD Index	1 DD = $20.00	12	CME
Des Moines CDD Seasonal	CME	X	X	Cooling Season — May through Sep	$20 × CDD Index	1 DD = $20.00	1	CME
Des Moines HDD Monthly	CME	X	X	Oct, Nov, Dec, Jan, Feb, Mar, Apr	$20 × HDD Index	1 DD = $20.00	20	CME
Des Moines HDD Seasonal	CME	X	X	Heating Season — Nov through Mar	$20 × HDD Index	1 DD = $20.00	8	CME

281

Commodity	Exchange	Futures	Options	Months Traded	Contract Size	Tick Size & Value	Daily Futures and Options Volume	Source
Houston CDD Monthly	CME	X	X	Apr, May, Jun, Jul, Aug, Sep, Oct	$20 × CDD Index	1 DD = $20.00	13	CME
Houston CDD Seasonal	CME	X	X	Cooling Season — May through Sep	$20 × CDD Index	1 DD = $20.00	2	CME
Houston HDD Monthly	CME	X	X	Oct, Nov, Dec, Jan, Feb, Mar, Apr	$20 × HDD Index	1 DD = $20.00	2	CME
Houston HDD Seasonal	CME	X	X	Heating Season — Nov through Mar	$20 × HDD Index	1 DD = $20.00	0	CME
Kansas City CDD Monthly	CME	X	X	Apr, May, Jun, Jul, Aug, Sep, Oct	$20 × CDD Index	1 DD=$20.00	11	CME
Kansas City CDD Seasonal	CME	X	X	Cooling Season — May through Sep	$20 × CDD Index	1 DD = $20.00	0	CME
Kansas City HDD Monthly	CME	X	X	Oct, Nov, Dec, Jan, Feb, Mar, Apr	$20 × HDD Index	1 DD = $20.00	4	CME
Kansas City HDD Seasonal	CME	X	X	Heating Season — Nov through Mar	$20 × HDD Index	1 DD = $20.00	0	CME
Las Vegas CDD Monthly	CME	X	X	Apr, May, Jun, Jul, Aug, Sep, Oct	$20 × CDD Index	1 DD = $20.00	4	CME
Las Vegas CDD Seasonal	CME	X	X	Cooling Season — Mar through Sep	$20 × CDD Index	1 DD = $20.00	0	CME
Las Vegas HDD Monthly	CME	X	X	Oct, Nov, Dec, Jan, Feb, Mar, Apr	$20 × HDD Index	1 DD = $20.00	8	CME
Las Vegas HDD Seasonal	CME	X	X	Heating Season — Nov through Mar	$20 × HDD Index	1 DD = $20.00	0	CME

Commodity	Exchange	Futures	Options	Months Traded	Contract Size	Tick Size & Value	Daily Futures and Options Volume	Source
Minneapolis CDD Monthly	CME	X	X	Apr, May, Jun, Jul, Aug, Sep, Oct	$20 × CDD Index	1 DD = $20.00	26	CME
Minneapolis CDD Seasonal	CME	X	X	Cooling Season — May through Sep	$20 × CDD Index	1 DD = $20.00	0	CME
Minneapolis HDD Monthly	CME	X	X	Oct, Nov, Dec, Jan, Feb, Mar, Apr	$20 × HDD Index	1 DD=$20.00	10	CME
Minneapolis HDD Seasonal	CME	X	X	Heating Season — Nov through Mar	$20 × HDD Index	1 DD = $20.00	0	CME
New York CDD Monthly	CME	X	X	Apr, May, Jun, Jul, Aug, Sep, Oct	$20 × CDD Index	1 DD = $20.00	35	CME
New York CDD Seasonal	CME	X	X	Cooling Season — May through Sep	$20 × CDD Index	1 DD = $20.00	5	CME
New York HDD Monthly	CME	X	X	Oct, Nov, Dec, Jan, Feb, Mar, Apr	$20 × HDD Index	1 DD = $20.00	28	CME
New York HDD Seasonal	CME	X	X	Heating Season — Nov through Mar	$20 × HDD Index	1 DD = $20.000	2	CME
Philadelphia CDD Monthly	CME	X	X	Apr, May, Jun, Jul, Aug, Sep, Oct	$20 × CDD Index	1 DD = $20.00	11	CME
Philadelphia CDD Seasonal	CME	X	X	Cooling Season — May through Sep	$20 × CDD Index	1 DD = $20.00	0	CME
Philadelphia HDD Monthly	CME	X	X	Oct, Nov, Dec, Jan, Feb, Mar, Apr	$20 × HDD Index	1 DD = $20.00	6	CME
Philadelphia HDD Seasonal	CME	X	X	Heating Season — Nov through Mar	$20 × HDD Index	1 DD = $20.00	0	CME

Commodity	Exchange	Futures	Options	Months Traded	Contract Size	Tick Size & Value	Daily Futures and Options Volume	Source
Portland CDD Monthly	CME	X	X	Apr, May, Jun, Jul, Aug, Sep, Oct	$20 × CDD Index	1 DD = $20.00	2	CME
Portland CDD Seasonal	CME	X	X	Cooling Season — May through Sep	$20 × CDD Index	1 DD = $20.00	0	CME
Portland HDD Monthly	CME	X	X	Oct, Nov, Dec, Jan, Feb, Mar, Apr	$20 × HDD Index	1 DD = $20.00	4	CME
Portland HDD Seasonal	CME	X	X	Heating Season — Nov through Mar	$20 × HDD Index	1 DD = $20.00	0	CME
Sacramento CDD Monthly	CME	X	X	Apr, May, Jun, Jul, Aug, Sep, Oct	$20 × CDD Index	1 DD = $20.00	0	CME
Sacramento CDD Seasonal	CME	X	X	Cooling Season — May through Sep	$20 × CDD Index	1 DD = $20.00	0	CME
Sacramento HDD Monthly	CME	X	X	Oct, Nov, Dec, Jan, Feb, Mar, Apr	$20 × HDD Index	1 DD = $20.00	1	CME
Sacramento HDD Seasonal	CME	X	X	Heating Season — Nov through Mar	$20 × HDD Index	1 DD = $20.00	0	CME
Tucson CDD Monthly	CME	X	X	Apr, May, Jun, Jul, Aug, Sep, Oct	$20 × CDD Index	1 DD = $20.00	4	CME
Tucson CDD Seasonal	CME	X	X	Cooling Season — May through Sep	$20 × CDD Index	1 DD = $20.00	0	CME
Tucson HDD Monthly	CME	X	X	Oct, Nov, Dec, Jan, Feb, Mar, Apr	$20 × HDD Index	1 DD = $20.00	1	CME
Tucson HDD Seasonal	CME	X	X	Heating Season — Nov through Mar	$20 × HDD Index	1 DD = $20.00	0	CME

Interest Rates

Commodity	Exchange	Futures	Options	Months Traded	Contract Size	Tick Size & Value	Daily Futures Volume	Daily Options Volume	Source
30 Year T-Bond	CBOT	X	X	Mar., June, Sep., Dec.	$100,000	1/32 pt = $31.25	276,322	52,230	Futures
10 Year T-Bond	CBOT	X	X	Mar., June, Sep., Dec.	$100,000	1/2 of 1/32 pt = $15.625	742,876	215,447	Futures
5 Year T-Note	CBOT	X	X	Mar., June, Sep., Dec.	$100,000	1/2 of 1/32 pt = $15.625	399,505	65,212	Futures
2 Year T-Note	CBOT	X	X	Mar., June, Sep., Dec.	$200,000	1/4 of 1/32 pt = $15.625	35,814	39	Futures
Eurodollar	CME	X	X	Mar., June, Sep., Dec. (Next 4)	$1,000,000	0.01 = $25	1,127,212	494,615	Futures
30-day Fed Funds	CBOT	X	X	Next 24 months	$5,000,000	1/2 of 1 basis pt = $20.835	45,228	17,830	Futures
LIBOR	CME	X		12 months	$3,000,000	0.005 = $12.50	10,936	0	Futures

285

Commodity	Exchange	Futures	Options	Months Traded	Contract Size	Tick Size & Value	Daily Futures Volume	Daily Options Volume	Source
Foreign Exchange									
Euro	CME	X	X	Mar., June, Sep., Dec.	€ 125,000	0.0001=$12.50	77,487	5,655	Futures
Japanese Yen	CME	X	X	Mar., June, Sep., Dec.	¥12,500,000	0.000001=$12.50	28,013	1,762	Futures
Canadian Dollar	CME	X	X	Mar., June, Sep., Dec.	C$100,000	0.0001=$10.00	21,255	724	Futures
British Pound	CME	X	X	Mar., June, Sep., Dec.	£62,500	0.0002=$12.50	17,714	630	Futures
Swiss Franc	CME	X	X	Mar., June, Sep., Dec.	SF125,000	0.0001=$12.50	15,408	211	Futures
Mexican Peso	CME	X	X	13 months	MP500,000	0.000025=$12.50	12,300	14	Futures
Australian Dollar	CME	X	X	Mar., June, Sep., Dec.	A$100,000	0.0001=$10.00	10,124	230	Futures
Brazilian Real/Dollar	BM&F	X	X	All Months	R$50000	R$0.001/$1.000=R$0.05	90,696	10261	Futures

Commodity	Exchange	Futures	Options	Months Traded	Contract Size	Tick Size & Value	Daily Futures Volume	Daily Options Volume	Source
Equity									
S&P 500	CME	(Futures)	CBOE (Options)	Mar., June, Sep., Dec.	$250 X Index	0.1=$25	61,271	187,394	Futures
Dow Jones	CBOT	(Futures)	CBOE (Options)	Mar., June, Sep., Dec.	$10 X Index	1 pt=$10	9,762	27,830	Futures

Notes

*Assume 252 day trading year for determining daily trading volume.

Exchange Abbreviations	Exchange	Country	Other Abbreviations	
BM&F	Bolsa de Mercadorias & Futuros	Brazil	CFTC	Commodities Futures Trading Commission
CBOE	Chicago Board Options Exchange	USA	Futures	*Futures* Magazine
CBOT	Chicago Board of Trade	USA		
CME	Chicago Mercantile Exchange	USA		
IPE	International Petroleum Exchange	UK		
NYMEX	New York Mercantile Exchange	USA		

Sources:

Zwick, Steve. "Why Can't We All Just Get Along?" *Futures* Magazine, April 2005, pp. 66-71.

Commodity Futures Trading Commission, CFTC Annual Report 2004.

Chicago Mercantile Exchange website and correspondence.
Thanks to Felix Carabello and David Smith. *http://www.cme.com.*

New York Mercantile Exchange website, *http://www.nymex.com.*

Value at Risk (VaR) and Other Risk Measures

The risk management profession overflows with jargon that bewilders both novice and experienced practitioners. In reality, many popular risk measurements are simple, and in some cases may not be that useful. Still, they are widely used in risk reports for management and documents disclosed to the public, so managers, directors, and investors, can benefit from familiarizing themselves with the common measures and should be wary of those who place great faith in Value at Risk and its offspring. An understanding of these measures will better prepare the reader to understand risk reports.

Value at Risk

One of the most common risk measurements is **Value at Risk (VaR).**[1] "VaR measures the worst expected loss over a given horizon under normal market conditions at a given confidence level."[2]

How is it Figured?

Value at Risk can be figured in three ways: using historical data, parametric means, and Monte Carlo simulations.[3]

Method 1 — Empirical

One simple way to calculate VaR is to collect and analyze data on the portfolio's value over a selected time period. It helps to graph the distribution as a histogram to observe whether it appears to be normally distributed, and in some cases to test that assumption formally. Histograms show the range of values that occur over the year. (Figure B-1). VaR is usually measured as the worst expected loss that will occur 95% of the time (although the confidence intervals can be adjusted to any desired level). When using a 95% confidence interval, the Value at Risk occurs at the line that separates the worst 5% of performances from the rest of the sample (as seen in Figure B-1). Another way of thinking about the 5% level is to consider a period of 20 trading days. The 95% confidence interval implies that, on average, 19 days out of 20, the portfolio will trade above the Value at Risk cutoff. On average, one day out of 20, the worst loss will exceed the Value at Risk — by an unknown amount. It could be just over the line, or very, very bad.

Consider an investor that has $100 at the beginning of the year that he will commit to the markets. He wishes to maintain the value of the portfolio throughout the year, which totals 250 trading days. Figure B-1 shows what happens during the year. The expected value of the portfolio is $100 and 5% of the time, the portfolio would be expected to fall below $40. Consequently the value at risk is $60. On average, one day out of 20 (or 12.5 days in a year of 250 trading days), the portfolio can fall through $40 VaR cutoff — to $39.50 or zero — the loss can not be known from VaR.

Method 2 —Parametric

Instead of using a complete historical data set, the parametric method uses the standard deviation of a portfolio along with the initial value of the portfolio to calculate Value at Risk.[4] Here is a simplified example based on the data used in Method 1. The initial value of the portfolio is $100 and the standard deviation is $36.47. The Value at Risk for a 95% confidence interval is, by definition, the difference between the initial value of the portfolio ($100) and cutoff point ($40) that occurs 1.645 standard deviations below the initial value. Thus the VaR is $60. Here is the calculation:

$$VAR = \$100 - \$40 = \$60$$

This calculation is highly simplified and readers are advised to consult a VaR text such as Jorion to go through the detailed calculations.[5]

Method 3 — Monte Carlo

The Monte Carlo method provides an estimate of VaR by simulating random scenarios and then calculating the effects of those scenarios on the value of the portfolio. Monte Carlo simulations approximate the behavior of the prices of the instruments through the use of an algorithm that creates a random price path.[6]

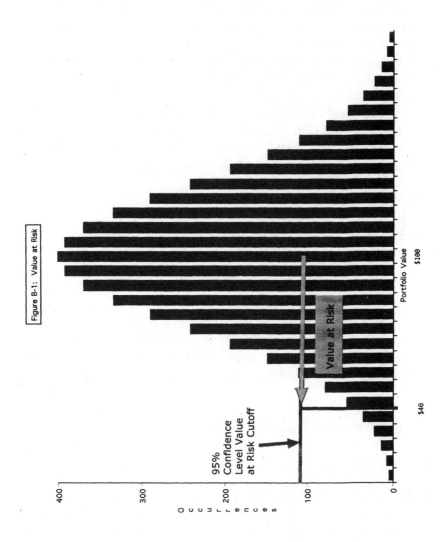

Figure B-1: Value at Risk

The concept of Value at Risk has also been extended to other measures such as Cash Flow at Risk and Credit Value at Risk.

Cash Flow at Risk (CFaR)

Cash Flow at Risk is the worst expected level of cash flow for a given time horizon at a specified statistical level. Cash Flow at Risk applies the VaR methodology to looking at the probability of having cash flow fall beneath a given level.[7] Again, it is modeled in the same form as Value at Risk, with the difference that Value at Risk looks at the worst expected loss of an asset class, while Cash Flow at Risk indicates potential low levels of cash flow over a given time horizon. CFaR is more applicable to businesses that are not financial institutions, where the significant risks to the firm come from drop-offs in cash flows, rather than the valuation of portfolios of securities.

Credit Value at Risk (CVaR)[8]

Over time, it is likely that an organization will sustain losses due to failure of counterparties in deals to make good on payment for a sale, or by not delivering what was purchased. A distribution can be plotted, similar to Figure B-1, that depicts the risk of losing money from a counterparty default. Once one of these distributions is assembled, from either historical, parametric, or Monte Carlo methods, the Credit Value at Risk can be calculated. Typically CVaR, or unexpected loss, is the difference between the expected loss over a particular time horizon and the loss at the 5% confidence level cutoff, as seen in Figure B-1.

Limitations of VaR and its Methodology

Although VaR is widely used, it is also abused and used to confuse. One of the strongest arguments against reliance (or over reliance) on VaR comes from the renowned mathematician Benoit Mandelbrot, who has questioned a number of the tenets that underlie modern financial thinking.[9] One major failing is that the returns in financial markets may not always follow a symmetrical, normal bell curve, which underlies VaR methodology. Oftentimes, financial events have curves that are asymmetrical, with extreme value events on one side of the curve having greater probabilities of occurring than those on the other side of the curve.

The appeal of VaR lies in the fact that it provides one number for those who want a quick take on an organization's risk profile. Those who read VaR reports need to understand that VaR, CFaR, or Credit at Risk, are merely numbers based on a simple methodology, and that VaR limits can and will be exceeded, regularly.

Looking at VaR, remember that those traders who understand how VaR works can game the system to create a deceptive picture of the actual risks they incur, not to mention commit fraud. In 1995, Barings Bank, one of the oldest in the UK, was brought down by the rogue trading of one employee, Nick Leeson, whose positions had a VaR of zero two days before $1.4 billion in losses were discovered. Because he controlled both the back office operations and trading, he made sure that his losses were entered as errors into the trading system, and the errors were not reported to the Barings risk system, creating a deceptive picture of the risk to which he exposed the firm. The VaR numbers are only as good as the data that are entered into the systems.[10]

There are other fundamental weaknesses behind these numbers. Ultimately VaR, CFaR, or Credit at Risk are based on historical rates of risk and return. Those rates may not recur, in which case, the model may set risk levels that are irrelevant to present operations.

There are more fundamental weaknesses that underlie the VaR model. The main one is the assumption of normality that underlies these models, with their nice, symmetrical bell curves. As noted before, research by Benoit Mandelbrot questions many of the assumptions that underlie modern finance, including Value at Risk. As he describes VaR, "The same false assumptions that underestimate stock-market risk, misprice options, build bad portfolios, and generally misconstrue the financial world are also built into the standard risk software used by many of the world's banks."[11] Mandelbrot points out that Value at Risk doesn't describe potential losses — what happens for example if you are beyond the 5% level? Your losses could be much worse.[12] In addition, Mandelbrot observes that many of the models consistently underestimate the risks of adverse market events. According to Mandelbrot, modern financial theorists have significantly underestimated the risk in financial markets. Understanding these limitations will help produce better consumers of these relatively simplistic numbers.[13]

Risk Adjusted Return on Capital

Another often talked about measure is Risk Adjusted Return on Capital (RAROC). This is a simple way to adjust returns for risk levels, and better understand past investments and incorporate risk into planning for future spending.

The concept underlying RAROC can be understood through an example of two traders who work in a speculative trading venture at a large financial firm. Trader A deals in low volatility Treasury Bills and Trader B deals in the highly volatile oil markets. In the calendar year, both bring in $10 million of income. However, Trader A has a Value at Risk of $100 million, while Trader B has a value of risk of $500 million.

RAROC is calculated as follows:

$$\text{RAROC} = \frac{\text{Expected Return}}{\text{VaR}}$$

RAROC for Trader A is: $10 Million/$100 million = 10%

RAROC for Trader B is: $10 Million/$500 million = 2%

Essentially, Trader A uses risk more effectively than Trader B. When determining how to compensate traders, this type of analysis could be useful in pointing compensation toward traders that may make more efficient use of the capital with which they are entrusted.

Conclusion

The measurements discussed above provide a snapshot of risk. They are simply one piece of the overall risk puzzle and should not be considered as the definitive risk measures, if there are any. They can be manipulated.

Often these measurements may provide no more than a representation of risk based on assumptions about markets that may be weak, at best, or useless at worst. In no way should the desire for an easy to digest number do away with the hard work of trying to understand the risks that the organization faces — which can't be distilled into one easy number. Although measures may appear scientific, the reality is that relying on inaccurate numbers that create misleading pictures of corporate health may lead to worse decisions than relying on accurate, but qualitative, information — such as the fact that a trader is not entering his losing trades in the corporate risk management system. The realization of these weaknesses, however, will make the reader a better consumer of information that portrays the risks a firm faces.

Notes

[1] One reason that Value at Risk is widely used is that it is one of the three options that the Securities and Exchange Commission (SEC) in the United States requires to disclose derivatives risk. The Commission requires registrants to disclose: "quantitative information about market risk sensitive instruments using one or more of the following alternatives:

i. Tabular presentation of fair value information and contract terms relevant to determining future cash flows, categorized by expected maturity dates;

ii. Sensitivity analysis expressing the potential loss in future earnings, fair values, or cash flows from selected hypothetical changes in market rates and prices; or

iii. Value at risk disclosures expressing the potential loss in future earnings, fair values, or cash flows from market movements over a selected period of time and with a selected likelihood of occurrence."

Source: Securities and Exchange Commission. 17 CFR Parts 210, 228, 229, 239, 240, and 249 [Release Nos. 33-7386; 34-38223; IC-22487; FR-48; International Series No. 1047; File No. S7-35-95]. RIN 3235-AG42. RIN 3235-AG77. *Disclosure of Accounting Policies for Derivative Financial Instruments and Derivative Commodity Instruments and Disclosure of Quantitative and Qualitative Information about Market Risk Inherent in Derivative Financial Instruments, other Financial Instruments, and Derivative Commodity Instruments.* p. 8. Available on the World Wide Web at: *http://www.sec.gov/rules/final/33-7386.txt*

Frank Partnoy, in his book, *Infectious Greed*, writes that firms chose to use VaR in their risk disclosures because it was the easiest of the three options to implement. Source: Frank Partnoy, *Infectious Greed: How Deceit and Risk Corrupted the Financial Markets* (New York: Times Books, 2003).

[2] Philippe Jorion, *Value at Risk: The New Benchmark for Managing Financial Risk,* Second Edition (New York: McGraw-Hill, 2001), p. xxii.

In statistics a confidence level describes the probability that the result is reliable. A 95% confidence level implies there is a 5% (1-0.95) chance that the result is unreliable. (Collins Reference. *Dictionary of Mathematics,* E.J. Borowski and J.M. Borwein, editors (London: Collins, 1989). Definition for *confidence level,* p. 107.

[3]A detailed discussion of the latter two methods of arriving at VaR are beyond the scope of this book. Those who desire more information on these two methods are advised to consult the following references: (1) Philippe Jorion, *Value at Risk: The Benchmark for Managing Financial Risk* (New York: McGraw-Hill, 2001). (2) Committee of Chief Risk Officers Valuation and Risk Metrics Working Group. *Valuation and Risk Metrics.* White Paper, November 19, 2002, Committee of Chief Risk Officers.

[4]The standard deviation measures the dispersion of a distribution. A larger standard deviation tends to imply a more variable distribution.

[5]Philippe Jorion, *Value at Risk: The New Benchmark for Managing Financial Risk.* Second Edition (New York: McGraw-Hill), 2001.

[6]CCRO, *op. cit.,* p. 2. Many of these simulations are based on the assumption that prices behave in ways that assume Brownian motion, which may be a flawed assumption according to Benoit Mandelbrot.

[7]Didier Cossin, "A Route Through the Hazards of Business," *FTMastering Corporate Governance,* 10 June 2005, p. 5.

[8]Committee of Chief Risk Officers Credit Risk Management Working Group. *Credit Risk Management.* White Paper, November 19, 2002, Committee of Chief Risk Officers, pp. 13-15.

[9]Benoit Mandelbrot and Richard L. Hudson, *The (Mis)behavior of Markets: A Fractal View of Risk, Ruin, and Reward* (New York: Basic Books, 2004). *See* chapters 3, 4, and 5.

[10]Frank Partnoy, *Infectious Greed: How Deceit and Risk Corrupted the Financial Markets* (New York: Times Books, 2003), p. 243.

[11]Benoit Mandelbrot and Richard L. Hudson, *op. cit.,* p. 272.

[12]Benoit Mandelbrot and Richard L. Hudson. *op. cit.,* pp. 272-274.

[13]Author (*Fooled by Randomness*) and trader, Nicholas Nassim Taleb equates VAR with charlatanism — "the concealment of a poor understanding of economics with mathematical smoke." Source: "Against Value-at-Risk," Nassim Taleb Replies to Philippe Jorion." Available on the World Wide Web at: *http://www.fooledbyrandomness.com/jorion.html.* Taleb is an adjunct professor at NYU'S Courant Institute of Mathematical Sciences, so his criticism of VaR cannot be disputed for lack of quantitative background. He criticizes those who use VaR and, "replace 2,500 years of market experience with a co-variance matrix that is still in its infancy. We made a tabula rasa of market lore that was picked up from trader to trader and crammed everything into a co-variance matrix." Source: "The World According to Nassim Taleb." *Deriva-*

tives Strategy, December 1996/January 1997. Available on the World Wide Web at: *http://www.derivativesstrategy.com/magazine/archive/1997/1296qa. asp.*

Taleb proposes these rules of thumb as guides to risk:

"Trader Risk Management Lore: Major Rules of Thumb

Rule 1 — Do not venture in markets and products you do not understand. You will be a sitting duck.

Rule 2 — The large hit you will take next will not resemble the one you took last. Do not listen to the consensus as to where the risks are (*i.e.* risks shown by VAR). What will hurt you is what you expect the least.

Rule 3 — Believe half of what you read, none of what you hear. Never study a theory before doing your own prior observation and thinking. Read every piece of theoretical research you can — but stay a trader. An unguarded study of lower quantitative methods will rob you of your insight.

Rule 4 — Beware of the trader who makes a steady income. Those tend to blow up. Traders with very frequent losses might hurt you, but they are not likely to blow you up. Long volatility traders lose money most days of the week. (Learned name: the small sample properties of the Sharpe ratio).

Rule 5 — The markets will follow the path to hurt the highest number of hedgers. The best hedges are those you are the only one to put on.

Rule 6 — Never let a day go by without studying the changes in the prices of all available trading instruments. You will build an instinctive inference that is more powerful than conventional statistics.

Rule 7 — The greatest inferential mistake: this event never happens in my market. Most of what never happened before in one market has happened in another. The fact that someone never died before does not make him immortal. (Learned name: Hume's problem of induction).

Rule 8 — Never cross a river because it is on average 4 feet deep.

Rule 9 — Read every book by traders to study where they lost money. You will learn nothing relevant from their profits (the markets adjust). You will learn from their losses."

Source: *http://www.fooledbyrandomness.com/jorion.html.*

Explanation of Glossary

This glossary contains terms gleaned from the organizations listed below. The source of each term is denoted, when applicable. A key to the abbreviations of the sources follows:

CFTC: Commodity Futures Trading Commission

CCRO: Committee of Chief Risk Officers

EIA: Energy Information Administration

NYMEX: New York Mercantile Exchange

Cross-References: To make the glossary more useful to those who are unfamiliar with the key terms of energy trading, references to other definitions are *italicized*. If a definition contains two-or-more words, that term is *italicized* and *underlined.*

a

abandon: To elect not to *exercise* or *offset* a *long option position.* [CFTC]

accommodation trading: Non-competitive *trading* entered into by a *trader*, usually to assist another with illegal trades. [CFTC]

actively traded: Any energy *commodity* for which a *buyer* and seller can be found in a relatively short time frame. [CCRO]

actuals: The physical or *cash commodity,* as distinguished from a *futures contract.* See *cash commodity* and *spot commodity.* [CFTC]

adequate assurance: Any additional information, security interest, or collateral that provides the requesting party with assurance that its *counterparty* will fulfill its obligations under contracts between the parties. (See article 2 part 6 of the UCC [Uniform Commercial Code] for a formal legal definition.) [CCRO]

aggregation: The principle under which all *futures positions* owned or controlled by one *trader* (or group of traders acting in concert) are combined to determine reporting status and compliance with *speculative position limits.* [CFTC]

aggregator: Any marketer, *broker*, public agency, city, county, or special district that combines the loads of multiple end-use customers in negotiating the purchase of electricity, the *transmission* of electricity, and other related services for these customers. [EIA]

all-or-none: An order which must be *filled* in its entirety or not at all. [NYMEX]

allowances: The *discounts (premiums)* allowed for *grades* or *locations* of a *commodity* lower (higher) than the *par* (or *basis) grade* or location specified in the *futures contract.* See *differentials.* [CFTC]

alternative delivery procedure (ADP): A provision of a *futures contract* that allows *buyers* and sellers to make and take *delivery* under terms or conditions that differ from those prescribed in the contract. An ADP may occur at any time during the delivery period, after *long* and *short futures positions* have been matched by the *Exchange* for the purpose of delivery. [NYMEX]

American option: An *option* that can be *exercised* at any time prior to or on the *expiration date.* See *European option.* [CFTC]

American Petroleum Institute (API): The primary U.S. oil industry trade association, based in Washington, D.C. API conducts research and sets technical standards for industry equipment and products from wellhead to retail outlet. It also compiles statistics which are regarded as industry benchmarks. [NYMEX]

American Society for Testing & Materials (ASTM): *Grade* and quality *specifications* for *petroleum* products and metals are determined by the ASTM in test methods. [NYMEX]

ancillary services: Services that ensure *reliability* and support the *transmission* of electricity from generation sites to customer loads. Such services may include: load regulation, *spinning reserve,* non-spinning reserve, replacement reserve, and voltage support. [EIA]

anthracite: Sometimes called hard *coal,* it has the highest energy content of all coals, and is generally mined in the Appalachian region of Pennsylvania. [NYMEX]

API: The *American Petroleum Institute,* a trade association. [EIA]

API gravity: *American Petroleum Institute* measure of *specific gravity* of *crude oil* or condensate in degrees. An arbitrary scale expressing the gravity or density of liquid *petroleum* products. The measuring scale is calibrated in terms of degrees *API*; it is calculated as follows: Degrees API = (141.5 / sp. gr. 60° F/60° F) − 131.5 [EIA]

approved delivery facility: Any bank, stockyard, mill, storehouse, plant, elevator, or other depository that is authorized by an *exchange* for the *delivery* of commodities *tendered* on *futures contracts.* [CFTC]

arbitrage: The simultaneous entering into of offsetting *transactions* that completely eliminate market *price risk* and lock in either an immediate riskless profit at no cost today or a return on investment greater than the risk-free rate. This sort of opportunity is generally short lived, as market arbitrageurs force prices back in line with each other and arbitrage away the opportunity. In practice, arbitrage may still contain credit and *operational risks.* There are a number of market activities referred to as "arbitrage like." Merger arbitrage, dividend arbitrage, etc., are not true arbitrage because future price movements can eliminate profits and/or cause losses. [CCRO]

Asian option/average price option: An *option* whose value at expiration is determined by the average price of the *underlying instrument* over some specified period of time. [CCRO]

ask: The lowest price an investor will accept to sell an asset or product. Practically speaking, this is the quoted offer at which an investor can buy the asset or product; also called the offer price. [CCRO]

assay: To test a metal or an oil for purity or quality. [NYMEX]

assignment: Designation by a *clearing organization* of a *writer* who will be required to buy (in the case of a *put*) or sell (in the case of a *call*) the *underlying futures contract* or *security* when an *option* has been *exercised*, especially if it has been exercised early. [CFTC]

Associated Person (AP): An individual who solicits or accepts (other than in a clerical capacity) orders, *discretionary accounts,* or participation in a *commodity pool,* or supervises any individual so engaged, on behalf of a *Futures Commission Merchant,* an *Introducing Broker,* a *Commodity Trading Advisor,* a *Commodity Pool Operator,* or an Agricultural Trade Option Merchant. [CFTC]

ASTM: The acronym for the *American Society for Testing and Materials.* [EIA]

at-the-market: An order to buy or sell a *futures contract* at whatever price is obtainable when the order reaches the *trading floor.* Also called a *market order.* [NYMEX]

at-the-money: An *option* or *derivative* whose *exercise price* is equal to the current price of the *underlying* asset or *contract.* [CCRO]

audit trail: The record of *trading* information identifying, for example, the *brokers* participating in each *transaction*, the firms *clearing* the trade, the terms and time or sequence of the trade, the order receipt and execution time and, ultimately, and when applicable, the customers involved. [CFTC]

automatic exercise: A provision in an *option contract* specifying that it will be *exercised* automatically on the *expiration date* if it is *in-the-money* by a specified amount, absent instructions to the contrary. [CFTC]

b

back months: *Futures delivery months* other than the *spot* or *front month* (also called deferred months). [CFTC]

back office: The department in a financial institution that processes and deals and handles *delivery*, settlement and regulatory procedures. [CFTC]

back pricing: Fixing the price of a *commodity* for which the commitment to purchase has been made in advance. The *buyer* can fix the price relative to any monthly or periodic *delivery* using the *futures markets.* [CFTC]

back spread: A *delta-neutral ratio spread* in which more *options* are bought than sold. A back spread will be profitable if *volatility* increases. See *delta.* [CFTC]

backwardation: Market situation in which *futures prices* are progressively lower in the *distant delivery months.* For instance, if the gold *quotation* for January is $360.00 per ounce and that for June is $355.00 per ounce, the backwardation for five months against January is $5.00 per ounce. (Backwardation is the opposite of *contango*). See *inverted market.* [CFTC]

barrel: A unit of volume measure used for *petroleum* and refined products. 1 barrel = 42 U.S. *gallons.* [NYMEX]

basis: The differential that exists at any time between the cash, or *spot*, price of a given *commodity* and the price of the nearest *futures contract* for the same or a related commodity. Basis may reflect different time periods, product forms, qualities, or *locations.* Cash minus *futures* equals basis. [NYMEX]

basis grade: The *grade* of a *commodity* used as the standard or *par* grade of a *futures contract.* [CFTC]

basis quote: Offer or sale of a *cash commodity* in terms of the difference above or below a *futures price* (*e.g.,* 10 cents over December corn). [CFTC]

303

basis risk: The risk associated with an unexpected widening or narrowing of *basis* between the time a *hedge position* is established and the time that it is lifted. [CFTC] (2) The risk that the value of a *futures contract* (or an *over-the-counter* hedge) will not move in line with that of the *underlying exposure*. Alternatively, it is the risk that the cash-*futures spread* will widen or narrow between the times that a hedge position is implemented and liquidated. There are various types of basis risk. For example, a *heating oil* wholesaler selling its product in Baltimore will be exposed to basis risk if it hedges using the New York Harbor Heating oil futures contract listed by the NYMEX. This is a locational basis risk. Other forms of basis risk include product basis, arising from mismatches in type or quality of hedge and underlying (*e.g.*, hedging *jet fuel* with *heating oil*); and time or calendar basis (*e.g.*, hedging an exposure to physical product in December with a January futures contract). Basis *differentials* are generally due to differences in geography, quality, *delivery*, time, and *options* valuations. [EPRM] [CCRO]

basis swap: A *swap* whose cash *settlement price* is calculated based on the *basis* between a *futures contract* and the *spot price* of the *underlying commodity* or a closely related commodity on a specified date. [CFTC]

bbl: The abbreviation for *barrel*(s). [EIA]

bbl/d: The abbreviation for *barrel*(s) per day. [EIA]

bcf: The abbreviation for billion cubic feet. [EIA]

b/d: *Barrels* per day. Usually used to quantify a *refiner's* output *capacity* or an oil field's rate of flow. [NYMEX]

bear: One who anticipates a decline in price or *volatility*. Opposite of a *bull*. [EIA]

bear market: A market in which prices generally are declining over a period of months or years. Opposite of *bull market.* [CFTC]

bear market rally: A temporary rise in prices during a *bear market.* See *correction*. [CFTC]

bear spread: (1) The simultaneous purchase and sale of two _futures contracts_ in the same or related commodities with the intention of profiting from a decline in prices but, at the same time, limiting the potential loss if this expectation is wrong. This can usually be accomplished by selling a _nearby delivery_ and buying a _deferred_ delivery. (2) A _delta_-negative _options position_ composed of _long_ and _short_ options of the same type, either _calls_ or _puts_, designed to be profitable in a declining market. An options _contract_ with a lower _strike price_ is sold and one with a higher strike price is bought. [NYMEX]

bear vertical spread: See _bear spread._ [CFTC]

beta (beta coefficient): A measure of the variability of rate of return or value of a stock or _portfolio_ compared to that of the overall market, typically used as a measure of riskiness. [CFTC]

bid: A motion to buy a _futures_ or _options contract_ at a specified price. Opposite of _offer._ [NYMEX]

bid-ask spread: The difference between what _buyers_ are willing to pay and what sellers are asking for in terms of price. [CCRO]

bilateral agreement: A written statement signed by two parties that specifies the terms for exchanging energy. [EIA]

bilateral electricity contract: A direct contract between an electric power producer and either a user or _broker_ outside of a centralized _power pool_ or _power exchange._ [EIA]

bituminous: Sometimes called "soft" _coal_, it has a higher _heating value_ than sub-bituminous and is the most commonly used coal for electric power generation in the United States. It is mined chiefly in Appalachia and the Midwest. [NYMEX]

Black-Scholes model: An _option pricing model_ initially developed by Fischer Black and Myron Scholes for securities _options_ and later refined by Black for options on _futures._ [CFTC]

board order: See _market-if-touched_ order. [CFTC]

board of trade: Any organized *exchange* or other _trading facility_ for the trading of *futures* and/or *option contracts*. [CFTC]

boe: abbreviation for *barrels* of *oil* equivalent (used internationally). [EIA]

booking out: A procedure for financially settling a *contract* for the physical *delivery* of energy. For example, booking out occurs when one party appears more than once in a contract path for the sale and purchase of energy. In that instance, the intervening counterparties may agree that they will not *schedule* or deliver physical energy that originates and ends with the same *counterparty*, but rather will settle in cash the amounts due to or from each intervening counterparty, thus booking out the *transaction*. [CCRO]

bookout [system operator definition]: A scheduling convenience allowing a purchaser or seller to avoid sending an electricity *schedule* to a system operator that normally does not relieve either party of financial responsibility. [CCRO]

book transfer: (1) A series of accounting or bookkeeping entries used to settle a series of _cash_ _market_ *transactions*. [CFTC] (2) Transfer of title without actually delivering the product. [NYMEX]

booking the basis: A forward pricing sales arrangement in which the _cash_ _price_ is determined either by the *buyer* or seller within a specified time. At that time, the previously-agreed *basis* is applied to the then-current *futures quotation*. [CFTC]

bottled gas, LPG, or propane: Any fuel *gas* supplied to a building in liquid form, such as _liquefied_ _petroleum_ _gas,_ _propane,_ or butane. It is usually delivered by tank truck and stored near the building in a tank or cylinder until used. [EIA]

bottom sediment and water (bs&w): Often found in *crude oil* and residual fuel. [NYMEX]

box spread: (1) An *options* market *arbitrage* in which both a _bull_ _spread_ and a _bear_ _spread_ are established for a risk-free profit. One *spread* includes _put_ _options_ and the other includes *calls*. [NYMEX] (2) An option *position* in which the owner establishes a *long* call and a *short put* at one _strike_ _price_ and a short call and a *long put* at another strike price, all of which are in the same *contract month* in the same *commodity*. [CFTC]

break: A rapid and sharp price decline. [CFTC]

breakeven point: The *underlying futures price* at which a given *options* strategy is neither profitable nor unprofitable. For *call options,* it is the *strike price* plus the *premium*. For *put options,* it is the strike price minus the premium. [NYMEX]

British thermal unit (BTU): The amount of heat required to increase the temperature of one pound of water one-degree *Fahrenheit*. A Btu is used as a common measure of *heating value* for different fuels. Prices of different fuels and their units of measure (dollars per *barrel* of crude, dollars per ton of *coal*, cents per *gallon* of gasoline, dollars per thousand cubic feet of *natural gas)* can be easily compared when expressed as dollars and cents per million Btus. [NYMEX]

broker: A person paid a fee or *commission* for executing buy or sell orders for a customer. In *commodity futures trading*, the term may refer to: (1) *Floor Broker* — a person who actually executes orders on the *trading floor* of an *exchange*; (2) Account Executive or *Associated Person* — the person who deals with customers in the offices of *Futures Commission Merchants;* or (3) the Futures Commission Merchant. [CFTC]

bs&w: See *bottom sediment and water*. [NYMEX]

Btu: The abbreviation for *British thermal unit*(s). [EIA]

Btu conversion factors: *Btu* conversion factors for *site energy* are as follows:

- Electricity. . . .   3,412 Btu/kilowatthour
- *Natural Gas* . . . .   1,031 Btu/ *cubic foot*
- *Fuel Oil* No.1 . . . . 135,000 Btu/*gallon*
- *Kerosene* . . . .   135,000 Btu/gallon
- Fuel Oil No. 2 . . . .   138,690 Btu/gallon
- *LPG (Propane)* . . . . 91,330 Btu/gallon
- Wood . . . .   20 million Btu/cord [EIA]

Btu per cubic foot: The total *heating value,* expressed in *Btu,* produced by the combustion, at constant pressure, of the amount of the gas that would occupy a volume of 1 *cubic foot* at a temperature of 60 degrees F if saturated with water vapor and under a pressure equivalent to that of 30 inches of mercury at 32 degrees F and under standard gravitational force (980.665 cm. per sec. squared) with air of the same temperature and pressure as the gas, when the products of combustion are cooled to the initial temperature of gas and air when the water formed by combustion is condensed to the liquid state. (Sometimes called gross heating value or total heating value.) [EIA]

bucketing: Directly or indirectly taking the opposite side of a customer's order into a *broker's* own account or into an account in which a broker has an interest, without open and competitive execution of the order on an *exchange.* Also called "trading against." [CFTC]

bucket shop: A brokerage enterprise that "books" (*i.e.,* takes the opposite side of) *retail customer* orders without actually having them executed on an *exchange.* [CFTC]

bulge: A rapid advance in *futures prices.* [NYMEX]

bull: One who anticipates an increase in price or *volatility.* Opposite of a *bear.* [NYMEX]

bull market: A market in which prices generally are rising over a period of months or years. Opposite of *bear market.* [CFTC]

bull spread: 1) The simultaneous purchase and sale of two *futures contracts* in the same or related commodities with the intention of profiting from a rise in prices but, at the same time, limiting the potential loss if this expectation is wrong. This can be accomplished by buying the *nearby delivery* and selling the *deferred.* 2) A *delta*-positive *options position* composed of both *long* and *short* options of the same type, either *calls* or puts, designed to be profitable in a rising market. An options contract with a lower *strike price* is bought and one with a higher strike price is sold. [NYMEX]

bull vertical spread: See *bull spread.* [CFTC]

bunched order: A discretionary order entered on behalf of multiple customers. [CFTC]

buoyant: A market in which prices have a tendency to rise easily with a considerable show of strength. [CFTC]

business day: For electric utilities, as determined by the *North American Electric Reliability Council* (NERC), the business day typically begins at 6 A.M. (the hour ending 0700) for a 24-hour period. Holidays are also determined by NERC and are separate from U.S.-designated holidays. For *futures* and *options contracts*, business days are *trading* days as determined by the *Exchange* board prior to the start of the year. [NYMEX]

butterfly spread: A three-legged *option spread* in which each leg has the same *expiration date* but different *strike prices.* For example, a butterfly spread in soybean *call options* might consist of one *long* call at a $5.50 strike price, two *short* calls at a $6.00 strike price, and one *long* call at a $6.50 strike price. [CFTC]

buyer: A market participant who takes a *long futures position* or buys an *option.* An *option buyer* is also called a *taker*, holder, or owner. [CFTC]

buyer's call: A purchase of a specified quantity of a specific *grade* of a *commodity* at a fixed number of points above or below a specified *delivery month futures price* with the buyer allowed a period of time to fix the price either by purchasing a *futures contract* for the account of the seller or telling the seller when he wishes to fix the price. See *seller's call.* [CFTC]

buyer's market: A condition of the market in which there is an abundance of goods available and hence buyers can afford to be selective and may be able to buy at less than the price that previously prevailed. See *seller's market.* [CFTC]

buying hedge (or **long hedge**): Hedging *transaction* in which *futures contracts* are bought to protect against possible increases in the cost of commodities. See *hedging.* [CFTC]

buy (or sell) on close: To buy (or sell) at the end of the *trading* session within the *closing price range.* [CFTC]

buy (or sell) on opening: To buy (or sell) at the beginning of a *trading* session within the open price *range.* [CFTC]

C

C & F: "Cost and Freight" paid to a point of destination and included in the price quoted; same as C.A.F. [CFTC]

calendar spread: (1) The purchase of one *delivery month* of a given *futures contract* and simultaneous sale of a different delivery month of the same futures contract; (2) the purchase of a *put* or *call option* and the simultaneous sale of the same type of *option* with typically the same *strike price* but a different *expiration date.* Also called a *horizontal spread* or *time spread* [CFTC]

call: (1) An *option contract* giving the *buyer* the right but not the obligation to purchase a *commodity* or other asset or to enter into a *long futures position*; (2) a period at the *opening* and the close of some *futures markets* in which the price for each *futures contract* is established by auction; or (3) the requirement that a *financial instrument* be returned to the issuer prior to maturity, with principal and accrued interest paid off upon return. See *buyer's call, seller's call.* [CFTC]

called: Another term for *exercised* when an *option* is a *call.* In the case of an option on a physical, the *writer* of a call must deliver the indicated *underlying commodity* when the option is exercised or called. In the case of an option on a *futures contract,* a futures *position* will be created that will require *margin,* unless the writer of the call has an offsetting position. [CFTC]

call option: See call.

call spread: Buying or owning a *call option* with a certain *strike price* and selling or owning a call option at a different strike price. Both *options* have the same *expiration date.* [CCRO]

cap: A supply *contract* between a *buyer* and a seller, whereby the buyer is assured that he will not have to pay more than a given maximum price. This type of contract is analogous to a *call option.* [NYMEX]

capacity: In general, the maximum volume of liquid or *gas* that can be pumped through a *pipeline*, or the maximum load that a generating unit or station can carry under specified conditions for a given period of time, or the total storage space or volume of a warehouse or storage container or tank farm. [NYMEX]

capital: In the long term, owner's claims to assets in the business reflected in *equity* or net worth. In the short term, capital or credit capital includes cash or its equivalents (letters of credit, *margin* and leases) to support the merchant business. [CCRO]

capital adequacy: The estimate of *capital* required to support the business. Capital adequacy requirements for (energy) *trading* and marketing firms provide stakeholders with a certain amount of confidence that various types of potential events and event externalities will not drive the business into a bankruptcy. [CCRO]

carrying broker: An *exchange* member firm, usually a *Futures Commission Merchant,* through whom another *broker* or customer elects to clear all or part of its trades. [CFTC]

carrying charges: Cost of storing a physical *commodity* or holding a *financial instrument* over a period of time. These charges include insurance, storage, and interest on the deposited funds, as well as other incidental costs. It is a carrying charge market when there are higher *futures prices* for each successive *contract maturity*. If the carrying charge is adequate to reimburse the holder, it is called a "full charge." See *negative carry, positive carry,* and *contango*. [CFTC]

carry market: A market situation in which prices are higher in the succeeding *delivery months* than in the nearest delivery month. Also known as *contango*, it is the opposite of *backwardation*. [NYMEX]

cash commodity: The physical or actual *commodity* as distinguished from the *futures* *contract,* sometimes called *spot* *commodity* or *actuals*. [CFTC]

cash flow: Cash from operations (*i.e.*, cash receipts and disbursements during the specified reporting period). Also known as cash *earnings*, which are cash revenues less cash expenses. [CCRO]

Cash Flow at Risk (CFaR): (1) The application of *value* *at* *risk* (VaR) methodology to a nonfinancial firm's business operations. In this context, the VaR is defined in terms of *earnings* or *cash flow* and expressed as the probability that the company will fail to meet its business targets. Typically, a CFaR model would be used to simulate future financial statements, taking as its input the projected values of the financial prices relevant to the company. In this way, it would be possible to build up a probabilistic picture of the impact of various risks on the company's cash flow or profitability in much the same way as financial institutions use VaR to find the probability of losses on a *portfolio* of assets. [JP Morgan]; (2) A statistical measure of the variability of cash earnings from a portfolio of *positions* or a given economic activity due to potential changes in the market prices of the commodities or other variables underlying the portfolio or activity. Two parameters are typically associated with CFaR, the *degree* *of* *confidence,* and the *holding period.* [CCRO]

cash forward sale: See *forward* *contract.* [CFTC]

cash market: The market for the *cash* *commodity* (as contrasted to a *futures* *contract*) taking the form of: (1) an organized, self-regulated central market (*e.g.*, a *commodity exchange*); (2) a decentralized *over-the-counter* market; or (3) a local organization, such as a grain elevator or meat processor, which provides a market for a small region. [CFTC]

cash price: The price in the marketplace for actual cash or *spot* *commodities* to be delivered via customary market channels. [CFTC]

cash-settled: *Futures* *contracts* that are settled in cash without the option to deliver the *underlying* *commodity.* [NYMEX]

CDD: See *cooling degree-days* below. [EIA]

CEA: *Commodity Exchange Act* or Commodity Exchange Authority. [CFTC]

certificated or certified stocks: *Stocks* of a *commodity* that have been inspected and found to be of a quality deliverable against *futures contracts*, stored at the *delivery points* designated as regular or acceptable for delivery by an *exchange*. In grain, called "stocks in deliverable position." See *deliverable stocks*. [CFTC]

CFTC: See *Commodity Futures Trading Commission*. [CFTC]

CFO: Cancel Former Order. [CFTC]

charting: The use of graphs and charts in the analysis of market behavior, so as to plot *trends* of price movements, average movements of price, volume, and *open interest*, in the hope that such graphs and charts will help one to anticipate and profit from price trends. Contrasts with *fundamental analysis*. [NYMEX]

chartist: Technical *trader* who reacts to signals derived from graphs of price movements. [CFTC]

chooser option: An *exotic option* that is transacted in the present, but that at some specified future date is chosen to be either a *put* or a *call option*. [CFTC]

churning: Excessive *trading* of a *discretionary account* by a person with control over the account for the purpose of generating *commissions* while disregarding the interests of the customer. [CFTC]

CIF: See *cost, insurance, freight*. [EIA]

city gate: Generally refers to the location at which *gas* changes ownership or transportation responsibility from a *pipeline* to a *local distribution company* or gas utility. [NYMEX]

class of options: All *call options*, or all *put options*, exercisable for the same *underlying futures contract* and which expire on the same *expiration date*. [NYMEX]

clearing: The procedure through which the *clearing organization* becomes the *buyer* to each seller of a *futures contract* or other *derivative*, and the seller to each buyer for *clearing members.* [CFTC]

clearing association: See *clearing organization.* [CFTC]

clearing house: See *clearing organization.* [CFTC]

clearing member: *Clearing* members of the New York Mercantile Exchange accept responsibility for all trades cleared through them, and share secondary responsibility for the *liquidity* of the Exchange's clearing operation. They earn *commissions* for clearing their customers' trades, and enjoy special *margin* privileges. *Original margin* requirements for clearing members are lower than for non-clearing members and customers, and clearing members may use letters of credit posted with the *clearinghouse* as original margin for customer accounts as well as for their own trades. Clearing members must meet a minimum *capital* requirement. [NYMEX]

clearing organization: An entity through which *futures* and other *derivative transactions* are cleared and settled. It is also charged with assuring the proper conduct of each *contract's delivery* procedures and the adequate financing of *trading*. A clearing organization may be a division of a particular *exchange*, an adjunct or affiliate thereof, or a freestanding entity. Also called a *clearing house, multilateral clearing organization,* or *clearing association.* See *derivatives clearing organization.* [CFTC]

clearing price: See *settlement price.* [CFTC]

close: The *exchange*-designated period at the end of the *trading* session during which all *transactions* are considered made "at the close." See *call.* [CFTC]

closing-out: Liquidating an existing *long* or *short futures* or *option position* with an equal and opposite *transaction*. Also known as *offset.* [CFTC]

closing price (or **range**): The price (or price *range*) recorded during *trading* that takes place in the final period of a trading session's activity that is officially designated as the "*close*." [CFTC]

coal: A readily combustible black or brownish-black rock whose composition, including inherent moisture, consists of more than 50 percent by weight and more than 70 percent by volume of carbonaceous material. It is formed from plant remains that have been compacted, hardened, chemically altered, and metamorphosed by heat and pressure over geologic time. [EIA]

coal grade: This classification refers to coal *quality* and use.

• **Briquettes** are made from compressed *coal* dust, with or without a binding agent such as asphalt.

• **Cleaned coal** or **prepared coal** has been processed to reduce the amount of impurities present and improve the burning characteristics.

• **Compliance coal** is a coal, or a blend of coal, that meets *sulfur* dioxide emission standards for air quality without the need for flue-gas desulfurization.

• **Culm and silt** are waste materials from preparation plants. In the *anthracite* region, culm consists of coarse rock fragments containing as much as 30 percent small-sized *coal*. Silt is a mixture of very fine coal particles (approximately 40 percent) and rock dust that has settled out from waste water from the plants. The terms culm and silt are sometimes used interchangeably and are sometimes called refuse. Culm and silt have a heat value ranging from 8 to 17 million *Btu* per ton.

• **Low-sulfur coal** generally contains 1 percent or less *sulfur* by weight. For air quality standards, "low sulfur coal" contains 0.6 pounds or less sulfur per million *Btu*, which is equivalent to 1.2 pounds of sulfur dioxide per million Btu.

• **Metallurgical coal** (or **coking coal**) meets the requirements for making coke. It must have a low ash and *sulfur* content and form a coke that is capable of supporting the charge of iron ore and limestone in a blast furnace. A blend of two or more *bituminous* coals is usually required to make coke.

- **Pulverized coal** is a coal that has been crushed to a fine dust in a grinding mill. It is blown into the combustion zone of a furnace and burns very rapidly and efficiently.

- **Slack coal** usually refers to *bituminous* coal one-half inch or smaller in size.

- **Steam coal** refers to coal used in boilers to generate steam to produce electricity or for other purposes.

- **Stoker coal** refers to coal that has been crushed to specific sizes (but not powdered) for burning on a grate in automatic firing equipment. [EIA]

coal rank: The classification of *coals* according to their degree of progressive alteration from lignite to *anthracite*. In the United States, the standard ranks of coal include lignite, subbituminous coal, *bituminous* coal, and *anthracite* and are based on fixed carbon, volatile matter, *heating value,* and agglomerating (or caking) properties. [EIA]

coal stocks: *Coal* quantities that are held in storage for future use and disposition. Note: When coal data are collected for a particular reporting period (month, quarter, or year), coal *stocks* are commonly measured as of the last day of this period. [EIA]

coal type: The classification is based on physical characteristics or microscopic constituents. Examples of *coal* types are banded coal, bright coal, cannel coal, and splint coal. The term is also used to classify coal according to heat and *sulfur* content. See *coal grade* above. [EIA]

collar: A supply *contract* between a *buyer* and a seller of a *commodity* whereby the buyer is assured that he/she will not have to pay more than some maximum price, and whereby the seller is assured of receiving some minimum price. Equivalently, a *cap* and *floor* at different *strike prices.* [CCRO]

combination: Puts and *calls* held either *long* or *short* with different *strike prices* and/or expirations. Types of combinations include *straddles* and *strangles.* [CFTC]

commercial: An entity involved in the production, processing, or merchandising of a *commodity*. [CFTC]

commission: (1) The charge made by a *futures commission merchant* for buying and selling *futures contracts*; or (2) the fee charged by a *futures broker* for the execution of an order. Note: when capitalized, the Commission usually refers to the *CFTC*. [CFTC]

commitment or **open interest:** The number of open or outstanding *contracts* for which an individual or entity is obligated to the *Exchange* because that individual or entity has not yet made an offsetting sale or purchase, an actual contract *delivery*, or, in the case of *options*, *exercised* the option. [NYMEX]

Commitments of Traders Report (COT): A weekly report from the *CFTC* providing a breakdown of each Tuesday's *open interest* for markets in which 20 or more *traders* hold *positions* equal to or above the *reporting levels* established by the CFTC. Open interest is broken down by aggregate *commercial*, non-commercial, and non-reportable holdings. [CFTC]

commitments: See *open interest.* [CFTC]

commodity: A commodity, as defined in the *Commodity Exchange Act,* includes the agricultural commodities enumerated in Section 1a(4) of the Commodity Exchange Act and all other goods and articles, except onions as provided in Public Law 85-839 (7 U.S.C. § 13-1), a 1958 law that banned *futures trading* in onions, and all services, rights, and interests in which *contracts* for future *delivery* are presently or in the future dealt in. [CFTC]

Commodity Exchange Act: The Commodity Exchange Act, 7 U.S.C. § 1, *et seq.*, provides for the federal regulation of *commodity futures* and *options trading*. See *Commodity Futures Modernization Act.* [CFTC]

Commodity Futures Modernization Act: The Commodity Futures Modernization Act of 2000 (CFMA), Pub. L. No. 106-554, 114 Stat. 2763, reauthorized the *Commodity Futures Trading Commission* for five years and overhauled the *Commodity Exchange Act* to create a flexible structure for the regulation of *futures* and *options trading.* Significantly, the CFMA codified an agreement between the *CFTC* and the *Securities and Exchange Commission* to repeal the 18-year-old ban on the trading of single stock futures. [CFTC]

Commodity Futures Trading Commission (CFTC): A federal regulatory agency authorized under the Commodity Futures Trading Commission Act of 1974 to regulate *futures trading* in all commodities. The commission has five commissioners, one of whom is designated as chairman, all appointed by the President, subject to Senate confirmation. The *CFTC* is independent of the Cabinet departments. [NYMEX]

commodity-linked bond: A bond in which payment to the investor is dependent to a certain extent on the price level of a *commodity*, such as *crude oil,* gold, or silver, at maturity. [CFTC]

commodity option: An *option* on a *commodity* or a *futures contract.* [CFTC]

commodity pool: An investment trust, syndicate, or similar form of enterprise operated for the purpose of *trading commodity futures* or *option contracts.* Typically thought of as an enterprise engaged in the business of investing the collective or "pooled" funds of multiple participants in trading commodity futures or options, where participants share in profits and losses on a pro rata basis. [CFTC]

Commodity Pool Operator (CPO): Acts as a general partner of *commodity pools.* CPOs hire independent *commodity trading advisors* to handle daily *trading* decisions. Responsible for the pool's administration, structure, and selecting and monitoring the *traders* who conduct *transactions* using the fund's money. [NYMEX]

commodity price index: Index or average, which may be weighted, of selected *commodity* prices, intended to be representative of the markets in general or a specific subset of commodities, *e.g.*, grains or livestock. [CFTC]

Commodity Trading Advisor (CTA): A person who, for pay, regularly engages in the business of advising others as to the value of *commodity futures* or *options* or the advisability of *trading* in commodity futures or options, or issues analyses or reports concerning commodity futures or options. [CFTC]

component value at risk: The contribution of an asset or a subset of a *portfolio* to the total portfolio *value at risk.* Component VaRs are usually added to the total portfolio VaR. Note that component VaR can be negative if the asset provides a *hedge* relative to the entire portfolio. Also called del value at risk, diversified value at risk, incremental value at risk, or marginal value at risk. [CCRO]

compressed natural gas (CNG): *Natural gas* which is comprised primarily of methane, compressed to a pressure at or above 2,400 pounds per square inch and stored in special high-pressure containers. It is used as a fuel for natural gas powered vehicles. [EIA]

confidence level or interval: A measure of the *degree of confidence,* or equivalently the probability that is associated with the set of outcomes, for a random variable (or a stochastic process) of interest. A confidence level of a is defined as the probability that, given the underlying distribution of the random variable (or process), the set of possible outcomes will lie in a range greater than or equal to a predetermined value. Equivalently, a confidence level of $(1 - a)$ is defined as the probability that the set of outcomes will lie in a range less than or equal to a predetermined value. As an example, a confidence level of 5% is used to assess the set of possible outcomes and assign a probability of 1 in 20 that the actual outcome will lie above a predetermined value, the latter being a function of the underlying distribution and the level of confidence being used. Alternatively, a confidence level of 95% is used to assess the set of possible outcomes and assign a probability of 19 out of 20 that the actual outcome will lie below the predetermined value. [CCRO]

confirmation statement: A statement sent by a *futures commission merchant* to a customer when a futures or *options position* has been initiated which typically shows the price and the number of *contracts* bought and sold. See *P&S* (Purchase and Sale). [CFTC]

congestion: (1) A market situation in which shorts attempting to *cover* their *positions* are unable to find an adequate supply of *contracts* provided by *longs* willing to liquidate or by new sellers willing to enter the market, except at sharply higher prices (see *squeeze, corner*); (2) in *technical analysis,* a period of time characterized by repetitious and limited price fluctuations. [CFTC] (3) A condition that occurs when insufficient transfer *capacity* is available to implement all of the preferred *schedules* for electricity *transmission* simultaneously. [EIA]

contango: A market situation in which prices are higher in the succeeding *delivery months* than in the nearest delivery month. Also known as a *carry market,* it is the opposite of *backwardation.* [NYMEX]

contingency order: An order which becomes effective only upon the fulfillment of some condition in the marketplace. [NYMEX]

contract: (1) A term of reference describing a unit of *trading* for a *commodity* future or *option*; (2) an agreement to buy or sell a specified commodity, detailing the amount and *grade* of the product and the date on which the contract will mature and become deliverable. [CFTC]

contract grades: Those *grades* of a *commodity* that have been officially approved by an *exchange* as deliverable in settlement of a *futures contract.* [CFTC]

contract market: A *board of trade* or *exchange* designated by the *Commodity Futures Trading Commission* to trade *futures* or *options* under the *Commodity Exchange Act.* A contract market can allow both institutional and retail participants and can list for *trading futures contracts* on any *commodity*, provided that each *contract* is not readily susceptible to *manipulation*. Also called *Designated Contract Market.* See *derivatives transaction execution facility.* [CFTC]

contract month: See *delivery month.* [CFTC]

contract price: The *delivery price* determined when a *contract* is signed. It can be a fixed price or a base price escalated according to a given formula. [EIA]

contract size: The actual amount of a *commodity* represented in a *contract.* [CFTC]

contract unit: See _contract size._ [CFTC]

control area: A portion of the electric grid that *schedules*, dispatches, and controls generating resources to serve area load (ultimate users of electricity) and coordinates scheduling of the flow of electric power over the *transmission* system to neighboring control areas. A control area requires entities that serve load within the control area to demonstrate ownership or contractual rights to *capacity* sufficient to serve that load at time of peak demand (usually annual) and to provide a reserve margin to protect the integrity of the system against potential generating unit outages in the control area. [CCRO]

controlled account: An account for which *trading* is directed by someone other than the owner. Also called a _managed account_ or a _discretionary account._ [CFTC]

convergence: The tendency for prices of physicals and *futures* to approach one another, usually during the *delivery month.* Also called a "narrowing of the *basis.*" [CFTC]

conversion: A _delta-neutral_ *arbitrage transaction* involving a *long futures contract,* a *long put option,* and a *short call option.* The put and call *options* have the same _strike price_ and same _expiration date._ [NYMEX]

conversion factors: Numbers published by *futures exchanges* to determine _invoice prices_ for debt *instruments* deliverable against bond or note _futures contracts._ A separate conversion factor is published for each deliverable instrument. Invoice price = _Contract Size_ × Futures Settlement Price × Conversion Factor + Accrued Interest. [CFTC]

cooling degree-days: A measure of how warm a location is over a period of time relative to a base temperature, most commonly specified as 65 degrees *Fahrenheit.* The measure is computed for each day by subtracting the base temperature (65 degrees) from the average of the day's high and low temperatures, with negative values set equal to zero. Each day's cooling degree-days are summed to create a cooling degree-day measure for a specified reference period. Cooling degree-days are used in energy analysis as an indicator of air conditioning energy requirements or use. [EIA]

corner: (1) Securing such relative control of a *commodity* that its price can be manipulated, that is, can be controlled by the creator of the corner; or (2) in the extreme situation, obtaining *contracts* requiring the *delivery* of more commodities than are available for delivery. See *squeeze, congestion.* [CFTC]

correction: A temporary decline in prices during a _bull_ _market_ that partially reverses the previous *rally*. See _bear_ _market_ _rally._ [CFTC]

correlation: A measure of how closely two variables move together through time. For example, electricity and _natural_ _gas_ prices tend to be highly correlated because natural gas is an input in the production of electricity. However, there are factors such as seasonality and location that affect the correlation of the two. Conversely, gold prices are not closely correlated with *gas* or electricity prices because the two are influenced by very different factors. The most important property of correlation is that its value is always between 1 and −1. The closer the relationship between assets, the closer the correlation coefficient is to 1 and vice versa. [CCRO]

cost, insurance, freight (CIF): A type of sale in which the *buyer* of the product agrees to pay a unit price that includes the _f.o.b._ _value_ of the product at the point of origin plus all costs of insurance and transportation. This type of *transaction* differs from a "*delivered*" purchase in that the buyer accepts the quantity as determined at the loading port (as certified by the Bill of Loading and Quality Report) rather than pay on the basis of the quantity and quality ascertained at the unloading port. It is similar to the terms of an f.o.b. sale except that the seller, as a service for which he is compensated, arranges for transportation and insurance. [EIA]

cost of tender: Total of various charges incurred when a *commodity* is certified and delivered on a _futures_ _contract._ [CFTC]

COT: See _Commitments of Traders Report._ [CFTC]

counterparty: The opposite party in a _bilateral agreement_, contract, or transaction. In the retail foreign _exchange_ (or forex) context, the party to which a _retail customer_ sends its funds; lawfully, the party must be one of those listed in Section 2(c)(2)(B)(ii)(I)-(VI) of the _Commodity Exchange Act._ [CFTC]

counterparty performance risk: See _market risk._ [CCRO]

counterparty risk: The risk associated with the financial stability of the party entered into _contract_ with. _Forward contracts_ impose upon each party the risk that the _counterparty_ will _default_, but _futures contracts_ executed on a _designated contract market_ are guaranteed against default by the _clearing organization._ [CFTC]

counterparty VaR: _Value-at-risk_ calculated at the _counterparty_ level. Counterparty VaR measures how _mark-to-market_ exposure to specific counterparties can change for a given time horizon and _confidence level._ [CCRO]

cover: (1) Purchasing _futures_ to _offset_ a _short position_ (same as _short covering);_ see _offset, liquidation;_ (2) to have in hand the physical _commodity_ when a short futures sale is made, or to acquire the commodity that might be deliverable on a short sale. [CFTC]

covered option: A _short call_ or _put option_ position that is _covered_ by the sale or purchase of the _underlying futures contract_ or other underlying _instrument._ For example, in the case of _options_ on _futures_ contracts, a covered call is a short call position combined with a _long_ futures position. A covered _put_ is a short put position combined with a short futures position. [CFTC]

covered writing: The sale of an _option_ against an existing _position_ in the _underlying futures contract._ For example, a _short call_ and _long futures_ position. [NYMEX]

Cox-Ross-Rubinstein option pricing model: An _option pricing model_ developed by John Cox, Stephen Ross, and Mark Rubinstein that can be adopted to include effects not included in the _Black-Scholes Model_ (_e.g._, early _exercise_ and price supports). [CFTC]

CPO: See *Commodity Pool Operator.*

cracking: The process of breaking down the molecular structure of a substance into smaller units. *Petroleum* is cracked as part of the refining process to extract products such as *heating oil* and gasoline. [NYMEX]

crack spreads: The simultaneous purchase or sale of *crude oil* against the sale or purchase of *refined petroleum products.* These *spread differentials* which represent refining margins are normally quoted in dollars per *barrel* by converting the product prices into dollars per barrel (divide the cents-per-*gallon* price by 42) and subtracting the crude oil price. [NYMEX]

credit default option: A *put option* that makes a payoff in the event the issuer of a specified reference asset *defaults*. Also called *default option.* [CFTC]

credit default swap: A bilateral *over-the-counter* (OTC) *contract* in which the seller agrees to make a payment to the *buyer* in the event of a specified *credit event* in *exchange* for a fixed payment or series of fixed payments; the most common type of *credit derivative*; also called *credit swap*; similar to *credit default option.* [CFTC]

credit derivative: An *over-the-counter* *(OTC) derivative* designed to assume or shift *credit risk,* that is, the risk of a *credit event* such as a *default* or bankruptcy of a borrower. For example, a lender might use a credit derivative to *hedge* the risk that a borrower might default or have its *credit rating* downgraded. Common credit derivatives include *Credit Default Options, Credit Default Swaps, Credit Spread Options, Downgrade Options*, and Total Return Swaps. [CFTC]

credit event: An event such as a debt *default* or bankruptcy that will affect the payoff on a *credit derivative. ISDA* has published a definition of a credit event. [CFTC]

credit rating: A rating determined by a rating agency that indicates the agency's opinion of the likelihood that a borrower such as a corporation or sovereign nation will be able to repay its debt.

The rating agencies include Standard & Poor's, Fitch, and Moody's. [CFTC]

credit risk: See *market risk.* [CCRO]

credit spread: The difference between the *yield* on the debt securities of a particular corporate or sovereign borrower (or a class of borrowers with a specified *credit rating)* and the yield of similar maturity Treasury debt securities. [CFTC]

credit spread option: An *option* whose payoff is based on the *credit spread* between the debt of a particular borrower and similar maturity Treasury debt. [CFTC]

credit swap: See *credit default swap.* [CFTC]

Credit Value at Risk (CVaR): The largest likely loss expected to be suffered due to a *counterparty default* over a given period of time with a given probability. The time period is known as the *holding period,* and the probability is known as the *confidence interval.* For example, a company might estimate its credit value at risk over ten days to be $100 million with a *confidence level* of 95%. This would mean there is a 1 in 20 (5%) chance of a loss larger than $100 million in the next ten days. If the *portfolio* has been charged for expected loss, CVaR reflects the unexpected credit loss. If no credit charge or reserve has been applied, CVaR reflects the total credit loss. (Note: This definition is provided with the caveat that there currently is not a consensus in the industry on CVaR. For further discussion and examples of some other notions of CVaR, see the Credit Risk Management white paper.) [CCRO]

cross-acceleration: Similar to a *cross-default,* but the third party *defaulted* against in financial agreements or *instruments* must accelerate the indebtedness and take proceedings to terminate their agreement before the non-defaulting party to the *contract* can do so. [CCRO]

cross-default: Event of *default* under a particular *contract* triggered by (1) a default or similar event to a third party under financial agreements or *instruments*, resulting in indebtedness (above a specified amount) that may be accelerated and terminated by that third party, (2) a failure to make payments (above a specified amount) on their due date under financial agreements or instruments after notice or the expiry of a grace period. [CCRO]

cross-hedge: *Hedging* a *cash market position* in a *futures* or *option contract* for a different but price-related *commodity*. [CFTC]

cross-margining: A procedure for margining related securities, *options*, and *futures contracts* jointly when different *clearing organizations* clear each side of the *position*. [CFTC]

cross rate: In foreign *exchange*, the price of one currency in terms of another currency in the market of a third country. For example, the *exchange rate* between Japanese yen and Euros would be considered a cross rate in the US market. [CFTC]

cross trading: Offsetting or noncompetitive match of the buy order of one customer against the sell order of another, a practice that is permissible only when executed in accordance with the *Commodity Exchange Act, CFTC* regulations, and *rules* of the *exchange*. [CFTC]

crude oil: A mixture of hydrocarbons that exists as a liquid in natural underground reservoirs and remains liquid at atmospheric pressure after passing through surface separating facilities. Crude is the raw material which is refined into gasoline, *heating oil, jet fuel, propane, petrochemicals*, and other products. [NYMEX]

crude oil qualities: Refers to two properties of *crude oil,* the *sulfur* content, and *API gravity*, which affect processing complexity and product characteristics. [EIA]

crude oil stocks: *Stocks* of *crude oil* and lease condensate held at *refineries*, in *pipelines*, at pipeline terminals, and on leases. [EIA]

CTA: See *Commodity Trading Advisor.* [CFTC]

cubic feet per day (CF/D): Usually used to quantify the rate of flow of a *gas* well or *pipeline*. [NYMEX]

cubic foot: The most common measure of gas volume, referring to the amount of gas needed to fill a volume of one *cubic foot* at 14.73 pounds per square inch absolute pressure and 60° *Fahrenheit*. One cubic foot of *natural gas* contains, on average, 1,027 *Btus*. [NYMEX]

curb trading: *Trading* by telephone or by other means that takes place after the official market has closed and that originally took place in the street on the curb outside the market. Under the *Commodity Exchange Act* and *CFTC rules*, curb trading is illegal. Also known as *kerb trading.* [CFTC]

currency swap: A *swap* that involves the exchange of one currency (*e.g.*, US dollars) for another (*e.g.*, Japanese yen) on a specified schedule. [CFTC]

current delivery month: The *futures contract* which ceases *trading* and becomes deliverable during the present month or the month closest to delivery. Also called the *spot month.* [NYMEX]

d

daily earnings at risk (DEaR): A (statistical) measure of the variability in the current *earnings* estimate due to potential changes in the prices of the *underlying commodities* over a one-day interval. The objective in using the daily earnings at risk is to assess the potential loss of value or reduction over a single day during which the price movements could be adversely affecting the value of the *positions* or *portfolio* of interest. As with VaR, daily earnings at risk also uses a *degree of confidence* and a *holding period* that, unlike in VaR, does not have the connotation of a liquidation time. Rather, this one-day interval is a time over which the potential changes to earnings or value are estimated. [CCRO]

daily price limit: The maximum price advance or decline from the previous day's settlement price permitted during one *trading* session, as fixed by the *rules* of an *exchange*. [CFTC]

daily profit and loss: Change in the *mark-to-market* value from period to period. [CCRO]

day ahead: See *next day.* [CFTC]

day-ahead and hour-ahead markets: *Forward markets* where electricity quantities and *market clearing prices* are calculated individually for each hour of the day on the basis of participant bids for *energy sales* and purchases. [EIA]

day-ahead schedule: A *schedule* prepared by a scheduling coordinator or the *independent system operator* before the beginning of a *trading* day. This schedule indicates the levels of generation and demand scheduled for each settlement period that trading day. [EIA]

day order: An order that expires automatically at the end of each day's *trading* session. There may be a day order with time contingency. For example, an "off at a specific time" order is an order that remains in force until the specified time during the session is reached. At such time, the order is automatically canceled. [CFTC]

day trade: The purchase and sale of a *futures* or an *options contract* on the same day. [NYMEX]

day trader: A *trader*, often a person with *exchange trading* privileges, who takes *positions* and then offsets them during the same trading session prior to the *close* of trading. [CFTC]

DCM: See *designated contract market.* [CFTC]

decatherm: Ten *therms* or 1,000,000 *Btu.* [EIA]

deck: The orders for purchase or sale of *futures* and *option contracts* held by a *floor broker.* Also referred to as an *Order Book.* [CFTC]

declaration date: See *expiration date.* [CFTC]

declaration (of options): See *exercise.* [CFTC]

328

dedicated reserves: The volume of recoverable, salable *gas* reserves committed to, controlled by, or possessed by the reporting *pipeline* company and used for acts and services for which both the seller and the company have received certificate authorization from the *Federal Energy Regulatory Commission* (FERC). Reserves include both company-owned reserves (including owned gas in underground storage), reserves under contract from independent producers, and short-term and emergency supplies from the intrastate market. Gas volumes under contract from other interstate pipelines are not included as reserves, but may constitute part or all of a company's gas supply. [EIA]

default: Failure to perform on a *futures contract* as required by *exchange rules*, such as failure to meet a *margin call,* or to make or take *delivery.* [CFTC]

default option: See *credit default option.* [CFTC]

deferred futures: See *back months.* [CFTC]

degree day: A measure of the coldness of the weather *(heating degree day)* or its heat (cooling degree day) based on the extent to which the daily mean temperature falls below or rises above 65° *Fahrenheit.* [NYMEX]

degree of confidence: See *confidence level.* [CCRO]

dekatherm: See *decatherm* [NYMEX]

deliverable grades: See *contract grades.* [CFTC]

deliverable stocks: *Stocks* of commodities located in *exchange*-approved storage, for which receipts may be used in making *delivery* on *futures contracts.* Also see *certificated or certified stocks.* [CFTC]

deliverable supply: The total supply of a *commodity* that meets the *delivery specifications* of a *futures contract.* [CFTC]

delivered: Often regarded as synonymous with *cost, insurance, and freight* in the international cargo trade, its terms differ from the latter in a number of ways. Generally, the seller's risks are greater in a delivered *transaction* because the *buyer* pays on the basis of landed quality/quantity. Risk and title are borne by the seller until such time as the *commodity*, such as *oil*, passes from shipboard into the connecting flange of the buyer's shore installation. The seller is responsible for clearance through customs and payment of all duties. Any in-transit contamination or loss of cargo is the seller's liability. In delivered transactions, the buyer pays only for the quantity of oil actually received in storage. [NYMEX]

delivery: Delivery generally refers to the change of ownership or control of a *commodity* under specific terms and procedures established by the *Exchange* upon which the *contract* is traded. Typically, except for energy, the commodity must be placed in an approved warehouse, depository, or other storage facility, and be inspected by approved personnel, after which the facility issues a *warehouse receipt,* shipping certificate, demand certificate, or due bill, which becomes a transferable *delivery instrument.* Delivery of the *instrument* usually is preceded by a notice of intention to deliver. [NYMEX]

delivery, current: *Deliveries* being made during a present month. Sometimes current delivery is used as a synonym for *nearby* delivery. [CFTC]

delivery date: The date on which the *commodity* or *instrument* of *delivery* must be delivered to fulfill the terms of a *contract*. [CFTC]

delivery instrument: A document used to effect *delivery* on a *futures contract,* such as a *warehouse receipt* or shipping certificate. [CFTC]

delivery month: The specified month within which a *futures contract* matures and can be settled by *delivery* or the specified month in which the delivery period begins. [CFTC]

delivery, nearby: The nearest traded month, the *front month.* In plural form, one of the nearer *trading* months. [CFTC]

delivery notice: The written notice given by the seller of his intention to make *delivery* against an open *short futures position* on a particular date. This notice, delivered through the *clearing organization,* is separate and distinct from the *warehouse receipt* or other *instrument* that will be used to transfer title. Also called *notice of intent to deliver* or Notice of Delivery. [CFTC]

delivery option: A provision of a *futures contract* that provides the short with flexibility in regard to timing, *location*, quantity, or quality in the *delivery* process. [CFTC]

delivery point: A location designated by a *commodity exchange* where *stocks* of a commodity represented by a *futures contract* may be delivered in fulfillment of the contract. Also called *location*. [CFTC]

delivery price: The price fixed by the *clearing organization* at which deliveries on *futures* are invoiced—generally the price at which the *futures contract* is settled when deliveries are made. Also called *invoice price.* [CFTC]

delta: (1) The sensitivity of an *option's* value to a change in the price of the *underlying futures contract,* also referred to as an option's *futures-equivalent position.* Deltas are positive for *calls,* and negative for *puts.* Deltas of deep *in-the-money* options are approximately equal to one; deltas of *at-the-money* options are 0.5; and deltas of deep *out-of-the-money* options approach zero. [NYMEX] (2) The expected change in an option's price given a one-unit change in the price of the underlying *futures* contract or physical commodity. For example, an option with a delta of 0.5 would change $.50 when the *underlying commodity* moves $1.00. [CFTC]

delta equivalent: Measuring a *position* in terms of its *delta. Notional* position of the *option* times the option's delta expresses the option *exposure* in terms of the *underlying* asset or *commodity.* In other words, the change in the value of the option will equal the change in the value of the delta equivalent underlying asset as the price of the underlying asset moves. [CCRO]

delta margining or **delta-based margining:** An *option* margining system used by some *exchanges* that equates the changes in option *premiums* with the changes in the price of the *underlying futures contract* to determine *risk factors* upon which to base the *margin* requirements. [CFTC]

delta neutral: A *position* where the sum of all positive and negative *deltas* add up to approximately zero. [CCRO]

delta neutral spread: A *spread* where the total *delta position* on the *long* side and the total *delta* on the *short* side add up to approximately zero. [NYMEX]

demand bid: A *bid* into the *power exchange* indicating a quantity of energy or an ancillary service that an eligible customer is willing to purchase and, if relevant, the maximum price that the customer is willing to pay. [EIA]

demand interval: The time period during which flow of electricity is measured (usually in 15-, 30-, or 60-minute increments.) [EIA]

dependable capacity: The load-carrying ability of a station or system under adverse conditions for a specified period of time. [EIA]

deposit: The initial outlay required of a client by a *futures position* to open a futures position, returnable upon *liquidation* of that position. See also *margin*. [CFTC]

depository or **warehouse receipt:** A document issued by a bank or warehouse indicating ownership of a *commodity* stored in a bank depository or warehouse. In the case of many commodities deliverable against *futures contracts,* transfer of ownership of an appropriate depository receipt may affect contract *delivery*. [NYMEX]

deregulation: The elimination of some or all regulations from a previously regulated industry or sector of an industry. [EIA]

derivative: A *financial instrument,* traded on or off an *exchange*, the price of which is directly dependent upon (*i.e.*, "derived from") the value of one or more *underlying* securities, *equity* indices, debt *instruments*, commodities, other derivative instruments, or any agreed upon pricing index or arrangement (*e.g.*, the movement over time of the Consumer Price Index or freight rates). Derivatives involve the *trading* of rights or obligations based on the underlying product, but do not directly transfer property. They are used to *hedge* risk or to exchange a floating rate of return for fixed rate of return. Derivatives include *futures, options*, and *swaps*. For example, *futures contracts* are derivatives of the physical contract and options on futures are derivatives of futures contracts. [CFTC]

derivatives clearing organization: A *clearing organization* or similar entity that, in respect to a *contract* (1) enables each party to the contract to substitute, through novation or otherwise, the credit of the derivatives clearing organization for the credit of the parties; (2) arranges or provides, on a multilateral basis, for the settlement or netting of obligations resulting from such contracts; or (3) otherwise provides clearing services or arrangements that mutualize or transfer among participants in the derivatives clearing organization the *credit risk* arising from such contracts. [CFTC]

designated contract market: See *contract market.* [CFTC]

designated self-regulatory organization (DSRO): *Self-regulatory organizations* (*i.e.*, the *commodity exchanges* and registered *futures* associations) must enforce minimum financial and reporting requirements for their members, among other responsibilities outlined in the *CFTC's* regulations. When a *Futures Commission Merchant* (FCM) is a member of more than one *SRO*, the SROs may decide among themselves which of them will assume primary responsibility for these regulatory duties and, upon approval of the plan by the Commission, be appointed the *"designated self-regulatory organization"* for that FCM. [CFTC]

diagonal spread: A *spread* between two *call options* or two *put options* with different *strike prices* and different *expiration dates.* See *horizontal spread, vertical spread.* [CFTC]

diesel fuel: A fuel composed of distillates obtained in *petroleum* refining operation or blends of such distillates with residual *oil* used in motor vehicles. The boiling point and *specific gravity* are higher for diesel fuels than for gasoline. [EIA]

differentials: The *discount* (*premium*) allowed for *grades* or *locations* of a *commodity* lower (higher) than the *par* or *basis grade* or location specified in the *futures contract.* See *allowances.* [CFTC]

directional trading: *Trading* strategies designed to speculate on the direction of the *underlying* market, especially in contrast to *volatility trading.* [CFTC]

disclosure document: A statement that must be provided to prospective customers that describes trading strategy, potential risk, *commissions*, fees, performance and other relevant information. [CFTC]

discount: (1) The amount a price would be reduced to purchase a *commodity* of lesser *grade*; (2) sometimes used to refer to the price differences between *futures* of different *delivery months,* as in the phrase "July at a discount to May," indicating that the price for the July futures is lower than that of May. [CFTC]

discretionary account: An arrangement by which the holder of an account gives written power of attorney to someone else, often a *Commodity Trading Advisor,* to buy and sell without prior approval of the holder; often referred to as a " *managed account*" or *controlled account.* [CFTC]

dispatching: The operating control of an integrated electric system involving operations such as (1) the assignment of load to specific generating stations and other sources of supply to effect the most economical supply as the total or the significant area loads rise or fall; (2) the control of operations and maintenance of high-voltage lines, substations, and equipment; (3) the operation of principal tie lines and switching; (4) the scheduling of energy *transactions* with connecting electric utilities. [EIA]

distant or **deferred months:** See *back months.* [CFTC]

distillate fuel oil: Products of *refinery* distillation sometimes referred to as *middle distillates; kerosene, diesel fuel,* and home *heating oil.* [NYMEX]

downstream: An industry term referring to commercial *oil* and *gas* operations beyond the production phase; oil refining and marketing, and *natural gas* transmission and distribution. [NYMEX]

DSRO: See *designated self-regulatory organization.* [CFTC]

dual trading: Dual trading occurs when: (1) a *floor broker* executes customer orders and on the same day, trades for his own account or an account in which he has an interest; or (2) a FCM carries customer accounts and also trades or permits its employees to trade in accounts in which it has a proprietary interest, also on the same trading day. [CFTC]

duration: (1) The average life of the present values of the *cash flows* or revenue streams that comprise a *portfolio* of *positions.* In the context of an energy *commodity* portfolio receiving a *mark-to-market* treatment, duration represents the average time over which the *unrealized* values will be recovered given the current structure of the portfolio and market conditions. A short duration means that either the portfolio of positions does not extend very far into the future in terms of values to be received or that a greater proportion of the value will be received in the near term as opposed to the longer term. (2) The average life of the present values of all future cash flows from a bond or an interest rate-sensitive *instrument.* [CCRO] (3) A measure of a bond's price sensitivity to changes in interest rates. [CFTC]

dynamic hedging: A procedure for *hedging* which involves periodically changing the derivatives held in relation to the *underlying* assets; the objective is usually to maintain a *delta neutral position.* [CCRO]

e

earnings: Net operating income from accrual and *fair value* accounting activities. For activities subject to accrual accounting, income and expense items are recognized as they are earned or incurred, even though they may not have been received or actually paid for in cash. For activities subject to fair value accounting, *realized* and *unrealized* gains and losses would be included in earnings. [CCRO]

Earnings at Risk (EaR): (1) A (statistical) measure of the variability of *earnings* from a *portfolio* of *positions* or a given economic activity due to potential changes in the market prices of the commodities or other variables underlying the portfolio or activity. Two parameters are typically associated with earnings at risk, the *degree of confidence* and the *holding period;* (2) A certain number of standard deviations of the distribution of earnings. [*Managing Bank Capital*, 2000, John Wiley] [CCRO]

ease off: A minor and/or slow decline in the price of a market. [CFTC]

efficient market: In economic theory, an efficient market is one in which market prices adjust rapidly to reflect new information. The degree to which the market is efficient depends on the quality of information reflected in market prices. In an efficient market, profitable *arbitrage* opportunities do not exist and *traders* cannot expect to consistently outperform the market unless they have lower-cost access to information that is reflected in market prices or unless they have access to information before it is reflected in market prices. See *Random Walk.* [CFTC]

EFP: See *exchange for physicals.* [CFTC]

electric system reliability: The degree to which the performance of the elements of the electrical system results in power being delivered to consumers within accepted standards and in the amount desired. *Reliability* encompasses two concepts, adequacy and security. Adequacy implies that there are sufficient generation and *transmission* resources installed and available to meet projected electrical demand plus reserves for contingencies. Security implies that the system will remain intact operationally (*i.e.*, will have sufficient available operating *capacity*) even after outages or other equipment *failure*. The degree of reliability may be measured by the frequency, duration, and magnitude of adverse effects on consumer service. [EIA]

electric utility: An enterprise that is engaged in the generation, *transmission*, and/or distribution of electric energy primarily for use by the public and is the major power supplier within a designated service area. Electric utilities include: investor-owned, publicly owned, cooperatively owned, and government-owned entities. [NYMEX]

electric zone: A portion of the grid controlled by the *independent system operator.* [EIA]

electricity broker: An entity that arranges the sale and purchase of electric energy, the *transmission* of electricity, and/or other related services between *buyers* and sellers but does not take title to any of the power sold. [EIA]

electricity congestion: A condition that occurs when insufficient *transmission capacity* is available to implement all of the desired *transactions* simultaneously. [EIA]

electricity demand bid: A *bid* into the *power exchange* indicating a quantity of energy or an ancillary service that an eligible customer is willing to purchase and, if relevant, the maximum price that the customer is willing to pay. [EIA]

electronic trading facility: A *trading facility* that operates by an electronic or telecommunications network instead of a *trading floor* and maintains an automated *audit trail* of *transactions*. [CFTC]

eligible commercial entity: An *eligible contract participant* or other entity approved by the *CFTC* that has a demonstrable ability to make or take *delivery* of an *underlying commodity* of a contract; incurs risks related to the commodity; or is a dealer that regularly provides *risk management, hedging* services, or market-making activities to entities *trading* commodities or *derivative* agreements, contracts, or *transactions* in commodities. [CFTC]

eligible contract participant: An entity, such as a financial institution, insurance company, or *commodity pool,* that is classified by the *Commodity Exchange Act* as an eligible contract participant based upon its regulated status or amount of assets. This classification permits these persons to engage in *transactions* (such as *trading* on a *Derivatives Transaction Execution Facility*) not generally available to non-eligible contract participants, *i.e.*, *retail customers.* [CFTC]

embedded optionally: *Contracts* in which terms or conditions resemble *option* terms or conditions. [CCRO]

emergency: (1) Any market occurrence or circumstance which requires immediate action and threatens or may threaten such things as the fair and orderly *trading* in, or the *liquidation* of, or *delivery* pursuant to, any *contracts* on a *contract market.* [CFTC] (2) The *failure* of an electric power system to generate or deliver electric power as normally intended, resulting in the cutoff or curtailment of service. [EIA]

end-user: The ultimate consumer of *petroleum* products or *natural gas*; most commonly refers to large commercial, industrial, or utility consumers. [NYMEX]

energy deliveries: Energy generated by one *electric utility* system and delivered to another system through one or more *transmission* lines. [EIA]

energy sale(s): The transfer of title to an energy *commodity* from a seller to a *buyer* for a price or the quantity transferred during a specified period. [EIA]

equity: As used on a *trading* account statement, refers to the residual dollar value of a *futures* or *option* trading account, assuming it was liquidated at current prices. [CFTC]

equity (financial): Ownership of shareholders in a corporation represented by stock. [EIA]

equity capital: The sum of *capital* from retained *earnings* and the issuance of stock. [EIA]

European option: An *option* that may be *exercised* only on the *expiration date.* See *American option.* [CFTC]

even lot: A unit of *trading* in a *commodity* established by an *exchange* to which official price *quotations* apply. See *round lot.* [CFTC]

exchange: A central marketplace with established *rules* and regulations where *buyers* and sellers meet to trade *futures* and *options* *contracts* or securities. Exchanges include *designated contract markets* and derivatives transaction execution facilities. [CFTC]

exchange-certified stocks: *Stocks* of *commodities* held in depositories or warehouses certified by an *Exchange*-approved inspection authority as constituting good *delivery* against a *futures contract position.* Current total *certified stocks* are reported in the press for many important commodities such as gold, silver, copper, platinum, and palladium. [NYMEX]

exchange for physicals (EFP): A *transaction* in which the *buyer* of a *cash commodity* transfers to the seller a corresponding amount of *long futures contracts,* or receives from the seller a corresponding amount of *short futures*, at a price difference mutually agreed upon. In this way, the opposite *hedges* in futures of both parties are closed out simultaneously. Also called *exchange of futures for cash,* AA (Against *Actuals*), or *Ex-Pit* transactions. [CFTC]

exchange of futures for cash: See *exchange for physicals.* [CFTC]

exchange of futures for swaps (EFS): A privately negotiated *transaction* in which a *position* in a physical *delivery futures contract* is exchanged for a *cash-settled* swap position in the same or a related *commodity*, pursuant to the *rules* of a *futures exchange.* See *exchange for physicals.* [CFTC]

exchange rate: The price of one currency stated in terms of another currency. [CFTC]

execution risk: The potential for an extra cost in completing an order to buy or sell. Typically, this may include a slippage in price received or paid between when the strategy is communicated and when the final *transaction* occurs, the cost of not exercising an *option*, the internal cost of executing a transaction, or the failure to perform according to the *contract*. [CCRO]

exempt commodity: The _Commodity Exchange Act_ defines an exempt _commodity_ as any commodity other than an Excluded Commodity or an agricultural commodity. Examples include energy commodities and metals. [CFTC]

exercise: To elect to buy or sell, taking advantage of the right (but not the obligation) conferred to the owner of an _option contract_. [CFTC]

exercise price (strike price): The price, specified in the _option contract_, at which the _underlying futures contract, security, or commodity_ will move from seller to _buyer_. [CFTC]

exotic options: Any of a wide variety of _options_ with non-standard payout structures or other features, including _Asian options_ and _lookback options._ Exotic options are mostly traded in the _over-the-counter_ market. [CFTC]

expiration date: The date on which an _option contract_ automatically expires; the last day an option may be _exercised_. [CFTC]

exposure: The condition of being subjected to a source of risk. [CCRO]

extrinsic value/time value: That portion of an _option's premium_ that exceeds the _intrinsic value._ The time value of an option reflects the probability that the option will move into-the-money. Therefore, the longer the time remaining until expiration of the option, the greater its time value. [CCRO]

ex-pit: See _transfer trades_ and _exchange for physicals._ [CFTC]

f

Fahrenheit: A temperature scale on which the boiling point of water is at 212 degrees above zero on the scale and the freezing point is at 32 degrees above zero at standard atmospheric pressure. [EIA]

failure (or **hazard**): Any electric power supply equipment or facility failure or other event that, in the judgement of the reporting entity, constitutes a hazard to maintaining the continuity of the bulk electric power supply system such that a load reduction action may become necessary and reportable outage may occur. Types of abnormal conditions that should be reported include the imposition of a special operating procedure, the extended purchase of emergency power, other bulk power system actions that may be caused by a natural disaster, a major equipment failure that would impact the bulk power supply, and an environmental and/or regulatory action requiring equipment outages. [EIA]

fair value: (1) _Theoretical value._ [NYMEX] (2) The price that a willing _buyer_ and seller would accept assuming a reasonable time frame. Often this price may be observable, but sometimes it is estimated by modeling techniques. Fair value could also be the value of a _transaction_ or asset based on model and observable price. Fair value in this context is an economic valuation in contrast to the _GAAP_ definition. [CCRO]

FASB: _Financial Accounting Standards Board._ [EIA]

fast market: _Transactions_ in the _ring_ that take place in such volume and with such rapidity that price reporters may fall behind with price _quotations_, so they insert "Fast" and show a range of prices. [NYMEX]

fast tape: See _fast market._ [EIA]

Federal Energy Regulatory Commission (FERC): The Federal agency with jurisdiction over interstate electricity sales, wholesale electric rates, hydroelectric licensing, _natural gas_ pricing, oil _pipeline_ rates, and _gas_ pipeline certification. FERC is an independent regulatory agency within the Department of Energy and is the successor to the Federal Power Commission. [EIA]

feedstock: The supply of _crude oil, natural gas liquids,_ or _natural gas_ to a _refinery_ or _petrochemical_ plant or the supply of some refined fraction of intermediate product to some other manufacturing process. [NYMEX]

fence: A _long (short) underlying position_ together with a long (short) _out-of-the-money put_ and a short (long) out of-the-money _call._ All _options_ must expire at the same time. [NYMEX]

FERC: *The Federal Energy Regulatory Commission.* [EIA]

fictitious trading: *Wash trading, bucketing, cross trading,* or other schemes which give the appearance of *trading* but actually no bona fide, competitive trade has occurred. [CFTC]

fill: (1) The execution of an order. [CFTC] (2) The price at which an order is executed. [NYMEX]

fill-or-kill: An order which must be filled immediately, and in its entirety. Failing this, the order will be canceled. [NYMEX]

final settlement price: The price at which a *cash-settled futures contract* is settled at *maturity*, pursuant to a procedure specified by the *exchange.* [CFTC]

Financial Accounting Standards Board (FASB): An independent board responsible, since 1973, for establishing *generally accepted accounting principles.* Its official pronouncement are called "Statements of Financial Accounting Standards" and "Interpretations of Financial Accounting Standards." [EIA]

financial instruments: As used by the *CFTC*, this term generally refers to any *futures* or *option contract* that is not based on an agricultural *commodity* or a natural resource. It includes currencies, *equity* securities, fixed income securities, and indexes of various kinds. [CFTC]

financial risk: *Exposure* to a relevant financial uncertainty. [CCRO]

financial settlement: Cash settlement, especially for energy derivatives. [CFTC]

firm energy: The highest quality sales of electric *transmission* service offered to customers under a filed rate *schedule* that anticipates no planned interruption. [NYMEX]

firm liquidated damages: A *contract* that requires firm *delivery* of the *commodity* or its equivalent financial value. The delivery can only be excused by a *force majeure* event commonly defined under financial agreements. [CCRO]

firm power: Power or power-producing *capacity*, intended to be available at all times during the period covered by a guaranteed commitment to deliver, even under adverse conditions. [EIA]

firm service: Utility service which assumes no interruption except if residential customers' supply is threatened. Opposite of *interruptible service.* [NYMEX]

first notice day: The first day on which notices of intent to deliver actual commodities against *futures market positions* can be received. First notice day may vary with each *commodity* and *exchange.* [CFTC]

floor: 1) The main *trading* area of an *exchange.* 2) A supply *contract* between a *buyer* and seller of a *commodity*, whereby the seller is assured that he will receive at least some minimum price. This type of contract is analogous to a *put option.* [NYMEX]

floor broker: A person with *exchange trading* privileges who, in any *pit, ring*, post, or other place provided by an exchange for the meeting of persons similarly engaged, executes for another person any orders for the purchase or sale of any *commodity* for future *delivery.* [CFTC]

floor trader: A person with *exchange trading* privileges who executes his own trades by being personally present in the *pit* or *ring* for *futures* trading. See *local.* [CFTC]

F.O.B.: See *free on board.* [NYMEX]

F.O.B. price: The price actually charged at the producing country's port of loading. The reported price should be after deducting any rebates and *discounts* or adding *premiums* where applicable and should be the actual price paid with no adjustment for credit terms. [EIA]

F.O.B. value (coal): Free-on-board value. This is the value of *coal* at the coal mine or of coke and breeze at the coke plant without any insurance or freight transportation charges added. [EIA]

force majeure: A *contract* clause that allows the supplier to forgo his/her obligation to supply in extreme circumstances, such as political crisis, war, or strikes that disturb production. It also applies to a purchaser who is unable to take *delivery* of the product (*e.g.*, a *refiner* whose *refinery* is shut down following a fire or other disaster). [CCRO]

forced liquidation: The situation in which a customer's account is liquidated (open *positions* are *offset*) by the brokerage firm holding the account, usually after notification that the account is under-margined due to adverse price movements and failure to meet *margin calls.* [CFTC]

forced outage: The shutdown of a generating unit, *transmission* line, or other facility for *emergency* reasons or a condition in which the generating equipment is unavailable for load due to unanticipated breakdown. [EIA]

forecast: Prediction of future events based on market data, assumptions, and model results. [CCRO]

foreign currency hedge: See *hedge*. [CCRO]

foreign currency transaction gains and losses: Gains or losses resulting from the effect of *exchange rate* changes on *transactions* denominated in currencies other than the functional currency (for example, a U.S. enterprise may borrow Swiss francs or a French subsidiary may have a receivable denominated in kroner from a Danish customer). Gains and losses on those foreign currency transactions are generally included in determining net income for the period in which exchange rates change unless the transaction *hedges* a foreign currency commitment or a net investment in a foreign entity. Intercompany transactions of a long-term investment nature are considered part of a parent's net investment and hence do not give rise to gains or losses. [EIA]

foreign currency translation effects: Gains or losses resulting from the process of expressing amounts denominated or measured in one currency in terms of another currency by use of the *exchange rate* between the two currencies. This process is generally required to consolidate the financial statements of foreign affiliates into the total company financial statements and to recognize the conversion of foreign currency or the settlement of a receivable or payable denominated in foreign currency at a rate different from that at which the item is recorded. Translation adjustments are not included in determining net income, but are disclosed as separate components of consolidated *equity*. [EIA]

forwardation: See *contango*. [CFTC]

forward: See *forward* *contract.*

forward contract: A supply *contract* between a *buyer* and seller, whereby the buyer is obligated to take *delivery* and the seller is obligated to provide delivery of a fixed amount of a *commodity* at a predetermined price on a specified future date. Payment in full is due at the time of, or following, delivery. This differs from a *futures* *contract* where settlement is made daily, resulting in partial payment over the life of the contract. [NYMEX]

forward market: The *over-the-counter* market for *forward* *contracts.* [CFTC]

forward months: *Futures* *contracts,* currently *trading*, calling for later or *distant delivery.* See *deferred futures, back months.* [CFTC]

forward price curve: Graphical depiction of the future value of one *commodity* and one location over time. The curve can be based on information from third party and/or *exchange* settled price quotes for large, *liquid markets;* models for illiquid markets with little or no external quotes; or interpolated markets where some third party data exists. [CCRO]

fossil fuel: An energy source formed in the earths crust from decayed organic material. The common fossil fuels are *petroleum, coal,* and *natural gas.* [EIA]

free on board (FOB): A *transaction* in which the seller provides a *commodity* at an agreed unit price, at a specified loading point within a specified period; it is the responsibility of the *buyer* to arrange for transportation and insurance. [NYMEX]

front month: The *spot* or *nearby delivery month,* the nearest traded *contract month.* See *back months.* [CFTC]

front months: Depending on the *commodity*, each of which tends to have its own level of *trading* activity, front months may refer to any of the first few *contract months.* [NYMEX]

front running: With respect to *commodity futures* and *options*, taking a futures or option *position* based upon non-public information regarding an impending *transaction* by another person in the same or related future or option. Also known as *trading ahead.* [CFTC]

front spread: A *delta-neutral ratio spread* in which more *options* are sold than bought. Also called *ratio vertical spread.* A front spread will increase in value if *volatility* decreases. [CFTC]

fuel oil: *Refined petroleum products* used as a fuel for home heating and industrial and utility boilers. Fuel oil is divided into two broad categories, *distillate fuel oil,* also known as No. 2 fuel, gas oil, or *diesel fuel;* and residual fuel oil, also known as No. 6 fuel, or, outside the United States, just as fuel oil. No. 2 fuel is a light oil used for home heating, in compression ignition engines, and in light industrial applications. No. 6 oil is a heavy fuel used in large commercial, industrial, and *electric utility* boilers. [NYMEX]

full carrying charge, full carry: See *carrying charges.* [CFTC]

full forced outage: The net capability of main generating units that are unavailable for load for *emergency* reasons. [EIA]

full power day: The equivalent of 24 hours of *full power operation* by a reactor. The number of full power days in a specific cycle is the product of the reactor's capacity factor and the length of the cycle. [EIA]

full power operation: Operation of a unit at 100 percent of its design *capacity*. Full-power operation precedes commercial operation. [EIA]

fundamental analysis: The study of pertinent supply and demand factors which influence the specific price behavior of commodities. Also see *technical analysis.* [NYMEX]

fungibility: The characteristic of interchangeability. *Futures contracts* for the same *commodity* and *delivery month* traded on the same *exchange* are *fungible* due to their standardized *specifications* for quality, quantity, *delivery date,* and delivery *locations.* [CFTC]

fungible: Interchangeable. Products which can be substituted for purposes of shipment or storage. [NYMEX]

futures: See *futures contract.* [CFTC]

Futures Commission Merchant (FCM): Individuals, associations, partnerships, corporations, and trusts that solicit or accept orders for the purchase or sale of any *commodity* for future *delivery* on or subject to the *rules* of any *exchange* and that accept payment from or extend credit to those whose orders are accepted. [CFTC]

futures contract: A *contract* between a *buyer* and seller, whereby the buyer is obligated to take *delivery* and the seller is obligated to provide future delivery of a fixed amount of a *commodity* at a predetermined price at a specified *location.* Futures contracts are most often liquidated prior to the *delivery date* and are generally used as a financial *risk management* and investment tool rather than for supply purposes. These contracts are traded exclusively on regulated *exchanges* and are settled daily based on their current value in the marketplace. [NYMEX]

futures-equivalent: A term frequently used with reference to *speculative position limits* for *options* on *futures contracts.* The futures-equivalent of an option *position* is the number of options multiplied by the previous day's *risk factor* or *delta* for the option series. For example, ten deep out-of-money options with a delta of 0.20 would be considered two futures-equivalent contracts. The delta or risk factor used for this purpose is the same as that used in *delta-based margining* and risk analysis systems. [CFTC]

futures market: A trade center for quoting prices on *contracts* for the *delivery* of a specified quantity of a *commodity* at a specified time and place in the future. [EIA]

futures option: An *option* on a *futures contract.* [CFTC]

futures price: (1) Commonly held to mean the price of a *commodity* for future *delivery* that is traded on a *futures exchange*; (2) the price of any *futures contract.* [CFTC]

g

GAAP: See *Generally accepted accounting principles.* [EIA]

gallon: A volumetric measure equal to 4 quarts (231 cubic inches) used to measure *fuel oil.* One *barrel* equals 42 gallons. [EIA]

gamma: A measurement of how fast the *delta* of an *option* changes, given a unit change in the *underlying futures price;* the "delta of the delta." [CFTC]

gas: A non-solid, non-liquid combustible energy source that includes *natural gas,* coke-oven gas, blast-furnace gas, and *refinery* gas. [EIA]

gas oil: European and Asian designation for No. 2 *heating oil* and No. 2 *diesel fuel.* [EIA]

gasoline grades: The classification of gasoline by octane ratings. Each type of gasoline (conventional, oxygenated, and reformulated) is classified by three *grades* — Regular, Midgrade, and Premium. *Note:* Gasoline sales are reported by grade in accordance with their classification at the time of sale. In general, automotive octane requirements are lower at high altitudes. Therefore, in some areas of the United States, such as the Rocky Mountain States, the octane ratings for the gasoline grades may be 2 or more octane points lower.

- **regular gasoline:** Gasoline having an antiknock index, *i.e.*, octane rating, greater than or equal to 85 and less than 88. *Note*: Octane requirements may vary by altitude.

- **midgrade gasoline:** Gasoline having an antiknock index, *i.e.*, octane rating, greater than or equal to 88 and less than or equal to 90. *Note*: Octane requirements may vary by altitude.

- **premium gasoline:** Gasoline having an antiknock index, *i.e.*, octane rating, greater than 90. *Note*: Octane requirements may vary by altitude. [EIA]

gasoline, motor (leaded): Contains more than 0.05 grams of lead per *gallon* or more than 0.005 grams of phosphorus per gallon. The actual lead content of any given gallon may vary. Premium and regular *grades* are included, depending on the octane rating. Includes leaded gasohol. Blendstock is excluded until blending has been completed. Alcohol that is to be used in the blending of gasohol is also excluded. [EIA]

gasoline, motor (unleaded): Contains not more than 0.05 grams of lead per *gallon* and not more than 0.005 grams of phosphorus per gallon. Premium and regular *grades* are included, depending on the octane rating. Includes unleaded gasohol. Blendstock is excluded until blending has been completed. Alcohol that is to be used in the blending of gasohol is also excluded. [EIA]

gasoline, Straight-Run: Also known as raw gasoline. Gasoline which is obtained directly from *crude oil* by fractional distillation. Straight-run gasoline generally must be upgraded to meet current motor fuel *specifications*. [NYMEX]

generally accepted accounting principles (GAAP): Defined by the *FASB* as the conventions, rules, and procedures necessary to define accepted accounting practice at a particular time, includes both broad guidelines and relatively detailed practices and procedures. [EIA]

giga: One billion. [EIA]

gigajoule (GJ): One billion *joules*, approximately equal to 948,211 *British thermal units.* One million *Btus* equals 1.0546175 GJ. [NYMEX]

gigawatt (GW): One billion watts or one thousand *megawatts.* [EIA]

gigawatt-electric (GWe): One billion watts of electric *capacity.* [EIA]

gigawatthour (GWh): One billion watthours. [EIA]

Ginzy trading: A non-competitive trade practice in which a *floor broker,* in executing an order — particularly a large order — will *fill* a portion of the order at one price and the remainder of the order at another price to avoid an *exchange's* rule against *trading* at fractional increments or "split *ticks.*" [CFTC]

give up: A *contract* executed by one *broker* for the client of another broker that the client orders to be turned over to the second broker. The broker accepting the order from the customer collects a fee from the *carrying broker* for the use of the facilities. Often used to consolidate many small orders or to disperse large ones. [CFTC]

good this week order (GTW): Order which is valid only for the week in which it is placed. [CFTC]

good 'til canceled: An order to be held by a *broker* until it can be *filled* or until canceled. [NYMEX]

government-owned stocks: *Oil stocks* owned by the national government and held for national security. In the United States, these stocks are known as the *Strategic Petroleum Reserve.* [EIA]

grades: Various qualities of a *commodity.* [CFTC]

grading certificates: A formal document setting forth the quality of a *commodity* as determined by authorized inspectors or graders. [CFTC]

grantor: The maker, *writer,* or issuer of an *option contract* who, in return for the *premium* paid for the option, stands ready to purchase the *underlying commodity* (or *futures contract*) in the case of a *put option* or to sell the underlying commodity (or futures contract) in the case of a *call option.* [CFTC]

greeks: Measures of the sensitivity of the *option* value to small changes in the parameters used to value the option. The key Greek measures are defined below.

 • **delta:** A measure of the sensitivity of the option value to a small change in the price of the *underlying* asset/*contract*. The delta is the ratio of the change in the value of the option and the (small) change in the price of the underlying. Delta is called the first derivative of the option value with respect to the price of the underlying.

 • **gamma:** A measure of the sensitivity of the option delta value to a small change in the price of the *underlying* asset/*contract*. Gamma is called the second derivative of the option value with respect to the price of the underlying.

 • **rho:** A measure of the sensitivity of the option value to a small change in the risk-free interest rate.

 • **theta:** A measure of the sensitivity of the option value to a small change in the time to expiration.

 • **vega:** A measure of the sensitivity of the option value to a small change in the *implied volatility* of the *underlying* asset/*contract*. [CCRO]

gross margin: Sales revenue less cost of goods sold expense. For *transactions* reported under accrual accounting, gross margin is profit from sales revenue before deducting the other variable expenses of making the sales. For transactions reported under *mark-to-market* accounting, gross margin is the change in *fair value* during the period, reduced by direct incremental transaction-related expenses. In either case, gross margin excludes general and administrative or other operating expenses, depreciation, interest income or expense, and taxes. [CCRO]

gross margin at risk: The *value at risk* associated with the asset *portfolio* over the period where market *liquidity* exists while simulating *risk factors* impacting price and volume. This metric gives the measure of the degree of variability over the period where market liquidity exists. [CCRO]

gross processing margin (GPM): Refers to the difference between the cost of a *commodity* and the combined sales income of the finished products that result from processing the commodity. Various industries have formulas to express the relationship of raw material costs to sales income from finished products. See *crack spreads* and *spark spread.* [CFTC]

GTC: See *good 'til canceled* order. [CFTC]

GTW: See *good this week order.* [CFTC]

Guaranteed Introducing Broker: An *Introducing Broker* that has entered into a guarantee agreement with a *Futures Commission Merchant,* whereby the FCM agrees to be jointly and severally liable for all of the Introducing Broker's obligations under the *Commodity Exchange Act.* By entering into the agreement, the Introducing Broker is relieved from the necessity of raising its own *capital* to satisfy minimum financial requirements. In contrast, an independent Introducing Broker must raise its own capital to meet minimum financial requirements. [CFTC]

GW: See *gigawatt.*

GWe: See *gigawatt-electric* above. [EIA]

GWh: See *gigawatthour.*

h

haircut: In computing the value of assets for purposes of *capital*, segregation, or *margin* requirements, a percentage reduction from the stated value (*e.g.*, book value or market value) to account for possible declines in value that may occur before assets can be liquidated. [CFTC]

hardening: (1) Describes a price which is gradually stabilizing; (2) a term indicating a slowly advancing market. [CFTC]

hazard: See *failure.* [EIA]

head and shoulders: In _technical analysis,_ a chart formation that resembles a human head and shoulders and is generally considered to be predictive of a price _reversal._ A head and shoulders top (which is considered predictive of a price decline) consists of a high price, a decline to a _support_ level, a _rally_ to a higher price than the previous high price, a second decline to the support level, and a weaker rally to about the level of the first high price. The reverse (upside-down) formation is called a head and shoulders bottom (which is considered predictive of a price rally). [CFTC]

heat content [natural gas]: Measurement: The gross heat content (or _heating value),_ is the number of _British thermal units (Btu)_ produced by the combustion, at constant pressure, of the amount of the gas that would occupy a volume of one _cubic foot_ at a temperature of 60 degrees _Fahrenheit,_ if saturated with water vapor and under a pressure equivalent to 30 inches of mercury at 32 degrees Fahrenheit and under standard gravitational force (980.665 cm per sec.^{2}), with air of the same temperature and pressure as the gas, when the products of combustion are cooled to the initial temperature of gas and air and when the water formed by combustion is condensed to the liquid state. [EIA]

heat rate: A measure of generating station thermal efficiency, generally expressed in _Btu_ per net kilowatthour. It is computed by dividing the total Btu content of fuel burned for electric generation by the resulting net kilowatthour generation. [EIA]

heating degree-days (HDD): A measure of how cold a location is over a period of time relative to a base temperature, most commonly specified as 65 degrees _Fahrenheit._ The measure is computed for each day by subtracting the average of the day's high and low temperatures from the base temperature (65 degrees), with negative values set equal to zero. Each day's heating degree-days are summed to create a heating degree-day measure for a specified reference period. Heating degree-days are used in energy analysis as an indicator of space heating energy requirements or use. [EIA]

heating oil: No. 2 _fuel oil,_ a _distillate fuel oil_ used either for domestic heating or in moderate capacity commercial or industrial burners. [NYMEX]

heating value: The average number of *British thermal units* per *cubic foot* of *natural gas* as determined from tests of fuel samples. [EIA]

heavy: A market in which prices are demonstrating either an inability to advance or a slight tendency to decline. [CFTC]

heavy crude: *Crude oil* with a high *specific gravity* and a low *API gravity* due to the presence of a high proportion of heavy hydrocarbon fractions. [NYMEX]

heavy gas oil: *Petroleum* distillates with an approximate boiling range from 651 degrees to 1000 degrees *Fahrenheit*. [EIA]

heavy oil: The *fuel oils* remaining after the lighter oils have been distilled off during the refining process. Except for start-up and flame stabilization, virtually all *petroleum* used in steam plants is heavy oil. Includes fuel oil numbers 4, 5, and 6; crude; and topped crude. [EIA]

hedge (economic): The initiation of a *position* in a *futures* or *options* market that is intended as a temporary substitute for the sale or purchase of the actual *commodity*. An example is the sale of *futures contracts* in anticipation of future sale of cash commodities as a protection against potential price declines or the purchase of futures contracts in anticipation of future purchases of cash commodities as a protection against the possibility of increasing costs. [CCRO]

hedge (accounting): Under *GAAP,* derivatives meeting certain specific requirements are recorded as assets or liabilities at *fair value* on the balance sheet, but all or a portion of the changes in fair value of those *contracts* is recorded in the *equity* section of the entity's balance sheet prior to the occurrence of the *transaction* being hedged. When the hedge transaction occurs, the cumulative change in fair value of the hedge is reclassified from equity and recorded as a component of *earnings*. (The requirements of GAAP for hedge accounting are detailed and complex, and this definition is provided only as a basis for general understanding and should not be considered a complete discussion of the hedge accounting requirements.) [CCRO]

hedge exemption: An exemption from _speculative position limits_ for bona fide _hedgers_ and certain other persons who meet the requirements of _exchange_ and _CFTC rules._ [CFTC]

hedge fund: A private investment fund or pool that trades and invests in various assets such as securities, commodities, currency, and derivatives on behalf of its clients, typically wealthy individuals. Some _Commodity Pool Operators_ operate hedge funds. [CFTC]

hedger: A _trader_ who enters the market with the specific intent of protecting an existing or anticipated physical market _exposure_ from unexpected or adverse price fluctuations. [NYMEX]

hedge ratio: 1) Ratio of the value of _futures contracts_ purchased or sold to the value of the _cash commodity_ being _hedged,_ a computation necessary to minimize _basis risk._ 2) The ratio, determined by an _option's delta,_ of _futures_ to options required to establish a risk-free _position._ For example, if a $1/_barrel_ change in the _underlying futures price_ leads to a $0.25/barrel change in the options _premium,_ the hedge ratio is four (four options for each futures contract). [NYMEX]

hedging: Taking a _position_ in a _futures market_ opposite to a position held in the _cash market_ to minimize the risk of financial loss from an adverse price change; or a purchase or sale of futures as a temporary substitute for a cash _transaction_ that will occur later. One can _hedge_ either a _long_ cash market _position_ (_e.g.,_ one owns the _cash commodity)_ or a _short_ cash market position (_e.g.,_ one plans on buying the cash commodity in the future). [CFTC]

hedging contracts: _Contracts_ which establish future prices and quantities of electricity independent of the short-term market. Derivatives may be used for this purpose. [EIA]

Henry Hub: A _natural gas pipeline_ hub in Louisiana that serves as the _delivery point_ for New York Mercantile Exchange natural gas _futures contracts_ and often serves as a benchmark for wholesale natural gas prices across the U.S. [CFTC]

historical volatility: The annualized standard deviation of percent changes in _futures prices_ over a specific period. It is an indication of past _volatility_ in the marketplace. [NYMEX]

holding period: A time interval or horizon over which the variability in the value of a *portfolio* or estimated *earnings* from an economic activity is assessed. During the holding period, changes in the market prices of the commodities or other variables underlying the portfolio or activity drive the corresponding changes in the value or earnings estimates used at the beginning of the time interval. In the case of *daily earnings at risk,* the holding period is naturally one day. In the case of *value at risk* (VaR), the holding period can vary and be different for different components of the portfolio of *positions* or types of economic activity. Holding period in the case of VaR is generally supposed to be representative of the length of time it would take to liquidate the portfolio, and hence it is also called the *liquidation* period. Another interpretation of the holding period is that it is a measure of the length of time that would elapse while strategies are implemented and actions are taken to remove the variability in the value or earnings (*i.e.*, to render the portfolio of *positions* or economic activity risk-free). [CCRO]

horizontal spread (also called *time spread* or *Calendar Spread*): An *option spread* involving the simultaneous purchase and sale of options of the same class and *strike prices* but different *expiration dates.* See *diagonal spread, vertical spread.* [CFTC]

hybrid instruments: *Financial instruments* that possess, in varying combinations, characteristics of *forward contracts, futures contracts,* option contracts, debt *instruments*, bank depository interests, and other interests. Certain hybrid instruments are exempt from *CFTC* regulation. [CFTC]

i

IB: See *Introducing Broker.* [CFTC]

imbalance energy: Discrepancy between the amount that a seller contracted to deliver and the actual volume of power delivered. Imbalances are resolved through monetary payment. [NYMEX]

immediate-or-cancel (IOC): An order which must be *filled* immediately or be canceled. IOC orders need not be filled in their entirety. [NYMEX]

implied volatility: The *volatility* of a *futures contract,* *security*, or other *instrument* as implied by the prices of an *option* on that instrument, calculated using an options pricing model. [CFTC]

inadvertent energy: The imbalance of energy flows back and forth that are on-going and routine between a generator of power and the centers of demand. These imbalances are typically settled through *exchanges* of physical product. [NYMEX]

inadvertent power exchange: An unintended power exchange among utilities that is either not previously agreed upon or in an amount different from the amount agreed upon. [EIA]

independent power producer: A corporation, person, agency, authority, or other legal entity or instrumentality that owns or operates facilities for the generation of electricity for use primarily by the public, and that is not an *electric utility.* [EIA]

independent system operator (ISO): ISOs are responsible for overseeing the operation and scheduling of power through regional power grids. Tasks may include scheduling, managing emergency demands, and balancing generation and dissemination of power. [NYMEX]

indirect bucketing: Also referred to as Indirect Trading Against. Refers to when a *floor broker* effectively trades opposite his customer in a pair of non-competitive *transactions* by buying (selling) opposite an accommodating *trader* to *fill* a customer order and by selling (buying) for his personal account opposite the same accommodating trader. The accommodating trader assists the floor broker by making it appear that the customer traded opposite him rather than opposite the floor broker [CFTC]

initial deposit: See *initial margin.* [CFTC]

initial margin: Customers' funds put up as security for a guarantee of *contract* fulfillment at the time a *futures market position* is established. See *original margin.* [CFTC]

injections: *Natural gas* injected into storage reservoirs. [EIA]

in position: Refers to a *commodity* located where it can readily be moved to another point or *delivered* on a *futures contract.* Commodities not so situated are *"out of position."* Soybeans in Mississippi are out of position for delivery in Chicago, but in position for export shipment from the Gulf of Mexico. [CFTC]

in sight: The amount of a particular *commodity* that arrives at terminal or central locations in or near producing areas. When a commodity is "in sight," it is inferred that reasonably prompt *delivery* can be made; the quantity and quality also become known factors rather than estimates. [CFTC]

instrument: A tradable asset such as a *commodity, security*, or *derivative*, or an index or value that underlies a derivative or could underlie a derivative. [CFTC]

integration: A term that describes the degree in, and to, which one given company participates in all phases of the *petroleum* industry. [NYMEX]

interchange energy: Kilowatthours delivered to or received by one *electric utility* or pooling system from another. Settlement may be payment, returned in kind at a later time, or accumulated as energy balances until the end of the stated period. [EIA]

intercommodity spread: A *spread* in which the *long* and *short* legs are in two different but generally related *commodity* markets. Also called an *intermarket spread.* See spread. [CFTC]

interdelivery spread: A *spread* involving two different months of the same *commodity*. Also called an *intracommodity spread.* See *spread.* [CFTC]

intermarket spread: See *spread* and *intercommodity spread.* [CFTC]

intermediary: A person who acts on behalf of another person in connection with *futures trading*, such as a *Futures Commission Merchant, Introducing Broker, Commodity Pool Operator, Commodity Trading Advisor,* or *Associated Person.* [CFTC]

intermediate grade gasoline: A *grade* of unleaded gasoline with an octane rating intermediate between "regular" and "premium." Octane boosters are added to gasolines to control engine pre-ignition or "knocking" by slowing combustion rates. [EIA]

International Swaps and Derivatives Association (ISDA): A New York-based group of major international *swaps* dealers, that publishes the Code of Standard Wording, Assumptions and Provisions for Swaps, or Swaps Code, for US dollar interest rate swaps as well as standard master interest rate, credit, and *currency swap* agreements and definitions for use in connection with the creation and *trading* of swaps. [CFTC]

in-the-money: An *options contract* that can be *exercised* and immediately closed out against the *underlying* market for a cash credit. The option is in-the-money if the underlying *futures price* is above a *call option's strike price,* or below a *put option's* strike price. [NYMEX]

interruptible gas: *Gas* sold to customers with a provision that permits curtailment or cessation of service at the discretion of the distributing company under certain circumstances, as specified in the service contract. [EIA]

interruptible load: This Demand-Side Management category represents the consumer load that, in accordance with contractual arrangements, can be interrupted at the time of annual peak load by the action of the consumer at the direct request of the system operator. This type of control usually involves large-volume commercial and industrial consumers. Interruptible Load does not include Direct Load Control. [EIA]

interruptible or **curtailable rate:** A special electricity or *natural gas* arrangement under which, in return for lower rates, the customer must either reduce energy demand on short notice or allow the electric or natural gas utility to temporarily cut off the energy supply for the utility to maintain service for higher priority users. This interruption or reduction in demand typically occurs during periods of high demand for the energy (summer for electricity and winter for natural gas). [EIA]

interruptible power: Power and usually the associated energy made available by one utility to another. This *transaction* is subject to curtailment or cessation of delivery by the supplier in accordance with a prior agreement with the other party or under specified conditions. [EIA]

interruptible service: Utility service which expects and permits interruption on short notice, generally in peak-load periods, in order to meet the demand by *firm service* customers. Interruptible service customers usually pay a lower rate than firm service customers. Opposite of *firm service.* [NYMEX]

intracommodity spread: See *spread* and *interdelivery spread.* [CFTC]

intrastate companies: Companies not subject to *Federal Energy Regulatory Commission* (FERC) jurisdiction. [EIA]

intrinsic value: The amount by which an *option* is *in-the-money.* An option which is not in the-money has no intrinsic value. For *calls*, intrinsic value equals the difference between the *underlying futures price* and the option's *strike price.* For puts, intrinsic value equals the option's strike price minus the underlying *futures price.* Intrinsic value is never less than zero. [NYMEX]

Introducing Broker (or IB): A person (other than a person registered as an *Associated Person* of a *Futures Commission Merchant)* who is engaged in soliciting or in accepting orders for the purchase or sale of any *commodity* for future *delivery* on an *exchange* who does not accept any money, securities, or property to *margin*, guarantee, or secure any trades or *contracts* that result therefrom. [CFTC]

inverted market: A *futures market* in which the nearer months are selling at prices higher than the more *distant* months; a market displaying "inverse *carrying charges,"* characteristic of markets with supply shortages. See *backwardation.* [CFTC]

invisible supply: Uncounted *stocks* of a *commodity* in the hands of wholesalers, manufacturers, and producers that cannot be identified accurately; stocks outside commercial channels but theoretically available to the market. See *visible supply.* [CFTC]

invoice price: The price fixed by the *clearing house* at which deliveries on *futures* are invoiced — generally the price at which the *futures contract* is settled when deliveries are made. Also called *delivery price.* [CFTC]

ISDA: See *International Swaps and Derivatives Association.* [CFTC]

j

jet fuel: A refined *petroleum* product used in jet aircraft engines. It includes *kerosene-type jet fuel* and naphtha-type jet fuel. [EIA]

jobber: A middleman. A gasoline jobber, for example, might buy from *refiners* and would resell to small distributors or consumers. [NYMEX]

job lot: A form of *contract* having a smaller unit of *trading* than is featured in a regular contract. [CFTC]

joule: A metric unit of energy. [NYMEX]

k

kerb trading or **dealing:** See *curb trading.* [CFTC]

kerosene: A light *petroleum* distillate that is used in space heaters, cook stoves, and water heaters and is suitable for use as a light source when burned in wick-fed lamps. Kerosene has a maximum distillation temperature of 400 degrees *Fahrenheit* at the 10-percent recovery point, a final boiling point of 572 degrees Fahrenheit, and a minimum flash point of 100 degrees Fahrenheit. Included are No. 1-K and No. 2-K, the two *grades* recognized by *ASTM* Specification D 3699 as well as all other grades of kerosene called range or stove oil, which have properties similar to those of No. 1 *fuel oil.* Also see *kerosene-type jet fuel* below. [EIA]

kerosene-type jet fuel: A *kerosene*-based product having a maximum distillation temperature of 400 degrees *Fahrenheit* at the 10-percent recovery point and a final maximum boiling point of 572 degrees Fahrenheit and meeting *ASTM* Specification D 1655 and Military *Specifications* MIL-T-5624P and MIL-T-83133D (*Grades* JP-5 and JP-8). It is used for commercial and military turbojet and turboprop aircraft engines. [EIA]

l

large traders: A large *trader* is one who holds or controls a *position* in any one future or in any one *option* expiration series of a *commodity* on any one *exchange* equaling or exceeding the exchange or *CFTC*-specified *reporting level.* [CFTC]

last notice day: The final day on which notices of intent to deliver on *futures contracts* may be issued. [CFTC]

last trading day: The final *trading* day for a particular *delivery month futures contract* or *options contract.* Any futures contracts left open following this session must be settled by delivery. [NYMEX]

leverage: The ability to control large dollar amounts of a *commodity* or *security* with a comparatively small amount of *capital.* [CFTC]

licensed warehouse: A warehouse approved by an *exchange* from which a *commodity* may be delivered on a *futures contract.* See *regular warehouse.* [CFTC]

life of contract: Period between the beginning of *trading* in a particular *futures contract* and the expiration of trading. In some cases, this phrase denotes the period already passed in which trading has already occurred. For example, "The life-of-contract high so far is $2.50." Same as *Life of Delivery* or *Life of the Future.* [CFTC]

limit (up or down): The maximum price advance or decline from the previous day's settlement price permitted during one *trading* session, as fixed by the *rules* of an *exchange*. In some *futures contracts*, the limit may be expanded or removed during a trading session a specified period of time after the contract is *locked limit*. See *daily price limit*. [CFTC]

limit move: See *locked limit*. [CFTC]

limit only: The definite price stated by a customer to a *broker* restricting the execution of an order to buy for not more than, or to sell for not less than, the stated price. [CFTC]

limit order: An order in which the customer specifies a minimum sale price or maximum purchase price, as contrasted with a *market order*, which implies that the order should be *filled* as soon as possible at the market price. [CFTC]

linear instruments: *Instruments* whose value varies linearly with *underlying* market price moves. These would include *forwards, futures*, and fixed for floating *swaps*. [CCRO]

liquefied natural gas (LNG): *Natural gas* which has been made liquid by reducing its temperature to minus 258° *Fahrenheit* at atmospheric pressure. Its volume is 1/600 of gas in vapor form. [NYMEX]

liquefied petroleum gas (LPG): *Propane*, butane, or propane-butane mixtures derived from *crude oil* refining or *natural gas* fractionation. For convenience of transportation, these gases are liquefied through pressurization. [NYMEX]

liquid market: a market in which selling and buying can be accomplished with minimal effect on price. [CFTC]

liquidation: The closing out of a *long position*. The term is sometimes used to denote closing out a *short position*, but this is more often referred to as covering. See *cover, offset*. [CFTC]

liquidation value: The estimated amount of money that a *transaction*, trade, asset, liability, or *portfolio* could be quickly sold for such as if it were about to go out of business. [CCRO]

liquidity: The ease with which assets or products can be traded without dramatically altering their current quoted prices. [CCRO] (2) A market is said to be "liquid" when it has a high level of *trading* activity and *open interest.* [NYMEX]

liquidity risk: *Exposure* to the inability to effectively/timely liquidate open *positions* in the marketplace. [CCRO]

local: An individual with *exchange trading* privileges who trades for his own account on an exchange *floor* and whose activities provide market *liquidity*. See *floor trader.* [CFTC]

location: A *delivery point* for a *futures contract.* [CFTC]

locked-in: A *hedged position* that cannot be lifted without offsetting both sides of the hedge (*spread*). See *hedging.* Also refers to being caught in a *limit* price move. [CFTC]

locked limit: A price that has advanced or declined the permissible *limit* during one *trading* session, as fixed by the *rules* of an *exchange.* Also called *limit move.* [CFTC]

local distribution company (LDC): Company that distributes *natural gas* primarily to *end-users.* A *gas* utility. [NYMEX]

locked market: A market where prices have reached their daily *trading limit* and trading can only be conducted at that price or prices which are closer to the previous day's settlement price. [NYMEX]

long: 1) The market *position* of a *futures contract buyer* whose purchase obligates him to accept *delivery* unless he liquidates his contract with an offsetting sale. 2) One who has bought a futures contract to establish a market position. 3) In the *options* market, position of the buyer of a *call* or *put options* contract. Opposite of short. [NYMEX] (4) one who owns an inventory of commodities. See *Short.* [CFTC]

long hedge: Purchase of *futures* against the future market price purchase or fixed price forward sale of a *cash commodity* to protect against price increases. See *Buying Hedge.* [NYMEX]

long position: A *position* that is purchased, such as buying a stock, *forward, futures, swap,* or *option.* [CCRO]

long the basis: A person or firm that has bought the *spot commodity* and *hedged* with a sale of *futures* is said to be long the basis. [CFTC]

long ton: A unit that equals 20 long hundredweight or 2,240 pounds. Used mainly in England. [EIA]

lookalike option: An *over-the-counter* option that is cash settled based on the settlement price of a similar *exchange*-traded *futures contract* on a specified *trading* day. [CFTC]

lookalike swap: An *over-the-counter* swap that is cash settled based on the settlement price of a similar *exchange*-traded *futures contract* on a specified *trading* day. [CFTC]

lookback option: An *exotic option* whose payoff depends on the minimum or maximum price of the *underlying* asset during some portion of the life of the option. [CFTC]

lot: A specific quantity of a *futures commodity* of uniform *grade*; the standard *contract* unit of *trading.* See *even lot, job lot,* and *round lot.* [NYMEX]

lower partial moment: A measure of downside risk computed as the average of the squared deviations below a *target return.* This measure of downside risk is more general than semi-variance, which is computed as the average of the squared deviations below the mean return. [CCRO]

m

macro fund: A *hedge fund* that specializes in strategies designed to profit from expected macroeconomic events. [CFTC]

maintenance margin: See *margin.* [CFTC]

major: A term broadly applied to those multinational *oil* companies which by virtue of size, age, or degree of *integration* are among the preeminent companies in the international *petroleum* industry. [NYMEX]

major electric utility: A utility that, in the last 3 consecutive calendar years, had sales or *transmission* services exceeding one of the following: (1) 1 million *megawatthours* of total annual sales; (2) 100 megawatthours of annual sales for resale; (3) 500 megawatthours of annual gross interchange out; or (4) 500 megawatthours of wheeling (deliveries plus losses) for others. [EIA]

managed account: See *controlled account* and *discretionary account.* [CFTC]

manipulation: Any planned operation, *transaction*, or practice that causes or maintains an artificial price. Specific types include *corners* and *squeezes* as well as unusually large purchases or sales of a *commodity* or *security* in a short period of time in order to distort prices, and putting out false information in order to distort prices. [CFTC]

many-to-many: Refers to a *trading* platform in which multiple participants have the ability to execute or trade commodities, derivatives, or other *instruments* by accepting *bids* and offers made by multiple other participants. In contrast to *one-to-many* platforms, many-to-many platforms are considered trading facilities under the *Commodity Exchange Act.* Traditional *exchanges* are many-to-many platforms. [CFTC]

margin: The amount of money or collateral deposited by a customer with his *broker*, by a broker with a *clearing member,* or by a clearing member with a *clearing organization.* The margin is not partial payment on a purchase. Also called *performance bond.* (1) *Initial margin* is the amount of margin required by the broker when a *futures position* is opened; (2) *Maintenance margin* is an amount that must be maintained on *deposit* at all times. If the *equity* in a customer's account drops to or below the level of maintenance margin because of adverse price movement, the broker must issue a *margin call* to restore the customer's equity to the initial level. See *variation margin. Exchanges* specify levels of initial margin and maintenance margin for each *futures contract,* but *Futures Commission Merchants* may require their customers to post margin at higher levels than those specified by the *exchange. Futures* margin is determined by the SPAN margining system, which takes into account all positions in a customer's *portfolio.* [CFTC]

margin call: (1) A request from a brokerage firm to a customer to bring *margin* deposits up to initial levels; (2) a request by the *clearing organization* to a *clearing member* to make a *deposit* of *original margin,* or a daily or intra-day *variation margin* payment because of adverse price movement, based on *positions* carried by the clearing member. [CFTC]

marked-to-market: See *mark-to-market*

market clearing price: The price at which supply equals demand for the day-ahead or hour-ahead markets. [EIA]

market correction: In *technical analysis,* a small *reversal* in prices following a significant *trending* period. [NYMEX]

market depth: Concentration of market volumes. See *liquidity.* [CCRO]

market-if-touched (MIT) order: An order that becomes a *market order* when a particular price is reached. A sell MIT is placed above the market; a buy MIT is placed below the market. Also referred to as a *board order.* Compare to *stop order.* [CFTC]

market maker: A professional securities dealer or person with *trading* privileges on an *exchange* who has an obligation to buy when there is an excess of sell orders and to sell when there is an excess of buy orders. By maintaining an offering price sufficiently higher than their buying price, these firms are compensated for the risk involved in allowing their inventory of securities to act as a buffer against temporary order imbalances. In the *futures* industry, this term is sometimes loosely used to refer to a *floor trader* or *local* who, in speculating for his own account, provides a market for *commercial* users of the market. Occasionally a futures exchange will compensate a person with exchange trading privileges to take on the obligations of a market maker to enhance *liquidity* in a newly listed or lightly traded *futures contract.* [CFTC]

market-on-close: An order to buy or sell at the end of the *trading* session at a price within the *closing range* of prices. See *stop-close-only* order. [CFTC]

market-on-opening: An order to buy or sell at the beginning of the *trading* session at a price within the *opening range* of prices. [CFTC]

market order: An order to buy or sell a *futures contract* at whatever price is obtainable at the time it is entered in the *ring, pit*, or other *trading* platform. [CFTC]

market risk: Potential fluctuations in prices, volumes exchanged, and market *rules* that may affect a company's buying and selling activities. Usually, this is composed of:

• **price risk:** Potential fluctuations in prices of the *underlying* energy *commodity.*

• **credit risk:** Potential adverse occurrence of a *counterparty's* ability to pay its obligations.

• **counterparty performance risk:** Potential adverse occurrence of a *counterparty's* ability to operationally perform on an agreement or obligation.

• **volumetric risk:** The risk that *commodity* volumes will vary from expected volumes and result in a potential loss due to changing commodity market prices. For example, a generating unit sells projected electric generation production forward and at the time of delivery a unit is forced out and cannot deliver. This results in a loss if the price to purchase electricity to cover the sales is higher than the electricity sale price. [CCRO]

mark-to-market (MTM): (1) The value of a *financial instrument* (or a *portfolio* of such *instruments*) at current market rates or prices of the *underlying.* Marking *transactions* to market on a daily (or more frequent) basis is often recommended in *risk management* guidelines. [CCRO] (2) Part of the daily *cash flow* system used by US *futures exchanges* to maintain a minimum level of *margin equity* for a given futures or *option contract position* by calculating the gain or loss in each contract position resulting from changes in the price of the futures or option contracts at the end of each *trading* session. These amounts are added or subtracted to each account balance. [CFTC]

mark-to-model (MTMO): The value of a *financial instrument* (or a *portfolio* of such *instruments*) using, in addition to available prices of the *underlying commodities,* approved models for developing both the prices of the underlying commodities where the prices are not readily observable in the marketplace and the valuation and risk metrics of the instruments themselves where the instruments are complex combinations of standard products. [CCRO]

material adverse change (MAC): Broadly defined, any negative event that is deemed material by a creditor. In some *contracts*, material adverse change is undefined, but its occurrence leads to defined changes in the relationship. In other contracts, examples of what would be considered MAC events are provided. [CCRO]

maturity: Period within which a *futures contract* can be settled by *delivery* of the actual *commodity.* [CFTC]

maximum price fluctuation: A *commodity exchange's* established maximum *limits* for movements in *futures prices* during any one *trading* session. See *limit (up or down)* and *daily price limit.* [NYMEX]

Mcf: One thousand cubic feet. [EIA]

mean reversion: The tendency of a market variable to revert back to some long-run average level. [CCRO]

megawatt (MW): One million watts of electricity. [EIA]

megawatt electric (MWe): One million watts of electric *capacity.* [EIA]

megawatthour (MWh): (1) One thousand kilowatt-hours or 1 million watt-hours. [EIA] (2) Amount of electricity needed to light 10,000 100-watt light bulbs for a one-hour period. One million watts used for one hour. [NYMEX]

member rate: *Commission* charged for the execution of an order for a person who is a member of or has *trading* privileges at the *exchange*. [CFTC]

metric ton: A unit of weight equal to 2,204.6 pounds. [EIA]

midstream: The sector of *oil* and *gas* business devoted to processing, storage, and transportation of *crude oil, natural gas,* and *natural gas liquids* (e.g. ethane, *propane,* and butane). The midstream sector also includes gas processing (fractionation) plants that remove natural gas liquids from oil and gas. *Pipeline* operations fall in the midstream sector.

middle distillate: Hydrocarbons that are in the so-called "middle boiling range" of *refinery* distillation. Examples are *heating oil, diesel fuels,* and *kerosene.* [NYMEX]

mill: A monetary cost and billing unit used by utilities; it is equal to 1/1000 of the U.S. dollar (equivalent to 1/10 of 1 cent). [EIA]

mini: Refers to a *futures contract* that has a smaller *contract size* than an otherwise identical futures contract. [CFTC]

minimum price fluctuation (minimum tick): Smallest increment of price movement possible in *trading* a given *contract.* [CFTC]

MMbbl/d: One million *barrels* of *oil* per day. [EIA]

MMBtu: One million *British thermal units,* equal to one *dekatherm.* Approximately equal to a thousand cubic feet (*Mcf*) of *natural gas.* [NYMEX]

MMcf: One million cubic feet. [EIA]

momentum: In *technical analysis,* the relative change in price over a specific time interval. Often equated with speed or velocity and considered in terms of relative strength. [CFTC]

money market: The market for short-term debt *instruments.* [CFTC]

multilateral clearing organization: See *clearing organization.* [CFTC]

MW: See *megawatt.* [EIA]

MWe: See *megawatt electric.* [EIA]

MWh: See *megawatthour.* [EIA]

n

naked: A *long* or *short* market *position* taken without having an off-setting short or *long position.* For *options*, the term "uncovered" is used interchangeably and refers to a position that is taken without the benefit of an offsetting position in the *futures market.* A *trader* who executes one side of a *spread* is said to be naked until he executes the other side. [NYMEX]

naked option: The sale of a *call* or *put option* without holding an equal and opposite *position* in the *underlying instrument.* Also referred to as an *uncovered option, naked* call, or naked *put.* [CFTC]

National Futures Association (NFA): A *self-regulatory organization* whose members include *Futures Commission Merchants, Commodity Pool Operators, Commodity Trading Advisors, Introducing Brokers,* commodity exchanges, commercial firms, and banks, that is responsible — under *CFTC* oversight — for certain aspects of the regulation of FCMs, *CPOs*, CTAs, IBs, and their *Associated Persons,* focusing primarily on the qualifications and proficiency, financial condition, retail sales practices, and business conduct of these *futures* professionals. NFA also performs arbitration and dispute resolution functions for industry participants. [CFTC]

natural gas: A naturally occurring mixture of hydrocarbon and non-hydrocarbon gases found in porous rock formations. Its principal component is methane. [NYMEX]

natural gas liquids (NGL): A general term for all liquid products separated from _natural gas_ in a _gas_ processing plant. NGLs include _propane_, butane, ethane, and natural gasoline. [NYMEX]

nearbys: The nearest _delivery months_ of a _commodity futures market._ [CFTC]

nearby delivery month: The month of the _futures contract_ closest to _maturity_; the _front month_ or lead month. [CFTC]

negative carry: The cost of financing a _financial instrument_ (the short-term rate of interest), when the cost is above the current return of the financial instrument. See _carrying charges_ and _positive carry._ [CFTC]

NERC: _North American Electric Reliability Council._ [NYMEX]

net asset value (NAV): The value of each unit of participation in a _commodity pool._ [CFTC]

netback: Industry term referring to the net _free on board_ cost of product offered on a _delivered_ or _cost, insurance, and freight_ basis. It is derived by subtracting all costs of shipment from the landed price. [NYMEX]

net position: The difference between the open _long contracts_ and the open _short_ contracts held by a _trader_ in any one _commodity_. [CFTC]

netting out: For credit purposes, the adding of current dollar amounts owed less current dollar amounts to be received from a _counterparty_. As opposed to offsetting, netting can be accomplished only via formal legal agreement between counterparties. [CCRO]

NFA: _National Futures Association._ [CFTC]

next day: A _spot contract_ that provides for _delivery_ of a _commodity_ on the next calendar day or the next _business day_. Also called _day ahead._ [CFTC]

neutral spread: Another name for a _delta neutral spread_. _Spreads_ may also be _lot_ neutral, where the total number of _long contracts_ and the total number of _short_ contracts of the same type are approximately equal. [NYMEX]

nominal price (or **nominal quotation**): Computed price _quotation_ on a _futures_ or option _contract_ for a period in which no actual _trading_ took place, usually an average of _bid_ and _asked_ prices or computed using historical or theoretical relationships to more active contracts. [CFTC]

nomination: (1) The process whereby the holder of a _long Exchange petroleum_ product _futures position_ who has elected to stand for _delivery_ tells the seller (the _short_) where the product is to be delivered and the method of transport. (2) A shipper's offer to move _gas_ on a _pipeline_ during a given period. Most nominations are made on a daily basis, although mid-day hourly nominations are possible on some systems. (3) A request for a physical quantity of gas under a specific purchase, sales or transportation agreement or for all _contracts_ at a specific point. [NYMEX]

non-firm energy: The quality sale of _transmission_ service offered to customers that anticipates possible interruption of deliveries. [NYMEX]

nonlinear instruments: _Instruments_ whose value does not vary linearly with _underlying_ price moves. This would include _options_. [CCRO]

non-member traders: _Speculators_ and _hedgers_ who trade on the _exchange_ through a member or a person with _trading_ privileges but who do not hold exchange memberships or trading privileges. [CFTC]

North American Electric Reliability Council (NERC): A group formed in 1968 by the _electric utility_ industry to promote the _reliability_ and adequacy of bulk power supply in the electric utility systems of North America. NERC consists of 10 regional reliability councils and encompasses essentially all the power regions of the contiguous United States, Canada, and Mexico. The NERC regions are: Alaskan System Coordination Council (AS-

CC); East Central Area Reliability Coordination Agreement (ECAR); Electric Reliability Council of Texas (ERCOT); Mid-America Interpool Network (MAIN); Mid-Atlantic Area Council, (MAAC); Mid-Continent Area *Power* *Pool* (MAPP); Northeast Power Coordinating Council (NPCC); Southeastern Electric Reliability Council (SERC); Southwest Power Pool (SPP); Western System Coordinating Council (WSCC). [NYMEX]

notice day: Any day on which notices of intent to deliver on *futures* *contracts* may be issued. See *delivery*. [CFTC]

notice of intent to deliver: A notice that must be presented by the seller of a *futures* *contract* to the *clearing* *organization* prior to *delivery*. The clearing organization then assigns the notice and subsequent *delivery* *instrument* to a *buyer*. Also *Notice of Delivery*. [CFTC]

notional: The principal amount used to calculate payments in a *derivative instrument*. The principal is notional because it is neither paid nor received. The notional amount is the number of currency units, shares, pounds, or other units specified in a derivative instrument. The notional position is the maximum volume of the position. [CCRO]

notional settlement: A reference price based on *trading* activity during a certain *range* close to the end of the day that is used to calculate the maximum daily price fluctuation for trading on the *NYMEX ACCESS®* electronic trading system when the regular settlement price has not been established in time for the start of the NYMEX ACCESS® session. The system is then updated with *final* *settlement* *prices* later in the session. [NYMEX]

NYMEX ACCESS®: NYMEX ACCESS® is an international electronic *trading* system offered by the New York Mercantile Exchange. The Exchange provides the user with the equipment, software, and services. ACCESS stands for American Computerized Commodity Exchange System and Services. [NYMEX]

NYMEX Lookalike: A *lookalike* *swap* or *lookalike* *option* that is based on a *futures* *contract* traded on the New York Mercantile Exchange (NYMEX). [CFTC]

NYMEX Swap: A *lookalike swap* that is based on a *futures contract* traded on the New York Mercantile Exchange (NYMEX). [CFTC]

O

OCO: See *one cancels the other order.* [CFTC]

offer: An indication of willingness to sell at a given price; opposite of *bid.* [CFTC]

off exchange: See *over-the-counter.* [CFTC]

off-peak: The load for the remaining hours that are not on-peak. (See *on-peak.*) [NYMEX]

offset: Liquidating a purchase of *futures contracts* through the sale of an equal number of contracts of the same *delivery month,* or liquidating a *short* sale of futures through the purchase of an equal number of contracts of the same *delivery month.* See *closing out* and *cover.* [CFTC]

oil: A mixture of hydrocarbons usually existing in the liquid state in natural underground pools or reservoirs. *Gas* is often found in association with oil. Also see *petroleum.* [EIA]

oil stocks: Oil *stocks* include *crude oil* (including strategic reserves), unfinished oils, *natural gas* plant liquids, and *refined petroleum products.* [EIA]

one cancels the other (OCO) order: A pair of orders, typically *limit orders,* whereby if one order is *filled,* the other order will automatically be canceled. For example, an OCO order might consist of an order to buy 10 *calls* with a *strike price* of 50 at a specified price or buy 20 calls with a strike price of 55 (with the same *expiration date*) at a specified price. [CFTC]

one-to-many: Refers to a *proprietary trading* platform in which the platform operator posts *bids* and *offers* for commodities, derivatives, or other *instruments* and serves as a *counterparty* to every *transaction* executed on the platform. In contrast to *many-to-many* platforms, one-to-many platforms are not considered trading facilities under the *Commodity Exchange Act.* [CFTC]

on-peak: Refers to hours of the *business day* when demand is at its peak. For example, the NYMEX Division California-Oregon border and Palo Verde electricity *futures contracts* define the on-peak period from the hour ending 0700 to the hour ending 2200 (6 A.M. to 10 P.M.), Pacific prevailing time. In the physical market, on-peak definitions vary by North America Electric Reliability Council region. Can also refer to the number of business days in any one month on which it is contracted that electricity is delivered. Patterns of the number of on-peak days in a week generally also vary by region. [NYMEX]

opening price (or range): The price (or price *range*) recorded during the period designated by the *exchange* as the official *opening*. [CFTC]

opening: The period at the beginning of the *trading* session officially designated by the *exchange* during which all *transactions* are considered made "at the opening." [CFTC]

open interest: The total number of *futures contracts* long or *short* in a *delivery month* or market that has been entered into and not yet liquidated by an offsetting *transaction* or fulfilled by delivery. Also called open *contracts* or open *commitments*. [CFTC]

open order (or orders): An order that remains in force until it is canceled or until the *futures contracts* expire. See *good 'til canceled* and *good this week orders.* [CFTC]

open outcry: A method of public auction, common to most US *commodity exchanges*, where *trading* occurs on a *trading floor* and *traders* may *bid* and offer simultaneously either for their own accounts or for the accounts of customers. *Transactions* may take place simultaneously at different places in the trading *pit* or *ring*. At most *exchanges* outside the US, open outcry has been replaced by *Electronic Trading Platforms*.

open trade equity: The *unrealized* gain or loss on open futures *positions.* [CFTC]

operational risk: The risk of direct or indirect loss resulting from inadequate or failed internal processes, people, and systems or from external events. [CCRO]

operations risk: The risks associated with physical asset or *delivery* of energy commodities. [CCRO]

options: A *contract* which gives the holder the right, but not the obligation, to purchase or to sell the *underlying futures contract* at a specified price within a specified period of time in *exchange* for a one-time *premium* payment. The contract also obligates the *writer*, who receives the premium, to meet these obligations. See *put* and *call.* [NYMEX]

option buyer: The person who buys *calls, puts,* or any *combination* of calls and puts. [CFTC]

option writer: The person who originates an *option contract* by promising to perform a certain obligation in return for the price or *premium* of the option. Also known as *option grantor* or *option seller.* [CFTC]

option pricing model: A mathematical model used to calculate the *theoretical value* of an *option.* Inputs to option pricing models typically include the price of the *underlying instrument,* the option *strike price,* the time remaining till the *expiration date,* the *volatility* of the underlying instrument, and the risk-free interest rate (*e.g.,* the Treasury bill interest rate). Examples of option pricing models include *Black-Scholes* and *Cox-Ross-Rubinstein.* [CFTC]

original margin: The *initial deposit* of funds, as good faith monies, when a *position* is initiated in order to guarantee fulfillment of its obligations. Also known as *initial margin.* [NYMEX]

OTC: See *over-the-counter.* [CFTC]

out of position: See *in position.* [CFTC]

out-of-the-money: An *option* which has no *intrinsic value.* For *calls*, an option whose *exercise price* is above the market price of the *underlying* future. For puts, an option whose exercise price is below the *futures price.* [NYMEX]

out trade: A trade that cannot be cleared by a *clearing organization* because the trade data submitted by the two *clearing members* or two *traders* involved in the trade differs in some respect (*e.g.*, price and/or quantity). In such cases, the two clearing members or traders involved must reconcile the discrepancy, if possible, and resubmit the trade for *clearing*. If an agreement cannot be reached by the two clearing members or traders involved, the dispute would be settled by an appropriate *exchange* committee. [CFTC]

overbought: A technical opinion that the market price has risen too steeply and too fast in relation to underlying fundamental factors. Rank and file *traders* who were bullish and *long* have turned bearish. [CFTC]

overnight trade: A trade which is not liquidated during the same *trading* session during which it was established. [CFTC]

oversold: A technical opinion that the market price has declined too steeply and too fast in relation to underlying fundamental factors; rank and file *traders* who were bearish and *short* have turned bullish. [CFTC]

over-the-counter (OTC): The *trading* of commodities, *contracts*, or other *instruments* not listed on any *exchange*. OTC *transactions* can occur electronically or over the telephone. Also referred to as Off-Exchange. [CFTC]

overwrite: The writing of more *options* than one expects to have *exercised. Call options* are overwritten because the *writer* considers the *underlying* overvalued. *Put options* are overwritten because the underlying is considered undervalued [NYMEX]

p

P&S (Purchase and Sale Statement): A statement sent by a *Futures Commission Merchant* to a customer when any part of a futures *position* is *offset*, showing the number of *contracts* involved, the prices at which the contracts were bought or sold, the gross profit or loss, the *commission* charges, the net profit or loss on the *transactions*, and the balance. FCMs also send P&S Statements whenever any other event occurs that alters the account balance including when the customer deposits or withdraws *margin* and when the FCM places excess margin in interest bearing *instruments* for the customer's benefit. [CFTC]

PAD (or PADD): *Petroleum* Administration for Defense District. The United States is divided into five distinct marketing regions in which prices might differ due to variations in the supply or demand. [NYMEX]

paper barrels: A term used to denote trade in non-physical *oil* (*futures, forwards, swaps*) markets which give a *buyer* or seller the right to a certain quantity and quality of *crude oil* or refined products at a future date, but not to any specific physical *lot*. [NYMEX]

paper profit or loss: The profit or loss that would be *realized* if open *contracts* were liquidated as of a certain time or at a certain price. [CFTC]

par: (1) Refers to the standard *delivery point(s)* and/or quality of a *commodity* that is deliverable on a *futures contract* at contract price. Serves as a benchmark upon which to base *discounts* or *premiums* for varying quality and delivery *locations*; (2) in bond markets, an index (usually 100) representing the face value of a bond. [CFTC]

path dependent option: An *option* whose valuation and payoff depends on the *realized* price path of the *underlying* asset, such as an *Asian option* or a *lookback option.* [CFTC]

pay/collect: A shorthand method of referring to the payment of a loss (pay) and receipt of a gain (collect) by a *clearing member* to or from a *clearing organization* that occurs after a futures *position* has been *marked-to-market.* See *variation margin.* [CFTC]

payment provision: Specifies a fixed or determinable settlement to be made if the *underlying* behaves in a specified manner. One of the parties is required to deliver an asset but that asset is readily convertible to cash or is itself a *derivative instrument.* [CCRO]

performance bond: See *margin.* [CFTC]

petrochemical: An intermediate chemical derived from *petroleum,* hydrocarbon liquids, or *natural gas,* such as ethylene, propylene, benzene, toluene, and xylene. [NYMEX]

petroleum: A generic name for hydrocarbons, including *crude oil, natural gas liquids,* refined, and product derivatives. [NYMEX]

petroleum refinery: An installation that manufactures finished *petroleum* products from *crude oil,* unfinished oils, *natural gas liquids,* other hydrocarbons, and alcohol. [EIA]

petroleum stocks, primary: For individual products, quantities that are held at *refineries,* in *pipelines* and at bulk terminals that have a *capacity* of 50,000 *barrels* or more, or that are in transit thereto. *Stocks* held by product retailers and resellers, as well as tertiary stocks held at the point of consumption, are excluded. Stocks of individual products held at *gas* processing plants are excluded from individual product estimates but are included in other oils estimates and total. [EIA]

pin risk: The risk to a *trader* who has sold an *option* that, at expiration, has a *strike price* identical to, or pinned to, the *underlying futures price.* In this case, the trader will not know whether he will be required to assume his options obligations. [NYMEX]

pip: The smallest price unit of a *commodity* or currency. [CFTC]

pipeline: A pipe through which oil or *natural gas* is pumped between two points, either offshore or onshore. [NYMEX]

pit: A specially constructed area on the _trading floor_ of some _exchanges_ where _trading_ in a _futures contract_ or _option_ is conducted. On other exchanges, the term _ring_ designates the trading area for _commodity_ contract. [CFTC]

pit brokers: See _floor broker._ [CFTC]

point or tick: The smallest monetary unit of change in a _futures price_ or an _options premium._ [NYMEX]

point-and-figure: A method of _charting_ that uses prices to form patterns of movement without regard to time. It defines a price _trend_ as a continued movement in one direction until a _reversal_ of a predetermined criterion is met. [CFTC]

point balance: A statement prepared by _Futures Commission Merchants_ to show profit or loss on all open _contracts_ using an official closing or settlement price, usually at calendar month end. [CFTC]

Ponzi Scheme: Named after Charles Ponzi, a man with a remarkable criminal career in the early 20th century, the term has been used to describe pyramid arrangements whereby an enterprise makes payments to investors from the proceeds of a later investment rather than from profits of the underlying business venture, as the investors expected, and gives investors the impression that a legitimate profit-making business or investment opportunity exists, where in fact it is a mere fiction. [CFTC]

population-weighted degree-days: Heating or _cooling degree-days_ weighted by the population of the area in which the _degree-days_ are recorded. To compute national population-weighted degree-days, the Nation is divided into nine Census regions comprised of from three to eight states that are assigned weights based on the ratio of the population of the region to the total population of the Nation. Degree-day readings for each region are multiplied by the corresponding population weight for each region, and these products are then summed to arrive at the national population weighted degree-day figure. [EIA]

portfolio: A collection of assets, liabilities, *transactions*, and/or trades. [CCRO]

portfolio insurance: A *trading* strategy that uses stock index futures and/or stock index *options* to protect stock *portfolios* against market declines. [CFTC]

portfolio neutralization: For purposes of *value at risk*, the concept of portfolio neutralization is meant to replace the commonly used reference to portfolio *liquidation*. The idea is that the risk in a *portfolio* can be effectively neutralized with a variety of financial and physical *trading instruments*, without actually having to estimate the time, cost, and capacity of the market to absorb a full liquidation of a given portfolio. By portfolio neutralization, what is implied is that through the process of entering into a variety of *transactions* around an asset or portfolio, the risk of change in the value of the asset or portfolio can be minimized. In the context of a portfolio of assets that may be illiquid in terms of liquidation, the value of the assets can be bound or monetized through active *hedging*. This process will involve a definite passage of time before the hedges are in place, during which the value of the assets can change. It is in this context that the concept of VaR can be applied with a suitable reinterpretation. [CCRO]

position: The net total of a *trader's* open *contracts*, either *long* or *short*, in a particular *underlying commodity*. [NYMEX]

position limit: See *speculative position limit*.

position trader: A *commodity trader* who either buys or sells *contracts* and holds them for an extended period of time, as distinguished from a *day trader*, who will normally initiate and *offset* a futures *position* within a single *trading* session. [CFTC]

positive carry: The cost of financing a *financial instrument* (the short-term rate of interest), where the cost is less than the current return of the financial instrument. See *carrying charges* and *negative carry*. [CFTC]

posted price: An announced or advertised price indicating what a firm will pay for a *commodity* or the price at which the firm will sell it. [CFTC]

potential exposure: Describes the range of values that current *exposure* could take over a given time horizon as a result of price and/or volumetric uncertainty. Current exposure includes both billed and unbilled receivables for product that has already been delivered, as well as MTM exposure for products yet to be delivered. [CCRO]

power exchange: An entity providing a competitive *spot market* for electric power through day-and/or hour-ahead auction of generation and *demand bids.* [EIA]

power exchange generation: Generation *scheduled* by the power exchange. See definition for *power exchange* above. [EIA]

power exchange load: Load that has been *scheduled* by the *power exchange* and is received through the use of *transmission* or distribution facilities owned by participating transmission owners. [EIA]

power marketer: A wholesale power entity that has registered with the *Federal Energy Regulatory Commission* to buy and sell wholesale power from and to each other and other public entities at market-derived prices. Power marketing companies include investor-owned, utility-affiliated companies; *natural gas* marketing companies; financial intermediaries; *independent power producers*; and entrepreneurs. Typically, power marketers do not own generating facilities. [NYMEX]

power pool: An association of two or more interconnected electric systems having an agreement to coordinate operations and planning for improved *reliability* and efficiencies. [EIA]

prearranged trading: *Trading* between *brokers* in accordance with an expressed or implied agreement or understanding, which is a violation of the *Commodity Exchange Act* and *CFTC* regulations. [CFTC]

premium: (1) The payment an *option buyer* makes to the *option writer* for granting an option *contract*; (2) the amount a price would be increased to purchase a better quality *commodity*; (3) refers to a futures *delivery month* selling at a higher price than another, as "July is at a premium over May." [CFTC]

price basing: A situation where producers, processors, merchants, or consumers of a *commodity* establish commercial *transaction* prices based on the *futures prices* for that or a related commodity (*e.g.*, an offer to sell corn at 5 cents over the December futures price). This phenomenon is commonly observed in grain and metal markets. [CFTC]

price discovery: The process of determining the price level for a *commodity* based on supply and demand conditions. Price discovery may occur in a *futures market* or *cash market.* [CFTC]

price gaps: A chart pattern of the price movement of a *commodity* when the low price of one bar on a chart is higher than the high of the preceding bar (or inversely, the high is lower than the low of the preceding bar); depicting a price or price *range* where no trades take place. The price patterns are used by technical analysts to try to recognize changes in a price *trend.* [NYMEX]

price movement limit: See *limit* (*up* or *down*). [CFTC]

price risk: See *market risk.* [CCRO]

primary market: (1) For producers, their major purchaser of commodities; (2) to processors, the market that is the major supplier of their *commodity* needs; and (3) in commercial marketing channels, an important center at which *spot commodities* are concentrated for shipment to *terminal markets.* [CFTC]

primary stocks: *Stocks* of *crude oil* or refined products held in storage at leases, *refineries, natural gas* processing plants, *pipelines*, tank farms, and bulk terminals that can store at least 50,000 *barrels* of refined products. [NYMEX]

program trading: The purchase (or sale) of a large number of stocks contained in or comprising a *portfolio.* Originally called program trading when index funds and other institutional investors began to embark on large-scale buying or selling campaigns or "programs" to invest in a manner that replicates a target stock index, the term now also commonly includes computer-aided stock market buying or selling programs, and index *arbitrage.* [CFTC]

prompt date: The date on which the *buyer* of an *option* will buy or sell the *underlying commodity* (or *futures contract*) if the option is *exercised*. [CFTC]

propane: A natural hydrocarbon occurring in a gaseous state under normal atmospheric pressure and temperature, however, propane is usually liquefied through pressurization for transportation and storage. Propane is primarily used for rural heating and cooking and as a fuel *gas* in areas not serviced by *natural gas* mains and as a *petrochemical* feed stock. [NYMEX]

proprietary account: An account that a *Futures Commission Merchant* carries for itself or a closely related person, such as a parent, subsidiary or affiliate company, general partner, director, *Associated Person,* or an owner of ten percent or more of the *capital* stock. The FCM must segregate customer funds from funds related to proprietary accounts. [CFTC]

proprietary trading: Standardized *contracts* entered into to take a view, capture market price changes, or put *capital* at risk. These activities are generally accounted for on a MTM basis under *generally accepted accounting principles (GAAP).* [CCRO]

proprietary trading group: An organization whose owners, employees and/or contractors trade in the name of accounts owned by the group and exclusively use the funds of the group for all of their *trading* activity. [CFTC]

public: In trade parlance, non-professional *speculators* as distinguished from *hedgers* and professional speculators or *traders*. [CFTC]

Purchase and Sale Statement: See *P&S*. [CFTC]

purchased power: Power purchased or available for purchase from a source outside the system. [EIA]

put: See *put option.*

put option: An *option* which gives the *buyer*, or holder, the right, but not the obligation, to sell a *futures contract* at a specific price within a specific period of time in exchange for a one-time *premium* payment. It obligates the seller, or *writer*, of the option to buy the *underlying* futures contract at the designated price, should an option be *exercised* at that price. See *call option* [NYMEX]

pyramiding: The use of profits on existing *positions* as *margin* to increase the size of the *position*, normally in successively smaller increments. [CFTC]

q

qualifying facility (QF): A generator or small power producer that meets certain ownership, operating, and efficiency criteria established by the *Federal Energy Regulatory Commission*, and has filed with *FERC* for QF status or has self-certified. QFs are physical generating facilities. [NYMEX]

quality or grade (of coal): An informal classification of coal relating to its suitability for use for a particular purpose. Refers to individual measurements such as heat value, fixed carbon, moisture, ash, *sulfur*, major, minor, and trace elements, coking properties, petrologic properties, and particular organic constituents. The individual quality elements may be aggregated in various ways to classify coal for such special purposes as metallurgical, *gas, petrochemical*, and blending usages. [EIA]

quick order: See *fill-or-kill.*

quotation: The actual price or the *bid* or *ask* price of either cash commodities or *futures contracts.* [CFTC]

r

rally: An advancing price movement following a decline in a market. [NYMEX]

Random Walk: An economic theory that market price movements move randomly. This assumes an *efficient market.* The theory also assumes that new information comes to the market randomly. Together, the two assumptions imply that market prices move randomly as new information is incorporated into market prices. The theory implies that the best predictor of future prices is the current price, and that past prices are not a reliable indicator of future prices. If the random walk theory is correct, *technical analysis* cannot work. [CFTC]

range: The difference between the high and low price of a *commodity*, futures, or *option contract* during a given period. [CFTC]

rating trigger: Any number of contractual clauses that call for some change in the *counterparty* relationship given a change in the debt ratings. Rating triggers often call for decreased unsecured credit limits. [CCRO]

ratio hedge: The number of *options* compared to the number of *futures contracts* bought or sold in order to establish a *hedge* that is neutral or *delta neutral.* [CFTC]

ratio spread: This strategy, which applies to both puts and *calls*, involves buying or selling *options* at one *strike price* in greater number than those bought or sold at another strike price. Ratio spreads are typically designed to be *delta neutral. Back spreads* and *front spreads* are types of ratio spreads. [CFTC]

ratio vertical spread: See *front spread.* [CFTC]

reaction: A downward price movement after a price advance. [CFTC]

realized: The occurrence of an activity required to entitle the entity to payment or obligating it to make payment. For *transactions* subject to accrual accounting, this will generally be when products or services are delivered or received. For transactions subject to *fair value* accounting, this will generally be when the transaction no longer is subject to *market risk.* [CCRO]

recovery: An upward price movement after a decline. [CFTC]

refined petroleum products: Refined *petroleum* products include but are not limited to gasolines, *kerosene*, distillates (including No. 2

fuel oil), liquefied petroleum gas, asphalt, lubricating oils, *diesel fuels,* and residual fuels. [EIA]

refiner: A firm or the part of a firm that refines products or blends and substantially changes products, or refines liquid hydrocarbons from *oil* and *gas* field gases, or recovers *liquefied petroleum gases* incident to petroleum refining and sells those products to resellers, retailers, reseller/retailers or ultimate consumers. "Refiner" includes any owner of products that contracts to have those products refined and then sells the refined products to resellers, retailers, or ultimate consumers. [EIA]

refiner-distributor: A company that acts as a wholesaler of gasoline, *heating oil,* or other products which operates its own *refinery*; may also retail and buy additional supplies to supplement its own refining output. [NYMEX]

refinery: An installation that manufactures finished *petroleum* products from *crude oil,* unfinished oils, *natural gas liquids,* other hydrocarbons, and oxygenates. [EIA]

refinery margin: The difference between a *refinery's* cost to produce a product and the amount it will procure from the sale of the product. [NYMEX]

regular warehouse: A processing plant or warehouse that satisfies *exchange* requirements for financing, facilities, capacity, and location and has been approved as acceptable for *delivery* of commodities against *futures contracts.* See *licensed warehouse.* [CFTC]

reliability (electric system): A measure of the ability of the system to continue operation while some lines or generators are out of service. Reliability deals with the performance of the system under stress. [EIA]

replicating portfolio: A *portfolio* of assets for which changes in value match those of a target asset. For example, a portfolio replicating a standard *option* can be constructed with certain amounts of the asset *underlying* the option and bonds. Sometimes referred to as a *synthetic asset.* [CFTC]

reportable position: The number of *futures* *contracts,* as determined by the *Exchange* or the *Commodity* *Futures* *Trading* *Commission,* above which a customer must be identified daily to the Exchange and to the Commission with regard to the size of his *position* by *commodity,* by *delivery* *month,* and by purpose of the *trading.* [NYMEX]

reporting level: Sizes of *positions* set by the *exchanges* and/or the *CFTC* at or above which *commodity traders* or *brokers* who carry these accounts must make daily reports about the size of the *position* by commodity, by *delivery* *month,* and whether the position is controlled by a *commercial* or non-commercial *trader.* [CFTC]

requirements power: The *firm* *service* needs required by designated load plus losses from the points of supply. [EIA]

resistance: In *technical* *analysis,* a price area where new selling will emerge to dampen a continued rise. See *support.* [CFTC]

resting order: A *limit* *order* to buy at a price below or to sell at a price above the prevailing market that is being held by a *floor broker.* Such orders may either be *day* *orders* or *open* *orders.* [CFTC]

retail customer: A customer that does not qualify as an *eligible* *contract* *participant* under Section 1a(12) of the *Commodity Exchange Act.* An individual with total assets that do not exceed $10 million, or $5 million if the individual is entering into an agreement, contract, or *transaction* to manage risk, would be considered a retail customer. [CFTC]

retender: In specific circumstances, some *exchanges* permit holders of *futures* *contracts* who have received a *delivery* *notice* through the *clearing* *organization* to sell a futures contract and return the notice to the clearing organization to be reissued to another *long;* others permit transfer of notices to another *buyer.* In either case, the *trader* is said to have retendered the notice. [CFTC]

retracement: A *reversal* within a major price *trend.* [CFTC]

reversal: A change of direction in prices. See *reverse conversion.* [CFTC]

reverse conversion or reversal: With regard to *options*, a *position* created by buying a *call option,* selling a *put option,* and selling the *underlying instrument* (for example, a *futures contract).* See *conversion.* [CFTC]

ring: A circular area on the *trading floor* of an *exchange* where *traders* and *brokers* stand while executing futures trades. Some exchanges use *pits* rather than rings. [CFTC]

risk-adjusted return on capital: A system that adjusts profits for *capital* at risk, defined as the amount of capital required to protect against 99% of potential economic losses over a year *holding period* or investment horizon, on an after-tax basis. In more developed RAROC systems, the same one-year horizon is used for all RAROC computations, regardless of the actual holding period, to allow meaningful comparisons across asset classes. [CCRO]

risk capital: Funds at risk in an enterprise, entity, or *trading* organization. [CCRO]

risk factor: See *delta.* [CFTC]

risk management: Risk management is a process to reduce a company's *exposure* to a relevant uncertainty. This typically involves reducing the prospect of losses which will interfere with the execution of a company's business strategy. A risk management program frequently involves: identifying the source of exposure; quantifying the exposure; clarifying the impact of the exposure on the company's overall business strategy; assessing the capability for managing the exposure; and selecting the appropriate risk management products. [CCRO]

risk/reward ratio: The relationship between the probability of loss and profit. This ratio is often used as a basis for trade selection or comparison. [CFTC]

risk tolerance/appetite: A company's ability and/or willingness to absorb declines in the value of an asset, liability, trade, *transaction*, or *portfolio*. [CCRO]

roll-over: A *trading* procedure involving the shift of one month of a *straddle* into another future month while holding the other <u>contract month.</u> The shift can take place in either the *long* or *short* straddle month. The term also applies to lifting a near futures *position* and reestablishing it in a more *deferred <u>delivery month.</u>* [CFTC]

round lot: A quantity of a *commodity* equal in size to the corresponding <u>futures</u> <u>contract</u> for the commodity, as distinguished from a <u>job</u> <u>lot,</u> which may be larger or smaller than the contract. [NYMEX]

round turn: A completed *transaction* involving both a purchase and a liquidating sale, or a sale followed by a *covering* purchase. [CFTC]

rulemaking (regulations): The authority delegated to administrative agencies by Congress or State legislative bodies to make rules that have the force of law. Frequently, statutory laws that express broad terms of a policy are implemented more specifically by administrative rules, regulations, and practices. [EIA]

rules: The principles for governing an *exchange*. In some exchanges, rules are adopted by a vote of the membership, while in others, they can be imposed by the governing board. [CFTC]

runners: Messengers or clerks who deliver orders received by phone clerks to *brokers* for execution in the *pit*. [CFTC]

S

sample grade: Usually the lowest quality of a *commodity*, too low to be acceptable for *delivery* in satisfaction of <u>futures</u> <u>contracts.</u> [CFTC]

scale down (or **up**): To purchase or sell a scale down means to buy or sell at regular price intervals in a declining market. To buy or sell on scale up means to buy or sell at regular price intervals as the market advances. [CFTC]

scalper: A *speculator* on the *trading floor* of an *exchange* who buys and sells rapidly, with small profits or losses, holding his *positions* for only a short time during a *trading* session. Typically, a scalper will stand ready to buy at a fraction below the last *transaction* price and to sell at a fraction above, *e.g.*, to buy at the *bid* and sell at the offer or *ask* price, with the intent of capturing the *spread* between the two, thus creating market *liquidity*. See *day trader, position trader.* [CFTC]

schedule: A statement of the pricing format of electricity and the terms and conditions governing its applications. [EIA]

seasonality claims: Misleading sales pitches that one can earn large profits with little risk based on predictable seasonal changes in supply or demand, published reports or other well-known events. [CFTC]

seat: An *instrument* granting *trading* privileges on an *exchange*. A seat may also represent an ownership interest in the exchange. [CFTC]

Securities and Exchange Commission (SEC): An independent agency that administers federal securities laws and regulates the firms that buy and sell those securities. [NYMEX]

security: Generally, a transferable *instrument* representing an ownership interest in a corporation (*equity* security or stock) or the debt of a corporation, municipality, or sovereign. Other forms of debt such as mortgages can be converted into securities. Certain derivatives on securities (*e.g.*, *options* on equity securities) are also considered securities for the purposes of the securities laws. Security Futures Products are considered to be both securities and futures products. *Futures* *contracts* on Broad-Based Securities Indexes are not considered securities. [CFTC]

security deposit: See *margin.* [CFTC]

self-regulatory organization (SRO): *Exchanges* and registered futures associations that enforce financial and sales practice requirements for their members. See *designated self-regulatory organizations.* [CFTC]

seller's call: Seller's call, also referred to as call purchase, is the same as the *buyer's call* except that the seller has the right to determine the time to fix the price. See *buyer's call.* [CFTC]

seller's market: A condition of the market in which there is a scarcity of goods available and hence sellers can obtain better conditions of sale or higher prices. See *buyer's market.* [CFTC]

seller's option: The right of a seller to select, within the limits prescribed by a *contract*, the quality of the *commodity* delivered and the time and place of *delivery.* [CFTC]

selling hedge (or **short hedge**): Selling *futures contracts* to protect against possible decreased prices of commodities. See *hedging.* [CFTC]

semi-variance: A measure of downside risk computed as the average of the squared deviations below the mean return. See also *lower partial moment.* [CCRO]

serial expiration: *Options* on the same *underlying futures contract* which expire in more than one month. NYMEX Division platinum options have serial expiration. [NYMEX]

series (of **options**): *Options* of the same type (*i.e.*, either *puts* or *calls*, but not both), covering the same *underlying futures contract* or other underlying *instrument*, having the same *strike price* and *expiration date.* [CFTC]

set-off close-out right: The right to net other amounts owed by the two parties to each other after calculation of the close-out amount on the early termination date. [CCRO]

settlement: The act of fulfilling the *delivery* requirements of the *futures contract.* [CFTC]

settlement or **settling price:** The price established by the *exchange* settlement committee at the *close* of each *trading* session as the official price to be used by the *clearinghouse* in determining net gains or losses, *margin* requirements, and the next day's price *limits*. The term "settlement price" is often used as an approximate equivalent to the term "*closing price*." The close in futures trading refers to a brief period at the end of the day, during which *transactions* frequently take place quickly and at a *range* of prices immediately before the bell. Therefore, there frequently is no single closing price, but a range of prices. In months with significant activity, the settlement price is derived by calculating the weighted average of the prices at which trades were conducted during that period. [NYMEX]

short: (1) The market *position* of a _futures_ _contract_ seller whose sale obligates him to deliver the *commodity* unless he liquidates his contract by an offsetting purchase; (2) A *trader* whose _net posi-_ _tion_ in the _futures_ _market_ shows an excess of open sales over open purchases; (3) The holder of a _short_ _position;_ (4) In the *options* market, the position of the seller of a *call* or a _put_ _option._ The short in the options market is obliged to take a futures position if he is assigned for *exercise*. Opposite of *long*. [NYMEX]

short covering: See *cover*. [CFTC]

short hedge: See _selling_ _hedge._ [CFTC]

short position: A *position* that is sold, such as selling a stock, *forward, futures,* *swap,* or *option*. [CCRO]

short selling: Selling a _futures_ _contract_ or other *instrument* with the idea of delivering on it or offsetting it at a later date. [CFTC]

short squeeze: See *squeeze*. [CFTC]

short-the-basis: A person or firm that has a commitment to sell in the cash or _spot_ _markets_ and *hedges* through the purchase of futures is said to be short-the-basis. [NYMEX]

short ton: A unit of weight equal to 2,000 pounds. [EIA]

site energy: The *Btu* value of energy at the point it enters the home, sometimes referred to as "delivered" energy. The site value of energy is used for all fuels, including electricity. [EIA]

small traders: *Traders* who hold or control *positions* in futures or *options* that are below the *reporting level* specified by the *exchange* or the *CFTC*. [CFTC]

soft: (1) A description of a price that is gradually weakening; or (2) this term also refers to certain "soft" commodities such as sugar, cocoa, and coffee. [CFTC]

sold-out-market: When *liquidation* of a weakly-held *position* has been completed, and offerings become scarce, the market is said to be sold out. [CFTC]

spark spread: (1) The difference between the price of electricity sold by a generator and the price (cost) of the fuel used to generate it, adjusted for equivalent units. The spark spread can be expressed in $/*MWh* or $/*MMBtu* (or other applicable units). To express in $/MWh, the *spread* is calculated by multiplying, for instance, the price of *gas* (in $/MMBTU), by the *heat rate* (in BTU/KWh), dividing by 1000, and then subtracting from the electricity price (in $/MWh). Also called spark *arbitrage*. [CCRO] (2) *Hedging* the spark spread currently involves the simultaneous purchase of *natural gas contracts* and sale of electricity contracts, or vice-versa, allowing market participants to procure a profit on the *margin* between the contracts, to *hedge* the cost of producing electricity. The spread itself is the difference between the market value of electricity and the cost of natural gas calculated in megawatt hours. The introduction of the *coal futures contract* will expand the spark spread *trading* opportunities. [NYMEX]

spark spread intrinsic value: Power price minus fuel cost times the *heat rate* summed over each of the hours of production. *Spark spreads* can be negative. A negative spark spread in the case of a generating unit or market structure implies that the unit, given the heat rate and the corresponding power and fuel prices, is out of the money. [CCRO]

specifications: (1) *Contract* terms specified by the *exchange.* (2) Term referring to the properties of a given *crude oil* or refined *petroleum* product, which are "specified" since they often vary widely even within the same *grade* of product. In the normal process of negotiation, the seller will guarantee the *buyer* that the product or crude to be sold will meet certain specified limits. Generally, the major properties of oil that are guaranteed are *API gravity, sulfur*, pour point, viscosity, and *BS&W*. [NYMEX]

specific gravity: The ratio of the density of a substance at 60° *Fahrenheit* to the density of water at the same temperature. [NYMEX]

speculative bubble: A rapid run-up in prices caused by excessive buying that is unrelated to any of the basic, underlying factors affecting the supply or demand for a *commodity* or other asset. Speculative bubbles are usually associated with a "bandwagon" effect in which *speculators* rush to buy the commodity (in the case of futures, "to take *positions*") before the price *trend* ends, and an even greater rush to sell the commodity (unwind positions) when prices reverse. [CFTC]

speculative limit: See *speculative position limit.* [CFTC]

speculative position limit: The maximum *position*, either net *long* or net *short*, in one *commodity* future (or *option*) or in all futures (or options) of one commodity combined that may be held or controlled by one person (other than a person eligible for a *hedge exemption)* as prescribed by an *exchange* and/or by the *CFTC.* [CFTC]

speculator: In *commodity* futures, an individual who does not *hedge*, but who trades with the objective of achieving profits through the successful anticipation of price movements. [CFTC]

spinning reserve: That reserve generating *capacity* running at a zero load and synchronized to the electric system. [EIA]

spot: Market of immediate *delivery* of and payment for the product. [CFTC]

spot commodity: (1) The actual *commodity* as distinguished from a *futures* *contract*; (2) sometimes used to refer to cash commodities available for immediate *delivery*. See *actuals* or *cash commodity*. [CFTC]

spot market: Also called *cash markets,* these are markets that involve the immediate delivery of a *commodity* or *security instrument*. For *fossil fuels,* this is daily. For U.S. power, this may be hourly or daily. [CCRO]

spot-market price: See *spot price*. [EIA]

spot month: (1) The *futures contract* that matures and becomes deliverable during the present month. Also called *current delivery month*. [CFTC] (2) The futures contract closest to maturity. The *nearby delivery month*. [NYMEX]

spot price: The price at which a physical *commodity* for immediate *delivery* is selling at a given time and place. See *cash price*. [CFTC]

spot purchases: A single shipment of fuel or volumes of fuel purchased for *delivery* within 1 year. Spot purchases are often made by a user to fulfill a certain portion of energy requirements, to meet unanticipated energy needs, or to take advantage of low-fuel prices. [EIA]

spread (or **straddle**): The purchase of one futures *delivery month* against the sale of another futures delivery month of the same *commodity*; the purchase of one delivery month of one commodity against the sale of that same delivery month of a different commodity; or the purchase of one commodity in one market against the sale of the commodity in another market, to take advantage of a profit from a change in price relationships. The term spread is also used to refer to the difference between the price of a futures month and the price of another month of the same commodity. A spread can also apply to *options*. See *arbitrage*. [CFTC]

spread (options): The purchase and sale of *options* which vary in terms of type (*call* or *put*), *strike prices, expiration dates,* or both. May also refer to an options *contract* purchase (sale) and the simultaneous sale (purchase) of a *futures contract* for the same *underlying commodity.* [NYMEX]

squeeze: A market situation in which the lack of supplies tends to force shorts to *cover* their *positions* by *offset* at higher prices. Also see *congestion, corner.* [CFTC]

SRO: See *self-regulatory organization.* [CFTC]

stock-type settlement: A settlement procedure in which the purchase of a *contract* requires immediate and full payment by the *buyer* to the seller. In stock-type settlement, the actual cash profit or loss from a trade is not *realized* until the *position* is liquidated. *Exchange options* have this type of settlement procedure, which differs from that in the *futures market* where gains and losses are realized on a daily basis. [NYMEX]

stocks: Inventories of fuel stored for future use. [EIA]

stop-close-only order: A *stop order* that can be executed, if possible, only during the closing period of the market. See also *market-on-close* order. [CFTC]

stop limit order: An order that goes into force as soon as there is a trade at the specified stop price. The order, however, can only be *filled* at the *limit* price or better. The stop price and the limit price can be the same or different. The stop price is the price level specified in the order. [NYMEX]

stop-loss: A *resting order* designed to close out a losing *position* when the price reaches a level specified in the order. It becomes an *at-the-market* order when the "stop" price is reached. Individuals also use stops to enter the market when the prices reach a specified level. [NYMEX]

stop order: This is an order that becomes a *market order* when a particular price level is reached. A sell stop is placed below the market, a buy stop is placed above the market. Sometimes referred to as *stop loss* Order. Compare to *market-if-touched* order. [CFTC]

storage additions: Volumes of *gas* injected or otherwise added to underground *natural gas* reservoirs or *liquefied natural gas* storage. [EIA]

storage withdrawals: Total volume of *gas* withdrawn from underground storage or from *liquefied natural gas* storage over a specified amount of time. [EIA]

straddle: (1) See *spread*; (2) an *option position* consisting of the purchase of *put* and *call options* having the same *expiration date* and *strike price.* [CFTC]

straddle (futures): Also known as a *spread*, the purchase of one futures month against the sale of another futures month of the same *commodity*. A straddle trade is based on a price relationship between the two months. [NYMEX]

straddle (options): The purchase or sale of both a *put* and a *call* having the same *strike price* and *expiration date.* The *buyer* of a straddle benefits from increased *volatility*, and the seller benefits from decreased volatility. [NYMEX]

strangle: An *option position* consisting of the purchase of *put* and *call options* having the same *expiration date*, but different *strike prices.* [CFTC]

Strategic Petroleum Reserve (SPR): *Petroleum stocks* maintained by the Federal Government for use during periods of major supply interruption. [EIA]

stress capital at risk: The amount of *capital* that is at risk derived from the process of ad hoc stress testing, scenario analysis, or sensitivity analysis of the *portfolio* based on certain conditions to determine various issues, such as outliers or low and high returns. [CCRO]

strike price: The price at which the *underlying futures contract* is bought or sold in the event an *options* contract is *exercised.* Also called an *exercise price.* [NYMEX]

strip: The simultaneous purchase (or sale) of an equal number of futures *positions* in consecutive months. The average of the prices for the *futures contracts* bought (or sold) is the price level of the *hedge*. A six-month strip, for example, consists of an equal number of futures contracts for each of six consecutive *contract months.* Also known as a calendar strip. [NYMEX]

strong hands: When used in connection with *delivery* of commodities on *futures contracts,* the term usually means that the party receiving the *delivery notice* probably will take delivery and retain ownership of the *commodity*; when used in connection with futures *positions*, the term usually means positions held by trade interests or well-financed *speculators*. [CFTC]

structured transaction: Nonstandard *contracts* not associated with owned or leased assets and involving significant tailoring of terms to meet customer needs. Thus, nonstandard contracts associated with owned or leased assets would be included in the owned asset category rather than in the structured contracts category. Structured contracts may be accounted for on either the accrual or MTM basis. [CCRO]

subportfolio: A subset of a *portfolio*. [CCRO]

sulfur: An element that is present in some *oil*, *gas*, and *coal* as an impurity in the form of its various compounds. [NYMEX]

support: In *technical analysis,* a price area where new buying is likely to come in and stem any decline. See *resistance*. [CFTC]

swap: (1) A custom-tailored, individually negotiated *transaction* designed to manage *financial risk,* usually over a period of one to 12 years. Swaps can be conducted directly by two counterparties, or through a third party such as a bank or brokerage house. The *writer* of the swap, such as a bank or brokerage house, may elect to assume the risk itself, or manage its own market *exposure* on an *exchange*. Swap transactions include interest rate swaps, *currency swaps,* and price swaps for commodities, including energy and metals. In a typical *commodity* or price swap, parties exchange payments based on changes in the price of a commodity or a market index, while fixing the price they effectively pay for the physical commodity. The transaction enables each party to manage exposure to commodity prices or index values. Settlements are usually made in cash. [NYMEX] (2) A bilateral *contract* between two counterparties to exchange *cash flows* in the future according to a prearranged/contracted formula. A swap can therefore be regarded as a *portfolio* of *forward contracts.* [CCRO]

swaption: An *option* to enter into a *swap* — *i.e.*, the right, but not the obligation, to enter into a specified type of swap at a specified future date. [CFTC]

sweet crude: *Crude oil* typically containing less than 1% *sulfur*, by weight. [NYMEX]

switch: Offsetting a *position* in one *delivery month* of a *commodity* and simultaneous initiation of a similar position in another delivery month of the same commodity, a tactic referred to as "rolling forward." [CFTC]

synthetic credit rating: An internal rating established by a company based on those factors that it deems most important to establishing *counterparty* credit quality. The synthetic rating may be the output from a scoring model or counterparty review. Agency ratings may be included in determining the synthetic rating. [CCRO]

synthetic futures: A *position* created by combining *call* and *put options.* A synthetic *long* futures position is created by combining a long *call option* and a *short* put option for the same *expiration date* and the same *strike price.* A synthetic short *futures contract* is created by combining a long *put* and a short call with the same expiration date and the same strike price. [CFTC]

systematic risk: *Market risk* due to factors that cannot be eliminated by diversification. [CFTC]

systemic risk: The risk that a *default* by one market participant will have repercussions on other participants due to the interlocking nature of financial markets. For example, customer A's default in X market may affect intermediary B's ability to fulfill its obligations in markets X, Y, and Z. [CFTC]

t

taker: The *buyer* of an *option contract*. [CFTC]

Tank Train: A procedure in the rail shipment of *crude oil,* refined products, and other liquids developed by General American Transportation (GATX). "Tank Train" tank cars are interconnected, which permits loading and unloading of the entire train of cars from one connection. [NYMEX]

target return: Usually the minimum return acceptable to an investor. [CCRO]

tariff: (1) A published volume of rate *schedules* and general terms and conditions under which a product or service will be supplied. [EIA] (2) A schedule of rates or charges permitted a common carrier or utility; pipeline tariffs are the charges made by *pipelines* for transporting *crude oil,* refined products, or *natural gas* from an origin to a destination. [NYMEX]

technical analysis: An approach to *forecasting commodity* prices that examines patterns of price change, rates of change, and changes in volume of *trading* and *open interest,* without regard to *underlying* fundamental market factors. Technical analysis can work consistently only if the theory that price movements are a *Random Walk* is incorrect. See *fundamental analysis.* [CFTC]

tender: To give notice to the *clearing organization* of the intention to initiate *delivery* of the physical *commodity* in satisfaction of a *short futures contract.* Also see *retender.* [CFTC]

tenderable grades: See *contract grades.* [CFTC]

tenor: Time to maturity of an asset, liability, trade, *transaction*, or *portfolio.* [CCRO]

terminal market: Usually synonymous with *commodity exchange* or *futures market,* specifically in the United Kingdom. [CFTC]

theoretical value: An *option's* value generated by a mathematical model given certain prior assumptions about the term of the options *contract*, the characteristics of the *underlying futures contract*, and prevailing interest rates. [NYMEX]

therm: 100,000 *British thermal units.* Ten therms, a *dekatherm*, is 1 million *Btus*. [NYMEX]

theta: The sensitivity of an *option's* value to a change in the amount of time to expiration. [NYMEX]

throughput: (1) A term used to describe the total volume of raw materials that are processed by a plant such as an oil *refinery* in a given period. (2) The total volume of *crude oil* and refined products that are handled by a tank farm, *pipeline*, or terminal loading facility. [NYMEX]

tick: Refers to a minimum change in price up or down. An up-tick means that the last trade was at a higher price than the one preceding it. A down-tick means that the last price was lower than the one preceding it. See *minimum price fluctuation.* [CFTC]

time decay: The tendency of an *option* to decline in value as the *expiration date* approaches, especially if the price of the *underlying instrument* is exhibiting low *volatility*. See *time value.* [CFTC]

time-of-day order: This is an order that is to be executed at a given minute in the session. For example, "Sell 10 March corn at 12:30 p.m." [CFTC]

time spread: The selling of a *nearby options contract* and buying of a more *deferred* options contract with the same *strike price.* [NYMEX]

time value: Part of the *options premium* which reflects the excess over the *intrinsic value,* or the entire premium if there is no intrinsic value. At given price levels, the option's time value will decline until expiration. It is this decrease in time value that makes options a wasting asset. Also called *extrinsic value.* [NYMEX]

403

to-arrive contract: A *transaction* providing for subsequent *delivery* within a stipulated time limit of a specific *grade* of a *commodity*. [CFTC]

tolling arrangement: An agreement between a power *buyer* and a power generator in which the buyer supplies the fuel and receives an amount of power generated based on an assumed *heat rate.* [CCRO]

trader: (1) A merchant involved in cash commodities; (2) a professional *speculator* who trades for his own account and who typically holds *exchange trading* privileges. [CFTC]

trading: Buying and selling. [NYMEX]

trading ahead: See *front running.* [CFTC]

trading around assets: Used in conjunction with *hedging* that reduces risk, the activity of selling more production or buying back more volumes than are currently *hedged.* [CCRO]

trading facility: A person or group of persons that provides a physical or electronic facility or system in which multiple participants have the ability to execute or trade agreements, *contracts,* or *transactions* by accepting *bids* and offers made by other participants in the facility or system. See *many-to-many.* [CFTC]

trading floor: A physical *trading facility* where *traders* make *bids* and offers via *open outcry* or the specialist system. [CFTC]

trading volume: The number of *contracts* that change hands during a specified period of time. [NYMEX]

transaction: The entry or *liquidation* of a trade. [CFTC]

transfer trades: Entries made upon the books of *Futures Commission Merchants* for the purpose of: (1) transferring existing trades from one account to another within the same firm where no change in ownership is involved; (2) transferring existing trades from the books of one FCM to the books of another FCM where no change in ownership is involved. Also called *Ex-Pit Transactions.* [CFTC]

transferable option (or **contract**): A *contract* that permits a *position* in the *option* market to be *offset* by a *transaction* on the opposite side of the market in the same contract. [CFTC]

transfer notice: A term used on some *exchanges* to describe a notice of *delivery*. See *retender*. [CFTC]

transmission: The movement of electricity across power lines. [NYMEX]

trend: The general direction, either upward or downward, in which prices have been moving. [CFTC]

trendline: In *charting*, a line drawn across the bottom or top of a price chart indicating the direction or trend of price movement. If up, the trendline is called bullish; if down, it is called bearish. [CFTC]

U

unable: Unless they are designated "*GTC*" (Good Until Canceled) or "Open," all orders not *filled* by the end of a *trading* day are deemed "unable" and void. [CFTC]

uncovered option: See *naked option.* [CFTC]

underlying: See *underlying commodity.*

underlying commodity: The *cash commodity* underlying a *futures contract.* Also, the commodity or futures contract on which a *commodity option* is based, and which must be accepted or delivered if the *option* is *exercised*. [CFTC]

unrealized: The activity required to entitle the entity to payment or obligating it to make payment has not occurred. For *transactions* subject to accrual accounting, this generally consists of the period prior to when products or services are delivered or received. For transactions subject to *fair value* accounting, this will generally consist of the period when the transaction is subject to *market risk.* [CCRO]

upstream: An industry term referring to commercial *oil* and *gas* operations dedicated to exploration for and production of oil and gas.

V

Value at Risk (VaR): Value at risk of a *position* or a *portfolio* is defined as the loss or change in value that is not expected to be exceeded with a given *degree of confidence* over a time period of interest called the *holding period.* VaR is therefore a statistical measure of variability in the value of a portfolio of positions or *earnings* from economic activity arising from the changes in the market prices of the commodities or other variables underlying the portfolio or activity. There are two parameters attached to any given VaR estimate, namely, the degree of confidence or *confidence level* and the holding period. The confidence level is associated with probability that is sought to be assigned to the range of outcomes, and the holding period is the time interval over which the market prices or other drivers undergo changes from the current levels and thereby affect the value currently placed on the portfolio. (Also see confidence level, *daily earnings at risk,* and holding period). In the context of analyzing *subportfolios*, see *component value at risk.* The change in VaR by adding a new *position* is commonly referred to as *delta* VaR. [CCRO]

variable price limit: A price *limit* schedule, determined by an *exchange*, that permits variations above or below the normally allowable price movement for any one *trading* day. [CFTC]

variation margin: Payment made on a daily or intraday basis by a *clearing member* to the *clearing organization* based on adverse price movement in *positions* carried by the clearing member, calculated separately for customer and proprietary positions. [CFTC]

vega: Coefficient measuring the sensitivity of an *option* value to a change in *volatility*. [CFTC]

vertical spread: Any of several types of *option spread* involving the simultaneous purchase and sale of options of the same class and *expiration date* but different *strike prices,* including *bull vertical spreads, bear vertical spreads, back spreads,* and *front spreads.* See *horizontal spread* and *diagonal spread.* [CFTC]

visible supply: Usually refers to supplies of a *commodity* in *licensed warehouses.* Often includes floats and all other supplies *"in sight"* in producing areas. See *invisible supply.* [CFTC]

volatile markets: *Commodity* markets with exceptional price movements in both directions, generally driven by the economic forces of supply and demand as well as world events. [NYMEX]

volatility: A statistical measurement of the rate of price change of a *futures contract, security,* or other *instrument* underlying an *option.* See *historical volatility, implied volatility.* [CFTC]

volatility quote trading: Refers to the quoting of *bids* and offers on *option contracts* in terms of their *implied volatility* rather than as prices. [CFTC]

volatility smile: A special situation in which *options* with different *strike prices* have different implied volatilities. With a smile, the *at-the-money* strike has the lowest *implied volatility.* If the strike price is plotted on the X-axis against the implied volatilities on the Y-axis, the low point of the graph will be close to the *underlying* price and the tails will rise as you move the *exercise prices* further away from the underlying price. [CCRO]

volatility skew: A modification to an *option* model allowing for different implied volatilities at different strikes. [CCRO]

volatility spread: A *delta-neutral* option spread designed to speculate on changes in the *volatility* of the market rather than the direction of the market. [CFTC]

volatility trading: Strategies designed to speculate on changes in the *volatility* of the market rather than the direction of the market. [CFTC]

volume of trade: The number of *contracts* traded during a specified period of time. It may be quoted as the number of contracts traded or as the total of physical units, such as bales or bushels, pounds or dozens. [CFTC]

volumetric risk: See *market risk* [CCRO]

W

warehouse receipt: A document certifying possession of a *commodity* in a *licensed warehouse* that is recognized for *delivery* purposes by an *exchange*. [CFTC]

warrant: An issuer-based product that gives the *buyer* the right, but not the obligation, to buy (in the case of a *call*) or to sell (in the case of a *put*) a stock or a *commodity* at a set price during a specified period. [CFTC]

wash sale: See *wash trading*. [CFTC]

wash trading: Entering into, or purporting to enter into, *transactions* to give the appearance that purchases and sales have been made, without incurring *market risk* or changing the *trader's* market *position*. The *Commodity Exchange Act* prohibits wash trading. Also called Round Trip Trading, Wash Sales. [CFTC]

weak hands: When used in connection with *delivery* of commodities on *futures contracts,* the term usually means that the party probably does not intend to retain ownership of the *commodity*; when used in connection with futures *positions*, the term usually means positions held by small *speculators*. [CFTC]

weather derivative: A *derivative* whose payoff is based on a specified weather event, for example, the average temperature in Chicago in January. Such a derivative can be used to *hedge* risks related to the demand for heating fuel or electricity. [CFTC]

West Texas Intermediate: A global benchmark *grade* of *crude oil* deliverable against the New York Mercantile Exchange light, *sweet* *crude* oil *contract* and used as the basis for an enymex^{sm} contract. [NYMEX]

wet barrel: A physical *barrel* of *crude oil* or refined product as opposed to a " *paper barrel.*" [NYMEX]

writer: The issuer, *grantor*, or seller of an *option contract.* [CFTC]

y

yield: (1) A measure of the annual return on an investment expressed as a percentage. (2) The proportion of heavy or light products which can be derived from a given *barrel* of *crude oil.* [NYMEX]

Acknowledgments

A book encompassing a field as broad as risk management could not have been written without calling upon the expertise of experts in other fields, who have been very generous with their time and knowledge.

The chapter on fraud proved a challenge to write. The study of fraud prevention is a whole field in itself. I benefited greatly from the input of two individuals, both CPAs, Mark Bell, a retired audit partner from PricewaterhouseCoopers and Dennis Chookaszian, former Chairman and CEO of CNA Insurance, both of whom extensively reviewed my writing, offered suggestions on how to improve the material and make it applicable in both the energy industry and the Sarbanes-Oxley environment. They helped assure that the material was relevant and accurate.

John Sodergreen of Scudder Publishing introduced me to the Committee of Chief Risk Officers (CCRO), served as a sounding board, and has been generous with his time and help with publicity for the book.

It was a great honor to have Robert Anderson, Executive Director of the Committee of Chief Risk Officers (CCRO) write the Foreword to this book. I am most thankful that he was able to take the time to do so. In making this happen, I was helped by Jim Pierobon, of Pierobon and Partners, who handled the CCRO's public relations at the time I was writing the book.

Thanks to the following people who have commented on the book:

- Phil O'Connor of Constellation New Energy.

- Blair Hull of Matlock Capital.

- David Koenig, Executive Director of the Professional Risk Managers International Association (PRMIA).

- Dan Doyle, Vice President and Chief Financial Officer, American Transmission Company.

Dan Gary, mathematician, attorney, and all around great guy was one of the forces that inspired this book. He offered great support during the writing process and as a person to bounce ideas off of.

Thanks to Felix Carabello and David Smith of the Chicago Mercantile Exchange for providing data on weather contracts.

Thanks to Steve Zwick and Daniel Collins of *Futures Magazine* for assisting with information on futures and options contracts volume.

I have learned a great deal about risk management from my involvement with the Professional Risk Managers International Association (PRMIA). (I urge anyone interested in risk management to join PRMIA to benefit from its many offerings and meetings. There is no charge to join: go to *http://www.prmia.org.*) As a member of the Chicago steering committee since its inception, and now as the co-chair of the Chicago Steering Committee, I have benefited greatly from the advice of my colleagues. Much thanks to Rizwan Kadir, our first chair, for getting me involved, providing insight on risk management and finding such informative speakers — one of whom helped me with the book: Dennis Chookaszian. In addition, it has been a pleasure to work with my co-chair, Timur Gök, of Northern Illinois University, on creating an active chapter in Chicago that reaches out to all types of businesses. Saurabh Narain, of Shorebank, has provided a great sounding board for ideas, and introduced my wife and me to the best in vegetarian Indian cuisine in Chicago. Hilary Till, Principal of PREMIA Capital Management, has been a very kind and supportive person to work with. James Clarke, former CRO of NiSource provided valuabe insight to the strengths and weaknesses of risk management operations at utilities, as well as being a great contrarian thinker. Ikhtiar Kazi, of Derivatives Solutions, has provided the sense of humor that has kept our meetings on track and focused.

David Koenig the Executive Director of PRMIA has been a great support while I wrote this book, providing perspectives on risk management and allowing me to interact with other PRMIA members and benefit from their knowledge.

Mark Abbott, of both Guardian Life Insurance and PRMIA, has been very supportive of my work at PRMIA, and I appreciate his input on risk management issues.

My editors at Public Utilities Reports proved most patient as this book grew and grew. First, great thanks to Phil Cross, Vice President of Public Utilities Reports for taking a chance on a book on risk, and providing the support necessary to bring it to fruition. Rose Ann Loechler has proved of great help in creating a book that is a pleasure to see as well as read.

My brother Robert C. Hyman proved a first-rate sounding board in bouncing ideas off of, and most importantly in giving his honest opinion about the book, as he wouldn't tolerate a fluff job.

Charles Chen, a fellow PRMIA member, has always been great to bounce ideas off of about risk management.

In addition to friends, I have been fortunate to have family members here in Chicago who have always taken a keen interest in my book and offered helpful suggestions based on their time in the academy. My cousins David, Charlotte, and Michael Reiter have offered a great deal of support and conviviality during the writing process. Attendance at one of their legendary poker nights proved most instructive about application of statistics in real world situations.

In addition, during the somewhat arduous times when progress was slow, it was always a pleasure to have a visit from, or call from my Miami family — the Bravermans, Aunt Debbie, Uncle Mort, Jeff and Mike, who always have a kind word and a great sense of humor.

I would like to thank Trish Harris of the Institute of Internal Auditors for allowing me permission to use a copy of the COSO cube as featured on their website in their newsletter, *Tone at the Top*, which is worthwhile reading, and available at no charge from the IIA's website: *http://www.theiia.org*.

Much thanks to Jennifer Semenza of the New York Mercantile Exchange for allowing permission to use materials from NYMEX's glossary.

Many thanks to Eugene Esposito, noted insurance attorney of PROactive Strategies, for enlightening me on insurance and risk, and showing me Mehr and Cammack's classic on insurance, that provided the framework for managing risk on which this book is built.

As anyone who has a little child knows, it can be very difficult to work and take care of a child at the same time. The child comes first. Fortunately my wife and I were able to secure the services of a marvelous babysitter, Ruby Lee Williams, now proprietor of "Ruby's Little Angels Daycare" in Chicago, who did a fabulous job of taking care of our daughter, Julia, as I was working on this book.

The City of Chicago offered a laboratory for risk management in the Winter of 2000/2001, when natural gas prices spiked, and many people were having trouble paying their natural gas bills. I was fortunate to work with William Abolt, the environment commissioner at the time, to put together a natural gas insurance system, based on derivatives, for lower income residents of the city, which Mayor Richard M. Daley, put forth as a way to help people manage price spikes. Mayor Daley showed how to use markets to help residents, at a time when other regulatory approaches were failing to help out the less-fortunate, a sign of his innovative approach to governance.

Of course, this book would not have happened without my co-authors. My father, Leonard S. Hyman proved a most valuable editor and co-contributor. Bradford Leach, of NYMEX, provided a tremendous insight into energy risk management and the colorful characters it produces. Michael Denton has also provided a considerable insight into what happens in energy risk management as it is practiced. Gary Walter has provided a great sounding board as well as a most detailed editor in assuring as few errors as possible appear on the pages of this book.

You can't mention one parent and not mention the other. My mother has been very supportive during the writing process, especially with helpful tips on getting our daughter to sleep.

Most of all has been the two lovely ladies that were there to support me as I was writing this book, and the amount of time and effort put into it, my lovely wife Adiel, and my daughter Julia. Adiel put up with months of my discussions about the various topics and editing and was very patient as this saga went on and on. Little Julia has taken well to risk management — she had her first birthday celebration at the Chicago Board of Trade.

Andrew S. Hyman
Chicago, Illinois